The
Languages
of Italy

THE HISTORY AND STRUCTURE OF LANGUAGES
General Editor, Eric Hamp

THE JAPANESE LANGUAGE Roy Andrew Miller (1967)

JAPANESE AND THE OTHER ALTAIC LANGUAGES
Roy Andrew Miller (1971)

THE PORTUGUESE LANGUAGE J. Mattoso Camara, Jr. (1972)

THE LANGUAGES OF ITALY Giacomo Devoto (1978)

The
Languages
of Italy

Giacomo Devoto

Translated by
V. Louise Katainen

The University of Chicago Press
Chicago and London

The late GIACOMO DEVOTO (1897–1974) taught at the universities of Florence, Cagliari, and Padua, and was president of the Accademia della Crusca in Florence and of the Tuscan Academy of Science and Letters. He received numerous honors and was the author of many books and articles.

THE UNIVERSITY OF CHICAGO PRESS, CHICAGO 60637
THE UNIVERSITY OF CHICAGO PRESS, LTD., LONDON

© 1978 by The University of Chicago
All rights reserved. Published 1978
Printed in the United States of America

82 81 80 79 78   5 4 3 2 1
Translated from Giacomo Devoto, *Il linguaggio d'Italia,* © 1974
Rizzoli Editore, Milano.

Library of Congress Cataloging in Publication Data

Devoto, Giacomo.
  The languages of Italy.

  (The History and structure of languages)
  Translation of Il linguaggio d'Italia.
  Includes index.
  1. Italian language—History. 2. Latin
language—History. 3. Italic languages and
dialects. I. Title.
PC1075.D3913   450   78-3391
ISBN 0-226-14368-6

Contents

Contents

Maps

Translator's Note

I have kept my translation of *Languages of Italy* as close as possible to the original, both in meaning and style. English-speaking readers will, therefore, be aware of a style of writing somewhat foreign to modern American sensibility. They will undoubtedly note the extremely complex Latinate sentence construction, in which periods are often quite long and contain many dependent clauses. This is characteristic of Italian literary style in general, but Devoto's prose is particularly dense and, it must be added, occasionally unclear. The technical linguistic vocabulary did not present insuperable problems, since lists of parallel terms and expressions are available. Particularly useful to me in this regard was Rose Nash's *Multilingual Lexicon of Linguistics and Philology* (Miami: University of Miami Press, 1968). It is my observation that linguists, who almost on a daily basis must mentally translate from one language to another, have little hesitation about coining the obvious correspondent where it does not already exist. The verb *to lenite,* for example, is not listed in Webster's or in the *OED,* but is the acceptable English equivalent of the Italian verb *lenire. Nominalizzare* translates easily into *nominalize* and is infinitely less awkward than "to make into a substantive" or something of the sort.

Entirely within the realm of Devoto's personal style of writing are the many metaphors, sustained and not, that embroider the text. Some of these may strike the American reader as imbued with an old-fashioned sentimentality more characteristic of the Victorian age than our own. I recall, for instance, the repeated references in the early chapters of the book to the Latin of the Dark and Middle Ages as a threadbare but still regal cloak which inadequately covers the awkwardness of the growing vernacular. At another point in the book (chapter 3) the author refers to interplay of various languages as occurring on the "chessboard of primitive Indo-European."

Also characteristic of Devoto's stylistic preferences, at least in this book, is his frequent and, to me endearing, personification of the languages whose evolutions he describes. The author knew these languages so well and was so familiar with their interactions that he dealt with them as though they were characters in a play: the setting is the Italian peninsula; the plot is Italy's history; and the languages are agents of change in that history just as surely as people are. As Devoto notes in his Preface, this is not a book on linguistics, but a history of Italy seen through the evolution of its languages. In order to heighten the sense of immediacy of these linguistic evolutions, the author makes frequent use of the historical present tense, which I have retained throughout the book, except in those passages where its use would have seemed wholly unnatural in English.

This brings me to the title, which in the original is *Il linguaggio d'Italia*. The English title, *The Languages of Italy,* is rather a compromise, because of the impossibility of easily translating the distinction between the Italian nouns *lingua* and *linguaggio*.

Readers interested in the appendixes by Luciano Agostiniani and A. L. Prosdocimi should refer to the Italian edition.

Although the responsibility for this project rests entirely on my shoulders, I must nevertheless thank the many persons whose help was not only supportive but indeed vital to its conclusion. To begin with, I must thank Professor Ruggero Stefanini of the University of California at Berkeley, without whose recommendation I should never have launched on this project which for me has constituted a formative education in many ways. My thanks also go to Professor Henry Hoenigswald, of the University of Pennsylvania, who consulted Professor Stefanini when the project was first conceived. Professors Yakov Malkiel and Madison S. Beeler were most kind in answering some questions of a technical nature. Laura Stortoni made helpful suggestions on idiomatic expressions. Dr. Patricia Clark read chapters 11 and 12, making many useful comments; later Professor Emeritus Arthur E. Gordon scrutinized all the chapters in the section entitled "Latinitas" and found many inaccuracies which were dutifully corrected. Miss Catherine King was endlessly patient and professionally generous as well as expert in the typing of the manuscript. Finally, the help of Laina Jarvela and Valma Mynzie was indispensable in the proofing, which, on the many pages containing lists of words in numerous foreign languages ranging from Greek to Faliscan, consisted in reading the text aloud letter by letter.

This translation is dedicated to the memories of my brother Lennard William Katainen and Henry St. George.

Preface

This book is not a book on linguistics, but a book on history, albeit a history colored by, tinged with, interpreted through the phenomena of language. These phenomena are meager, apparently individual, and of little importance. They are, however, "continuous," and they alone permit the uninterrupted welding that we call tradition, that is, history. Continuity is represented here first of all by a geographic notion, the image of Italy as Nature formed her, as external events defined her, but as only the words of men, in the alternation of disruptive and reconstructive forces, have ultimately made her alive and united. If we do not exploit or relive linguistic experiences, we cannot write the history of Italy or of any other nation.

In the obvious decadence of the scientific spirit, which is clearly distinguished from the purely external progress of technology, in the light of the prevalence of shortsighted egotism, in the light of so many forewarnings of a medieval abdication, these pages aspire, precisely for their maximalism and unitary policy, to present themselves as an act of faith in the capacity of the human intellect, in its capacity to project itself in time, to converse, to make itself the promoter of civilized life. This act of faith is rendered topical by the coincidence of the centennial of the death of Alessandro Manzoni, who was the greatest user and the most fervent cultivator of Italian linguistic institutions.

Generous in their advice and help to me were Professor Aldo Prosdocimi and Dr. Luciano Agostiniani in the chapters on epigraphy and Dr. Fabrizio Tausini on the technical plane. To all go my heartfelt thanks.

Introduction

Italy has been inhabited for half a million years, but how long ago did its inhabitants learn to speak? One might say when their life had a minimum of the kind of organization that required coordination of individual actions and the exchange of messages. Yet it was only at the end of the Ice Age that messages were transmitted according to regular codes which could be transformed and indeed replaced by other codes without lapsing into a barbarous confusion.

In how many nuclei, in how many forms did these first linguistic institutions appear? Not even this is known. What we do know is that Italy is a geographic entity which has had the destiny of realizing, possessing, and then losing and regaining a unity which is ethnic, cultural, political, and consequently also linguistic.

In *The Languages of Italy* I shall not insist on the unity of linguistic institutions and on their subsequent evolutions, but rather on that treasury of expressive power which was able over the centuries to change its linguistic codes without ever making it impossible to transmit messages, and on that potentiality of expression which knew how to take advantage of the coexistence of various codes now tending to congeal, now to disperse, and now to become stratified.

This complex of codes consists not only of alternating phases of linguistic unity and variety but also of alternating rates of development. At times these phases are so slow moving as to allow of structural analyses and descriptions as if they were in effect immobile, or at least comparable to slow-motion film.

At other times the development of the language is so rapid, so tumultuous, that all of one's interest is concentrated on the modalities and qualities of a breathless change.

The principal phases of Italian linguistic development are the following:

1. Relics of forms anterior to the first millennium B.C. (§§1–15)
2. Beginning of a continuous linguistic tradition from the founding of Rome (§§16–40)
3. Involution and splintering of this first development in the fifth century B.C. (§§41–50)
4. Ascent—not only in the Italian peninsula—toward linguistic unity from the fourth century B.C. to the second century of the Christian era (§§51–100)
5. Involution and splintering during the early Middle Ages (§§101–25)
6. New ascent—this time limited to Italy—through unification (§§126–250)

In view of this rapidly changing linguistic situation, this book is not primarily concerned with the centrifugal and centripetal forces at work or in historical or structural analysis. It concentrates realistically on what the documents of Italy clearly show or suggest to the reader interested in the linguistic experiments, achievements, and limitations of the ancestors of Italians.

Part One

From the Origins
to 500 B.C.

One

Man and the Linguistic Materials of the Mediterranean

1 THE PALEOLITHIC AGE

Italy, it has been said, has been inhabited for half a million years: a mere second compared with the age of the earth, a relatively short period with respect to other European regions, but a very long period with respect to the possibility of even an approximate indirect reconstruction, not to speak of documentation of its linguistic history.

Direct evidence of man is much more recent, however. In the 1920s and 1930s two Neanderthal skulls associated with Mousterian industry were found in Rome on the Via Nomentana in the Saccopastore cave. The skulls date from the last Ice Age, approximately 150,000 years ago. In the Guattari grotto in Mount Circeo a Neanderthal skull and mandibles were found with an industry somewhat more recent than the Mousterian, namely, the Pontic.[1] According to Eickstedt, the Neanderthal period lasted up to 70,000 B.C.[2] but the question of whether Neanderthal man spoke, and if so, how he spoke, still remains elusive and almost futile. Only with the repopulation of central Europe in the postglacial period and with the subsequent migrations from the southwest and the southeast of Europe of peoples who had been saved from glaciation[3] did there appear a new human race, the Neanthropic, otherwise known as *Homo sapiens.* The movement had begun from Asia and had spread toward Europe by various routes, principally along the coast of northern Africa to the Straits of Gibraltar and also through the region of the Caspian Sea by way of the steppes of Russia in the direction of Central Europe.[4] The idea that the Balkans also played a part in the repopulation is not to be rejected. At the end of this long period of settlement, the human types which concern Italy are the Cro-Magnon and the Combe-Capelle. These humans lived approximately 25,000 years ago—a very long period with respect to possible linguistic documentation and reconstruction, since even the most indirect evidence pertinent to this kind of study does not date back more than 5,000 years.

These first evidences of Cro-Magnon man appear in a group of caves in the Balzi Rossi (Red Terraces) region of the extreme western part of Liguria, very close to the French border near Menton. Only as recently as the last century several skeletons were found in the Barma Grande grotto, and skeletons of children were found in the so-called Grotta dei Fanciulli (Children's Grotto). These finds are at the level of the upper Paleolithic man of the Aurignacian type.[5] The fact that the age of these skeletons is definitely postglacial allows us to recognize the beginning of a tradition which has continued uninterrupted for 20,000 years, right up to our own time. About 80 kilometers to the west, in the Arene Candide (White Sands) grotto, there also appeared skeletons belonging to the parallel Combe-Capelle type of the upper Paleolithic level. The following facts—that at the Balzi Rossi sites shells and bone ornaments were discovered with the skeletons, that with the children's skeletons were found evidences of garments decorated with sea shells, that the head of a youth of negroid race was protected by stone slabs forming a hollow filled with ochre—make it clear to us that such activities were not accompanied by animallike noises, but that some form of language, however rudimentary, was indispensable.[6]

From that time, all through the Mesolithic Age, from 13,000 to 5,000 B.C., we see before us burial grounds in which almost all of the skeletons are in crouching positions, in Liguria as well as in Apulia, in Veneto and in the Abruzzi, in Emilia and in Latium, in the Marches and in Sicily;[7] and the fact that they are all accompanied by rather rich accoutrements leads up to assume both elaboration and dialogue.

2 SEMIOTIC ELEMENTS IN THE AENEOLITHIC AGE

By the end of the Neolithic Age, linguistic communication is not only a well motivated presumption, but a certainty, if not yet on the "grammatical" level, at least on the "semiological" level. Again in the extreme northwest corner of Italy, on Mount Bego, in what is now French territory, more than forty thousand drawings from the Aeneolithic Age, of weapons, of plows and other utensils, of oxen, as well as geometrical figures, were excavated.[8]

3 INDIRECT SOURCES

In the absence of direct documents, we must approach the problem of giving form to these sure but elusive linguistic entities with certain established tenets: (1) With the beginning of the Neolithic Age, Italy was populated by men who had at their disposal organized linguistic tools. (2) These linguistic structures seem to have existed for a long time before they were recorded in direct linguistic-grammatical documents. We cannot come even close to them through normal procedures of reconstruction because there are no valid fulcrum points which connect presumed relationships and which permit a comparison that is not just typological. (3) And yet grammatical structures and lexical units which were rooted for millennia in the soil of Italy could not have disappeared without leaving a trace, as if they had been swept away by enormous brooms or scraped clean by sharp razors. Under these conditions it is necessary to proceed by degrees, by attempting to isolate or extract from the traditionally affirmed linguistic heritage of sure Indo-European origin those elements which can be "suspected" of having been decanted from the more ancient stratum (which we shall provisionally call "Mediterranean"), elements which are accepted and "recognized" even if emanating from an illegitimate source.

To avoid groping in the dark, we shall begin by defining three areas of research. The first is represented by the mass of place names both ancient and modern, the etymologies of which are not evident, but which find correspondences in a vast area beyond the limits of the areas that had already become Indo-European in the prehistoric age. We shall soon see numerous examples of such a linguistic procedure which was first applied on a large scale by Francesco Ribezzo and then perfected by Vittorio Bertoldi and Benvenuto Terracini.[9] The second area of research is made up of words attested only in the modern age, confined to remote dialects especially in the Alpine region, which evade any sort of connection either with Latin or with any other languages of our era, from Arabic, to the Germanic languages, to French. The pioneer in these studies has been the Swiss scholar Jakob Jud.[10] The third area concerns Latin designations which attract our attention because they do not permit satisfactory comparison with forms in other Indo-European languages and especially because they show in their structure phonetic and morphological peculiarities which are foreign to the usual Indo-European models.

4 PHONETIC INDICATIONS

In order to facilitate the selection of an adequate number of homogeneous examples, it seems right to indicate here several "signposts" which will attract our attention as we choose from these large masses of words or as we concentrate on restricted questions which though tentative may yet prove fertile.[11] From the phonetic point of view the characteristic signpost that is most trusted is the one furnished by words containing the sequence A . . . A, such as is found in the place name *Vara* (river), in an Alpine word such as *malga,* and in the Latin designation *alga.*

This signpost—external but significant—has been used by the German scholar H. Krahe as characteristic of a specific area and of a certain phase called "ancient European" in the context of Indo-European antiquity.[12] Krahe's supposition is not, however, legitimate because A . . . A types are diffused throughout an area much vaster than the primary Indo-European areas. Krahe's theory can be utilized only in an extra-Indo-European, and therefore also in a pre-Indo-European, context.

As we do for Indo-European languages, we must also admit the possibility of alternations in the Mediterranean system. Naturally we must proceed with greater caution because in the Indo-European system the validity of the correspondences between alternating forms leans heavily on its conformity with constant morphological characteristics which the Mediterranean systems do not employ. Examples of admissible alternations are those of the type BARGA, which is inseparable from the type BERGA(MO). So we have the possibility of an A/E alternation, which is evidenced again in the Italian designations *tarma* 'clothes moth' and *tèrmite* 'termite'. An opposing alternation, more limited but persistent, is the A/O type, which appears in the name of two rivers which run in opposite directions and spring from neighboring sources: AMRA *Ambra* and OMRO *Ombrone.*

Another alternation in vowels must be considered graphic, owing to the difference between the Mediterranean phonetic system on the one hand and the Latin or Greek on the other. The fact that the Latin word *menta* finds a correspondence with the Greek *minthe* attests the existence in an earlier stage of a vowel which, to the Greek or Latin ear, could not be easily classified, as if it were a vowel intermediary between the E and the I of these languages. As for the consonants, oscillations between voiced and unvoiced are inadmissible in the Indo-European world, which clearly distinguishes them, whereas in the Mediterranean world they appear as inevitable, at least in the central eastern sector. Besides Barga (Lucca) we have Parga (Florence); as opposed to Bergamo in Lombardy we have Pergamo in Asia Minor. Finally, the difference between simple and geminate articulation establishes in the Indo-European world a certain relationship of balance which also takes into account the quantity of the preceding vowel. In the reproduction and the reception of Mediterranean words in an Indo-European system, there are instead uncertainties, so that a type BAKA is reproduced not only as Latin *baca* but also as *bacca* (§7).

5 MORPHOLOGICAL INDICATIONS

The structure of themes and the processes of derivation must be examined with similar criteria. There is a series of Latin words which end in -K and which all lack valid Indo-European etymologies.

This list, an imposing one, consists of FAIK Latin *faex,* 'grounds, sediment'; THALK Latin *falx* 'sickle, scythe'; FAUK Latin *fauces* 'gullet, throat'; FRAK Latin *fraces* 'dregs of pressed oil'; KALK Latin *calx* 'heel'; KRUK Latin *crux* 'cross'; LANK Latin *lanx* 'plate, platter'; MERK Latin *merx* 'merchandise.'

In the field of suffixes, too, the problem is not so much a matter of singling out those which are positively "Mediterranean" as it is one of specifying suffixes which are clearly not Indo-European (for these see §9).

A group apart is represented by K suffixes preceded by the consonants S or N: place names such as Carasco (Genoa) or Malosco (Novara), common nouns such as *verbasco* and *lentisco,* the ancient name for the Po, *Bodincus,* a modern place name such as Bognanco (Novara), and a modern common noun like *calanco* "series of falls of land."

There are other types which in themselves could be Indo-European (like those ending in -NT), but which are sometimes found in nominal derivations of a non-Indo-European nature: examples are nouns ending in -NT preceded by a vowel other than E/O, as in the word Taranto, or even by the vowel E but linked to a nonverbal root, as, for example, in Ferento. There are also the types characterized by -P, for example Osoppo (Udine).[13]

The final type has endings which are not suffixes but actually grammatical endings. An example of this is the -AR ending, the Etruscan signpost for the plural which combines to form place names still used today even outside of former Etruscan territory, for example, in the modern toponyms Chiarvar(i), Barvar(i), and Crevar(i); the final -I is nothing more than the neo-Latin confirmation of the plural value which was no longer adequately indicated by -AR, the old Etruscan ending by now welded into a single unit with the theme.

Two

Unity and Variety in the
Mediterranean World

6 STRUCTURES

On the basis of these soundings and of other materials that have been gathered, it is possible to attempt some partial description of Mediterranean linguistic structures. A first diagram of the vocalic system, which is dissymetrical,[1] brings into opposition a palatal vocalic system in which the vocal E gravitates toward the A, and a velar system in which the intermediate vowel O gravitates instead toward the U. The pattern that results from these tendencies is the following:

$$
\begin{array}{c}
\text{A} \\
\text{Ä} \ldots \ldots \\
\ldots \ldots \text{O} \\
\text{I} \ldots \ldots \text{U}
\end{array}
$$

Alternations of the type Barga/Bergamo and Parga/Pergamo are more frequent than those of the other type cited. Ambra/Ombrone. In relationship with the prevalence of the first type we find the prevalence of the themes AU as found in AUSA, in which the two components of the diphthong are in sharp contraposition, in comparison with the AI types, in which the two elements are less sharply opposed, as in SAITA 'bristle' (Latin *saeta*).

The development of the vowel A in the opposite direction, indicated by the second alternation, would lead to a system which would no longer be triangular but quadrangular, of the type

$$\text{Ä} \qquad \text{Å}$$
$$\text{E/I} \qquad \text{O/U}$$

The inverse development, directed toward attaining a total simplified symmetry, ought to lead to the elimination of the difference between the intermediate and extreme vowels, and of the two series, as is demonstrated by the following diagram:

$$\text{A}$$
$$\text{E/I} \qquad \text{O/U}$$

A clue is given by the uncertain fixation of Mediterranean themes in Greek and Latin forms: as in the case of *menta/minthē,* of the Latin *citrus* and the Greek *Kédros,* and of the Latin *cupressus* and the Greek *kypárissos* 'cypress'.

Not even in this direction, however, does one arrive at a definitive nonsymmetrical result: the O/U process of fusion is much more advanced than the E/I process.

One further suggestion is offered by the treatment of a Mediterranean word such as appears in the Greek *sŷkon* and the Latin *ficus.* For this it is very nearly certain that in the Mediterranean world or in certain of its areas there existed the mixed vowel ü. If, then, we take into consideration this final clue, we can arrive at a complete picture of Mediterranean vocalic nuclei and of their tendencies, which could be diagrammed in this way:

$$\text{Ä} \qquad \text{Å}$$
$$\text{E/I} \qquad \text{O/U}$$
$$\text{Ü}$$

The infrequent distinction between voiced and unvoiced consonants and between simple and geminate consonants has already been mentioned. One particular and typical problem has been raised by the possible presence in the Mediterranean system of an unvoiced interdental consonant. These indications have been deduced from the following facts taken together:

1. Only in initial position (in Latin and Venetic) or in internal position (in the Osco-Umbrian tradition) do the Indo-European

languages of Italy resolve the ancient aspirated voiced Indo-
European consonants BH, DH, and GwH (to which list is sometimes added GH) into the bilabial F.

2. But many Latin words without Indo-European etymologies
begin with F: they can be attributed to the Mediterranean group
of words in which the F derives from a different Mediterranean
sound, one which has not been more closely identified because
there is no evidence of the existence of the primitive F.[2]

3. We do not come close to arriving at a definition of this Mediterranean sound (the unvoiced interdental consonant), unless we
take into account the two Mediterranean words which correspond to fixed parallel forms in both Latin and Greek. To the
Latin *ficus* corresponds the sibilant dental of the Greek form
sŷkon; to the Latin *falx* corresponds the Greek *Zánklē* (and its
variant *Dankle*[3]), a different sound, granted, but one that contains both dental and affricative sibilant elements. Under these
conditions it would seem reasonable to think that a synthesis
of the Latin F and the Greek s/z can be determined as a TH (P),
almost like a minimal common denominator.

7 SEMANTIC FIELDS

If certain orientations of an external nature define the first area of
study (§3) and certain formal characteristics make the likelihood of
Mediterranean reference appear greater, it is certain that another
important factor for both the definition of the Mediterranean world
and the recognition of its lexical elements consists of semantic values.
To this end, it is not simply a matter of deciding if certain groups
of meaning, taken in an abstract way, ought preferably to be considered as belonging to the Mediterranean group. Meanings must be
judged also from an external point of view, that is, from the point
of view of their transferability. It it not enough that they meet the
semantic requirements of the Mediterranean world or even that they
correspond to its geographical and sociocultural characteristics. They
must be shown to be incompatible with the exigencies of the Indo-
European world, considered from the point of view both of its
original structures and of circumstances connected with the long
period of transfer and settlements, which the Indo-European ascend-
ancy presumes. With regard to the elementary vocabulary compiled
by H. Breuil,[4] it seems proper to recognize the fact that all vocabulary
referring to the hunt and to the harvesting of fruit is surely linked
to the soil, and it is reasonable to presume that newcomers would
easily learn the terminology in use in their new homes. But elementary notions such as number and all that refers to quantity and mea-

sure are, as abstract notions, equally necessary in all climates and conditions, in a nomadic society as well as in a society of fixed location and are thus easily preserved by newcomers without contamination.

The preferential semantic fields for a Mediterranean interpretation of the lexical heritage of which the historical age made use, can be ordered in the following way: of prime importance is the notion of the natural shelter, the "cave"; next in degree of importance come the contours of the land, the waterways, the springs (preliminary conditions of subsistence); third, the variety of fruit; fourth, the animals from which man had to defend himself and which he could use as food; fifth, artificial protection, and I include in this category clothing and elementary utensils; finally, at least in theory, the way in which the dead were disposed of and magical rites, in the narrow limits within which they can be recognized in lexical units. Here then are some Mediterranean bases arrived at by applying these devices and classified in this way: Natural land formations: ALBA/ALPA 'stone' is found in fixed form in the Latin *Alpes,* in the place name Alba Longa, and in other toponyms still in use today such as the Italian Alba. ARMA 'shelter, protection' is exemplified in the modern place name Arma (di Taggia), which is near San Remo. ARNA 'bed hollowed out by a river' is found in the name of the river Arno, in the medieval Latin term arna 'vas apium' (tenth century), in the Istrian designation *arne* 'cavern'[5] and even in the modern Italian word *arnia* 'beehive'. AUSA 'spring, fountain' is found in the name of the Tuscan river which is *Aus(er)* in Latin and Serchio in modern Italian and in the ethnic *Ausones,* which refers to 'the people who live in the vicinity of the spring',[6] and was diffused throughout the area between Ireland and Arabia. BALMA 'cave' continues in the modern place name Balme (in the province of Vercelli) and in the Ligurian dialect form Barma Grande or 'Great Grotto' near Menton (§1). BRATTA 'mud' is alive today in the Ligurian form *bratta,* having the same meaning, and in the Italian verb *(im)brattare*[9] 'to soil, stain'. GLARA we find in the Latin *glarea* 'gravel'. Derivations of KAR(R)A 'stone'[7] are found throughout an immense territory: from the Irish *carr* 'cliff' to the Armenian *kar* and the Sumerian *har;* it is also found in Italian place names such as Car(asco) (Genoa). KLAVA 'alluvial cone, delta of stones' remains in the place names Chiav(ari) and Chiav(enna). LAMA 'marshy plain' we have in the place names Lama dei Peligni, which is located in the Abruzzi, and in Lama Mocogno in Emilia. PALA 'rotundity of earth' is found in Latin *palatum* 'vault' or 'roof of the mouth' as well as in modern place names such as Mount Cimon della Pala. RAVA 'landslide' is exemplified in the modern toponym of the Bolognese Apennines Bocca del Ravari,[8] Ravarano (Parma), and in the designation *ravaneto* 'a pile of marble rubble'. TAURA 'dune, cairn' we note in place names such as Taurasi (Avellino) or Gioia Tauro (Reggio, Calabria).[9] VARA 'water' is a frequent name for rivers, for example in La Spezia province; other examples have been cited above (§4).

Less typical from the point of view of structure, but well documented not only as toponyms are the following forms: LIMA 'river with a rocky bed' in the Latin *lima*, in the Italian *lima*, and in the Lima River, which flows near Pistoia and Lucca; KRODA 'rock' in the Venetian dialect *croda* and in Croda, a town in the province of Como. BODO 'base, bottom' still lives with its Ligurian suffix in the Latin form *Bodincus* 'Po'; ROKKA is a very widely used place name (there are seventy-five county towns which incorporate it) in addition to the appellative; POPLO 'hillock, knoll' we find in the Etruscan toponym *Pupluna* 'Populania', in the Latin *populus*, meaning 'progeny, issue', and in Mount Boplo found in the Polcévera Valley according to the *Sententia minuciorum* (CIL I² 584); KUKKO 'pointed relief of land'[10] has been shown to have a wide diffusion from the Basque *kukur* 'comb' to the Slovenian or the Caucasian *kuk; finally* M(O)LU(M)B- 'lead' is *plumbus* in Latin but *mólybdos* in Greek.

By making use of the same procedure, we can isolate the following structural types related to the category of vegetation: BAK(K)A Latin *bac(c)a* 'fruit, berry', Italian *bacca* with the same meaning; MAGA, the word from which the Lombard term *mag(iustra)* 'strawberry' is derived, and which is also evident in the extreme west of Europe, for example in the Basque *mag(uri)*;[11] SRAGA 'strawberry' is also found in the Latin *fraga* 'strawberry'; AMPA 'raspberry' is evident in the Italian *lampone* in which the article has been combined with the stem. In addition we find the following terms, no longer related to fruits and berries, but still within the category of vegetation: ALGA Latin *alga* 'seaweed', GALLA Latin *galla* 'gall-nut, oak-apple', LAPPA Latin *lappa* 'burr', MALVA Latin and Italian *malva* 'mallow', LAURA Latin *laurus* and Italian *(al)loro* 'laurel', NAPA 'cabbage' Latin *napus*, TAKSA Latin *taxus* and Italian *tasso* 'yew'. Beyond the typical forms we meet in the category of wild vegetation: KIDRO/KEDRO Latin *citrus*, Greek *kédros;* ILEK 'variety of oak' Latin *ilex* 'live oak'; KUPAR 'cypress' Latin *cupressus*, Greek *kypárissos;* LEIRIO[12] Latin *lilium*, Greek *leírion*, Italian *giglio* 'lily'; WRODJA 'rose' Latin and Italian *rosa*, Greek *rhódon*. In the category of edible vegetation the notion of hunger or appetite appears: THAM Latin *fames.* MINT(H)A 'mint' finds correspondences in the Latin and Italian *menta* and in the Greek *mínthē.* The vocabulary of oil and wine includes ELAIWO, which in Latin becomes *oleum* and in Greek *élaion,* and WOINO 'wine', which gives the Latin *vinum* and the Greek *Foînos.* Other words pertaining to the category of edible vegetation are FAIK Latin *faex* 'grounds, sediment', THONGO 'mushroom' Latin *fungus* and Greek *spóngos,* and finally THÜKO 'fig' Latin *ficus* and Greek *sŷkon.*

In the category of animals we find the typical forms TALPA Latin *talpa* 'mole'; TARMA Latin *tarmes,* Italian *tarma* 'clothes moth'; BLATTA 'insect', with which we can compare the Italian *piatt(ola)* 'crab louse'. Outside of the typical forms we can admit LAB/LEP 'hare' Latin *lepus*[13] and thus the Latin *(cam)ox,* an Alpine animal, *(i)bex* 'chamois', Latin *cab(allus)* 'work horse'.

In the field of artificial protection we find the following words: KASA 'shed, hut' Latin and Italian *casa* 'house'; BAITA and MALGA 'rustic house in Alpine pastures'; BARGA 'shed, hut', which insists on the rotundity of the form, is very widely used as a place name and is also present in the Latin and Italian words *barca* 'boat'.

As names of instruments characterized by the form A . . . A or the ending in -K we find: BARRA Italian *barra* 'bar'; THALK 'sickle, scythe' Latin *falx* and Italian *falce;* LANK 'platter, plate', Latin *lanx.*

8 "Nostratic" and "Indo-Mediterranean"

Certain of these similarities and contacts are so widespread that it is legitimate to speak of the remains of an ancient unity which is extra-Italian. Even if this is not of direct relevance to the "languages of Italy," still it is advisable to keep in mind certain distinctions in terminology. There are stems such as AUSA, which have corresponding forms throughout a vast area—from the Basque territory, to Ireland, to Italy, to the Near East, and to Arabia—and which are comprised in the very general term "Nostratic."[14] There are those words which are found more often in a northerly zone which stretches from the Pyrenees to the Alpine region, from the Balkans right to the Caucasus, and are called "Paleo-European." An example from this group is KUK (§7). There are others which, on the other hand, are found in the south of Europe and North Africa, thrusting themselves all the way to India: these are called "Indo-Mediterranean." According to V. Pisani,[15] this accounts for the diffusion of the vigesimal numerical system and the value of certain Greek and Italian correspondences, such as the Greek *erébinthos* 'chick-pea' as opposed to the ancient Indian *aravinda.*

9 Paleo-European

Of greater interest from the Italian point of view is the opposite situation, whereby we encounter differences within the Mediterranean stratum and particularly within its Italian testimony.

If we have to choose between the tendency of B. Gerola, who is reluctant to admit this variety, and that of M. Durante,[16] who is, on the contrary, inclined to extol and even to exaggerate it, the latter merits our preference.

A fundamental example of variety has been recognized in Sardinia by B. Terracini. On the one hand, particularly in the South, there appear place names such as *Ittiri* and *Isili,* which are comparable to the African *Gilgili,* and to the Iberian *Bilbili.* On the other hand, we find names such as *Orotelli* and *Bosincu,* which echo Ligurian stems in -ELLO- and -INCO-,[17] as in *Vercelli* or *Bodincus* 'Po'.

The correct interpretation, however, attempts at the same time to recognize in the abstract that certain large areas or centers of attraction are at work within the Italian peninsula and that at the same time certain characteristic signposts do not respect rigid confines but rather continuously expand and contract. These centers of attraction can be defined in the following way: Liguria of northwestern Italy, the Euganean and Rhaeto-Euganean region of the northeast, the Tyrrhenian area of the western part of the peninsula, and the Picena area of the eastern part. Sicily and Sardinia open up partly toward the Tyrrhenian and the Ligurian areas and partly toward Africa.

As examples of linguistic boundaries which are not barriers, we cite certain suffixes. Suffixes in -s include Suessa and Sinuessa in southwestern Italy, but Atessa in the southeast. Suffixes in -ss and in -NTH are characteristic, according to Krahe,[18] in south central Italy and are connected with the Aegean-Anatolian world.[19] Examples of suffixes in -R(R)- are Lipara and Mazara in Sicily, Acerra on the outskirts of Naples, Suburra in Rome. Liguria is the center for suffixes in L, AL(L)O-, EL(L)O-, IL(L)O-; and examples such as (Tituk)-alos and (Popp)alus (§31) are found in the Leponzie inscriptions. In the *Sententia minuciorum* (CIL I 584) we have rivo Tudel(asca); in toponymy we have Rapallo, Varallo, Vercelli; Lake Regillo near Rome and Roselle in Etruria, and finally Entella, which exists both in Liguria and in western Sicily.

For suffixes having the root N, in the variant -E(N)NA, we find toponyms in Etruria as well as in surrounding areas, such as Bolsena and Rasenna in the provinces of Macerata and Modena, Ravenna and Cesena in Romagna, Chiavenna in Emilia and in the central Alps, Valbrevenna in Liguria, and Palena in the Abruzzi.

The suffix -ONA has a broad distribution. Beginning in Dertona in Liguria, and passing by Cremona, we find examples in the Rhaeto-Euganean territory, in Verona and Gemona, as well as in Ortona in the Abruzzi along the Adriatic coast, and in Albona, Fianona, and Salona along the eastern coast.

Similarly the suffix -TE has its center of attraction in northeastern Italy, for example in Terges-te 'Trieste' or in Ates-te 'Este', but they are also found toward the south in Tea-te 'Chieti', in Rea-te 'Rieti', and finally in Mount Sorac-te 'Soratte', which is located north of Rome.

10 CONNECTIONS WITH CENTRAL EUROPE

Archeological studies have proven that in earliest times—in the Neolithic and Aeneolithic Ages—human societies were not isolated but, on the contrary, had established contacts with each other often over great distances. In deposits of Danubian coil pottery which can be dated to the Neolithic Age, there were found mollusk shells (the *Spondylus gaederopus*[20]) meant to be used as ornaments. In later deposits of the Aeneolithic civilization of Unětice (Bohemia) there appear shells of another mollusk, the *Columbella rustica*.[21] Thus, from the Mediterranean and from Italy there emanated currents of culture and commerce which have been defined as "pre-Indo-European."[22]

The Aeneolithic civilizations of Serraferlicchio (Agrigento)[23] and Rinaldone in upper Latium with their war axes[24] and of Gaudo in Campania near Paestum with their dotted-ribbon motif bear witness to distant connections in the opposite direction,[25] sometimes trans-Adriatic. The civilization of Remedello (Brescia), which, because of the "bell-shaped" form of their glasses, can be dated toward the end of the Aeneolithic Age and the beginning of the Bronze Age, was directed toward the west.[26] Finally, as we approach the Terramare civilization (middle and recent Bronze Ages),[27] the conspicuous contacts are again with central Europe. From one direction and the other, Italy in the second millennium, with regard both to giving and to receiving, is always in contact by sea or by land with the rest of the continent.[28]

Three

The Establishment of
Indo-European

11 INDO-EUROPEAN LINGUISTIC INSTITUTIONS
At a certain point in history, after this originally uniform earth had been continually exposed to innumerable differentiating forces, a new tradition became established, a tradition which was subsequently modified and altered, but which put down roots that were never again to be disturbed. Unlike the Mediterranean linguistic patrimony, and notwithstanding vicissitudes and fractures, this linguistic tradition, the Indo-European tradition, succeeded in retaining an organic quality even though its impact in Italy was neither unitary nor instantaneous (§15).

The salient characteristics of the linguistic heritage which now makes its presence felt are the following.[1] From the point of view of phonetics, the vowel system is based on three timbres: E, O, and A. of the three the E, alternating with O, was dominant, while the A appeared either as a vowel of nonalternating forms, characteristic of "popular" vocabulary according to Antoine Meillet,[2] or as a helping or supporting vowel when, for reasons of accentuation or morphology, the normal timbres grew weaker. The consonant system was originally based on a quadripartition among occlusive consonants, simple voiced and unvoiced consonants on the one hand and aspirated voiced and unvoiced consonants on the other; from the point of view of articulation the occlusives were further differentiated into the four-part series of labial, dental, guttural, and labiovelar. The continuants were limited to the sibilant s, which could possibly also be sonorized into z, Intermediate between the vowels and the consonants were the sonants, which were articulations capable of functioning either as vowels or as consonants according to the phonetic context. There were six sonants: the vowel ı alternating with the consonant ʏ (= ᴊ); the vowel ᴜ alternating with the consonant w; the vowel ʟ̥ alternating with the consonant ʟ, and similarly the vowel ʀ̥ with the consonant ʀ, ᴍ̥ with ᴍ, and ɴ̥ with ɴ. Also necessary from the point of view of the system is the so-called laryngeal, which cannot be defined phonetically, but which is conventionally designated by ǝ ; it can function with vocalic value (ǝ̣ beside the consonantal ǝ) and is traditionally called the "schwa."[3] When it has vocalic value, it merges with ᴀ in most areas and with ı in the Aryan world; when it has consonantal value, it merges with the preceding vowel and gives life to the long quantity of the same. The difference between long and short quantity is not therefore a primitive property of Indo-European vowels, but an acquired characteristic.

12 Indo-European Innovations

When it appeared on Italy's doorstep, however, the Indo-European tradition was no longer a primitive tradition for reasons other than those already mentioned. Two principal transformations had already been partially realized in the Indo-European world and in all the linguistic currents that had reached Italy, and both are related to the consonant system. On the one hand we find the transformation of the system of degree of articulation from a quadripartite to a tripartite scheme, as a consequence of the alignment of unvoiced occlusives, voiced and fricative occlusives, heirs of the aspirated. On the other hand, we find the dissolution of the category of sonants which separate into the vowels ı and ᴜ and the consonants ᴊ, ᴠ, ʟ, ʀ, ᴍ, and ɴ, without further possibility of alternation. The vocalic forms of the four sonants ʟ̥, ʀ̥, ᴍ̥, and ɴ̥ are represented principally by the groups ᴏʟ, ᴏʀ, ᴇᴍ, and ᴇɴ. The consonants called labiovelar are preserved better in the proto-Latin tradition than they are in all the other Indo-European languages, and they are energetically labialized in Osco-Umbrian (§27).

In the field of morphology, the fundamental characteristic was that of the alternation of roots between a normal state ᴇ, a strong state ᴏ, and a reduced state with no vowel. In special phonetic situations, in place of a reduced degree (of articulation) with no vowel, there was a semireduced degree, which was treated in different ways in the

Italian peninsula. In Italy this morphological system has been the victim of subsequent phonetic alterations, owing both to the effect of the intensity of the accent and to a different gradation of vocalic timbres. The morphology of the noun was based on a declension of eight cases, of which the instrumental and the locative have left only scant traces in Italy. The morphology of the verb was based on the coexistence, not necessarily total, of the three fundamental themes of the present, perfect, and aorist, which defined the tense and the quantity of the action (or aspect) of the verb, and of the moods which defined the quality, with relative nominal forms of participles, infinitives and so on. The diathesis of the verb aimed at setting up a counterbalance between the active and the middle voices, while the passive was assigned to a secondary system of conjugation, parallel to the causative, desiderative, and intensive forms. In the category of "moods" there was a distinction between the subjunctive, which was the signpost for possibility, and the optative, which expressed desirability. There remained traces of a "primitive" mood[4] which played no part in the Indo-Europeanization of Italy, except perhaps in the formation of the paradigm of the substantive verb *s-u-m*.

13 LEXICAL GROUPS

It is very important to have a picture of the Indo-European lexical heritage in its philological and social stratifications. From the philological point of view, the vocabulary which arrived in Italy can be divided into three categories. The first[5] was made up of those lexical units which, because they are found in all or in almost all the different Indo-European areas, constituted a "compact" whole: in this group we find such verbal roots as ES 'to be' Latin *esse,* DŌ 'to give' Latin *dare,* STHĀ 'to stop, halt' Latin *stare,* WEID 'to see' Latin *videre,* GEUS 'to taste' Latin *gustus,* and finally all the numerals, already inclined toward a decimal system.

A second logical stratum[6] is represented by words which tended to gravitate toward the northwest, that is, to the left side of the chessboard of primitive Indo-European. From the point of view of climate, these words apply to the humid forested areas of central Europe and set themselves in counterpoint to the arid steppes of southeastern Europe. A case in point is GWRANO-, which in the Latin *granum* indicates something (advantageously) dry, while in the more easterly regions it has the value of something which is (injuriously) dry, that is, 'the old man'. Similarly, in the West IWYTI- has the meaning of '(bearable) thirst', while in the East, for example in the Greek *phthisis,* it means '(insufferable) consumption'.

A third lexical stratum[7] is represented by words that survived in areas not contiguous but rather peripheral and escaped the alterations and substitutions that asserted themselves in the central areas. Such was the case with the Latin words *rex, jus,* and *credo,* which find correspondences possibly in the Celtic world (which is indeed contiguous), but otherwise only in the Indo-Iranian world, located at the opposite extreme. In general the words of this stratum pertain to culture, religion, and social order; they call to mind, therefore, social upheavals that resulted in the replacement of ancient institutions, beginning in the interior and working outward to its peripheries. It is strange that qualified scholars find it difficult to accept the fruitful principle of constraposition of marginality and centrality,[8] which constitutes the great step between unidimensional and bidimensional linguistics,[9] while awaiting the arrival of tridimensional linguistics bequeathed to modern sociolinguistics.

Of much greater import is the stratification of words not so much on the basis of their external documentation as in relation to the phases of civilization where they occur. We find echoes from the primitive "food gatherer" stage, for example, in the terminology BHRATER 'brother', which crosses with the terminology BHER 'to carry, bear'. We also find the root LEG meaning 'to gather' and also 'to choose', which is a term pertaining to gatherers, but not to farmers. We find YEM, which survives in its abstract value in the Latin *imago,* but which originally indicated the 'double fruit' or 'twin'. LEIGH, found in the Latin *lingere* 'to lick', is better preserved than terms for eating and drinking precisely because it is connected with a diet which leans toward the consumption of honey and fruit juices.

Memories of the hunt are found in the root SAG 'to go hunting', which survives in an intellectualized form in the Latin *sagax,* and in GHWER, preserved in the Latin *ferus,* which indicates the wild animal, the object of the hunt.

The lexical family AG 'to lead to pasture' is strictly related to sheep rearing. From AG we derive the Latin *agere,* from the root AL 'to nourish' the Latin *alere,* and similarly from PEKU 'flock' the Latin *pecu,* from VAK(K)A 'milk cow' the Latin *vacca,* from (G)LAKT 'milk' the Latin *lac,* and finally from WLENA the Latin and Italian *lama.*

Mythical memories of agriculture have resulted in the passage of the root AGRO- from 'pasture to 'field'; similarly, ARŌ, which is derived from the family ERĒ 'to row, paddle' has profited from the image of plowing as 'rowing the earth'; SE 'to sow' and MET 'to reap, mow', however, have values which are entirely encompassed by the world of farming.

Quite apart from the philological and sociocultural stratification, the vocabulary can be divided into large groups of meaning, artificial though these may be. While maintaining the division of vocabulary into ten large groups which have been presented elsewhere,[10] we may make a further broad distinction into two groups: the first, referring to general psychological, meteorological, and anatomical terminology and including immediate family relationships, endures the consequences of great geographic displacements well; the other is economic, technical, and alimentary and has to do with nature, both domestic and wild, and with larger social units which have obviously felt the greatest repercussions of the geographic displacements. The vocabulary of the first broad category cited is fairly well preserved, but that of the second major grouping has come down to us in a weary and ravaged form, rather like a warrior returning from the battlefield.

It is evident that the lexical voids of Indo-European, or those areas of least resistance, should constitute a source of great attraction for the Mediterranean lexical units with which the Indo-European lexical patrimony came into contact. The following contrasts are most interesting: while in Indo-European we find NAWI-, Latin absorbs the form *barca;* as opposed to WESTI 'attire, garment' Latin accepts *palla* 'woman's outergarment, cape'; compared with KELLA 'hut' Latin has *casa* and, in Alpine regions, the MALGA types; along with AUSO 'gold', ARGNTO 'silver', and AYES 'copper', Latin accepts *plumbum* 'lead'. As regards instruments, Latin absorbs both *serra* 'saw' and *falx* 'sickle, scythe'. In the matter of land forms Latin welcomes the various toponyms of the type *Alba, Alpes,* in addition to *mons* 'mountain'; in contrast to *aqua,* numerous toponyms of the type AUSA 'fountain, spring' are accepted. In the area of vegetation Latin resists *flos* 'flower', but at the same time accepts the Mediterranean *bac(c)a;* beside the names of the great species of the forest, which are dominated by the oak PERKWU- Latin *quercus,* stands the Mediterranean term *taxus.* The 'bee' and its 'honey' offer resistance in the Latin forms *apis* and *mel,* but the technical vocabulary of the apian industry is taken from the Mediterranean world, as we see in the Latin forms *favus* 'honeycomb' and *fucus* 'drone' and even in the surviving Italian form *arnia* 'beehive'. The rodent family, as represented by *mus* 'mouse', is enriched by the company of TALPA 'mole'; among insects, *pulex* 'flea' stands beside BLATTA 'insect'; the word TARMA 'clothes moth' is absorbed along with *vermis* 'worm'. The contact between the Indo-European and the Mediterranean worlds was not, at least in Italy, a violent collision; its consequences were not destructive, but rather integrating and enriching.

14 FIRST FOCI IN ITALY

These new structures, these new lexical units did not, therefore, obliterate or submerge Italy's original linguistic heritage. At the beginning they appear in strongholds or in bridgeheads, which, despite irrepressible linguistic needs, can be identified only by means of archaeology. One preliminary requisite is that the events we are dealing with be so distant that they permit the arrival in Italy of lexical units prior to that internal upheaval of Indo-European society of which we have written above (§13). And since the Greek language appears in the Aegean world already in autonomous form in the fifteenth century B.C., it behooves us to identify a more or less contemporary, initial focal nucleus for the establishment of Indo-European in Italy.[11] The answer to this need is simple. The extra-Italian contacts of the northern Italian prehistoric stations (Emilia and Veneto) belong to a relatively recent period, because they were connected with the central European civilization of fields of urns, that is, following the democratic movement already established in that period.

Farther to the south, halfway down the coast of the Adriatic, other archaeological deposits were found which are rich in trans-Adriatic correspondences and communications, but belong to the Iron Age civilization and therefore are more recent. There remain for our consideration only the deposits of the so-called Matera civilization from the end of the middle Neolithic Age.[12] The Indo-European phase in Italy starts therefore from Apulia, and it is to this first very ancient testimony that the artificial name of "proto-Latin" refers. Ceramics found in the caves of Pertusa and Zachito in Salerno province[13] and resembling the style of the second stratum of Vinča in Yugoslavia show trans-Adriatic similarities.[14] On the banks of the Gargano wedge-shaped stones and painted ceramics of the Turdos type (Transylvania)[15] were found, and in Apulia coil pottery which corresponds to the second period of the Apennine civilization has also been uncovered.[16]

The northern focal nucleus is concentrated first around the prehistoric settlements of the Po Valley, known as terramare, and later mostly around Este. The terramare, which date from the end of the second millennium, bear witness to the middle and recent Bronze Age.[17] The next stage, called "proto-Villanovan," belongs to the late Bronze Age and has its most ancient bases at Fontanella di Casalromano (Mantua) and Bismantova (Reggio Emilia). During this stage there is a tendency to expand toward Pianello di Genga, Monteleone di Spoleto[18] as far as Latium. The Atestine culture of the first Iron Age is the most brilliant; we find evidence of this culture dating from the ninth century and showing associations with Venetic epigraphic remains. In the first phase of this complex we find the following evidence of contact with central Europe: fibulae (§25),[19] the rite of cremation, and the absence of decoration;[20] in more recent phases gibbous, grooved pottery is prominent.

Even from the coasts of the Marches and the Abruzzi, ninth-century finds attest an Iron Age civilization which shows trans-Adriatic connections both in its burial rite and in its grave goods such as the large rings and small spheres found at Cupra and Grottamare on the one hand, and the pendants formed of tiny spheres discovered in Glasinac in Bosnia[21] on the other. These correspondences retrace the old routes already established through the connections between the most ancient civilizations of Rinaldone and Belverde, on the one hand, and of Vučedol, on the other, as has been illustrated by Pia Laviosa Zambotti (§10).[22]

15 THEIR ORGANIZATION

To understand the significance of these movements, it is necessary to have a clear idea of how this new linguistic tradition came to assume a dominant position. It did not have to do with colonization in a demographic sense, nor with conspicuous migrations of peoples; either of these would have left some traces in legend, as the "nostoi" or "returns" of the soldiers of the Trojan War or the descent of the Dorians into the Peloponnesus did. It was not even a matter of the establishment of a cultural aristocracy; this would have left us some record in the form of manuments. The Mediterranean world, in which we include Italy, was culturally superior; the idea of an Indo-European cultural conquest is unthinkable.

And yet, some kind of force, whatever its nature, must have been at work to permit the conquest or at least the establishment of Indo-European. Such a force was all the more necessary, inasmuch as the transplant of a linguistic system from regions so different as those of central Europe must have put it in crisis. This force could only have been social. The nuclei of Indo-European tradition, devoid of any demographic or cultural force, were on the contrary organized into tribes which were solid, if small, and which, wherever they arrived, not only maintained their compact nature but also constituted a force of attraction and confrontation for the indigenous peoples: first, as a source of curiosity, and next as models of a psychologically urban life, then as a solid, fixed point of reference in the change of daily life, something comparable to a "market." Only in this way is it possible to understand an achievement so potent and durable, and at the same time invisible. From this point on, the languages of Italy manifest themselves in new forms, according to a tradition which is full of misfortunes and obstacles, but which is never again interrupted.

Four

Pre-Indo-European
Epigraphic Evidence

16 NON-ETRUSCAN

Only after the first millennium is it possible to pass from the "confrontation" of pre-Indo-European structures to the "comparison" of linguistic units that are historically established and comprehensible to us. Naturally the outcome of this turning point was not immediate, but rather took shape gradually in a tripartite form.

First we must take into account the more or less organic evidence of pre-Indo-European languages which date through and beyond the first half of the millennium. Our second task is to discover within these languages the first signs of "skirmishes" with the Indo-European tradition (i.e., Indo-European penetration), especially in the Etruscan world, where it is legitimate to speak of a peri-Indo-European belt (§§17ff.). Our third and final problem is that of defining the individual Indo-European traditions within the context of the regions and the forms from which they sprang to be diffused throughout Italy with greater and lesser success. We must consider, for example, the linguistic foci of proto-Latin (§§22ff.), Venetic (§25), Osco-Umbrian (§26), Messapic, Lepontic, and Gallic (§§31ff.), and the traditions that in some cases descended from them.

The Punic inscription discovered in 1964 at Pyrgi near Civitavecchia is the first in a series of examples of non-Indo-European languages in ancient Italy. It is also the easiest document to interpret historically, inasmuch as it records the consecration of a temple to the goddess Astarte by Tiberius Veliana, tyrant of Caere, at the beginning of the fifth century B.C. The inscription consists of approximately ten lines which have ample correspondence with two similar but not identical Etruscan versions. The inscription proves the importance of the relations that existed between Carthage and Etruria in that epoch, and not the existence in ancient Italy of a region which was linguistically Punic.[1]

Of much greater significance is the "Sicanian" inscription of Sciri near Caltagirone, Sicily, published by Francesco Ribezzo in 1933. It dates from the sixth century B.C. and is made up of 58 Greek letters which correspond partially to the most ancient Greek alphabet of Syracuse.[2] According to Ribezzo the inscription belongs to a period in which Indo-European was already making itself felt in Sicily. Other authors, Pisani for example,[3] consider it instead as belonging to the Indo-European level of the Siculi. In reality the inscription is still Mediterranean: words such as *nendas, tebeg, pra arei, pagosti kealte,* and *inrubo* do not lend themselves to an Indo-European interpretation. The meaning Ribezzo has attributed to the inscription is: 'Nenda Pureno destroyed in war the citadel in the city of Burena and conquered five territories'. This interpretation is, however, rather uncertain.

The celebrated sixth-century inscription of Capestrano, discovered in 1934, presents problems of a similar sort. It contains approximately forty symbols without division into words and has been read by Radke[4] in the following manner: *Ma Kaprih K. Oram opsu Tr Minis R akinebihi pomp.... II.* Of the eleven words thus isolated, six should be personal nouns, two are numerals, *oram* should be a pronoun, *opsu* a verb, and *akinebihi* would indicate a magistracy. Even if we cannot exclude the possibility of some degree of Indo-European infiltration, the Indo-European stamp of Radke's interpretation seems premature. The alphabet used is common to that employed in archaic Umbrian (or "proto-Sabellian") inscriptions (§26).

The nature and significance of the inscription at Novilara, discovered in 1889,[5] are indubitable. Carved in a block of sandstone on which has been portrayed a wheel with five spokes, the inscription is made up of twelve lines composed of approximately forty words. The first two lines are as follows: *mimnis' erut gaares 'tades'/rotnem uvlin parten us.* Despite the most exhaustive kinds of studies, this inscription has resisted every attempt at interpretation. To this internal difficulty must be added the profound difference between the language of the inscription and Etruscan (geographically close), not only from the morphological and lexical points of view, but also because of the presence of the vowels O and U (reciprocally independent) and the voiced consonants, in an alphabet of Etruscan origin.

The seventy-odd inscriptions of northern Italy which are called Rhaetic belong to a region bounded by the Trentino Alto-Adige and the pre-Alpine base, ranging from the Lago di Garda to Padua. These inscriptions are not so very old, but the difference between their language and Etruscan is too noticeable to permit their being considered as relics of the Etruscan culture of the Po Valley, which was forced to migrate northward after the Gallic invasion of the fifth century. The alphabets are, however, of a northern Etruscan stamp and are divided into two types, Bolzano and Sondrio. Published in the collections of Whatmough and Pisano,[6] the most important of these inscriptions are no. 215 of Caslìr, found in the Val Cembra near Trento, consisting of sixty letters; no. 244, the "paletta di Padova," containing approximately thirty letters; and the "spada di Verona," no. 247, with about forty words. The descent of these alphabets from Etruscan is clear because of the absence of voiced consonant signs and the vowel O and also because of the vacillating use of both voiced and unvoiced aspirated consonants. Characteristic forms are of the type *trinaχe, tinaχe,* which recall forms of the Etruscan perfect.[7]

17 ETRUSCAN

The inscription of the lituus of Collalbo (Bolzano)[8] represents a text which is definitely Etruscan, indeed an Etruscan which was "driven" northward by the Gallic invasion, according to the accounts of Livy and Pliny.[9]

In this way we come to the principal problem of pre-Indo-European linguistics in Italy, that of the Etruscan language! Of all pre-Indo-European linguistic testimony throughout the length and breadth of Europe, none comes close to equalling the richness and the significance of Etruscan. We have at our disposal almost ten thousand inscriptions, the majority of which are extremely brief, a few of which are bilingual, and in addition some scores of isolated glosses, all of which have been gathered together in the *Corpus inscriptionum etruscarum* (CIE), begun in 1890 and not yet finished.[10] The inscriptions are written in alphabets which are not homogeneous, and their prototypes are as follows: the ivory tablet of Marsiliana d'Albegna and two vases, one from Formello and another from Carveteri. These prototypes show the influence of western Greek models and are perfectly legible; some signs have become superfluous, like the consonants B and D, the vowel O, and

the sibilant "samech." In later inscriptions (fourth to first centuries
B.C.) the K and Q, and X as the sign of the sibilant, are also abandoned.
The remaining valid signs define a phonetic system characterized by
four vowels A, E, I, and U and the semivowel V, the aspirate H, three
simple occlusive consonants (C, T, and P) and three aspirated occlusives (chi, theta, and phi), the labiodental F, the three sibilants s, s',
and z, the two liquids L and R, and the nasals M and N. Apart from
minimal corrections, these readings have been well established for a
century.[11]

The first inscriptions date back to the seventh century. But it
will be shown below (§36) that alphabetic possibilities existed in
certain focal areas of Etruria as far back as the Mycenaean age. According to M. Lejeune,[12] these very ancient traces of Etruscan, characterized by syllabic punctuation, were exhumed and reutilized, enjoying their greatest value at the high point of Etruscan history (sixth
and fifth centuries B.C.); from Etruria they spread toward Venetia,
where they were generally accepted (§25), and to the Oscan and
Umbrian areas where the Etruscan alphabet was established in following centuries (fifth and fourth) when it was no longer so fashionable. The principal linguistic monuments of Etruscan are the following: (1) the text of the mummy of Zagreb, a book on linen which
contains 530 words, taking into account repetitions; (2) the roof
tile of Capua, with 62 lines preserved and about 300 legible words;
(3) the cippus of Perugia (CIE 4538), containing 46 lines and 130
words; (4) the lamina of Magliana (CIE 5237), consisting of approximately seventy words; (5) the inscription of Pulena (from Tarquite
CIE 5430), with about sixty words; (6) the two laminae found at
Pyrigi along with the Punic inscription described above (§14) and
also containing approximately sixty words.

18 RELATIONS BETWEEN ETRUSCAN AND INDO-EUROPEAN
The interest which the Etruscans and their languages have aroused
has its roots in antiquity: from Dionysius of Halicarnassus, who defined Etruscan as being different from all other languages,[13] to the
Emperor Claudius, who collected literary examples of Etruscan in
a work now lost. Among modern scholars who have renewed this
interest stands the Englishman Thomas Dempster (seventeenth century), whose work *De Etruria regali* was published only in 1723.
Among Italian antiquaries, it was Luigi Lanzi (1732–1810)[14] who
picked up the thread; among the Germans Carlo Ottofredo Muller
in 1828.[15] The first incentive was to assign to Etruscan a genealogical
definition, whether Italic or not. Corssen, Lattes, and Nogara belonged to the first school; to the second, Deecke, Skutsch, and all the

moderns. Reevaluation in favor of Indo-European is evident in Goldmann, in a resolute manner,[16] and in Vetter in a more vacillating way.[17]

A third avenue of study was indicated about some thirty years ago by P. Kretscher with the theory of "protindogermanische Schicht"[18] or "proto-Indo-European stratum," which I myself have transferred from the historical to the geographic plane with the notion of "peri-Indo-European." The words *Tinia* 'Jove' and *tiv* 'moon' might be precocious developments of the Indo-European root *di(n)* which means 'light', energetically immersed and metamorphosed in the Etruscan world,[19] after a slow and gradual rapprochement on the part of proto-Latin (§23) and Umbrian (§30) tribes.

19 ETRUSCAN LINGUISTIC STRUCTURES
That there are Indo-European elements in Etruscan is undeniable; but this does not prove a kinship between the two languages. *Lautni* 'freedman' can be traced to the proto-Latin tradition (§22); *etera* 'foreign, extraneous' comes from Osco-Umbrian (§20); *aisar* 'gods' goes back to the North Italic tradition (§37); *-umno-*, as for example in the word *Vertumno*,[20] is another example from protoLatin. Although we are not able to trace their evolutionary paths, we must also remember *turce* 'he gave' from the Indo-European root DO, which in Greek (*doron*) is expanded by R, and which takes the suffix *-ce* in the perfect tense; similarly *-c* from the Indo-European KWE; *ta* from the Latin *(is)to-d; mi* from the Latin *me; -th* as the signpost of the locative from an Indo-European tradition *-dhi*, subsequently lost in Latin; and finally the elaboration of a declension in which the individual cases are not quite fixed or established by the signposts which ought to define them.[21]

The stages according to which the fundamental values of certain Etruscan words have been isolated, or at least according to which the semantic field has been defined, have been three in number. In the first phase an etymological method was followed, by comparing in turn first the Italic languages, and then also Armenian (Bugge), Basque and Caucasic (Thomsen), Ugro-Finnic (Martha), even Dravidic (Konow), and more recently Greek (Coli)[22] and Hittite (Georgiev).[23]

The second stage of Etruscan linguistic study is represented by the opposite method, which is called the "combinatory method" because it does not take into account external relations with other languages, but restricts itself to making internal comparisons and to determining the value of words according to internal relationships, with the contexts to which they periodically return. This is the method by which Emil Vetter and Massimo Pallottino have proven themselves.

The third phase is represented by the combination of the first two methods, within a context that is broader than that of the "combinatory," but much more restricted than the etymological. This is the "bilinguistic" method which operates again on the level of external comparison of the language under investigation, not so much by tracing etymological identities as by establishing structural correspondences between the language under investigation and one other language. This is the method which younger scholars, such as the recently deceased K. Olzscha and especially A. Pfiffig,[24] are successfully applying, but it must not be forgotten that the praiseworthy precursor of this structural comparative method was E. Goldmann.[25] I myself have been influenced in the interpretation of the Tablets of Gubbio[26] by both the study of structures and the bilinguistic comparative method.

20 ETRUSCAN INTERPRETATIONS

Apart from those phonetic features which emerge from the transformations of alphabets, the scholar's attention must be directed toward three fundamental points regarding the linguistic structure of Etruscan. In phonetics the theory of the influence of the intensive accent has with the passage of time become more established; by this phenomenon the internal vowels are eliminated; an example is the development of *Clutmsta* from the Etruscan form *Cluthumusta* through the Greek *Klytaiméstra*.[27] In the field of morphology, we must bear in mind the progressive arrangement of a declension, as well as the diffusion of the process of morphological redetermination;[28] there is a passage from the original absence of a "motion" (that is, of an alternative designation of masculine and feminine gender) to some trace of grammatical gender. Here is a list of words from the Etruscan lexicon which may be considered to be correctly interpreted.

In religion: *ais* 'god', *aisar* 'gods', *fler* 'offering', *sacni* 'sacred place', 'sacred action', *mul* 'to dedicate', *tur* 'to present, bestow', *trutnvt* 'augur', *nets'vis* 'soothsayer', *cletram* 'truck or carriage for offerings'.

Regarding funerary rites: *thaura* 'tomb', *cela* 'cell', *mutna* 'sarcophagus', *lupu* 'to die', *hinthia* 'soul, shade', *phersu* 'mask'.

Words denoting familial relationship: *clan* 'son', *s'ec* 'daughter', *puia* 'wife', *nefts* 'grandchild', *prumths* 'great grandchild'.[29] Among verbs we have *am* 'to be', *sval* 'to live', *zich* 'to write'.

Words relating to society: *lautn* 'family', *lautni* 'freedman', *etera* 'foreign', 'inferior', *lauchume* (Latin *lucumo*) 'Etruscan chief', *lucairce* 'former Etruscan chief', *zilc* 'praetor', *maru* 'magistrate', *cepen*

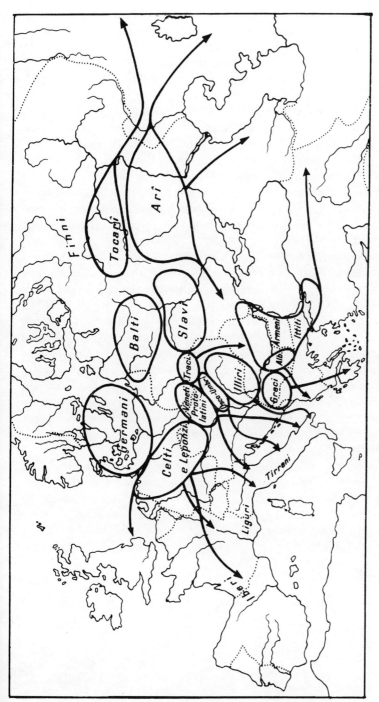

Map 1. The Indo-European Lexical Areas in the Second Millennium B.C.

'priest', *macstrevc* 'master', *spur* 'city', *tuthi* 'state'; *par* (*parchis*) 'equal', that is 'citizen with full rights' (see *etera*), *mechl* 'nation', *rasna* 'Etruria', *tular* 'boundaries', *rumach* 'Roman', *frontac* 'from Ferentum',[30] *naper* (unit of linear measure).

Terms of domestic life: *vinum* 'wine', *verse* 'fire', *cape* 'container', *pruchum* 'jug, pitcher', *sren* 'figure'.

Regarding the calendar: *tin* 'day', *thesan* 'morning', *tivr* 'month', *avil* 'year', *ril* 'at the age of', *acale* 'June', *celi* 'September', Latin *velcitanus* 'March', Latin *traneus* 'July', *ermius* 'August'.

Names of animals: *andas* 'eagle', *arakos* 'sparrowhawk', *arimos* 'monkey', *capu* 'falcon', *damnos* 'horse', *thevru* 'bull'.[31]

Here are two examples of inscriptions that have been interpreted:

Partunus Vel 'Partunu Vel' *Velthurus Stanlnal-c Ramthas clan* 'of Velthur and Satlnei Ramtha son' *avila lupu XXIIX* 'died at the age of 28' (CIE 5424).

Arnth Churcles Larthal clan 'Arnth Churclo son of Larth' *Pevthial* 'and of Pevthi', *zilc parchis amce* 'praetor of the peers', *marunuch spur a na cepen tenu* 'he acted as the priest of the city Marus', *avils machs semphalchls lupu* 'dead at the age of seventy-five' (CIE 5811).

In connection with the opening of the frontiers of Etruria to Greek artistic products, the Etruscan vocabulary became receptive to many Greek terms—first of all to proper nouns concerning the Greek myths which had spread to Etruria through Greek art; and then to the appellatives which were related to the material objects of this commercial traffic (such as *Achmenrun* from the Greek *Agamémnōn, Telmun* from the Greek *Telamōn,* and *phersu* from the Greek *prósōpon*),[32] and above all to the fundamental acquisition of the alphabets (§17).

The prestige of the Etruscan civilization, above all in the sixth century B.C., has coordinated cultural life in central Italy; it has diffused words such as *populus, par, spurius,* or formulae such as the onomastic form which consists of the first name, a noun, followed by the family name, an adjective (see §27).[33]

Five

Indo-European Traditions:
Proto-Latin and Venetic

21 FOCAL NUCLEI IN APULIA: THE OENOTRIANS AND THE OPICI
The contacts between Indo-European nuclei and the indigenous peoples of Italy not only began in limited areas but also were established in a very gradual way. The first phase probably consisted in rudimentary linguistic forms that can be likened to a simple, variable "lingua franca," from which the newcomers began to learn a terminology that reflected the peculiarities of the places they had come to inhabit. A second phase is represented by the fact that frequenters of the "markets" (as they have been called above) did not limit themselves to the exchange of tools of linguistic communication, but also learned adequate structures, functions, and means of expression. The Indo-Europeanized area in this second phase does not yet expand geographically, but rather takes deeper root, and is consolidated; it acquires prestige on a sociological level.

Only in the third stage does an extension take place, although it is not necessary to think of it in terms of a solid demographic expansion. Small nuclei—more or less organized—established a network of contacts in areas which were farther and farther away from the coast, and they left as records of these most ancient achievements names which were no longer related only to isolated tribes, but to peoples. Within the framework of what has been defined above as peri-Indo-Europeanism,[1] isolated words, the avant-garde of these movements, precede human achievements, and like test pilots, enter preexisting linguistic spheres without altering their original character.

In the preliminary phase, in which indigenous ethnic names had not yet become established, the technical term which best defines the situation, though in an artificial way, is "proto-Latin." The expansion of this tradition from Apulia was in a westerly direction, and it affected the whole of southern Italy, subsequently sustaining the pressures and indeed the superimposition of successive linguistic currents. In Apulia this succession was realized by way of the Illyrian stratum to which the Messapic tradition bears witness (§33). The Oenotrians settled in the region immediately adjacent (although none of their linguistic documents have come down to us),[2] and they were replaced in the fifth century B.C. by the Lucanians. Beyond this region and to the south, other currents flowed even into Sicily.

22 SICULAN

In the first millennium B.C. the Mediterranean character of Sicily was not entirely pure (§9). Recent discoveries indicate that it is no longer possible totally to identify the local notion of "Siculan" with that of the proto-Latin stratum defined above. In western Sicily between Segesta and Montelepre, approximately two hundred graffiti inscriptions were discovered,[3] one of which contains the series *ataitukai emi*; in other words, a morphological signpost of Indo-European stamp like *emi* surfaces. The complexity of the situation must be evaluated by taking into consideration the fact that northeastern Sicily has toponymical ties even with Liguria (Segesta-[Sestri], Eryks-Lerici, Eentella, §9) while the Thucydidean tradition associates the Elymi with earlier pressure from the Aegean. Final conclusions about these linguistic remains must not be compromised because of terminology. M. Durante considered these inscriptions to be testimonies of an Oenotrio-Bruttian avant-garde,[4] G. Alessio defined them more generically as "Italic";[5] R. Ambrosini, however, saw in them an autonomous Indo-European tradition linked in some way with Anatolia.[6] M. Lejeune[7] has recently seen in them an Italic tradition once again, one which he would like to consider autonomous, both with regard to the Venetic, Faliscan, and Latin traditions, and the Osco-Umbrian tradition. The most reasonable position seems to be an intermediate one between Durante and Lejeune in the sense that the inscriptions display a generic Italic character inclining toward the proto-Latin complex rather than toward the Osco-Umbrian, a character which in the first half of the millennium was still very distant from Sicily. As for contacts with the East, it is necessary to remember that the years which span the first and second millennia are the years of Mycenaean expansion —both linguistic and nonlinguistic—which justified the rise in antiquity of the theory of the "Pelasgians" (§36).[8] The notion of Siculan in the strict sense is based principally on three inscriptions, the most important of which is that of the "guttus" or pitcher of Centorbi.[9] The interpretation of this inscription is not entirely clear, but the form *nunus*, which is identical to the Latin Nonus, excludes the possibility of any connection whatever with the Osco-Umbrian current which would have rendered NOVIO.[10] Glosses permit the delineation of other characteristics important to the proto-Latin tradition in Sicily.

There is an evident connection between a form like AITNA 'Etna' (in Greek transcription) and the Indo-European root AIDH 'to burn'; it proves the passage of DH to T. Thus we have at the same time proof of the difference between proto-Latin and Latin (in which we find *aedes* with a D), and the possibility of explaining a Latin adjective such as *rutilus* or a local name such as *Liternum* (which can be traced back to the root forms RUDH and LUDH, respectively) as vestiges of a proto-Latin tradition which remained undisturbed. An analogous case is found in the Siculan *litra* as compared to the Latin *libra*. Other interesting glosses attributed to the Siculan language are *ūnkia* 'uncia', *moîton* 'mutuum', *kýbiton* 'cubitus'. The phoneme F (Mediterranean TH; §6) does not appear at this point.[11]

To the north and west of the Oenotrian territory lies that of the Opici. While from a linguistic point of view the Oenotrian zone has remained mute, the Opici area, as we know thanks to the perspicacity of F. Ribezzo, has left some traces which survived the arrival of the Samnite superstratum and the Oscan language (§29). The form *hipid* for 'habuit' can be suspected of Opician influence because of the presence of an internal unvoiced consonant in the place of an ancient aspirated one.

23 FALISCAN

To the north of the territory of the Opici lies the Ausonian zone, and at its extreme northern wing the Latin area. This is anything but uniform. North of Rome, through the Faliscan zone, there is a surviving (proto-)Latin territory which has been subject to both Etruscan and Sabine influences. Our knowledge of Faliscan today is founded on the work of G. Giacomelli.[12] The important inscriptions edited by Giacomelli number about one hundred and fifty. They take up 600 entries in the CIE (8000–8600); a few of them are in Etruscan. The alphabet is archaic Latin, although with a different form of the F. The spelling, influenced in part by Etruscan, has z for s and T for D, and sometimes U for O, K for G, as for example in *eko* for the personal pronoun 'I'. Archaisms in Faliscan (not necessarily proto-Latin) are: *neven* Latin 'novem', *peparai* Latin 'peperi', *eti* Latin 'ET', -*osio* genitive singular ending (Latin -ī). On the lexical level *lecet* 'he/she/it lies' Greek *lékhetai* is important. An innovation common to Latin is that of the substitution of the diphthong -OI for -OU, as for example in *loi(fırta)* Latin 'libertas'.

We must remember that, with regard to consonants, Faliscan like Latin belongs to the area that developed the sound F (see §27), which in Faliscan undergoes an even greater development than in Latin, as is evident in the word *foied* for 'hodie' (§41) in which the initial H has been replaced by an F, and in which we also note the evolution of the group *die* into *ie*. The presence of F in internal position is a proof of Sabine influence, since it takes the place of the simple voiced consonant which, instead, corresponds in Latin to the Indo-European aspirated voiced consonants: this is the case of the Faliscan *loifırta* as compared with the Latin 'libertas', and of the Faliscan *efiles* as compared with the Latin 'aediles'; this is also the case of the forms of the future tenses *carefo, pipafo* in B (Latin *carebo*) which were similarly subjected to the Sabine F, even if the form of the Osco-Umbrian future tense did not end in BH but in s (§27).

24 LATIN DIALECTS

Apart from Faliscan we do not have organic testimonies of Latin dialects, but only indications of dialectal variety, which must have been large. In Lanuvium the aspirated voiced labiovelar consonant did not give life to a G as it did in Rome, but to a B, as the word *neBrudines* 'testicles' proves. The small size of the territory available to Latin results in the fact that even in the Latin of Rome, words of rustic (rather than urban) stamp are granted citizenship; cases in point are *bos* 'ox, bullock', which ought to have been VOS in Latin, *lupus* 'wolf', instead of LUKOS, *forfex* 'scissors' instead of FORBEX. That this last urban form did exist is proved by the present-day Italian form *forbice*.

The situation for Latin is destined to worsen again when its linguistic scantiness is again fattened—no longer by the influx of Latin dialectal varieties, but by the infiltration of other languages which, like Volscian, appear on the scene in later periods (§46).[13]

25 VENETIC

One of the first Indo-European currents which played a part in the formation of Latin leads back to the north Italic tradition of Venetic.

What we now know of Venetic has been collected in the great work of G. B. Pelligrini and Aldo Prosdocimi.[14] Today Venetic inscriptions number 270, of which 119 come from Este, 15 from Adria, 19 from Padua, 73 from Cadore, and 23 from Gail valley, which is situated on the other side of the Carnic Alps in Austrian territory. They date from the sixth century B.C. to the dawn of the Roman Age in the second century.

Their alphabet, of Etruscan origin, was adopted in the period between 550 and 450 B.C., along with all the problems that stem from its adaptation to a significantly different phonetic system. The principal difficulty is posed by the makeshift expedient adopted to indicate the voiced consonants (not denoted in the Etruscan alphabet); namely, the use of those signs which in Etruscan indicate the aspirated consonants: khi for G, phi for B, zeta for D. Signs for the sibilants abound: s' and š are frequently interchanged, but they are distinguished from the simple S. In Latin s' and š are transcribed with ss, as we can see in the example *sselboisselboi* (Belluno 1). The sign which at one time was read as H is now read as I: the name of one of the goddesses is Reitia, not *Rehtia*. In labiovelar series (or in labiovelar equivalents) the appended component is reinforced to a notable degree as the examples *kvidor* (Cadore 64) and *ekvon* (Este 71) show. Of fundamental importance is the syllabic punctuation,[15] taken organically from the Etruscan (§17) and dating back, from all appearances, to the Mycenaean Age (§36).

On the phonetic level, the importance of Venetic lies in the passage from aspirated voiced consonants to simple voiced consonants in internal positions: this pattern indicates an affinity with Latin and an opposition to the Umbro-Samnite solution (see §27); the Venetic form *louderobos* reflects the point of departure LOUDHEROBHOS (dative-ablative plural) 'liberis'. On the morphological level the following forms are typical: the pronouns *ego mego* as compared to the Latin forms 'ego' 'me' (in Gothic *ik mik*); the sigmatic aorist *donasto* 'donavit', *fagsto* 'fecit'; the so-called injunctives such as *kvidor* 'he/she paid' or *toler* 'he/she placed'. In declension the case ending *-bos* is prominent, being applied even to the declension in -o, as we have seen in the above-cited *louderobos* 'liberis'.

In vocabulary the number of words of which we find evidence is close to one hundred and fifty. To be remembered are the archaic *deivos* 'dei' (accusative plural); *doto* athematic aorist of the root DŌ 'to give', *ekvon* Latin 'equom', *dono* Latin 'donum'; *aisu-* the central Indo-European stem with religious value, penetrated even into Etruscan; the well-known root TEUTA 'people'; the stem *foug*, which goes back to the Indo-European root BHEUG; the two names of femi-

nine divinities LOUDHERA, Latin 'Libera', and *Reitia,* which is semantically equivalent to the Greek *Horthia.* Another important but
less clear stem is represented by *iorobos* if it can be connected with
the German *Jahr* 'year'. Finally the preposition *op(i)* Latin 'ob',
and *per,* identical to its Latin correlative, appear. An extension from
the Venetic world is represented by the inscriptions from the Val
Camonica, in which we witness the Indo-Europeanization of an
originally Euganean population. These inscriptions date from 350
to 70 B.C. The man who first shed light on them, F. Altheim, wanted
to emphasize their Latinity; G. Radke[16] preferred rather to connect
them with the Umbrian world. In reality the only Italic-type words
are *Sanco Leima Ju'vila,* an insufficient number to permit their being
assigned to a determined genealogical group. Some Indo-European
traces are, however, discernible (e.g., *tiez,* perhaps to be read *dies,*
in the context of a scene of solar cult), but they do not provide any
definite clue to their genealogic position.

Moreover, the Venetic area maintains its importance in a broad
sense, inasmuch as it is connected to a major communication system.
If, in a more ancient phase, linguistic and cultural currents moved
southward from Veneto as far as Latium (and *Venetulani* is in fact
the name of a tribe of Latium), then in a more recent stage, the
region has been the crossroads of another current going in the
opposite direction, which carried the alphabetic tradition of the
rune to the north.[17]

Six

Indo-European Traditions:
Umbro-Samnite

26 ARCHAIC UMBRIAN

The Umbrian community stands next to the Etruscan in historical importance. It is not essential to our purpose to insist on the original Mediterranean root of the name, which was subsequently assumed as a technical linguistic term.[1]

In this sense we are using the term "Umbrian" when we speak of the linguistic tradition which began on Italian soil halfway down the Adriatic coast in the provinces of Ascoli, Piceno, and Teramo, and which became established in the interior, between Gubbio and Rieti. From there, through successive expansions connected in the historiographic tradition to the practice of the rites of spring, it gave life to successive linguistic and cultural crystallizations, which reached even the Straits of Messina. The traditional name given to this complex is "Osco-Umbrian," to which I feel the term "Umbro-Samnite" is to be preferred only for formal reasons.

The earliest linguistic testimony of this tradition appears in epigraphy through the inscriptions called "proto-Sabellic," or preferably "ancient Umbrian," whose bonds with the classical testimony of the Tables of Gubbio[2] have only recently been recognized. Their alphabet, which already appears in the inscription of the warrior of Capestrano (§16), exhibits different connections with the Greek

Corcyrian models, even though disparities in the reading of a few signs do exist, as in the case of the sign which Pisani reads as F and Radke as H.[3] In spite of these uncertainties, they guarantee the kinship of some proto-Sabellic words such as *petro-, puqlo-, patere, matere, postin, estas,* which mean 'four', 'son', 'father', 'mother', 'after' or 'second', and finally a demonstrative pronoun, respectively. Only three differences appear in comparison with classical Umbrian: the voiced aspirates are not yet merged with F; the diphthongs are not yet fused, as the proto-Sabellic *svaipis* (in comparison with the Umbrian *svepir*) shows; and finally, there are nominal themes that take endings in *-es* instead of *-os*.[4]

The basic evidence of the Umbrian language was found far from the Adriatic coast, on the Tyrrhenian slope of the Apennines in Gubbio. There remains in the Iguvine Tablets a trace of a prior phase, in the name of a confraternity of the priests of Gubbio, who called themselves "the brothers of Atiedio" and who lived to the east of the Apennine watershed, in a locality near Fabriano which today is known as Attiggio.

The original name of this ethnic tradition must have come from the root SABH, but its derivatives were lost in the "proto-Sabellic" tradition cited above, and in that of the Umbrians of Gubbio. We do find derivatives in historical times in populations (for example, Sabines, Sabellians, Samnites) that settled more to the south, in the Abruzzi and in Sannio.

27 IGUVINE UMBRIAN

The Iguvine Tablets,[5] seven in number, are made of bronze, and are in part written in an alphabet of Etruscan origin, partially adapted to the needs of the Umbrian language, and to a (lesser) degree in a Latin alphabet also partially adapted to the exigencies of Umbrian. They were found in 1444 and have been preserved in Gubbio itself in the Palazzo dei Consoli. They date back to a period between the third and the first centuries B.C. The Etruscan alphabet does violence to the Umbrian language by not distinguishing between the vowels o and U, nor between the voiced and unvoiced consonants. The difference between the two spelling systems becomes apparent when one compares parallel passages: Tab. VI b 6, *rubine porca trif rofa* (in which we note a distinction in the Latin alphabet in B/P and O/U) is identical in content to Tab. I b 28, RUPINIE E TRE PURKA RUFRA (which does not contain these distinctions). In both passages the meaning is 'three young red pigs.' Two new signs, which we transcribe with ř and ç, were added to the Etruscan alphabet. The first indicates the pronunciation of the "rolled" intervocalic D; the second, the palatalized pronunciation of the unvoiced guttural consonant before E and I, evident in STRUCLA (a cake) which is derived from STRUK(E)LA = Latin 'struicula'. Even in the Latin alphabet there is recourse to two modifications or expedients. The digraph RS serves to indicate the same pronunciation of the postvocalic D, which has been described above as "rolled," as for example in *seRse* = Latin 'sedens'. s' indicates the palatalization of the guttural consonants before E and I; we cite as an example *Fiso S'a(n)cio* (Tab. VI b 3).

The language to which the Iguvine Tablets bear witness is Indo-European and rather close to Latin and the other languages of ancient Italy. Sometimes, however, it is more in agreement with Greek or other Indo-European languages other than Latin: *purom-en efurfatu* means 'Let it be taken off the (sacrificial) table and be thrown in the fire', because *purom* is the accusative of the theme PUR (Greek *pŷr* 'fire') and *efurfatu* is the imperative of a denominative verb taken from a theme FURFO- 'table', which survives in the Germanic languages in the form *bordo-* (English 'bord') and goes back to an Indo-European theme BHORDHO.

Words resembling Greek in genealogical kinship can be found next to words borrowed from Etruscan, as we note for example in Tab. Va II f., *esunes-ku vepurus . . . prehubia*, 'with the sacrificial words . . . prepare'. *Vepurus* is the dative-ablative plural of the same theme whence the Greek *wepos* 'word', derives, while *esunes-ku* shows an association of the postposition *com* with the dative-ablative plural of the root derived from the Etruscan *aisuna*. On the phonetic plane, the labiovelar consonants are labialized: Kw gives P, and Gw gives B. Common not only to Umbrian but also to the other languages of the group is the treatment of aspirated consonants regardless of their position in the word: from both DH and BH we always derive F, while in Latin the F appears only in initial position. Characteristics which are strictly Umbrian are the palatalization of the K and G before E and I, the passage of the long $\bar{u}$ to I, apparently by way of an intermediate phase *ü*, and finally the rhotacism of the s even in final position. Not only is there a genitive plural form *-arum* derived from ASOM, but also a dative-ablative plural such as *plener* as compared with the Latin 'plenis.'

In the field of morphology the characteristic forms, recognizable even today, are: in numerals, the dissimilar formation of the ordinals which in Umbrian are extracted from the "root," as for example NOVIO from **nov(em)*, while in Latin they are derived from the "theme," *nonus* from NOWEN-; in personal pronouns, the accusative case takes the ending *-om,* as we see in the Umbrian form *tiom* as compared with the Latin 'te', or the Oscan *siom* as compared with 'se'; among the demonstratives we find the ablative form *esu* (Latin 'hoc') which comes from the more ancient form EKSO, and *eru* (Latin 'eo') from the more ancient form EISO; in verb forms we note the formation of future tenses in -s- as in *pehast* (Latin 'piabit'), the formation of the future anterior in -F- as in *(an)dersafust* (Latin '-dederit'), the formation of infinitives in -o(m) as for example FAÇIU (Latin 'facere'). Among case endings the middle verbs in -r are characteristic, as for example *ferar* with an impersonal value.

Within this group of phenomena which are common to the entire Osco-Umbrian tradition, there are others peculiar only to Umbrian: these are the themes of the perfect tenses in -L-, as for example in ENTELUS from EN-TEND-LO (Latin 'imposueris') or in -nš- as for example in *(combifia)nšiust* (Latin '(nuntia)vĕrit'). It is noteworthy that Umbrian has case endings in -*tur*, in agreement with Latin, while Oscan has endings in -*ter*.[6]

The Umbrians also adopted the Etruscan onomastic formula which was composed of given name and family name (§20). But, like the Etruscans of the Po Valley, and unlike the Latins and the Etruscans of Tuscany, they placed the patronymic before the family name. The Oscan pattern is "Lucius, son of Titus Tetteius," while in Latin we would have "Lucius Tetteius, son of Tito" (see §41).

28 PROTO-SABINE, SABINE, POST-SABINE, SABELLIC

Various tribes broke away from the Umbrians and regrouped themselves in the following way beginning from the Rieti plateau: toward the west there were the proto-Sabines and Sabines who almost reached the gates of Rome; farther to the east there were the various Sabellis branches, and even farther, almost like a vanguard, the Samnites. Of the Sabine language there exists practically no whole text but only isolated words.[7] Indeed, the Sabine pressure on Rome lends itself to classification into two periods: a more ancient phase, proto-Sabine, which corresponds (in an early phase) to the founding and initial establishment of the city; and a more recent stage, Sabine in the strict sense, which culminates in the first century of the Roman republic (fifth century B.C., §46).[8] As E. Peruzzi has convincingly argued (§41), it was in all probability these "proto-Sabines" who brought to Rome the primitive Etruscan onomastic formula with the patronymic *after* the family name.

The most ancient testimony of a proto-Sabine or at least an Osco-Umbrian pressure in Latium is found in the Praenestine fibula (seventh century B.C.), which is characterized by two unequivocal features: (*a*) the dative singular ending in -OI (*Numasioi*) and (*b*) the doubled perfect tense, as attested in the Oscan language (*fhefhaked*).

This is opposed to the form which is not doubled, which can be traced back to an Indo-European aorist, and which indeed appears in the archaic Latin word *feced*.

Testimonies of Sabellic (from the third century on) are not homogeneous. In the Bottiglioni edition[9] they are represented by two examples of Vestinian testimony (nos. 119–20), one Marrucinian (121), ten Paelignian (122–31), and four Marsian (132–35). Most of them are limited to a few words, except for the bronze Marrucinian inscription of Rapino, which has twelve lines, and the Paelignian inscription of Herentas, which has seven. The passage from the original phase in which the diphthongs are still preserved to that in which the diphthongs are fused becomes clear when one compares the Marrucinian *totai* (in Umbrian 'tote') or the Paelignian *coisatens* (Latin 'cura-') to a Marsian form life *(iou)es* instead of *-ois*. A testimony apart is that of the Volscian language, which appears in the so-called Tablet of Velletri of the third century B.C.; although it consists of only four lines, these are sufficient to support its ·classification as Umbrian rather than Sabellic, despite the fact that it was found rather far south. In fact, the onomastic formula shows the patronymic before the family name as is the case in Umbrian and not in Latin (§41); guttural consonants alternate before a palatal vowel; diphthongs are absorbed.

29 OSCAN

Unlike the other Italic languages, Oscan is conspicuous for the breadth of its territory and for its linguistic unity, ensured in almost all of southern Italy from the fourth century B.C. on. The Oscan inscriptions number more than 200. The most important ones are the fourth-century tablet of Agnone, found in Molise and containing 48 lines and an important list of divinities;[10] the cippus of Abella in Campania, of 58 lines, which tells of the demarcation of a temple to Hercules on the boundary between Nola and Abella territories; the Tabula Bantina, a juridical text originating from Bantia in Lucania (north of Potenza), of 39 lines plus a fragment discovered in 1966; the Curse of Pacius Clovatius of 13 lines, and originating from Capua. Most of the minor inscriptions come from Campania. Finally, we have the inscriptions of Bruzio and Messina[11] in addition to the inscription of Adrano in Sicily.

The Oscan language is generally more conservative than Umbrian: it maintains diphthongs, as well as guttural consonants, intact, independent of the following vowel. In morphology the following feature should be noted: the theme of the demonstrative pronoun EKO-, as for example EKAS = Latin 'hae' and the perfect tenses in

-TT, as for example in PRUFATTED = Latin 'probavit'. In the field of vocabulary we note *feihos* 'wall', which is identical to the Greek *teîkhos,* but which is missing in Latin.

30 SURVIVING FEATURES

One of the alphabets used is of Etruscan-Campanian origin; the other is Latin. There are a few examples of the use of the normal Greek alphabet. The Etruscan-type alphabet incorporates an important innovation, in the sense that, in addition to the vowels I and E, the vowel I' is introduced; it was designed to indicate either a particularly closed E or a particularly open I. This phenomenon is one of the first clues to the distinction in degrees of openness that is characteristic of vulgar Latin.[12] The vowel U' also exists but serves more than anything else to reestablish the difference between O and U which the Etruscan alphabet had abandoned.

Seven

Indo-European Traditions:
Lepontic, Messapic,
and Gallic

31 LEPONTIC MONUMENTS
The first point which must be elaborated is the notion of "Lepontic."
In the normal epigraphic tradition Lepontic is the language of a
few inscriptions recently restudied by M. G. Tibiletti-Bruno;[1] num-
bering approximately eighty,[2] they cover the area defined by the
Toce and Adda rivers and are linked to the territory of the ancient
population of the Lepontii[3] and the present-day Val Leventina in the
Swiss canton of Ticino. The extension of this term, which postulates
an Indo-European tradition that is neither Italic nor Gallic, is justified by the fact that in the triangle encompassed by Genoa, Piacenza,
and Parma onomastic and toponomastic testimonies exist even today
which for other reasons pose the same problem of an Indo-European
character which is neither Italic nor Gallic.[4] This testimony appears
in two monuments written in Latin, the Sentential Minuciorum of
117 B.C. (CIL I² 584) and the list of foodstuffs found at Veleia and
dating from the era of Trajan (CIL XI 1147). The fact that the two
areas, though not contiguous, demonstrate common characteristics
justifies the hypothesis that the break between them was caused by
the invasion of the Celts at the beginning of the fifth century. The
need to designate the whole by an artificial term results in turn from
the need to reserve the term "Ligurian" for the pre-Indo-European

stratum of the region (see §4). One Lepontic feature, probably absorbed by the preceding Indo-European stratum is that of the derivatives in *-alo,* as in *Ritu-kalo* (§9).

32 INDIRECT TESTIMONY

Toponomastic correspondences extend beyond the area. The Latin *Genua* 'Genoa', which corresponds to the most inland point of a well-defined gulf can be separated only with the greatest difficulty from the Latin *Genava* 'Geneva', which is geographically located at the point where the waters of Lake Geneva return to form the river-bed of the Rhône. The name *Genavia,* which refers to one of the estates listed in the *tablet* from Veleia, completes the picture. The common point of departure of all these terms is the theme GENU 'knee': the "articulation" of the gulf is compared to the articulation of the knee.

In the case of the toponym *Bormio,* a locality of the central Alps to which the name of the Piedmontese-Ligurian river *Bormida* corresponds, a phonetic necessity obliges us to make recourse to an expedient foreign to the Italic and Celtic traditions. The theme BORMO- is certainly the same one that appears in the Irish *gorm* and the Latin *formus,* but the phonetic treatment of the voiced aspirated labiovelar GwH is different from its treatment in both the Italic and Celtic traditions. The dative-ablative plural *debelis,* found in the Veleia tablet, is part of the same series and comes from a root DHEGwH, which is the same root from which the Latin *foveo* comes, although in a rather different form. The same treatment of the voiced aspirated consonant appears in the form *fundus Roudelius,* to which the present-day Mount *Rudella* corresponds. The Latin name of the river Polcévera, which flows into the sea immediately west of Genoa, is *Porcobera,* and its structure is the result of the combination of the element *porca* 'clod, sod' and the theme *bero-* which is equivalent to the Latin *fero.* This treatment could be even Gallic, but the Gauls never settled in the Val Polcevera, and in any case they would not have tolerated the consonant P- in initial position.

An almost Germanic treatment of the vocalized nasal ON appears in the form *Blondelia* (a village mentioned in the Veleia tablet) and proves the existence of a theme BLUNDA, which was once held to be exclusively Germanic and was supposed to have penetrated the vocabulary in the period of the late Empire to indicate a reddish color in horses, although it was already present much earlier presumably to define 'reddish-colored earth'. A Lepontic theme appears to have spread in the direction of central Italy, reappearing in the Latin *bitumen.* It is a derivative of a theme BITU, which is found in more elementary forms in Lepontic territory: *Bittelus,* which today is 'Bettola' (Piacenza) and *Bettonianus,* which presupposes Betunia, today Bedonia (Parma).[5]

33 MESSAPIC MONUMENTS

The term "Illyrian" is as vague and exaggerated (and not only in ancient Italy) as the notion of "Lepontic" is strictly limited. Only within the last ten years has the term begun to be used again within reasonable boundaries. The notion of "Illyrian" is conventionally defined in a negative way. It describes the remains of the Indo-European tribes that did not migrate far from their places of origin after the Celts were established as a nation spreading toward the west, the Germans and Baltics toward the north, and the Slavs toward the east. Beside the Illyrians and directly to the east, the Thracians make up part of this group of "central" Indo-Europeans (see §12).[6] It is necessary to bring drastic reductions to bear on the attempts to give positive content to the notion of "Illyrian" through onomastic and toponomastic documentation, because this documentation deals in large part with "pre-Indo-European," and not Illyrian, elements.[7] This does not exclude the idea that trans-Adriatic correspondences exist in Italy; the study of Italian linguistics, because of the peninsula's Umbrian, Venetic, and proto-Latin ancestry, "calls for" trans-Adriatic connections (see §14). But these are always "Indo-European" connections which have not yet been differentiated and are not circumscribable by restricted terms such as "Illyrian." According to the adage of Festus (248 L), "Paeligni ex Illyrico orti" implies a geographic and not an ethnic dependence, as many have been tempted to establish.[8] In any case, when we enter the territory of Apulia, things change. The general notion of Iapyges, and the particular notions of Daunii, Peucetii, and Messapii follow each other, corresponding approximately to the general notion of Apulia and to her three historical provinces, Foggia, Bari, and Lecce, respectively. All together they represent an Indo-European stratum which is superimposed on the proto-Latin stratum, beginning with, let us say, the ninth or eighth century. It would appear that the Daunii settlement had some contact with the proto-Latin stratum insofar as the term *Fauni* is a Latin word distinguished as such only by the diverse treatment of the initial voiced aspirate: it becomes fricative in Latin while remaining devoid of aspiration in the land of the Daunii. Within this group, to which we may apply the name "Illyrian," the Messapic linguistic tradition, surviving in the Salentine Peninsula, and more precisely in the area of Lecce, excels in the richness of its linguistic testimony.

More than three hundred inscriptions which date from the sixth to the first centuries B.C. bear witness to the Messapic language. The features of this strain of Illyrian, pushed to extreme consequences by the influence of other more eastern Indo-European currents such as the Thracian-Phrygian ones, are characterized by the passage of the short o into a, the passage of the aspirated voiced consonants into simple voiced consonants, and finally by the assibilation of the gutturals.[9]

As R. Ribezzo well understood,[10] the distant ties of the language thus documented are to be sought in a relationship with Albanian. In the field of morphology one interesting characteristic is the ending of the genitive singular in *-ihi.*

The alphabet is essentially related to the Greek alphabet of Tarentum; a few uncertainties have been illustrated by O. Parlangeli.[11] Signs designating the ends of words do not exist; that is, there is no separation between words. The sign o, which was used less frequently because of the passage of the short o to a, still enjoyed some success because it came very close to the value of U and ultimately eliminated the Greek sign Y. In Parlangeli's classification[12] and from the point of view of alphabet the inscriptions can be divided into four stages: archaic, classic, late, and final. Here are some interesting words: *argora(pandes)* 'silver weigher', the name of a presumed magistrate, linked with the Greek 'argyro-'; *barzidihi,* a personal noun taken from the root BHERGH (277); *berada* and related words to be linked to the root BHER (279); *bilia,* which is commonly compared with the Latin 'filia' (280); *blavit* 'he offered' (past absolute) from the root BHLAU; *deranthoa* related to the Greek 'gerusia' according to Haas;[13] *dehatan,* adjective and verb linked to the root DHEIGH 'to mold, shape' (300); *deivas* 'god' (302ff.); *hazavathi* 'he/she pours out' (314) from the root GHEU 'to pour (out)' *kalatoras* (320), compare Latin 'calator'; *klaohi* (323) imperative from the root KLEU 'to listen'; *kos* interrogative pronoun from the root KwO-; *pido* 'he gave' (past absolute) from a root DO with the prefix *(e)pi* (350); *totthebis* dative and ablative plural connected with the theme TEUTA;[14] *-thi* (case ending) to be connected perhaps with the Greek *eti* (370); *veinan* (380) from SWEINO- 'his'; *venas* probably analogous to the Latin Venus (380); *zi* to be connected perhaps with Jove (386); and finally the noun *brendon,* to be connected with Brundisium (Brindisi) and with the meaning 'stag, deer'.

34 GALLIC MONUMENTS
At the beginning of the fifth century the Gallic linguistic tradition appears in an organic form, like a real invasion followed by coloniza-

tion. It breaks the former continuity between the central Alps and the Ligurian Apennines which was realized by the Lepontii (§31), and farther to the East it dominates the Etruscan colonies which had been established in the preceding century.

Gallic epigraphic testimonies are limited to the inscriptions of Briona (in the province of Novara), of Zignago near La Spezia, and finally to the bilingual document of Todi, which is a testimony to subsequent raids. The proper nouns of the inscription of Briona[15] —Anareuiseos, Tanotalos, Anokopokios, Satupokios—which have not yet been disturbed by the action of the intensive accent, stand as a testimony to a state that is still relatively archaic. A verb in the same inscription, *karnitus,* which is to be understood as 'they made (did)' (past absolute) is important. If we take into account the relatively late dating of the monument (second half of the second century B.C.), its importance appears to decrease. The fact remains, however, that even if Celtic linguistic characteristics (such as the passage of the long E to I or the passage of the voiced aspirated labiovelar from GWH to G, and even less the typical features of Britannic and continental Celtic labialization) did not become established in Cisalpine Gaul, the remnants of Gallic in Latin and in its final tradition in Italy are vast. Examples of words which have been gathered into Latin from Gallic are *ambactus* 'servant', *bracae* 'trousers', *brennus* 'minor sovereign', *bulga* 'purse', *benna* 'small vehicle', *carpentum* 'cart', *petorritum* 'cart with four wheels' *carrus* 'cart' (with an evident propensity for modes of travel), *veredus* 'horse', *alauda* 'lark'.

35 SURVIVING FEATURES

But this is a mere trifle in comparison with the impression the Gallic tradition left on Latin toward the end of the first century B.C. when the latter was accepted as the basic language in use and Gallic was abandoned. Even if not all of the features that characterize those dialects of northern Italy called precisely Gallo-Italic do not date back to this event but depend in part on influences of the imperial age (§97), nevertheless the processes of palatalization both of vowels (passage of A to Ä) and of consonants (from CT to IT and ĉ, see §126) definitely do date back to this linguistic stratum. It left a stamp on northern Italy which was never erased.[16]

Eight

The Origins of Rome

36 Mycenaean Currents

For several of the Indo-European linguistic traditions in Italy, the sea was the vehicle by which Italy was reached. Examples of such traditions were the proto-Latin and the Umbro-Samnite, both of which came to Italy from across the Adriatic Sea, the first to the shores of Apulia, the second to the coasts of the Marches and the Abruzzi (§14). In such cases these crossings were brief passages, almost like a ferry crossing. The other seas of Italy, the Ionian and the Tyrrhenian, although they did not constitute real migration routes, did permit and promote trade and the establishment of colonies, which later became entrenched in historiographic traditions and even in legend; these in turn had indirect but significant linguistic consequences. Among these occurrences the conspicuous Mycenaean element was the most ancient, though the most recent to be uncovered.

As is evident from the catalog of a recent exhibition at Taranto,[1] the Mycenaean finds, which have been made from time to time along the coastal trading route which extends from the Ionian islands to the Straits of Otranto, along the Salentine Peninsula and the Gulf of Taranto, to the eastern coast of Sicily and along the Tyrrhenian coast, are connected with the findings in Ischia, for example, where three fragments of Mycenaean ceramic of Mycenaean III A were unearthed, and at Luni sul Mignone (Viterbo), where five fragments of Mycenaean ceramic of Mycenaean III B and C were found in an Apennine hamlet. In Sardinia even copper bullion with signs in linear A writing were found.[2] This precocious expansion continues until the end of the thirteenth century B.C. Nevertheless, from the point of view of linguistics these finds do not produce results equal to those made on the Adriatic coast. These latter bring together technical-cultural aspects with ethnic-linguistic elements connected with the first achievements of Indo-European traditions. In the Tyrrhenian, even though Mycenaean words probably accompanied "objects," still as long as the Mycenaean expansion did not constitute real colonization, it was limited to the technical-cultural frame of reference: it is not yet feasible to speak of an encounter of the grafting of a Greek linguistic tradition to those traditions that are generically called Italic.

Nevertheless, one indirect linguistic consequence is evident, and it is an important one. The Tyrrhenian route was once known to have been followed only by the Phoenicians, and so long as no other competitors were in sight it remained accessible to more or less speculative though not absurd hypotheses regarding other displacements and migrations, such as those attributed to the Etruscans. But now, as a consequence of recent discoveries, this route became "occupied" by Mycenaean material; other presumable navigators, whether intruders or legitimate travelers, found the way already taken. The space which remains at the disposal of the Phoenicians tends toward different routes, along the coast of Africa and Sardinia with fulcrum points from Cyrenaica to Morocco, to the Balearic Islands.[3] All things considered, there remains of this archaic expansion—which in successive centuries was no longer recognized as Greek even by compatriots—on the one hand the name of the Pelasgians,[4] which keeps bobbing up and which later spread in legend as far as the basin of the Adriatic and the mouth of the Po,[5] and on the other some indirect traces preserved in legend; one such trace is provided by the first founding, around the middle of the eleventh century, of Cumae,[6] which was not yet a colony but only a refueling and supply station subsequently abandoned.

The picture takes on a different light, indirect but effective, if we take into consideration the legendary traditions which essentially fall into two categories. The earlier tradition comes from the legend of Ulysses[7] and is therefore Greek; it reaches Italy's shores as a consequence of the Trojan war; in other words, around the eleventh century. This first tradition is related to the coast of Apulia, which is the closest for the traveler coming from the Aegean. Hesiod,[8] however, is already familiar with a certain "Latinus," who is the brother of Agrius and a son of Ulysses, and so even this legend reaches Italy's Tyrrhenian coast.

The second category of legend is even more important and concerns the legend of Aeneas;[9] it consists of three elements: (1) the echo of the *nostoi,* that is, of the "returns" of the heroes of the Trojan war, even though in this case we are dealing with a Trojan and not a Greek hero; (2) the generic genealogical echo of cities whose origins are linked with Aeneas for etymological reasons, an example being the city of Aineia[10] in Macedonia; and (3) the crystallization of the epos after the Trojan war according to Stesichorus' poem (seventh and sixth centuries)[11] in which we find not only a point of departure but also the indication of a destination in a land to the west, Esperia. The first contacts with the West were established in Africa with the Dido episode and in Sardinia with the Ilienses population, whose name is etymologically related to the name of Ilium/Troy. The final link with Latium or Rome occurs in the fifth century, principally through the Sicilian historian Timaeus (fourth and third centuries). Finally the war with Latinus and the marriage with his daughter consolidates the Tyrrhenian tradition of Aeneas with the Adriatic tradition that goes back to Ulysses.[12]

The possibilities hidden in archaeological finds and the slow elaboration of a doctrine about the establishment of a Greek tradition in Rome find at a certain point in history a confirmation in the actual constitution of the first Greek colonies, two of which were more than any others destined to have even a linguistic significance: Ionian Cumae near Naples and Doric Taranto in the eighth century.[13]

In addition, the Mycenaean expansion is touched upon by another particular problem, that of the previous history of alphabets. The combined results of F. Slotty's[14] and E. Vetter's [15] investigations have led scholars to deduce, from indications of the use of punctuation in a central period of Etruscan epigraphy, the existence in Italy of a very ancient syllabic alphabet which is almost like an offshoot of the linear A and B writings of the Aegean-Mycenaean world and the Cypriot world. Through the latest work of A. Pfiffig[16] and M. Lejeune,[17] scholars have been able, if not to reconstruct a Tyrrhenian primer, at least to admit the possibility of a connecting link between the Greek testimonies, which date from the end of the second millennium, and Etruscan testimonies that reemerged in the form of a fashion from the shadows of the sixth and fifth centuries. Presumably this system of punctuation would then have passed organically into the Venetic environment (§25). Naturally time has flattened these two stratifications. In Tacitus (*Annals* XI.14) Demaratus of

Corinth, who is said to have taught the Etruscans the so-called historical alphabet (§17), is put on the same plane with Evander, who, according to Dionysius of Halicarnassus (I.31), is said to have arrived in Italy even before the Trojan war and who therefore could be considered as the first personification of the precocious legendary transmission of the syllabic alphabet mentioned above.

37 PROTO-VILLANOVAN CURRENTS

Undeniable, though more vague, is the part the Tyrrhenian played in the diffusion of elements linked not with Greece but with northern Italy. The so-called proto-Villanovan civilization could have followed an overland route from its places of origin in Emilia to Ancona (the hill of the Capuchins), and then inland to the Pianello di Genga, to Ponte San Pietro, to Tolfa and Allumiere, as far as the Roman Forum and even a little south of it.[18] Finds in southern Italy in the Taranta region[19] raised the first doubts, but were not sufficient, however, to ascertain or propose that passage was only by sea. But since in more recent times a proto-Villanovan settlement has been discovered in Milazzo[20] in Sicily and another has been found in Chiavari,[21] the maritime hypothesis has gained support and has permitted us to consider the thesis that the proto-Villanovans slowly became navigators,[22] that they were "Normans" twenty centuries ahead of their time. While they do not provide us with direct linguistic connections, these proto-Villanovan "Normans" do reinforce the idea that the maritime routes were on the itinerary of the "occupied" Tyrrhenian coast, impermeable to linguistic traditions that were neither Greek nor proto-Villanovan.[23]

38 TRIPARTITE ORIGINS OF ROME

All of these forces and peripheral currents, after they were blended and intertwined, found their final point of confluence and order in one well-defined area, Rome. It is only within the context of this settlement that we can speak of a continuous, rooted, illustrious tradition. The historical setting is the following. In the first half of the eighth century B.C. Etruria did not yet represent a far-reaching influential force, and Rome was far from being a metropolis; it was only a bridge, that is, a precondition to the life of Etruria and to her inclusion even in overland trade. If then we are not obliged to consider Etruria as an element and constitutive force in Rome at its beginning, the problem simultaneously broadens and becomes more simplified, when we keep in mind the tripartite[24] characteristics of the origins of Rome from the historiographic as well as the archaeological and linguistic points of view.

On the historiographic plane, the three primitive tribes recorded by Varro (L.L. V 55, L.L. V 89), *Tities Ramnes Luceres,* can (even though they are felt by the author to be Etruscan names) be connected on the ethnic-linguistic plane with the respective values of the proto-Sabines (not to be confused with the Sabines of the fifth century B.C.), the proto-Latins (connected with the settlements in the Alban hills), and the northern Italics, filtered through the territorial expansion of the ancient proto-Villanovans. This ethical and juridical element is paralleled by an archaeological element: on the one hand, the necropolis of the Esquiline is linked, according to Duhn[25] and MacIver,[26] to the Iron Age civilization of the Adriatic and would correspond to the proto-Sabine *Tities;* on the other hand, the huts of the Palatine are related to the trench tombs of the Alban hills and therefore lie on the plane of the *Ramnes* and of the proto-Latins in a strict sense; finally, the incinerators of the Roman Forum admit only of connections with the north and therefore are to be linked with the juridical notion of the *Luceres* and the ethnic-historic notion of the northern Italics. A pleasing parallel linguistic element is provided by the various surviving forms of the root REUDH 'red'. The type *rutilus,* which demonstrates the passage of the DH to T, is proto-Latin and documented even in Sicily; the type *rubro-,* with the voiced consonant in place of the voiced aspirate in internal position, is of Venetic, and therefore northern Italic, stamp; finally the type *Rufus,* with the fricative in internal position, is of the Osco-Umbrian, and therefore (proto-)Sabine, type.

Of the original elements there remains in traditional historiography only the partial echo of a Roman-(proto-)Sabine fusion. With the passage of time, and more precisely in the period of the Tarquin kings, we witness instead a quadripartite organization of the city into four regions: the suburban, the Esquiline, the hill, and the Palatine, the first mention of which we find in Varro.[27] With this expansion we recognize the decisive contribution of the Etruscan element.

39 THE LANGUAGE OF NUMA POMPILIUS

Linguistic references to these earlier historical facts outside of the etymological field do not exist. Nevertheless, the two following formulae are of some significance. *Senatus populusque romanus* shows us that the notion of *populus,* that is, of young people organized into armed units, is linked to the topographic notion of Rome; the senate as a council of elders existed before the establishment of the Latin tradition in Rome; similarly the formula *populus romanus Quirites* embraces not only the idea of armed "Roman" youth but also that of united citizens, and here it is not important whether this coalition was organized around a topographical seat or a divinity; in neither case was it yet associated with Rome.

A unitarian tradition having been established, we now face the problem of giving a precise name to its most archaic phase. The first suggestion might be that of "Latin of the monarchy." As we shall see below, however, the Latin of the monarchical period is divided into two clearly distinct phases of civilization, one corresponding to the Tarquin kings and another to the period preceding it. Since for the preceding stage the expression the "laws of Numa Pompilius" has endured in the tradition to indicate the first juridical texts, it seems proper to call this first stage of Latin, which by that time was already anchored in Rome, the Latin of Numa Pompilius. This definition has been developed by Emilio Peruzzi,[28] who emphasized its Sabinelike features, which ought more precisely to be called "proto-Sabine" (§28).

One of its characteristics consists in the dative-ablative plural of the first declension in -*as* (rather than in -*ais, is*) as is evident from the formula *devas corniscas sacrum,* which in classical form would be *diis cornicibus sacrum.* According to Peruzzi, this feature would have connections with the inscriptions of Pesaro (§80).

This does not mean that forms that have come down to us in adapted, altered, or translated form ought to be considered as contemporary with Numa Pompilius; examples of such forms are *paricidas,* which shows the insertion of vocalic apophony (which is fifth century, §47) as already having taken place, and *Tarpeius,* which is linked to the Capitol, but only "after" the latter had overcome the Etruscan phase of the Tarquins (§51).[29]

The return to a certain respect for and trust in the Livian tradition does not hinder our recognizing chronological distortion in it, which are easily comprehensible, given the hiatus which divided the events from the constitution of their first sources.

40 THE LATIN COMMUNITY

The Latin of the monarchy can be divided into two phases. The first phase, which has been defined as that of Numa Pompilius, comprises everything that was the result of the first phase of equilibrium among the proto-Latin, the proto-Sabine, and the northern Italic tradition. Of the second phase, the Latin of the monarchy, which begins with the reign of Tarquin the Elder, is characterized instead by its being placed in a broader frame of reference as a result of the following factors: the Etruscan presence throughout Italy, the Italic contacts which are no longer limited only to the Sabine element, and an active Greek presence. This is the period which has been correctly defined by Santo Mazzarino[30] as that of the Etruscan-Italic *koiné*.

Naturally, linguistic material cannot always be directly classified in the first rather than in the second phase. It is certain that the definitive treatment of *aedes* with D (instead of with T or F) already belongs to the Latin of the time of Numa Pompilius.[31] It is not certain if the action of the accent and especially the destructive buffets that profoundly altered the primitive structure of proto-Latin words are to be referred to the contact with the proto-Sabines in the time of Numa Pompilius or if they belong to the second phase of the *koiné*.

The most beautiful example of this phase comes from a text that is incorrectly called the most ancient Latin inscription. It concerns the Praenestine fibula which belongs to the seventh century B.C. Its text is *Manios med fhefhaked Numasioi*, which means 'Manius made me for Numasius'. The decisive form is *fhefhaked*, a doubled perfect which is attested to in the inscription of Bantia in the Oscan language and which is an old Indo-European perfect, while in Latin the form of the perfect was taken from the ancient aorist and appears as *feced* in the inscription of Dueno, which is a more recent document by more than a century. Even the dative *Numasioi*, with the ending in *-oi*, has an Oscan and not a Latin quality, since the dative of the latter is derived from *-o*. On the contrary, the form of the personal pronoun *med* is a Latin one.[32] Therefore, in the Praenestine fibula we have a direct documentation of the broadening of horizons and of a pervasive penetration which goes beyond the restricted boundaries defined by the age of Numa Pompilius.

If we can say that the age of Numa Pompilius brought an intensive accentuation through Sabine contacts, this tendency is further confirmed by the concentric action that was developed in the *koiné* period. In any case, contrary to what the manuals teach, it was not a case of a systematic action, but rather of violent and at the same time partial battering. This is the case with the form HOSTI-POTIS, which was transformed into *hospots (and later into *hospes*) with the elimination of *two* syllables (§47–49). Such cases, however, are definitely in a minority. We note, moreover, that internal syllables which in the following century (§47) will be the object of a different process remain immune from these destructive forces. Whatever the explanation one would want to give for this phenomenon, it can be stated with certainty that it presupposes that the internal syllables were still intact.

Nine

Blossoming in the Age
of the Monarchy

41 THE ETRUSCAN-LATIN COMMUNITY
During the sixth century there coincides a cultural with an economic blossoming which radiates from Etruria and spreads over Rome and her hinterland. The extension of horizons and the stability of the new relationships have one general consequence and several secondary results. The general consequence consists in the establishment of that phase that has traditionally been called the "common Italic language" period, which, contrary to what many manuals affirm, is not a historical antecedent to the establishment of the Latin and Osco-Umbrian traditions, but a secondary fact determined by the needs of the new society which was being established. The features of the common Italic language period consist essentially in the development of the ablative case, which is the same in Umbrian as it is in Latin in terms of importance and case endings: *poplu* as compared with 'populo', *karne* as compared with 'carne', *tota* with 'tota', and (with reference to adverbial derivations from the strumental or ablative cases) *rehte* as contrasted with 'recte', and *subra* as contrasted with 'supra'.[1]

The secondary consequences consist in the establishment of terms of comparison among the traditions destined to coexist without merging; for example, the relationship between voiced consonants in internal position (D or B) in the Latin of the time of Numa Pompilius as compared with the F of the Umbro-Samnite tradition: the Umbrian theme *mefio-* is translated into the Latin theme *medio-* just as the Latin theme *medio-* is transformed into the Umbrian *mefio-*.

Naturally the most interesting cases are those that do not result in total fusion but only demonstrate the beginning of the process. A prime example taken from the voiced consonants is the vocalization A (as in Greek) which we still find occasionally in place of the Latinate vocalization with E: an example is the Osco-Umbrian form *-an* as compared with the Latin *en-*, which then became *in-*. Nevertheless, there are cases in which Latin conserves very archaic structures which Umbro-Samnite adopts only in the more recent and functionally marginal cases. The Latin gerund,[2] for example, is a form which still retains the function of a verb, but tends to accentuate nominal features and therefore to be transformed into a gerundive adjective. In the Italic world only the gerundive exists, the gerund having been rejected like an old and by now useless tool.

The three-part story of the genitive singular of themes in *-o* is important. Latin, like Irish, conserves an archaic form which is not even included in the declension because the ending -ī is not added to the theme but to the simple or amplified root. In contrast with this form, which is a relic even from the Indo-European point of view, we find the classic Homeric Indo-European ending, attested to in Sanskrit, which is *-osio*.[3] In Osco-Umbrian in its turn, there is neither a sterile relic nor a serviceable vestige from the Indo-European tradition but an adjustment with the case ending of themes in -ī. Since Faliscan, because of its composite tradition (see §23), could not have preserved the case ending *-osio* without outside influence, *-osio* must be attributed to the Umbro-Samnite component of Faliscan and is seen as having been preserved only in Faliscan, having been substituted in its original environment (Osco-Samnite) by the analogous form *-eis*.

Finally, there are phenomena which evolve as partial and extreme tendencies, sometimes in the Latin zone and at other times in the Osco-Umbrian area. The most interesting example is that of the aspirates which, as has been said above, constitute an opposition between a strong F and a weak H. The equilibrium between the two elements is unstable. Quite independent of its stronger articulation power, the F is found in Indo-European words of different phonetic origin and even in Mediterranean words. The H is a reflection only of words derived from Indo-European GH and of no Mediterranean words. It is natural that there should have been a certain tendency toward the transformation of the relationship of these aspirates from a rapport of opposition to one of variation with consequences inside as well as outside of Rome. Examples of such cases are *foied* in Falerii as opposed to 'hodie' in Rome (§23), *fasena* in Sabina (Velio Longo VII 69.8) as contrasted with Latin 'harena', and the inverse example of *Foratia* (CIL I² 166) in Rome as compared with the normal form 'Horatia'.

The following reinforced forms are set in opposition within the Latin language: *fordeum* as compared with 'hordeum' (barley); *fariolus* as opposed to 'hariolus' (soothsayer); *folus* as contrasted with 'holus' (legume), and even *fostis* as opposed to 'hostis' (enemy). One reinforced form which completely gained the upper hand is *fel* 'bile, gall' from GHEL, which ought to have rendered HEL. At the other extreme we have the weakened variants of the Faliscan form *haba* instead of the Roman 'faba' (broad bean), *hordus* instead of 'fordus' (pregnant, full), *hebris* instead of 'febris' (fever), *horctus* instead of 'forctus' (valid; compare §55).

On the cultural plane, the major innovation is the acceptance by the Romans of the Etruscan onomastic formula, made up of the given name (substantive) followed by the family name (adjective) and then by the patronymic: *Marcus* (noun) *Tullius* (adjective) *Quinti filius* (see § 27). Emilio Peruzzi[4] has shown with convincing arguments that the Sabines must have been the necessary intermediaries in the development of the binominal formula, or to be more precise, the proto-Sabines, because only they could have introduced the patronymic in postposition. The Sabines, linked to the Umbrians, would have introduced it in prefixed position.

42 THE FIRST GRECISMS

The sphere of influence of focal nuclei, such as Taranto and Cumae on the linguistic as well as on the economic and cultural levels, is enormous. The first expansion was of alphabets of Greek origin (§17) which were introduced into Etrurian and by way of Etrurian into other languages, for example into Umbrian (§27). The second category is represented by the Latin alphabet, which is also of Greek origin, but which, unlike the alphabets of the other languages of ancient Italy, passed directly from the world of the Greek colonies to Rome, displaying a normal word movement from the left to the right in the inscriptions of the Praenestine fibula and a boustrophedonic mode of writing in the inscription of the Roman Forum. Contrary to present-day opinion, which is based on the studies of M. Hammarström,[5] the Etruscans played only a peripheral role in the material transmission of the alphabets. With regard to the alphabet of Chalcis, no new signs were necessary in Latin but three were superfluous (theta, phi, and khi), and they were used to indicate numbers. The difference between c and к was one of voice (voiced or unvoiced). But at a certain point it appeared more necessary, because of an Umbrian influence (and not because of an Etruscan influence as is commonly stated) to distinguish the gutturals according to the point of articulation which is determined by the vowel that follows, rather than according to the degree of openness; c, therefore, was employed before е and ı, while к was used before а, and Q before о and u. After that phase к became superfluous; c had the specialized function of indicating the unvoiced articulation (§89) while a new sound, G, was introduced to indicate the voiced articulation. The digamma ꟻ was also superfluous, but was used in association with н to indicate our ꟻ, an unvoiced bilabial, as it does also in the Etruscan and Venetic alphabets. After this, Latin once again became more simplified, adopting the simple ꟻ to indicate the very important unvoiced bilabial, and reserving the sign н to indicate a light aspiration of the type found in *homo*. In its acceptance of Greek words, aspiration is not at first indicated. For example, in comparison to the Greek *porphýra*, the Latin form *purpura* does not make a distinction between phi and pi; similarly in *calx* 'limestone, chalk' we find no trace of the initial Greek khi. Neither is there present in Latin any sign indicating the difference between the vowel u and the consonant u, or btween the vowel ı and the consonant j. The sign z indicated the voiced s; that is, the intervocalic s which had not yet been subjected to rhotacism (§51). The Greek sound zeta (§62) on the other hand became confused with s, and so in Latin *massa* renders the Greek *máza*, and *sona* 'belt, girdle' the Greek *zṓnē*. Turning our attention to the mixed Greek vowel y, we note that it became assimilated by the Latin u in the earliest period of contact. Later the sign y was introduced into the Latin alphabet (§87) and z was put at the end of the alphabet to distinguish the z sound in Greek words from the s sound. Finally, the Greek sound y was sometimes used to indicate that sound halfway between u and ı, which was characteristic of the internal vowel before м and other labial articulations, as we find in the example *lacrymis* (§62).[6]

43 PROBABLE INTERMEDIARIES

The wave of Grecisms that follows the spread of the alphabets at the beginning of the sixth century first appears in the legend about the Greek origins of Tarquinius Priscus and his connections with Demaratus and is related to the influx of proto-Corinthian vases[7] and to the first group of Greek words. These Greek words are not united by a common place of origin nor by a common route to Italy, but they are conspicuous for their abundance and for the sureness with which they can be assigned to this first period of Hellenism. Generally speaking, we can say that a "Doric" form with digamma, like that used in the Latin forms *oliva* and *Achivi,* presupposes an earlier period rather than an "Ionian" form without digamma, as we find in *oleum* and *Achaei.* Even the travel route of these words can be assumed to be more over land in the first case and more over sea in the second. Likewise the contraction of EA to A is Doric, and so a more recent Grecism such as *choragus* belongs to a Tarentine tradition in all likelihood, while the contraction of EA to E is Ionic and indicates Cumae as its place of origin. To this first classification two others may be added. The first, chronological in nature, characterizes Grecisms which are known definitely to have arrived in Italy during the period of the monarchy, because we find actual evidence of them at that time, as in the case of the temple of the Dioscuri of Lanuvium,[8] or because they were subjected to Latin phonetic changes[9] which were completed in the fifth century; examples of these are *trutina* 'balance' and *mac(h)ina* from the Greek forms 'trytánē' and 'mākhanā', *camera* from 'kamára', *balineum* from 'balaneîon', *talentum* from 'tálanton' and *Agrigentum* from 'Akrágas, -antos'. The second classification investigates whether or not the travel route of these words from the Greek to the Roman world included any contact or stopover in Etruria, where they might have undergone phonetic changes.[10] When there is a voiced consonant in Greek which in Latin is substituted by an unvoiced consonant, we can take it as a sure sign of Etruscan influence:[11] this is the case of the Greek *thríambos* and the Latin 'triumpe', of the Greek *amórgē* and the Latin 'amurca' (dregs of oil), of the Latin *cotonea* and the Greek 'kydónia (mala)', and of the Latin *sporta* and the Greek (accusative) 'spyrída'. The Etruscan word *phersu* in the sense of 'mask' can be interpreted as an adaptation of Greek 'prósōp(on)', and at the same time as the basis for the Latin *persona,* which could not possibly be considered a "direct" derivation from the Greek. Finally the Greek goddess *Persephónē* is attested to in Paelignian in an almost identical manner, *Perseponas.*[12] If we consider the Etruscan form, which is *Phersipnai,* we can see in it a link in the chain which through the presumed form PRSRPNA, would justify the Latin Proserpina.[13] In the case of the Dioscuri, however, Etruscan intervention is excluded. The Etruscan form of the Greek *Polydeúkēs* is 'Pultuke' with reinforcement of the voiced consonant, while the archaic Latin form is *Poloces* and the classical form 'Pollux', both of which presuppose a weakening of the same consonant,[14] namely, from *ld* to *l(l)*.

Certain other alterations in the degree of openness of articulation belong to the earlier period, even though there is some parallel in the development from Vulgar Latin to Italian: examples are *gobius* (fish) as compared with the Greek 'kóbios', *gamba* as compared with the Greek 'kampḗ', *Burrus* as contrasted with 'Pýrrhos', and *buxus* as contrasted with the Greek 'pýxos'. The words *ballaena* in contrast to a Greek form 'phállaina', and *Bruges* in comparison to a Greek 'Phrýges' lead to the assumption not only of an overland passage but also of Messapic intervention.

44 GREEK RHYTHMS

We find proof of the intensity of the Greek influence in this period also in rhythmical phenomena which have been put in their proper perspective by Giorgio Pasquali.[15] The Indo-European linguistic tradition was sensitive to the quantitative difference between long and short vowels and was in a position to transmit homogeneous rhythmic traditions to both the Greeks and the Latins. Nevertheless, in the Greek world[16] there is an evident distinction between an Aeolian tradition, in which isosyllabism plays a part, and the Ionian tradition, which leans toward isochronism; in the Latin world the lack of evidence is total. In Saturnian verse we no longer find these rigid accentual and alliterative patterns which clearly appear in prose and which at one time had been recognized as genuinely belonging to the presumed Latin rhythmic tradition. Pasquali's conclusions regarding Saturnian verse are the following: that it is *not* accentual; that important remnants of alliterative traditions are found in the Carmen Arvale and in the prayers to Mars on the occasion of the Suovetaurilia,[17] which correspond to the contribution of the Sabine component; and that in Saturnian verse there appear "cola" of Greek origin which when linked in pairs in Rome gave birth to Saturnian verse itself.

In other words, contrary to what is taught in the manuals,[18] the history of all that is Greek in Rome is not unitary; the archaic period is characterized by two features: (*a*) it is important up to the Tarquinian age, and (*b*) it is less foreign than one might expect because the accent, although it had endured blows of initial intensity and consequent syncope, had respected the bulk of Latin lexical material and had been able later to absorb those gentler alterations of which we must speak (§47).[19]

45 THE FIRST MOVEMENTS

We can still catch an echo of the disdainful tolerance of the classical age toward this period and even toward the whole of the archaic age;

we cite as examples Horace's comments on Livius Andronicus (*Ep.* II. I. 53), and even Plautus (*Ars Poetica* 270 ff.). There also remained the establishment of one fact, and that is the incomprehensibility of the Latin of the period preceding the "archaic" authors. Regarding the first treaty between Rome and Carthage, Polybius writes that he was able to decipher it only with the help of some Roman scholars.[20] The same difficulty was encountered regarding other treaties of the sixth[21] and fifth[22] centuries between the Romans and the Latins, and between Rome and Ardea.[23]

Facts that are recognized as having been due to external forces are integrated with archaic texts which have come down to us in a more or less faithful manner by way of texts that are close to us. The *Carmen saliare,* which has come down to us by way of Terentius Scaurus,[24] enriches the spectrum of archaisms with formulae such as *tonas Leucesie,* with the diphthong EU still intact and not confused with OU, and *prai ted tremonti* (§53) with the diphthong AI intact, the final -D persisting, and the ending *-onti* in place of the classical '-unt'; the phrase *duonos ceros* 'the good creator' shows a partial passage of the primitive groups DUE, which evolved into *duo-* but not yet into the classical *bo-* as appears in *bonus.*

The Carmen Arvale is a genuine document but its epigraphic copy belongs to the third century A.D. The cippus (sepulchral pillar) of the Roman Forum and the Duenos vase, however, are original documents which belong to the period between the end of the sixth and the beginning of the fifth century. The data available from the cippus of the Forum are essentially the forms *qoi* 'qui', relative pronoun with the diphthong still intact; *sakros* 'sacer', with the final syllable still intact; *esed* 'erit', again without rhotacism and with the final *-ed* instead of '-it'; *recei* 'regi', again with the diphthong intact and the slight change caused in the guttural consonant by the following E; *iouxmenta* 'iumenta', with the diphthong preserved and with the group KS preserved at the end of an internal syllable; *iovestod* 'iusto', with the triphthong and the ablative ending intact. The lessons learned from the Duenos vase are similar, with the preservation of both diphthongs and triphthongs, of consonants at the ends of words or syllables, as for example in *cosmis* 'loving'.[25] In the Carmen Arvale the reinforced form of the plural of the first person *enos,* the types *pleores* for 'plures', and the graphic uncertainties in the case of the vowels in final syllable, *-es/-is, -ar/-or,* and of the consonants p/b[26] should be noted.

Ten

First Latin
Systematization

46 SOCIOCULTURAL CHANGES

At the beginning of the fifth century the political scene inside Rome changed. The monarchy of Etruscan origin fell and was replaced by an oligarchical regime in which the large landowners, with their needs, interests, and mentality, established themselves.[1] The old regime, which was open to commerce directed toward Etruria and overseas goals and in which the plutocratic interests of those who would later be called "plebeians" prevailed, was replaced by the narrow-mindedness and shortsightedness of the patricians, who were little interested in such distant horizons. In the first twenty-four years of the Republic there were twelve consuls of plebeian ancestry; that is, the fall of the monarchy did not bring about an immediate reversal of the social situation. The figure of the king ceased to correspond to the maximum authority of the state and was replaced by two consuls with a status of resolutely equal sovereignty, a form belonging exclusively to Rome. The king continued to hold religious sovereignty (later assumed by the *pontifices*) with the title of *rex sacrorum*. The *Regia,* which was rebuilt in that period of transition, shows that the name was not dead but only that it had taken on a specialized meaning, just as in the Ottoman Empire a distinction was made at a certain point between the Sultanate and the Caliphate.

The reasons for the change were in large part external. On the one hand the prestige and influence of the Etruscan culture were beginning to decline; and on the other hand the pressure of the Italic "rites of spring"[2] from the mountains was making itself felt on the coastal populations. Thus in Campania we witness the descent of the Samnites, who superimposed their own settlements on the earlier Etruscan colonization;[3] the Volsci descended in the Pontine region, interrupting communications from Cumae and the other cities of Campania toward Rome.[4] The Volsci and the Aequi pressed down upon the area immediately south of Rome in the direction of the Alban hills. East of Rome, the Sabines made their presence felt in the episodes of Attius Clausus (Livy II 16) and Appius Herdonius, who succeeded in reaching the Capitol (Livy III 15), and with a regular war in the year 449 (Livy III 61).

The vital space left to the Latin of Rome was so reduced that to all appearances it was in this period moribund.

47 RAPID EVOLUTION IN THE FIFTH CENTURY

A comprehensive evaluation of these imbalances leads us to the following conclusions. (1) Among vowels, the process of the fusion of diphthongs begins under external, Sabinizing influence; it continues throughout the classical period, while AU merges only in the imperial period in *Vulgar* Latin (§87). The passage of the triphthong OUE to o or U also occurs in this movement. (2) In the vowels begins the obscuring of E and o in closed syllables toward I and U, especially before nasals and dentals: *feced* becomes 'fecit'; *tremonti* becomes 'tremunt'. (3) In the area of consonants rhotacism triumphs, as we see for example in the genitive plural ending *-arum,* which comes from ASOM. (4) Groups of the type DUE are labialized, and *duenos* is reduced to 'bonus'. (5) Consonant groups which contain an s are energetically simplified; IN STLOCO, for example, becomes *ilico,* MANTERGSLE becomes *mantele* 'napkin', LOUKSNA becomes *luna.*[5] (6) All the above is of secondary importance in comparison with the action of the accent, which reveals itself through the so-called Latin apophony.[6] During the monarchy Latin accentuation had undergone blows of initial intensity which had profoundly altered and rendered unrecognizable words such as HOSTIPOTIS, which was reduced to HOSPOTS (§40) and then to *hospes.* The great majority of Latin words had survived this period undamaged and thus were able to submit to the alterations of Latin apophony in an uncompromised condition. The general rule is the following: in every internal syllable that is open and contains a short vowel the latter assumes the value of I; if the syllable is closed, the internal short vowel assumes the value of E. If the vowel is long, it remains intact in both open and closed syllables. If we are dealing with a diphthong in I, it assumes the value of a long I; if the diphthong is in U, it assumes the value of a long U: CONFACIO, which in open syllable appears as *conflcio*, provides us with an example; its past participle has an internal vowel in a closed syllable and therefore appears as *confEctus*. *Impletus* remains intact because the E is long; one compound of 'caedere' is *inclidere*; one of 'causare' is *accUsare*.

Syncope, while extremely tenuous in Rome, is a common phenomenon in the language of the Italici, and a trend among the Etruscans. Apophony is typically Roman: there are two examples of it at Praeneste, on mirrors, with the forms *alixentrom* (CIL I² 553) and *Casenter(a)* (CIL I² 566) for Alexander and Cassandra, respectively. But at Falerii we find *cuncaptum* (CIE 8340): it is only in Rome that the form 'concEptum' appears.

48 PHONETIC CONCEALMENT

If at this point one attempts a summary comparison with the Indo-European structures as they have been delineated (in §§11–12), the Latin of Rome appears to be characterized by these differences with respect to the linguistic structures typical of the first Indo-European bridgeheads in Italy. On the phonetic plane[7] the stability of the vowel system in initial position is striking. The short A of *ago* 'I lead' endures unchanged, as do the long A of *mater* 'mother', the short E of *ego* 'I', the long E of *femina* 'woman', the short O of *octo* 'eight', and the long O of *donum* 'gift', in addition to the SCHWA represented by A in *pater* (from PƏTER). Moreover, we have the vocalized sonants: the short I in *video* 'I see' and the long I in *vidi* 'I saw', the short U in *jugum* 'yoke' and the long U in *fumus* 'smoke'; finally, there are the diphthongs of the archaic period: AI in *aidilis* 'aedile', EI in *deico* 'I say', OI in *oino* (for the classical 'unum'), AU in *augeo* 'increase', EU in *Leucesie* (§45), an epithet applied to Jupiter, OU in *loucom*. The other sonants are no longer susceptible to vocalic pronunciation and lean in these cases (see §11) on another, true vowel: MRTM became *mortem*; MLDM became *mollem*; KMTOM, *centum*; TNTOS, *tentus*. R, L̩, M̩, and N̩ no longer exist, and consonantal I and U are by now independent sounds—U, for example, *jugum* 'yoke' and V, for example, *vidi* 'I saw'—with no longer any possibility of change. The category of the sonant as a constitutive element of the phonetic system is eliminated.

With respect to articulation, the occlusive consonants preserve the four Indo-European distinctions: labials in *Potis* 'lord' and *deBilis* 'weak'; dentals in *Tres* 'three' and *Domus* 'house'; labiovelars in

Quis 'who' and *Vivus* 'alive'; gutturals in *Centum* 'hundred' and *Genus* 'kind, type'. With respect to the degree of articulation, these examples show that the distinction between voiced and unvoiced consonants is preserved, and moreover that in the case of the labiovelars the distinction is accentuated to the point that the first of the two constitutive elements of the voiced labiovelar is lost.

Aspiration, which originally constituted a puff of breath added to voiced or unvoiced articulation, comes to constitute an autonomous category, equidistant from both voiced and unvoiced consonants, as happened in Greece and in the Germanic area. In Latin the puff of breath comes to merge with the preceding articulation, giving life to a different articulation at the beginning and in the middle of a word; at the beginning of a word aspiration is usually reinforced and individualized, while in the middle of a word it tends to merge with the voiced consonant or is reduced to a simple H. We find examples of this phenomenon in the opposition of the labials in *Fero* 'I carry' and *neBula* 'cloud', of the dentals in *Fumus* 'smoke' and *aeDes* 'hearth', of the labiovelars in *formus* 'hot' and *ninGuit, niVem* 'it is snowing', 'snow'. Gutturals, however we find initially in *homo* 'man', medially in *veho* 'I transport'.

The unvoiced sibilant is preserved only in initial position, as for example in *Sedes* 'seat', but before R it gives life to a type of interdental, from which the group FR arises. Examples of this are *frigus* 'cold weather' and *funeBris* 'funeral' (adj.), which derive respectively from SRIGOS and FUNES-. Rhotacism occurs in intervocalic position (see §51). The voiced sibilant z disappears, sometimes leaving a trace through a compensatory lengthening of the preceding vowel.

Regressive assimilation is broadly diffused by unvoiced occlusives or even by continuant consonants, as in the cases of OBCAIDO, which becomes *occido* 'I kill', ADFERO, which becomes *aFFero* 'I bring, take, carry (a thing) to a place', and DISFERO, which becomes *diFFero* 'I disperse here and there, I scatter'; similarly we find ATNOS vis-à-vis *aNNus* 'year', SEDLA :: *seLLa* 'seat', and CORONLA :: *coroLLa* 'crownlet'. Partial assimilation is evident in LEGTOS, which was transformed into *lectus* 'chosen', and SOPNOS, which became *somnus*. Progressive assimilation promoted generally by liquid consonants is less diffused: from TOLNO we derive *tollo* 'I lift'; from TORSEO we get *torreo* 'I dry', and from VELSE, velle 'to wish, want'.

49 MORPHOLOGICAL CONCEALMENT OF THE NOUN

In morphology,[8] the efficacy of vocalic alternation in the middle of the root has been neutralized by the apophony described above. Rare traces of the E type, which alternates with zero grade, are found in the opposition between *EDo* 'I eat', and *D-ens* 'tooth' (that is, the eater). The E/O alternation is evident in the case of *tEgo* 'I cover,' which alternates with *tOga* 'toga'.

Nominal themes are structurally analogous to Indo-European themes, even though they are somewhat changed in the normative systematization of the grammarians. They are those ending in a consonant (*reX*), in -O, as in *lupus* (from LUPO-), in -A (*rotA* 'wheel'), in -I (*sitIs*) 'thirst' (these are confused with those ending in consonants), and in -U (*statUs*). In addition there is a heterogeneous category of themes apparently ending in a long E (*res*). In word formation the capacity for composition of nominal themes is greatly reduced, partly as a consequence of alterations in the middle of words which impede the recognition of their constitutive elements: it is no longer possible to recognize the constitutive elements *hosti-* and *potis* in 'hospes' (§40), which is derived from GHOSTI-POTIS. SAKRO-DHOT, reduced to 'sacerdos', does not permit an analysis of *sacer* followed by *-fex*. Timid attempts at resumption appear in corresponding types such as 'agri-cola' and 'sacri-legus'. It thus happens that the expression 'master of the house' is no longer a composite, as it is in Greek *de(m)s-pótēs*, but a derivative: *dominus* from 'domus' (house). There are suffixes of derivation to indicate the feminine gender in *genetrix* as compared with 'genitor', the collective as in *clientela* as compared with 'cliens', to create from verbs substantives that indicate the agent or 'actor', the action or "actio," or the instrument as in *aratrum* 'plow' from *arare*. In parallel fashion, abstract substantives such as *superbia* are drawn from adjectives (*superbus*), or adjectives from substantives as in *patrius* from *pater* 'father' or even from verbs as we see in *audax* 'daring, audacious' from the verb *audeo* 'I dare'.

Declension has been reduced to five cases, but the scope of the ablative (§41) has been expanded. Anomaly, well known also in the Celtic world, is characteristic in the case endings of the declension, with the result that the traditional signpost of the genitive of themes in -O (-OSYO), is replaced by a sort of adverb ending in -I, which does not follow the thematic marker -O but is put in place of it: *lupi*, rather than *lupo+i*. In this period the comparison of the adjective is in ferment. The original derivation by means of -YOS was the most ancient, drawn from the root and not from the adjectival theme, as in *maior,* which is taken from MAG, not from the theme of the positive *magnus*. Besides this form there remain only vestiges of the suffix -TERO, in *alter* 'the other', for example, and in *magister* 'master, teacher', which have lost their efficacy for purposes of comparison. As far as the superlative is concerned, there is a succession of suffixes from the most elementary sort to the most complex: -MO in *summus* (from SUPMO) 'the highest', -EMO in *plurimus* (from PLOIS-EMO-) 'the most', TEMO- in *intimus* 'intimate', SEMO- in *maximus* 'maximum', and finally IS-SEMO- in *longissimus* 'longest'. The fundamental pronoun is taken from the theme I/EI into *is, ea, id* and amplified in various ways; the theme SO-/TO- survives only in association with other themes, as for example *(is-)te/(is-)tud*. The theme *qui/quo* is not only an indefinite and interrogative pronoun but also a relative pronoun, taking the place of the lost YO- in this function. Personal pronouns and numerals are conspicuous for their stability. Like nouns, verbs are divided into primitive and derivative, among which are distinguished those drawn from nouns or demonstrative verbs: *laudare* from 'laus', *metuere* from 'metus' (fear).

50 MORPHOLOGICAL CONCEALMENT OF THE VERB

Division of the verb into conjugations is, like the declensions for the noun, late and artificial, but legitimate insofar as there did not exist an Indo-European conjugation but only single themes (of the present, the aorist, the perfect, and so on). A rational classification must first of all distinguish the opposition of athematic verbs *(fert* 'he carries') from thematic verbs *(leg-i-t* 'he chooses'). Within the category of thematic verbs, we must distinguish among those which have as a theme the traditional thematic vowel E/O *(legit* from LEG-E-T) and those characterized by other vowels, such as *laudAt, monEt, audIt,* 'he praises', 'he warns', and 'he hears'.

In the Latin verb the middle voice is formally characterized, being designated by archaic endings in -R, but these maintain their function only in a part of the transitive verbs which are called "deponent," while in the others it comes to indicate the passive voice.

Thus a dissymmetry is born between the functional opposition of transitive and intransitive verbs (without the passive) and the formal opposition of endings without R (active) and with R (deponent). The quality of the action of the verb, the so-called mode, no longer distinguishes between action possible, characteristic of the subjunctive, and the action desired, proper to the optative. Vestiges of forms of the optative survive in unrecognizable forms in the Latin subjunctive, as we find for example in the verb *esse: sim, sis,* and so on (ancient *siem, sies*).

The quantity of the action, the so-called aspect, loses its primitive preeminence. It is maintained in visible and effective form in the imperfect as opposed to the perfect, and this opposition is still alive today in Italian. In other situations it tends to escape toward the lexical field, utilizing possibilities of derivation offered by prefixes: *conficere* has the value of 'to complete, accomplish, execute', while *facere* remains anchored to its durative value.

The Latin conjugation, which was coming into being, in this period is characterized by: (1) rigidity and automatism in the relationships among the temporal themes of the regular verb. The so-called irregular verbs are verbs that have not accepted the systematization of one single verbal theme. (2) The Latin perfect tense is a composite formation, which uses unified Indo-European signposts of diverse value; examples are the -s- of the sigmatic aorist in *dixi*, and the original perfect tenses that are not doubled, such as *vidit* 'he saw', or those that are doubled, such as *tutudit* 'he struck'[9] or characterized by -w-, as in *noVit* 'he (has) learned, knows.' The theme of the perfect tense, thus constituted, is the basis of the indicative and subjunctive perfects and pluperfects (and, in part, of the infinitive), clearly being opposed to the parallel bonds between the theme of the present indicative and the present and imperfect tenses of the subjunctive and the infinitive. This opposition between "finished" and "unfinished," as it is called, must only in small part be understood as an aspectual opposition. As Alessandro Ronconi has shown,[10] the category of time quickly came to predominate. As a consequence the distinction in Latin between absolute and relative times develops and comes into harmony: *amavi* is past absolute; *amaveram* is relative past; *amabo* is future absolute; *amavero,* relative future.

From the point of view of the formation of single themes, the periphrastic procedure, by which the imperfects in -*Bam* and the futures in -*Bo* are formed, becomes prominent. We are dealing with elements taken from the very root of *fui,* treated according to the rule for the aspirates, which are reduced to voiced consonants in the middle of the word.

Innovations in nominal forms of the verb are important though impoverished in comparison with the vast possibilities offered by Indo-European structures. In the present participle only the active voice survives, *laudans* 'praising, he/she who praises'. Only isolated vestiges of the middle voice remain; for example, we have *alumnus* 'he who is reared', *columna* 'that which is raised'. Inversely, the past participle, an ancient verbal adjective, is passive when the verb is active and transitive, active when the verb is "deponent," and nonexistent when the verb is intransitive and active; cases in point are *laudatus* 'praised', and *hortatus* 'that/who has exhorted', but not **itus* 'gone', which is inadmissible. The future participle in -*turus,* which is only active, represents an important symmetrical improvement. The gerund of the type *legendo* and *amando* is a characteristic form of obscure origin but at the same time destined for a great future. It is accompanied by the adjectival form called the "gerundive"; in comparing *ad audiendum verbum* and 'audiendo verbum' we note that in the former the active action of the verb is translated into a passive value in the adjective. Only this adjectival form has been found in the Italic area, which ignores the gerund as a form of the verb (§41).

The infinitive is the result of an opposite procedure, which passes from a rigid nominal form of the ending of one particular case to a more "verbal" form; examples are the athematic Latin forms such as *es-SE* 'to be' or the thematic ones such as *lege-re* (from LEGE-SE), which seem to be ancient locatives of a theme with a sibilant.[11] The supine represents a form of the infinitive taken from nominal themes in -TU-M, TU, which had previously fallen into disuse.

This is the still fluid skeletal structure around which the difficult task of arrangement, ordering, and classification begins, which will assure to the now literary language a minimum of stability. It must be remembered, however, that successive political events that are frankly revolutionary will make profound impressions on the language and will ultimately define new imbalances.

Part Two

Latinitas:
From 500 B.C. to A.D. 500

Eleven

Standardization of
Phonetic Structures

51 ADDITIONAL SABINISMS
Before concluding its process of congealment, Latin undergoes in
the early Republic additional Sabine pressures. A number of Sabinisms in the Latin vocabulary is the first linguistic consequence. The
Sabine form *cascus* for 'old' appears alongside *vetus*; we also find
curis 'lance, spear' as compared with *hasta*; *februum*, which according to Varro means *purgamentum*; and *dirus,* which according to
Servius means *malus.* Similarly, we also discover *strebula, -orum* 'parts
of (sacrificial) victims', attributed by Festus to Plautus as clearly an
Umbrian word, and the divinity *Nerio,* connected with and wife of
Mars, whose name is derived from *ner* 'man' (in the Umbrian lan-
guage) just as *Virtus* in Latin is derived from *vir.* In any case, these
Sabinisms do not have a certain chronology. In themselves they can
even precede the republican revolution in Rome. The following
forms, however, certainly do belong to this phase of Roman history:
Tarpeius, the attribute of the famous cliff is a derivation of Sabine
type from a root TARP, which is the Sabine translation of a Latin
Tarqu(inius) and of an Etruscan TARKUNA.[1] Thus the Capitoline
Hill reveals its original toponomy before the period of Sabine influences and the advent of the republic. The second testimony is
given by *plebeius,* which is taken from the Latin *plebs,* but with a

Sabine suffix.[2] Moreover, Sabinisms and in general Italicisms appear in the following forms: (1) in place of a diphthong, single vowels appear, such as *levir* 'brother-in-law', which theoretically should have had the diphthong *ae,* as the Greek *daér* calls for; *edus* instead of *haedus* 'kid', which we find recorded by Varro (I.I. V 97); *Cecilius praetor* (for Caecilius), a rustic pronunciation recorded by Lucilius (1130); (2) the substitution of a liquid consonant for a voiced dental: examples are *solium* 'throne' as opposed to *seDere,* or *oLere* as compared with *odor,* according to an alteration generalized in the Umbrian language; (3) the extension of this process even at the beginning of a word, where in Umbrian the voiced dental remains intact; examples are *lingua, lacrima, levir,* which should have been DINGUA, DACRU, DAIVER. The case of the prefix AR instead of *ad-* also enters the picture here: examples are *arfuise* (CIL I[2] 581.21), *arvorsum* (581.24), *arvorsario* (583.20), and also *apur finem* (I[2] 5) instead of *apud* (§80).

So-called rhotacism appears again in this category; that is, the passage of s to R which at first occurs in intervocalic position but which then extends to other situations as well. The original focal area is once again the Umbrian zone, where it sometimes appears even in final position, as in the case of *sehmenier dequrier* (Tab. Ig. Vb *II, 16*) as compared with AVEZ ANSERIATES (T. Ia 1). Tradition assigns to 312 B.C. the orthographic reform of the censor Appius Claudius Caecus, who *R litteram invenit,*[3] 'who invented the letter R'. Examples of prerhotacistic situations are *Lases* for 'lares' in the Carmen Arvale and *esed* for 'erit' in the Roman Forum cippus (CIL I[2] I). A similar exaggerated form is *honor* instead of 'honos' (CIL I[2] 15) in the second century B.C. The contrast between intervocalic and nonintervocalic situations is seen in the comparison of *gero* and *gestus,* of *queror* and *questus, nefarius* and *nefas, dirimo* and *distineo,* and finally *cura* (from KOISA) and the Paelignian form *coisa(tens).*[4]

52 URBAN REACTIONS AND RESISTANCE

Notwithstanding the success and diffusion of these innovations, the linguistic particularism of Rome assumes its definitive physiognomy. And notwithstanding the two examples of apophony in the mirrors of Praeneste, this latter sets itself up in opposition to the linguistic particularism of Rome; we note the ancient Praenestine form *Numasioi* in contrast to the Roman *Aiscolapio* (CIL I[2] 26) without final diphthong; and the form *losna* (CIL I[2] 549) as compared with Latin 'luna'; and finally *Quorta* (I[2] 328) in contrast to Latin 'Quarta'. In Lanuvium at the foot of the Alban hills one says *nebrundines,* from NEGWHR-, which in Latin would have given *negr-.* At Tusculum we note the fusion of the diphthong in *Fortune* (CIL I² 48) instead of *Fortunae*. Beyond the Tiber Etruscan is spoken. In the Alban hills at Velletri Volscian is spoken, and this language remained in use until the third century b.c.[5] Thus the territory in which the Latin of Rome was spoken is restricted to an area smaller than the present-day municipal territory.

It is not only isolated rustic forms such as the ones noted above that penetrated Rome; morphological Italicisms also accumulated there, such as the following: *Caecilis* (CIL I² 1036) instead of *Caecilius; Clodis* (CIL I² 1050) instead of *Clodius; Mercuris* (563) instead of *Mercurius.*

In any case even before political circumstances changed the stifling picture of the vital space left to the Latin language, some manifestations of internal resistance did appear; some of these are confirmed later in the classical period, others only through the Vulgar Latin and Romance tradition.

The first manifestation lies in the resistance of the gutturals to the following vowel, which previously had influenced alphabetic particularities through the threefold distinction of the use of Q, K, and C. This distinction, valid during the monarchy, disappeared in the republican period; it had been imposed by certain kinds of Italic (and not Latin) pronunciation, which were reabsorbed. To discover a different pronunciation of the K before E and I, it was necessary either to move to Umbria or to go forward in time to the Christian (not pagan) Latinisms adopted by the Germanic languages (§89).

As for the lexicon, we have two examples of mute but eloquent resistance through the form FORBEX, which is not attested in all of classical antiquity, but instead lives on in Italian in the form 'forbice'; it is opposed to *forfex,* which is attested in the classical period, but in Italic form. Another example is *MACINA, which has survived even down to our own age in a nonaspirated, that is, a genuine and archaic form (*macina* = 'grindstone'), while during the classical period it was aligned with Greek models and assumed the aspiration and took on an independent development which resulted in our word *macchina* (§75).

The most beautiful example of urban revolt appears with the substitution of diphthong for nondiphthong forms even in a historically unjustified way; examples of this are *plaudo*[6] 'I applaud', which derives from a more ancient form PLODO, whether because its compounds are of the type *explOdo* (and not *explUdo,* as in the relationship *causare/accusare*), or because outside of Latin there is the counterproof of the existence of a primitive form in PLO(D) through the literary form *plóti* 'to clap one's hands, to applaud'. A similar case is furnished by *scaina* 'scene' from the Greek *skēnḗ;* the latter presupposes a previous form SKENA, which in turn was understood to be dialectical and hence corrected first into *scaina* and then into *scaena.*[7]

As for the pronunciation of the gutturals (which, under external stimuli, had been on the point of becoming distinguished in terms of the nature of the following vowel), by this time the generalized sign c for the unvoiced guttural became diffused: *ca* in *capio, ce* in *centrum, co* in *coctus.* There are remains of K *in Keri* (I² 445) and in *deKem(bris)* (1038).

The group NS, which by its nature tended to be reduced to a simple s[8] manifests, at least in writing, a tendency to "flourish again"; examples are *cosol* and *cesor* (I² 8), to which the forms *consul* and *censor* of the classical period are opposed; *cosentiont* as opposed to *consol censor* (I² 9); and again in 45 B.C. *cesendi* (I² 593.152) as compared with *censor* (I² 593.144).

Finally, the old tendency aimed at the total weakening of the final -M. This process—of which there exists some epigraphic evidence— is countered by a greater capacity of resistance in later times, even at the cost of diminishing the conspicuousness of the preceding vowel, obscuring its timbre from o to u. We find four examples of the loss of the final -M after o: *oino, duonoro, optumo, viro* (CIL I² 9) vis-à-vis only *Luciom* and the classical forms *unUm, bonorUm, optimUm, virUm, LuciUm,* or *sacrOm* (I² 607, 217 B.C.) and the classical *sacrUm; suom* (I² 593.34) :: *suUm* (593.32). The passage from *dederOnt* (I² 383, third century) and *cosentiOnt* (I² 9) to the classical forms *dederUnt* and *consentiUnt* are analogous.

On this same plane of reinforcement of final consonants, there were parallel developments with the substitution of the unvoiced consonant for the voiced; for example, in comparison with *feced, sied* (I² 4), we find *mitat* (I² 4), *velet, eset,* (I² 581.3, 10). Consolidation of the final articulation is favored, by analogy with the preceding phenomenon, when the timbre of the preceding vowel is obscured; thus we have the three phases of *dedet* (I² 9), *dede* (I² 477), and finally, the stable form (but with the vowel obscured) *dedit* (I² 561, third century B.C.) or, to give another illustration, *feced* (I² 4), but *fecid* (I² 561), and finally the classical *fecit.*

53 DIPHTHONGS AND ISOLATED PHONEMES
The most visible change, however, is that which leads to the fixed use of diphthongs and then to their gradual weakening and merging in a later age, immune to the rustic influences from which in this period Roman citizens still wanted to maintain their distance. Sur-

viving archaic forms of AI are *aidiles* (I² 8), *haice,* 'haec' (581.22), *aiquom,* 'aequum' (581.26), as compared with *AEdem* (581.1). The diphthong AU is preserved until the age of the empire (§82, 87). For EI there is *deicerent* (I² 581.4), as compared with generalized types in I. For EU there is only *Leucesie* in the prerepublican period (§45), insofar as the fusion between the diphthongs EU and OU became widespread also in the Italic languages. Manifestations of OI, which is slow in developing through the series OE > OU > U, are conspicuous; examples are *loidos* (I² 364, 200 B.C.), *oino,* 'unum' (I² 9.4), *comoine(m)* (581.91, 186 B.C.), *oitile* (I² 586.9) and *coiraverunt moiros* (I² 1722), in contrast to the partial solutions of *coeraverunt* (I² 672, 112–111 B.C.) and total solutions *utier* (I² 10) and *usura* (I² 632, 145 B.C.). Finally we have the conservative forms *adouxet* (CIL I² 2438), *indoucebamus* (586.6), *iousit* 'iussit' (614), and *ious* (583.19, 123–122 B.C.), as compared with the resolved forms already evident in *Lucius* (I² 7) and *iuset* (593.121). The interpretation of the dative *matuta* (I² 379), instead of *matutae, is dubious; it is perhaps due to an excess of Roman patriotism (see the dative singular masculine in -*o*).

As for triphthongs, we have conservative cases such as *coventionid* (I² 581.22), partial simplification as in *noundinum* (I² 581.23), contraction to O as in *nontiata* (586.5, 160 B.C.) and finally the classical form *nuntiata.* The passage from the intact form *Gnaivod* (I² 7) to the classical form *Gnaeo,* simplified through the elimination of V, is apparent again in an analogous process of simplification in the cases of *conflovont* (I² 584.23) or *tov(am)* (I² 1805) in comparison with the already simplified *tua* (I² 10), and *soveis* (I² 364) with V preserved as contrasted with the simplified *suos* (I² 583.50).

Uncertainties about alterations resulting from vocalic apophony, which occurred in the preceding period, are not of great importance. A result only partial with respect to the general rule is found in *inceideretis* instead of *incid-* (I² 581.26). The process of labialization is imposed on classical apophony in stable fashion in *occupare* from OB-CAPARE or in *recUperatores* (582.9, 125 B.C.); in a temporary form in *condUmnari* (CIL I² 582.10): *condemnatus.* In general there is a conflict between the "local" solution involving a labial and the "general" solution involving a palatal. For a certain time there was an awareness for example, of a single sound hovering between I and U, according to Quintilian.[9] Little by little the "general, palatal" solution had begun to prevail. It appears, for example, in a personal (labialized) Greek name in the form *Lusumacus* (CIL I² 2393), as compared with *Lusimacus* and a later classical form *Lysimachus;* similarly the passage from *maxUmum* (CIL I² 593.130) to the classical *maxImus;* from *infUmum* (584.10) to *infImo* (584.6), and similarly

optUmo (I² 9) and *facilUmed* (581.27) in contrast to the corresponding classical forms *optImo* and *facillIme*. Finally, let us note two
examples of excessive labialization and delabialization: *pontUfex*
for the classical *pontIfex* (I² 1488), in which the u has no phonetic
justification, and inversely *trebIbus* (398), which in the classical form
has not replaced the U because it is the sign of the fourth declension.
In a fashion parallel to what we have seen with the -м, with the
final -s the obscuring of the preceding vowel is generalized precisely
to allow more breath for the articulation of the consonant; as compared with the loss in *Cornelis* (I² 8) appears the classical *Cornelius;*
as compared with *militarE* (I² 49) with open vowel and loss of the
consonant, there is *aidilES* (I² 8) with open vowel and preservation
of the consonant; but an equilibrium is reached only with the classical type *militaris,* which has the vowel obscured. Finally we go from
VenerEs (451) to *honorIs* (612, 193 B.C.). The letter o behaves in a
similar way. The forms *maio* (I² 76) and *mino* (126), as compared
with the classical forms of the type *maius* and *minus* with consonants
preserved and vowel obscured, show an open vowel and loss of the
final consonant. In like manner we have the forms *praifectOs* (398),
Venos (550), *Novios, PlautiOs* (561) as contrasted to the classical
forms *praefectUs, VenUs, NoviUs,* and *PlautiUs.*

In cases in which morphological reasons intervene to render a
case-ending obsolete, our testimony is limited to archaic forms with
vowels not yet altered: *Diovos* (360) does not change a parallel form
*Diovus but *(D)iovis; nominOs* changes *nominUs* (581.7), but this
form is later eliminated by the different ending of the classical *nominIs;* from REGOS we go on to the form *regUs,* but this is later eliminated by *regis.*

Minor instances of standardization are those in O which change
to u before a velar L, as occurs in the transition from the archaic *consOluerunt* (I² 581) to the classical *consuluerunt;* and from *pocOlum*
(439) to the classical *pocUlum.* The group uo is differentiated in UE:
in 581.19 we have *oinVOrsei,* which changes to the classical *uniVErsi;*
in 581.24 we have *arVOrsun,* which is destined to become the classical
adversus. Even ov is differentiated in AV: in I² 573 we still have *fove*
which is destined to become the classical *fAve.*

Among consonants we are able to witness the transition of DJ to J
in initial position, for example, from *Diove* (I² 20) to the classical
Iovi; of DU- to B-, as we see for example in 581.2 *Duelonai* (186 B.C.),
which changes to the classical *Bellonae;* of GN- to N- (in I² 11, 583.13,
etc.), we have *gnatus,* which then becomes the classical *natus;* of STL-
to SL- and L-, for example, from *stlitium* (CIL IX 2845) to *slis* (I² 583.7)
and finally to *lis* (583.63, 123–122 B.C.).

Finally the progressive elimination of the final -D is important because it is connected with morphology: when it is the sign of the ablative it aligns forms such as *eod* with the -D and *quo* without (in CIL I² 366), or, to give another example, *sententiad* (I² 581.8, 186 B.C.) and *poplicod* (581.15), as compared with *in agro Teurano* (581.30). Outside of the paradigm proper and in contrast to the classical forms *me* and *se,* we note the archaic forms *med* (in Ennius, *var.* 45) and *sed* (CIL I² 582.21, 125 B.C.).

54 HYPERARCHAISMS

The effort at normalization, which aims at putting all texts on the same plane, conflicts with an opposing concern. The contents of a text can take on a special prominence through some linguistic particularism. One of the most efficient instruments toward this end is "archaism," and it is not important here to make a distinction between authentic or symbolic archaism. In the monuments at our disposal, the most conspicuous means for arousing the feeling of the archaism is provided by the improper employment of diphthongs lacking any historical justification whatsoever, and above all of EI. Cases in point are *pleib(ei)* (CIL I² 22), *pleibeium* (591), *preimus* (589, 71 B.C.), *peteita* (592 II 9), for *petita, feiat* (600.8) for *fiat, meilia* (638.4, 138 B.C.) for *milia, decreivit* (614, 189 B.C.) for *decrevit, seit* (756.11) for *sit, nolei* (2188) for *noli, eitur* (I² 1529) for *itur*. On grounds which are entirely different but still efficacious for archaistic purposes, we have the type *suntod* (I² 366), in which the final -D does not represent a past state of affairs (which in reality never existed) but rather behaves in comparison with the classical form *sunto,* as *estod* (which is instead a legitimate form) does in comparison with the classical *esto* (see I² 401).

In addition we have the forms *audeire* (CIL I² 583.71) 'audire'; *veneire* (588.9) 'venire'; *faxseis* (632) 'faxis'; *(Q)ueinctius* (1547) 'Quinctius'. Forms which are more exaggerated and, from the point of view of the archaism, arbitrary are those with AEI: *Caeicilius* (633) 'Caecilius' and *conquaeisivei* (638.11, 132 B.C.) 'conquisivi', because they presuppose a contamination between AE and E. We also note the diphthong in place of a short I, as in *seine* (583.54) 'sine', *parenteis* (1214.5, genitive singular) 'parentis' and finally *seibi* (1739) 'sibi'.

55 ASPIRATES, DOUBLED CONSONANTS, SYLLABIC PROBLEMS

Other questions seem minor and almost merely graphic, but at the same time they do prepare the ground for systematizations and distinctions which will become relevant in later periods. These are the problems of the weak consonants such as H and of doubled consonants.

The consonant H in Latin had come to be in a position of instability and one of external opposition to the F, which from the outside tended to gain ground over the overly weak H (§41). Within Latin the instances of H which had occurred are the following: (1) The H in a homogeneous intervocalic position can be eliminated: instead of *nihil* (I² 1219) we find *nil* (1212); instead of *mihi* we have *mi* (I² 1216). (2) Between different vowels we find H either only as a marker indicating hiatus: *ahenam* (I² 581.26, 186 B.C.), or eliminated, as in the case of DEHABEO, which becomes *debeo*. (3) After a consonant, H may have lost all force: already in the period of apophony, the H exercised no action, and from a compound of the type DIS-HABEO, we derived, with normal rhotacism and normal apophony, *dirhibeo*. (4) In initial position H ends up being omitted, in an anticipation of what will be the normal development of Vulgar and Romance Latin: *Oratia* (1124) instead of *Horatia*. (5) Under the influence of the archaisms an H can be introduced even before an initial vowel without historical justification. *havet* (1222), which corresponds to a classical form *avet* 'he greets'.[10]

The marking of the doubled consonants begins at the end of the third century,[11] and according to Festus (293) at the suggestion of Ennius. The use of double consonants has a different meaning according to whether its justification is historical or only emotional. The classic example is that of *quattuor,* for instance (CIL I² 587 II 18, 21; 81 B.C.), in which the double consonant can find an Indo-European justification precisely in connection with the semireduced grade of the roots in A, as opposed to the E grade in the other Indo-European languages. Vacillation between *litteras* (I² 588.10, 78 B.C.) and *leiteras* (I² 583.35, 123–122 B.C.) is explained by the uncertainty with which a word of distant Mediterranean origin was pronounced rather than by difference in chronology. *Caussa* (I² 589 II 9, 71 B.C.; 593.58, 45 B.C.) and *accussasse* (593.120) show original doubling of consonants which were then progressively dropped in later times. *Cottidie* (593.18) and *rettulerit* (593.15) correctly reflect the original formations QUOTITEI-DIE and RETETULERIT. Finally, in the case of *rellatum* (585.80, second century B.C.) and *relliquiae* (1297), we are dealing with analogous innovations. The consonant-doubling so characteristic of Italian in a later period does not yet have occasion to appear.

The assertion of a specifically Roman tradition appears also through facts lacking epigraphic confirmation. One of the most characteristic is the vocalization of groups consisting of a consonant followed by J (yod): in all of the Indo-European languages the type MEDHYO-, whatever its actual outcome, remains bisyllabic. In Latin it does not: the form *medius,* which derives from it, is trisyllabic.[12] This singularity, however, which also distinguishes the Latin of Rome from all the other Italic languages, is not only a difference of geographic order: it also constitutes a social difference. Inscriptions give testimony to the fact that a hiatus between vowels was not welcome. The most characteristic example is that of *pariat* (CIL I[2] 582.10) for *pareat* (125 B.C.). Parallel manifestations at Pompeii (§80) show that the latter form is already looking to the future. In these examples appears in tangible form the organizational effort toward phonetic normalization: intense, but belabored and resisted.[13]

Twelve

Standardization of Morphological, Syntactical, and Lexical Structures

56 SUFFIXES AND ENDINGS

In the field of morphology, the process of standardization is no less complex. As far as the first declension is concerned, the salient feature is given by the substitution of the genitive singular ending in -AS by the ending formed on the model of the genitive case of the second declension in -I. In contrast to *familias* (CIL I² 582.12, 125 B.C.) there are *Fortunai* (I² 433) and *Duelonai* (581.2, 186 B.C.). A contaminated form halfway between the primitive and the new forms results in the ending -AES, as we find in *Aquilliaes* 'Aquilliae' (1249), for example. A surviving locative exists in *Romai* (561). Ablatives with an analogous -D surviving are *sententiad* (581.8, 186 B.C.) and *Hinnad* (608, 211 B.C.). Datives in -A parallel to the masculines in -O are *Matuta* (379) and *Flaca* (477).[1] Singular datives and plural nominatives in -AI (not yet in -AE) are *Menervai* (I² 34), *Fortunai* (397) and *Poplicai*, and *tabelai* and *datai* (581.29). In the dative-ablative plural there are three phases: the original one in *libertabus* (1278); the analogous phase with regard to the second declension but still having the diphthong in *soveis* 'suis' (364); and the contracted phase which is not yet aligned in the definitive form -IS, in *manubies* (635, 135 B.C.) and *nuges* (1861).

In the second declension, the original ending -I of the genitive is clear right from the most ancient documents for both themes in -o and those in -io: *Volcani* (453), *Aisclapi* (440). Examples of the forceful introduction of false archaisms are *cogendei* and *dissolvendei* (632, 145 B.C.) and *suei* 'sui' (583.60, 123–122 B.C.). -D as the surviving ending of the ablative singular appears in *Gnaivod* (I² 7) and *meritod* (CIL I² 33). Genitive plural endings in -OM not yet in line with feminine genitives in -SOM are evident in *socium* 'sociorum' (581.7) and *sovum* 'suorum' (727, 80 B.C.); but the aligned form is already documented in the third century: *duonoro* 'bonorum' (I² 9). In the dative-ablative plural there is still a diphthong form *castreis* (614, 189 B.C.) in contrast to the contracted form *rostris* (583.43, 123–122 B.C.), and a deliberately archaic *suieis* 'suis' (2208).

In the third declension there are remains of the genitive singular in -os and -us instead of the normal ones in -ES and -IS: *diovos* 'Iovis' (360), *nominus* 'nominis' (581.7), *regus* 'regis' (730). There appear in the same inscription (I² 1430) the three successive forms of the dative ending -EI, -E, and -I: *Iunone, Seispitei matri.* In the ablative singular there are forms with and without -D: for example *conventionid* (581.22, 186 B.C.), but *sanctioni* (583.56, 123–122 B.C.).

The standardization of the pronouns is extremely laborious, and the situation chaotic for a long time. Here it is important only to note the distinction between the interrogative-indefinite pronoun and the relative pronoun in *sei ques esent quei . . . deicerent* (581.3ff), a distinction which the classical languages dissolves into the single plural *qui.*

As far as the verb is concerned, normalization appears through the elimination of themes of the subjunctive which have been separated from the normal themes of the present: there is still *atigas* (499) and the normalized *attingat* (583.20). In the formation of the perfect there are types in -II, sometimes in the archaic or archaizing form -IEI, as compared with the forms in -IVI that later become established: such are the cases of *petiei* (I² 15) and of *quaesierit* (583.62) as compared with *conquaesiverit* (583.34, 123–122 B.C.); such are the forms in -IVI destined to be replaced by forms in -UI, as for example, *poseivei* (638.3, 132 B.C.) and *posivi* as compared with *posuit* (1545). The systematization of the endings of the third person plural in -ERE and in -ERONT, destined to merge into the classical -ERUNT, is important: there is *censuere* (581.3) but in *consoluerunt* (581.1); and *coeravere, fecere* (687, 106 B.C.) as compared with *coiraverunt fecerunt* (675, 108 B.C.).

In the nominal forms of the verb, the standardization of the middle passive infinitive is particularly laborious. On the one hand there are the remains of the ending -IER in *figier gnoscier* (581.27), and *avocarier abducier* (583.71); on the other hand we find the archaizing graphics EI for -I, as, for example, in *solvei* and *mittei* (584.44, 117 B.C.).

A coexistence between gerund and gerundive forms of the type -UNDO- and those of the type -ENDO- in the third and fourth conjugations continues for a long time. The forms *exdeicendum* and *faciendam* (CIL I² 581.3, 25 186 B.C.) are premature; the forms *reficiUndas sternEndas* (593.26, 45 B.C.) coexist, as do *faciUndum* and *claudEndam* (I² 1565); the formula *iure dicundo* persists as a juridical archaism even in the first century of the Christian era.

57 DERIVATION OF WORDS

In the derivation and formation of words there are numerous processes of congealment, such as *tribunale* (593.34, 45 B.C.) as compared with the normal *tribunal,* because it is attracted by the normal ending of the neuter forms of adjectives in *-alis/ale.* More conspicuous are the adjustments between suffixes of connected, parallel, or intersecting meaning. For example, the suffix *-bilis,* well illustrated by J. Marouzeau,[2] gives life to verbal adjectives without denoting whether its primitive function was that of the active or passive voice: *terribilis* means 'capable of terrorizing' while *adorabilis* means 'worthy of being adored'. That is to say, linguistic standardization does not occur on a basis of grammatical coherence, but as if through individual crystallizations, which occur too late for it to be possible to guide their application and too early to be able to correct it and make it uniform.

The possibilities of derivation of abstract words are copious—both in the case of those derived from adjectives and originally little used (abstract in the strict sense) and in the case of those derived from verbal roots or themes, widely used even prehistorically, and more properly called "action nouns." Ancient abstract suffixes are those in *-tudo* and *-ities,* destined soon to become obsolete, but available at every return of archaizing fashion even in the Imperial Age.

The original form of action nouns, by now indeterminable, was in the Indo-European languages marked by the suffix *-ti,* as in the Latin *gens,* or *tussis.* This was very soon amplified into the form *-tio(n),* as, for example, in *natio* and *ratio.* Alongside these a third procedure comes forward, more tied to nominal forms of the verb, namely of nouns ending in *-tura, mercatura, scriptura,* and *textura.* Nouns ending in *-tio* in an early period preserved the possibility of being construed as verbs, as we note in the Plautine examples *manum iniectio hanc tactio,*[3] 'the action of touching this', and *huc ventio,* 'the action of coming here'. This is still a valid procedure in Italian, in which the infinitive, even when accompanied by the article and therefore clearly considered a substantive, takes a complementary object, as we see in the case of *l'amar la patria*. But this is possible in Italian only because in the beginning the article determined the entire syntagma: *l'amar-la-patria*.

With the passage of time the nominal value is accentuated and a suffix of derivation such as *-tu,* with its strongly nominal nature, is opposed to the suffix ending *-tio(n),* as the following examples demonstrate: *cultus regis* 'comportment of the king', which is completely nominal, in contrast to *cultio agri,* which is formally nominal but syntactically verbal because *agri* is an 'objective genitive' which replaces a direct object.

As for the elaboration of deponent verbs, the process appears to take place through the progressive renunciation of the active forms of certain verbs, which in the classical period are reduced to exclusive deponents: examples are *amplecto, contemplo, laeto, pacisco.*[4]

Finally, in contrast to the process by which action nouns accentuate their nominal nature, the infinitive accentuates its verbal nature. In the Plautine formulae *ire dixi, aio scire, dare promitto,* the infinitives are a kind of complementary object because they are equivalent in meaning to 'I declared the fact of going', 'I affirm the fact of knowing', 'I promise a gift'. In the classical period these formulae would have needed a subject in the accusative *me* before the infinitive.

58 SYNTACTICAL CONGEALMENTS
In the field of syntax the most important development of this period is hypotaxis, that is, the distinction between principal and dependent propositions. The successive stages through which the procedure is established are the following. The elementary phase appears through asyndetic alignment: in the Duenos inscription we read, "Duenos made me for a good purpose; to Duenos let not unpleasant circumstances come." At the other extreme we have Caesar's remark *veni vidi vici,* in which the syntactic elementariness acts as a factor of strong expressivity. The second stage is represented by cases in which a rapport of correlation is established; that is, the two propositions are still parallel, but have come to be considered as a group in comparison with all the others, through a marker of real or virtual liaison. The link is virtual, (or equivalent to zero) in Plautus for example: *ne me moneatis, memini ego officium meum* 'don't remind me of it, I know my duty' (*Miles* 1378). The marker of a real opposition or adversativeness is given by the personal pronoun *ego* with respect to the understood *vos* of the first part. Another example is *abi modo, ego dum hoc curabo recte* 'go ahead, in the meantime I'll attend to this properly' (*Rudens* 779). The element *dum* here has the value of an adverb that limits its action to the verb *curabo,* but is destined

to become a considerably more important syntactical marker. Finally, the marker is real in *quamquam hoc tibi aegre est, tamen fac accures* 'Even if it bores you, try to do it well' (*Casina* 421), in which the correlation is represented by *quamquam,* which is opposed to *tamen,* according to the traditional parallelism between interrogative and demonstrative themes. The third phase is that of crypto-hypotaxis included in the nominal forms of the verb. From a historical point of view we are dealing with an ancient situation, insofar as the nominal forms of the verb are of an Indo-European level: note the Plautine instances *quae hinc flens abiit* 'who went off crying' (*Cistellaria* 123), in which the present participle implies a hypotactic structure of the type 'while she went off she was crying', and *iam victi vicimus* 'already conquered, we have conquered' (*Casina* 510), which is equivalent to a hypotactic structure 'although conquered, we have conquered'. The fourth phase is realized when an element passes from a function of correlation to a marker of hypotactic rapport, as for example in the case of *dum* cited above, in which *dum* ceases to be an adverb and becomes a temporal conjunction. The fifth phase is finally realized when the main clause abandons the correlation marker, and the marker of the dependent clause definitively becomes a conjunction; note for example the definitive elaboration of passages of the law of Numa *SI qui hominem liberum dolo sciens morti duit,* ZERO *paricidas esto.* Or to cite another example *SI intestato moritur cui suus heres nec escit,* ZERO *adgnatus proximus familiam habeto* (XII Tab. V. 4). The particle SI changes from an element of correlation to a true conditional subordinate conjunction. In other words, behind the different subordinate conjunctions, there are always stems of demonstratives or interrogatives.

Taking full advantage of this device, the Latin period tends toward articulation of increasingly complex forms, which find their natural conclusion in Ciceronian syntax. The complexity of the relationships between different elements of the sentence thus established leads to a system of temporal bonds between the verbs of the principal and dependent propositions, which has been called *consecutio temporum.* It is not, however, a matter of a result of the elaboration of the hypotactic construction: the relative value of the tenses of the Latin verb is part of its fundamental structure from the time when it lost its aspectual basis, which had been proper to Indo-European antiquity and which was preserved in Greek.

59 Further Syntactical Imbalances
In addition to the structure of the sentence, the standardization of the Latin literary language takes advantage of the possibility of

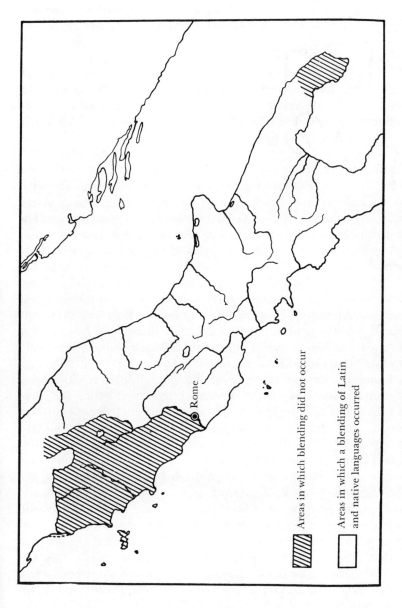

Areas in which blending did not occur

Areas in which a blending of Latin and native languages occurred

Map 2. Italy Immediately before the Diffusion of Latin

reinforcing the normal morphological markers by means of syntactical procedures. In Plautus' *Captivi* we find the following two passages close together: *Praecipe quae ad patrem vis nuntiari* (ll. 359–60), and *numquid aliud vis patri nuntiari* (ll. 400–401). The importance of the two parallel constructions is not relevant at this historical period. It does become relevant if one considers that the forms with *ad*, which are for the moment exceptional, are destined to gain more and more ground, and will end by eliminating the forms that are by nature only morphological. (§100).

60 LEXICAL PROBLEMS
The principal characteristic of Latin vocabulary in this period is its enrichment in conformity with the needs of a society in the process of transformation. The salient aspects are essentially two. The first consists in the consecration of a certain number of metaphors taken from the vocabulary of agriculture; *pecunia* 'money' from *pecu* 'livestock'; *ager,* which means not only 'meadow' or 'field' but also 'territory'; *laetamen* 'dung, manure' insofar as it indicates 'that which gladdens (the earth)'; *locuples* 'rich (in lands)'; *frugi* 'produce (of fruits)'; *egregius* 'chosen from the flock'; *rivalis* 'rival', that is, 'bordering on the irrigation canal'; *delirare* 'to rave', that is, 'to leave the beaten track'; *impedire* '(to impede, hinder) the foot'; *peccare* 'to act (inadequately) with the foot'.

In order to measure how alien the Latin tradition was with respect to abstract words, as compared with our own predilection for them, it suffices to gather together a few formulae: for 'I learned it in my youth', in Latin one says *adulescens didici*. A passage from the *Adelphoe* (ll. 987–90) by Terence contains a formula in which it is stated that something did not happen *ex aequo et bono, sed ex adsentando indulgendo et largiendo* 'from justice and goodness, but through complaisance, indulgence, and generosity'. In other words, what for us is represented by abstract nouns, Latin indicated with adjectives or gerunds.[5] In any case the formal structures emanating from action nouns existed, and at a certain moment, in connection with the raising of the intellectual level of society, the way was opened to them. One of the vehicles was the process of personification, which emanated from religious environments: *Pallor* and *Pavor* had temples according to Livy (I 27.7). Lucretius (III 65) records *Turpis enim fere Comptentus et acris Egestas;* Horace (*Odes* 1.24.6) *pudor ac iustitiae soror, incorrupta Fides nudaque Veritas.* But the decisive thrust in this direction depended on another very powerful factor, which we shall now study, Hellenism.

Thirteen

Hellenism

61 THE CULTURAL SETTING
Because of the disbanding of the Latin League, the year 338 B.C.
represents the beginning of the ascent of Rome as a political power
in Italy. The reestablishment of contact with the Greek world does
not take place for yet a few decades. With the end of the Samnite
wars, however, the breaking of the treaty with Tarentum (303 B.C.),
the entry of a Roman garrison in Thurii (285 B.C.), the submission
of Tarentum (272 B.C.), the acquisition of Sicily as a Roman province
in 241 B.C., the floodgates open to permit the penetration of Greek
linguistic elements after a long interruption, though indeed with the
delay of some decades. Thus all that follows later—the submission
of Greece in the year 146 B.C. and that of the kingdom of Pergamum
in 132—is the direct consequence of a thrust that is no longer
checked. The resumption of Greek cults begins with the cult of
Aesculapius (293 B.C.), who is attested in the inscription CIL I^2 440,
in the form *Aisclapi* (§56).
    The fundamental characteristic of the Grecism of this period is
that it acts like a pincer from both the highest and the lowest social
levels. The Greek cognomina taken by men such as Sempronius So-
phus (consul in 304 B.C.) or Furius Philus (consul in 223 B.C.), are
instances of the Greek influence at the highest level; the multitudes

of slaves, coming from the most diverse origins but all united by the universal language in use, Greek,[1] is an indication of its working at the lowest social level. The interjections found in literary works, largely diffused already at the time of Plautus, are the best testimony of this pressure from below: *heia, euge, eugepae, pax, papae, euax, attat pol.*[2]

62 PHONETIC MODIFICATION

The adaptation of Greek words is usually quite faithful. From an ancient Greek form without aspirate **ampora* had been taken the diminutive *ampulla*. In this second stratum, however, the Greek *amphoreús* appears with aspiration in the Latin *amphora*. The type *colapus* without aspirate survives, hidden in Vulgar Latin and re-appearing in the Italian 'colpo'; but in classical Latin, *colaphus* with the aspirate is in evidence. Some epigraphic evidence without aspiration continues: *pilemo* from Greek *Philémōn* (CIL I[2] 681), *Antioco* from Greek *Antiokhos* (I[2] 12); and beside the form Achaia (CIL I[2] 626) there is still Corinto. Aspiration, however, becomes the rule: instead of 'triumpe' there is *triumphus,* and similarly *phaselus, scapha, aether, thermae, schola, athleta, cithara,* and *spatha* abound. From the middle of the second century the matter becomes well regulated. In place of the U as a reflection of the Greek Y, as in the case of *purpura* (from the Greek *porphýra*), sometimes open to the point of being an O, as in *àncora* 'anchor' (from the Greek *ánkyra*), the Y was introduced, destined later to merge with the I. Note the forms *symbolus, syngraphus, symphonia, symposium, myrtus,* and *papyrus.* Only certain groups of consonants are resolved by means of an anaptyctic vowel, as we see for example in *techina* from the Greek 'tékhnē', *drachuma* from the Greek 'drakhmē', and similarly *mina* from 'mnâ', and *Alcumena* from 'Alkménē'. Finally, even the sound z is accepted after the preceding modification into s or ss. In an earlier stage the banker was the *tarpessita* in comparison with the Greek 'trapezítēs', while in later times we find the form *trapezita.* Along these lines the following forms become established: *oriza* 'rice', *zona* 'belt, girdle', *zephyrus* 'west wind'. This sensitivity to aspiration even penetrates words that are not Greek: it is firmly fixed in the case of *pulcher;*[3] it appears occasionally with unjustified exaggeration, as in the case of *lachrymis* (I[2] 1222) or *sepulchrum* (1225 and see §42).

63 MORPHOLOGY

In the field of morphology, the consequences of Hellenism are less conspicuous. In its adaptation to the declensions, the lower social class acts more energetically, and from the Greek type *kratér* it makes a theme of the first Latin declension *cratera, craterra* 'cup'. On the higher social level more fidelity is maintained and the same Greek form gives life to Latin *crater,* framed in the same declension as the Greek. From the point of view of the case endings, there can be examples of Greek words that maintain ties with the original Greek declension, as 'for example in the form of the accusative *aera* in Ennius *Ann.* 148. In the processes of word derivation the Greek suffix *-izo,* typical of denominative verbs, is accepted early on, first being Latinized in *-isso,* as for example in *badisso, cyatisso,* and *moechisso;* the last example is particularly important because the model of the Greek verb does not exist but only the substantive *moikhós* (Latin *moechus* 'adulterer'), from which the Latin verb is derived by means of a Greek suffix.

On the morphological plane, the most important contrast takes place with regard to nominal composition. The latter was present and vital in the Indo-European world, but in Italy and in archaic Latin it had been greatly damaged by the gusty blows of the intensive accent (§40), which had removed the possibility of recognizing the constituent elements of the word: regarding the word *hospes* no one was in a position any longer to recognize the components HOSTI and POTI. In Greek, however, compound words had preserved their vitality intact, and this appeared to the Romans as something distinctly foreign. Plautus, along with the models he had derived from Greek comedy, presents nominal composition even in humorous forms, in this way emphasizing their exotic qualities. Verses 702 ff. of Plautus' *Persa* are significant: "vaniloquidorus, virgines-vendonides/nugiepiloquides, argentumextenebronides/tedigniloquides, nugides, palponides/quodsemelarripides, numquameripides." The satire strikes not only at the passage and the personage, but at the entire morphological procedure of the composition. Even vocal apophony (§47) had contributed to making nominal composition difficult: in any case, by substituting ɪ (and, in closed syllable, ᴇ) for the loss of internal vowels, it had furnished an instrument which permitted the two constituent elements of a compound word to be distinct and at the same time linked: besides *sacerdos,* which was difficult to analyze, there is *sacrilegus,* which was analyzable; similarly we have *iuridicus* with respect to *iudex;* and *primigenius* with respect to 'princeps'; *agricola,* which did not become '*agercola', and *pontifex municeps,* which did not become '*ponfex', '*munceps'. As soon as the exotic quality of the procedure was overcome, Latin was able to develop its internal possibilities and furnish types such as *angiportus, pedisequa,* which were already Plautine, and *carnufex, furcifer, caeli-*

potens, and the typical compounds of the poetic fragments of **Cicero,** *altitonans, altisonus, horrificus, aurifer, ignifer, levipes,* and so on.

64 Syntax

On the syntactical level, from the beginning there are no facts which are comparable in importance. From the point of view of internal mechanism, however, the problem of the nominal forms of the verb, and in particular of the participles, is introduced. Participles, of Indo-European tradition, had at the beginning permitted a reduced form of subordination, which was related to their intermediate nature between verb and noun. The impoverishment of the nominal forms of the verb from the point of view of their variety, and the consequent spread of asyndetic parataxis, had devalued even the surviving forms. Now, on the basis of Greek models, Ennius shows examples of participles with full capacity for substituting subordinate clauses as for example in *Ann.* 77f.: *curantes magna cum cura, tum cupientes—Regni, dant operam simul auspicio augurioque (Ann.* 77–78); or *Haud doctis dictis certantes nec maledictis—Miscent inter sese inimicitias agitantes. (Ann.* 270–71).

65 Vocabulary

Naturally it is the lexicon which has the lion's share in producing a change in Italy's linguistic expression in the third through the first centuries (§43).[4] Besides the single words, which impose themselves individually, as instances of brute force, particularly among members of the lower classes, the problem is introduced among men of letters in a complex form. Livius Andronicus translated the Greek *polýtropos* of the first line of the *Odyssey* with *versutus.* It is an acceptable translation, which poses neither lexical nor morphological problems: *versutus* is not a compound word. The problem is born in the shadow of a certain amount of restraint, when Ennius supplies a Greek word with its Latin translation: *Sophiam sapientia quae perhibetur (Ann.* VII 218), or Afranius *Sophiam vocant me Grai, vos Sapientiam* (299). There are cases in which the Greek word does not triumph, but rather is held in reserve to underline a certain solemnity: *aether* is imposing, but it does not supplant *caelum.* At this point there arises the problem of calks, namely, the molding of a Latin word, in meaning or even form, after a Greek term. As an example of a calk in meaning, we note the establishment by convention of an equivalence between the Greek *tékhnē* and the Latin 'ars'; between the Greek *lógos* and the Latin 'ratio'; between the Greek *phýsis* and the Latin 'natura'; and even of *humanus* as an equivalent of the Greek 'philánthropos'. Similarly we have *causa* for the Greek 'aitía', and *locus* for 'tópos.' Formal calks that elegantly overcome even the difficulty of composition are *convenientia* for 'homología', *aequilibritas* for 'isonomía', *medietas* for 'mesótēs', *mulierositas* for 'philogýneia', *providentia* for 'prónoia', and finally *qualitas,* which comes from 'qualis', as the Greek *poiótēs* comes from 'poîos'. Not even in moments of greatest success, however, are Grecisms in a condition of true equality. They are more frequently accepted in common language, dialogues, and collections of letters than in literary works or in official documents. And within the category of literature, they are more readily accepted in poetry than in prose; more in comic poetry than in tragedy or epic. In philosophical works on the other hand, Grecisms can impose themselves as a technical necessity. It is not possible to make very long lists of lexical units of Greek origin. To give a sampling, I list some terms pertaining to the sea: *phaselus, lembus, scapha, prora, anquina, nauta, proreta, pirata, campsare* 'to double', *exantlare, pausa* (of oarsmen), *malacia* 'calm (at sea)', *nausea* 'seasickness', *pontus, pelagus, oceanus, isthmus, petra, antrum, spelunca, thalassicus* (from the Greek *thálassa* 'sea'), *cumatilis* (from *kŷma* 'wave'), and finally the names of the winds: *aura, eurus, notus, boreas, zephyrus.*

Here is a list of words pertaining to commerce: *emporia, danista, symbolus* 'identification card', *syngraphus* 'ticket', *dica* 'allotment', *arrabo* 'pledge, token', *poena* 'fine' (n.); and then different kinds of coins *nummus, mina, talentum, obolus; statera* 'weight'; containers such as *cupa cista, saccus, canistrum.* Examples from vegetable life are *malum* (also *melum*), *castanea, cerasus, platanus, papyrus, charta, sesamum, sinapis, oriza, tus.*

Fourteen

The Accent

66 THE POSITION OF THE ACCENT

In all the preceding periods, the urban accent had sought to defend its original nature, but had had to submit to two things: the intense buffets from the outside which had introduced certain drastic syncopes (§40), and after the end of the monarchy, the passage from an early freedom to the fixation of the accent on the first syllable, as the facts of apophony prove (§47). Not even this acceptance, however, led to a definitive congealment, and at the end of the fourth century, the period of apophonic action having been exhausted, Latin was simultaneously deprived of both the awareness of the historical accent and a solid automatic substitution like that of the generalized initial accent. Thus, from this void of power is born the accent that depends on the quantity of the penultimate syllable, which remained stable in words which survived in the passage from Latin to Italian. If the penultimate syllable is long, it takes the accent, while if it is short, the accent falls on the preceding syllable. The fact that one never finds the accent further back than on the antepenultimate syllable led to a belief in a similarity with Greek and to the application of a so-called law of the three syllables.[1] The similarity does not exist. In Greek we are dealing with the Indo-European accent subjected to restrictions in its liberty and negatively conditioned in the limits of the last three syllables. In Latin we are dealing with the application of a new discipline which imposes from the outside an "active" regulation on the penult, or on the antepenult. Latin receives a new accent. In order to insist on an interpretation of the nature of the Latin accent which would be in harmony with the preceding investigations about its intensive nature, studies have been made to prove that in prosody there had existed a certain tendency to make the position of the ictus coincide with that of the word accent. An illustrious German philologist, Eduard Fraenkel, has devoted an entire book to the problem.[2] A detailed review by Fraenkel's old school companion, Giorgio Pasquali,[3] has greatly restricted the scope of these coincidences and has pointed up the fact that the ictus of the line avoids more than anything else correspondence with the final syllable of the words. This does not mean that the ictus automatically coincides with the accented syllable, but only that the word has distinct and clearly discernible boundaries, and that the final syllable does not lend itself to be the rhythmical center of a foot. That the two movements are entirely independent is proved by the fact that the rhythm is liberated from all these restraints, not at the time when a weakening of the accent occurs, but on the contrary when, in Horace's time, the Latin accent is approaching a stage in which the tendency to become intensified and to center its action on the rest of the word will be all the more clear.

67 WEAK CENTRALIZING CAPACITY

There is at this point proof not only that the centralizing activity of the accent is weak, but that it is further weakened in the act of passing from the prehistoric to the historical stage. There are two proofs. The first lies in the harsh vocalization of the sonant of the type MEDHYO-, which in all the Indo-European languages is bisyllabic. In Latin, however, *medius* is (as we seen in §55) trisyllabic, and this could not have happened except through a relaxing of the centralizing capacity of the accent of the word. This occurs in all the series consisting of a consonant followed by J (yod): *capio*, 'I take', *venio* 'I come' are trisyllabic words.

The second example is given by the anaptyctic vowel which comes to divide groups of consonants plus L: STABLO- 'stable' becomes *stabulum;* TABLA, *tabula* 'table'; and POKLO- *poculum* 'drinking glass'. As soon as the accent of intensity appears (§87) an opposite movement will be realized: one of the first consequences will be the centralization of the word under the accent and the consequent weakening and loss of the internal atonic vowel.

The process of decentralization was therefore a "phase" in the development of the Latin structures, a phase which corresponds to its classical period. It remains in doubt whether this phase made an impact on the entire breadth of the linguistic system or only on its upper strata, which were more delicate and susceptible. A different process, which is verified in the fortunes of the form *spat(u)la,* which was assimilated in the Italian 'spalla', and those of *spec(u)lum,* which through a process of dissimilation becomes the Italian 'specchio', raises the doubt that the ancestor of the Italian word *specchio* was not a relatively recent vulgarism such as that disapproved by Probus (§87), but rather the archaism SPEKLO-, which the lower social strata of the population had refused to subject to the anaptyxis suggested by the upper classes.

68 IAMBIC SHORTENING

The systematization of the earlier inheritance did not consist only in the acceptance of a new, mechanical accent. In addition it necessarily included within its scope the translation into rhythmical terms of what had been the equilibrium determined by the application of apophony and its indirect consequences. In the field of word formation there remained, even after the cessation of apophonic activity, a model for word formation, and because of it, even in classical times, one continued to consider it normal that the easily analyzable compound *agri-cola* should continue to have the I in place of the thematic vowel O, because this had been imposed by the rule of apophony (§47), which allows in the second syllable only the vowel I in open syllable and the vowel E in closed syllable. It is only with the advent of Grecisms that this prejudice against the internal vowel is overcome, with particular attention to the vowel placed in second position.

If one accepts the possibility that in a nominal compound the thematic vowel should not have greater sonority than the initial vowel, then we should not be surprised if something similar now becomes evident also from the point of view of rhythmical series. In rhythmic terms, given a pattern of a compound word, or a formula, composed of four syllables, the first pair of syllables can be of the four following types: trochaic — ∪, spondaic — —, pyrrhic ∪ ∪, or iambic ∪ —. A trochaic, spondaic, or pyrrhic series does not conflict with the tradition resulting from apophony, because in none of the three cases does the second syllable have a rhythmic relevance which is superior to that of the first syllable. In the case of the iambic series, however, the second element, because it is long, prevails over the first. This prevalence cannot be tolerated by the system, and thus what has been called the law of the shortening of the iambic series intervenes: *malē* becomes 'malĕ', *modō* 'modŏ', *benē,* 'benĕ', and *abī*, 'abĭ'. Similarly, the shortening takes place in formulae which constitute a rhythmic unity such as *male dicere, bene facere, cito venire*.[4] Even within a word, without the intervention of morphological analysis, the shortening remains a possibility at the disposition of poets, as for example *vŏlŭptates, iŭvĕntute;* these are possibilities of which Plautus still avails himself at this time and which then are progressively allowed to fall into disuse (§83). The rule for iambic shortening has been used as a proof in favor of the prevalence of the intensity of the accent itself which determined it.[5] It must be objected that, if it had depended on the nature of the accent, there would have been all the more reason for a transformation in favor of a spondaic or a trochaic series, a transformation that did not occur.

69 RHYTHMIC PATTERNS IN PROSE
Apart from these well-defined deviations, the sensibility of Latin for quantity is quite refined. Cicero affirms in *De oratore* III 196 that the slightest quantitative irregularity evokes a reaction in the listeners; and in *Orator* 48.159 he invites the reader to rely with confidence on his sense of hearing, which does not fail in recognizing quantitative distinctions. The succession of long and short syllables gives life to the rhythm of the verse, which on that account is in perfect harmony with the listener's capacity to perceive it.[6] Theoretically, prose ought not to be linked to rhythmical measure. But, apart from the fact that a verse of Ennius can be transferred into the context of historical prose, even prose can be influenced by rhythmic models or ideals; as far as the Latin of this period is concerned, it is probable that the fashion came from Greece. The penetration of rhythmic factors in prose is concentrated in the final portions of propositions or clauses. There were several favorite patterns. Cicero liked to use the ditrochee — ∪ — ∪, the dicretic — ∪ — — ∪ —, the double spondee — — — —, the cretic plus spondee — ∪ — — —, and still others. The weight of the rhythmic patterns is such that they can impose the subjunctive in place of the indicative and vice versa: for example, *esse videatur* with the subjunctive is preferred to *esse videtur* with the indicative, while *dicere videtur* with the indicative is preferred to *dicere videatur* with the subjunctive.[7]

70 THE NATURE OF THE ACCENT
Finally we must consider the direct testimony of the ancients on the nature of the accent. This testimony must surely be taken into consideration with a critical spirit, but not with the systematic diffidence

with which L. R. Palmer expresses himself, for example, when he considers them "slavish imitators of Greeks."[8] There are three fundamental passages. The first comes from Varro, which we have received by way of Servius.[9] According to Varro, in the accent one must distinguish the material, which is the voice, the position, which is the syllable, and the quality, which can be either of high or low pitch.

If all the syllables are pronounced at the same pitch, there is no "prosody." The voice as material of the accent has three dimensions: the length (or quantity), the pitch or musicality, and finally the fullness, which can also be emphasis, aspiration, or intensity. There is no doubt that the voice, as material of the accent, possesses musical pitch.

The second passage comes from Nigidius Figulus, a contemporary of Varro. It is quoted by Gellius[10] and takes into consideration only the musical difference that occurs in the pronunciation of the name Valeri, when one is questioning (in which case there is a higher pitch in the second syllable) and when instead one is calling (in which case the first syllable has the more elevated pitch).

The third proof comes from Cicero. He states in *Orator* 18.58 that Nature, as if to modulate the speech of men, has placed in every word a "sharp tone (accent)"; and again in *Orator* 17.57 that the nature of the voice with its three modulations—intermediate, high, and low—is a wondrous thing; and finally, that Nature has placed in our ear the possibility of distinguishing between high- and low-pitched voices.

To this positive testimony there must be added a negative argument made by G. Pasquali.[11] The exaggerated emphasis of oratory of the eastern style was unpleasant to the Roman ear because, as Cicero once again says,[12] it inappropriately gave the impression of being a song. But no Roman ever had the occasion of criticizing the "song" of those who spoke normal Greek, evidently because the "song," part and parcel of languages with a musical accent, was the same for Romans as it was for Greeks, and therefore the "song" of the Greeks must have passed unnoticed.

Notwithstanding the learning and the seriousness of the arguments in favor of the intensity of the accent in the Latin of the classical period as they have been developed by V. Pisani[13] or L. R. Palmer,[14] the opposite theory of the musicality of the Latin accent is therefore to be recommended, as is that of the substantial continuity of the tradition of the Indo-European accent, as it has been expounded by J. Marouzeau,[15] for example.

Fifteen

The Classical Age

71 Bona Consuetudo

Linguistic standardization was not just a matter of eliminating the rustic forms which had become encrusted on the Latin of Rome, nor a matter of simple internal congealment. Because Rome was continually acquiring more prestige and it exercised an ever more far-reaching attraction, it favored the influx of foreign cultures and speakers of foreign languages. These people had at the same time the aspiration for a superior unity and brought together elements and tastes divergent and new. Only a firmly established superior cultural unity conditions, permits, and promotes the search for a unitary linguistic base. We may say that cultural unity was realized with Ennius and Plautus, or in the middle of the third century B.C. This unity brings together men of very diverse origins: in addition to Plautus, who is Umbrian, and Ennius, who is Salentine, there is Livius Andronicus from Tarentum, Naevius from Campania, and Terence, who is in fact African. The ideas and tastes that derive from them are in direct relation with the contrasting needs that make themselves felt. Archaism as a literary taste and linguistic embroilment is generally reflected in the literary world. In the epigraphic tradition, which is bound to the formalism and the ultraconservatism inherent in the legal formulations, archaisms—authentic or even false—maintain their positions and play their part. Rusticism is also rejected. But, urbanity is not born only from a negative operation. It develops through concrete criteria, which are not abandoned to occasional eclecticism, but rather are bound to a search for sensibility, gentility, and restraint. Lexical requirements are enormous. Lucretius, still in the first century B.C., deplores several times over the *sermonis patrii egestas*,[1] 'the poverty of the mother tongue'. As with the Grecism, however, the search for neologisms is always a process of sifting and selecting and does not sink into an uncontrolled amassing, at least not so far as the literary language is concerned. The situation is different in the lower social classes or in the familiar speech of cultured persons, because in these cases we are not dealing with an attitude of conscious search but with foreign elements which offer or impose themselves by their own force. The definition of this prudence, actuated before being rationally elaborated, is identified with what Cicero called the *bona consuetudo* 'good usage'.[2]

72 GRAMMATICAL DOCTRINES

Besides these tendencies, which were instinctive more than anything else, little by little the desire, if not the necessity, for a doctrine such as the Greek models offered began to make itself felt. Up to the time of Plato, the laying down of a grammatical doctrine appeared to the Greeks to be potentially twofold. What in Plato was the hypothesis of a language as *nómos* 'law' or 'convention' gave life to the concept of 'analogy'. What in Plato had been defined as creativity or *enérgeia* of language gave life to the doctrine of 'anomaly'. As grammatical doctrine, analogy was developed above all in Alexandria in Egypt, in the school of Aristarchus; anomaly was elaborated in the school of Pergamum and was made known in Rome by Crates of Mallos, who arrived before the middle of the second century B.C. Varro shows himself to be well informed regarding both doctrines.[3] The two principles, inherent in any linguistic system, are valid even for modern linguistics, which must accept their coexistence.

In Rome Caesar was a great follower of analogy: to indicate 'river', for example, he preferred a term such as *flumen,* which belonged to a long list of other terms ending in *-men,* rather than the synonyms *fluvius or amnis,* which did not have "analogous" forms to which they could be compared. Similarly the word *mortuus,* characterized by two u's, seemed to him to be acceptable only as an adjective. He had difficulty in using it as a participle, insofar as it could not be confronted with all the other participles that ended in *-tus,* that is with only one u.[4]

73 ANOMALIES

The standardization of the literary language, which was reached after complex exertion even without the reinforcement of such a doctrinal motivation as analogy, must have led to a position of resistance or even rejection of new centrifugal temptations which could ensue. It is worth illustrating two such temptations. The first problem has to do with the heaviness of the accent, which is suggested by a passage of Cicero in *Brutus* 259 on sonorous pronunciations which called to mind something uncultivated or rustic. The opposite quality, which deserves praise is, according to Cicero, the lightness or *subtilitas,* the *suavitas,* the *lenitas vocis,* which appears in *De oratore* III 42 ff., for example. According to Marouzeau,[5] this heaviness, this fullness of sound should be explained by the abundance of diphthongs, characteristic of the archaic way of speaking, as opposed to the normal orderliness of the Ciceronian age. This is impossible, however, because, as we have seen above, rusticity always coincided with premature fusion, that is, the elimination of dipthongs. This heaviness and excessive sonority can be explained very well if it is related to the heaviness of the intensive accent, characteristic of the peripheral and rural areas, with respect to the urban boundary of Rome. This heaviness, characteristic of the Umbrian, Sabine, and Etruscan areas, or up to the Ciceronian age, is destined to gain the upper hand from the beginning of the Imperial Age, following the diffusion of Latin throughout Italy and its superimposition on linguistic strata by now characterized in large part by the intensive accent (§80).

Besides heaviness, aspiration is condemned; Cicero accepts it only in certain exceptional examples, such as *pulcher, triumphus,* and *Cethegus.* But the aspirated forms reflect archaic or regional peculiarities of a high level, rather than rusticism. The removal of the aspiration as a relic of earlier strata of language is definitive (see above). Precisely because in closed circles (in Etruria, for example) aspiration was in use, we can explain examples of playfulness such as that for which Catullus in Ode 84 criticizes a certain Arrius, who pronounces *cHommoda* for 'commoda' and *hinsidias* for 'insidias'.

74 LEXICAL SELECTION

The repressive barrier does not stop in the face of problems of vocabulary. Words which appear to be more or less synonymous are subjected to social scrutiny even before being scrutinized for the strictness of their meanings and their subtle semantic distinctions. One famous example was pointed out by Eduard Norden[6] regarding the four-part series of synonyms pertaining to the notion of "swearing together, taking a common oath", contained in the text of the Senatus Consultum de Bacchanalibus (CIL I² 581): *coniurare, conspondere, convovere, compromittere*. Of these four lexical units only the first, *coniurare*, was deemed worthy to be continued in use in the classical age, not for technical reasons, but rather because of the higher social level which it connoted.

In reaction to the enrichment of the vocabulary which appeared to be so necessary to Lucretius, for example, "social censorship" introduces factors of both selection and paucity. In this matter of restraint, imposed by social criteria, Caesar and Cicero, so different in temperament and sensibility, find themselves in agreement. Caesar's constant preference for *perfugere* over its synonym *transfugere* for 'to desert' (while Cicero chose the latter) appears from our present-day perspective to be without motivation; *absumere* 'to dissipate, squander' is found in Cicero but never in Caesar; similarly the preference given to *externus* as opposed to *extraneus* in the sense of 'foreigner' seems to us to be entirely without motive.

In other words, a need which is selective, subjective, and based on class consciousness and which therefore tends to reduce the scope and breadth of the vocabulary carries more weight than the purely functional exigency which is aimed at enriching it. This class-based selectivity is a characteristic of the linguistic expression of Italy which will make itself felt throughout its long history, even, one might say, up to our own day.

75 THE HIDDEN TRADITION

These selective preoccupations, bolstered by a coherent doctrine and an analogous sensitivity, were able to give stability and harmony to the structure of Latin in a spatial as well as in a temporal sense. At first sight, we are not in a position to answer the question whether or not these preoccupations penetrated the whole social spectrum of the system. But a more detailed investigation proves that in fact total penetration was not the case. In an interesting work that dates back to the first years of this century, a German scholar, Marx,[7] concentrated his attention on linguistic elements that are documented in the archaic period, and then seem to have been forgotten, only to reappear in a later period. A Plautine word such as *canutus* 'white-haired' disappears for the entire classical period and then reappears later in the *Acta Andreae et Matthiae*[8] of the sixth century A.D.; *minaciae* is found in both Plautus and Arnobius, but not in the classical age. The construction with *quod* (§85), which presupposes the passage to Romance syntax (devoid of the accusative plus infinitive construction), is not a novelty in Vulgar Latin; it is found in the Latin of Plautus and in an anonymous text, the "Bellum hispaniense," which is attributed to Caesar.[9] *Fabulantur* instead of 'loquuntur' is found in the playwright Titinius at the beginning of the second century B.C.; then it disappears, but reappears in peripheral areas such as Spain and Friuli, where it survives in the modern phonetic forms of the Spanish *hablar* and the Friulian *favelà*, while in France and in the rest of Italy the term PAR(ABO)LARE, Italian 'parlare', took over. *Quaero,* in the sense 'I wish', is found in Terence in the second century B.C. and then in the Vulgar Latin of Spain. The declension *arva, arvae,* instead of 'arvum, arvi' appears in Naevius and Pacuvius in the age of the Republic, and then only in Venantius Fortunatus and in the Bible (Itala) in the second half of the Imperial Age; similarly *castra, castrae,* instead of 'castra, castrorum' (encampment) is found in Accius and then only in the Bible. A different example of an "underground" life is that of FORBEX, which is not documented because in the whole of the Latin tradition the form *forfex,* of rural origin, is used; and still it must have existed, because the Italian *forbice* is proof of it. Similarly, MACINA represents the more genuine form of the Greek *makhanã* (§43). In the classical age, however, this form was replaced by a more relevant one, *machina,* which in turn is represented in Italian by *màcchina.* The Italian *macina* demands an explanation independent of the more distant times of the arrival of the Greek word in Italy (§51).

The metaphorical image adopted by Marx is that of a river which freezes in a certain part of its course, while below the ice the original current continues to flow. There is some truth in this image. But what determines the continuity between archaic and late evidence is not a subterranean current. It was exactly the opposite, the immobility. Because of this, another metaphor seems better to me, that of the trunk of a tree, which in summer is covered with leaves and flowers—in short with vegetation—just as the Latin language is adorned in its golden age with new forms and qualities which hide the trunk. When summer is over and the vegetation disappears, the old trunk reappears, not entirely unchanged, but still a recognizable continuation of what was first seen.

For the language of Italy, it is a first test of resistance and continuity.

Sixteen

Latin in Italy

76 THE COLONIES

The linguistic unification of Italy was carried out over a period of approximately three centuries, from the time of the dissolution of the Latin League to the *lex Julia* (90 B.C), which confers citizenship on those living between Rome and the Po, and to the *lex Pompeia* (89 B.C.) which confers Latin citizenship as far as the Alps, and finally to 49 B.C., when Roman citizenship is extended to the Alps through the action of Caesar.

It was not an even expansion emanating from a central nucleus in ever larger circles. Rather, the peninsula was prepared for linguistic unity during these three centuries in a number of isolated focal nuclei, namely, the colonies under Latin law and those of Roman citizens, all of which were spreading their influence in all directions. Besides these direct diffusions, only the annexed territories represented a direct linguistic continuity with Rome. Moreover, even the city-states that were linked to Rome in unequal alliances, though they could not spread the Latin tradition because of the fact that they were locked into their forced particularism, constituted foci where the desire to be part of the Latin linguistic community was cultivated. These city-states facilitated the flow of currents that emanated from both the colonies and the annexed territories. In the

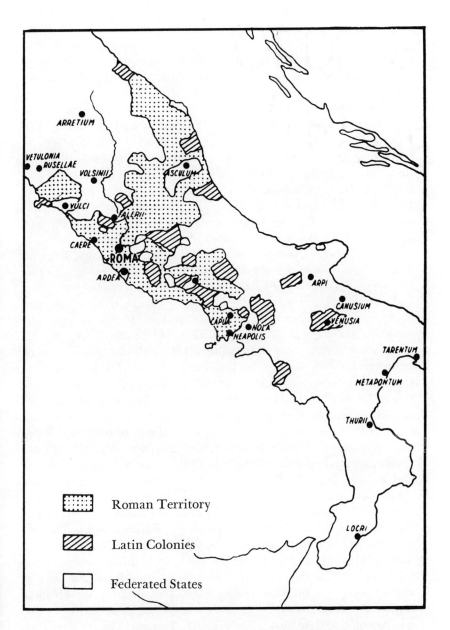

Map 3. First Foci of Latin in the Third Century B.C.
(From Devoto, *Storia della lingua di Roma,* table 7)

third century these gaps in the Latin linguistic continuity numbered at least 150; some were more ready than others to enter into the larger, linguistically united group.[1]

Most of the Latin colonies already established in 338 B.C. were immediately to the southeast of Rome, in the land of the Volsci. To these were added Fregellae, Setia, Pontiae, *Interamna Lirenas* (near Cassino), and Sora in the fourth century B.C., Suessa Aurunca, Cales, and Saticula (today Sant'Agata dei Goti) in the territory of the Caudine Samnites. Toward the northwest the first successes of this kind were at Nepete and Sutrium. Toward the east there was Alba Fucens (in 303 B.C.) in the territory of the Marsi, which had already been long preceded by the distant *Luceria,* founded in 314. In the third century the greatest efforts were directed above all toward the north: Narnia (299), Spoletium (241), Hadria (after 290), Firnum (264), Aromi (268), Cremona (218), and Placentia (218). To the east there were Carsioli (298) among the Aequii, the very distant Venusia in Apulia (291), Beneventum midway along the route of the future Via Appia (268), farther inland Aesernia (263), and finally Brundisium (246), the point of embarcation for the East and terminus of the Via Appia. Toward the southwest there was only Paestum (273), and toward the northwest only Cosa, in Etruscan territory. At the beginning of the second century the most distant ones are quite far away: to the south in Bruttium, at Thurii (193) and Vibo (192), to the north Bononia (189) and Aquileia (181), followed by nine others (after the *lex Pompeia*), all in Transpadane Gaul. The Roman colonies, which theoretically ought to have been more effective disseminators of Latin than the Latin colonies, were at first relatively rare: in the fourth century there were only two, Antium (338) and Terracina (329), both in the territory of the Volsci. In the third century, among the Ausones, there were Minturnae and Sinuessa; in Picenum, Castrum Novum; on the Adriatic side of Umbria, Aesis and Sena Gallica, and on the borders of Etruria, Alsium (247) and Fregenae (245). In the second century the colonies are by contrast numerous: Vulturnum (the present-day Capua), Liternum, Puteoli, and Salernum in Campania, all at the beginning of the century; Buxentum and Potentia in Lucania, Sipontum (194) and Tarentum (122) in Apulia, Temesa and Croto (194), Scolacium (122), in Bruttium; *Pyrgi* (191), Saturnia (183), and *Graviscae* in southern Etruria; Luna on the northern borders of Etruria; Pisaurum (184) in Umbria; Mutina, Parma, and Dertona in Cispadane Gaul, on the route of the future Via Aemilia and Auximum in Picenum. To these lists we must add also the veteran soldiers' colonies such as Eporedia (100), the Sullan colonies at Hadria, Interamna, Aretium, Praeneste, Nola, Abella, and Pompeii; and the Augustan ones at Augusta Praetoria, Brixia, Ateste, Concordia, Tergesto, and Pola. A category apart consists of the two provinces of Sicily and Sardinia, which were certainly suited to receive and transmit the Latin tradition, but only in discontinuous waves through links with the maritime frontiers. Their lines of communication passed through the offices of the governor (consul, proconsul, or praetor) with its entourage of legates, friends, and the *apparitores* (subordinate employees).

77 ROADS AND MARITIME ROUTES

A consideration of the static factors of this process must be accompanied by a description of its dynamic elements. One of these is curiosity, then the active desire on the part of the colonial populations not only not to resist, but on the contrary to welcome, and get even closer to, the linguistic-cultural influence of the constantly more famous metropolis. This aspiration, born in the linguistic and cultural milieu, extends then to the political field and even the military: the Social War (90–89 B.C.) did not flare up because of hatred but out of exasperated love for the Roman world, in which all the peoples of Italy aspired to be united and merged. The Social War is identified with a defeat on the military level but with full success as regards the political and linguistic aspirations of the peoples.

Overland routes constitute another dynamic aspect of the problem, in that they appear as a necessary condition for the diffusion and acceptance of the Roman tradition. During the republic and the first centuries of the empire, the distribution of these land routes is star-shaped: they are as many beams that radiate from a single star. For the first time, but not for the last, we realize the expression "all roads lead to Rome." The skeleton of the road system is as follows: (a) the Via Appia, from Rome to Brundisium; (b) the Via Popillia, which branched off from the Via Appia at Capua to make its way to the Straits of Messina; (c) the Via Aurelia, from Rome to the boundary of Transalpine Gaul; (d) the Via Flaminia, from Rome to Spoleto and Rimini, whence it continued as the Via Aemilia as far as Piacenza and beyond the passes of the Monginevro, San Bernardo, Spluga, and Giulio. From Rimini another Via Popillia branched off, which, by way of other branchlets, led to the passes of Resia, the Brenner, Monte Croce Carnico, Tarvisio, and Postumia. This system of roads is not the result of a single design but rather the consequence of isolated efforts carried out over the centuries. Maritime routes were necessary as regards Sardinia: but for technical reasons the roads from Rome through Provence or from Rome or Naples to Sicily were to be preferred.

78 GREEK RESISTANCES

This solid system of roads was not completely effective. The case of Calabria is typical; in the central and southern part there are still remains, though in vestigial form, of the Doric tradition of pre-Roman antiquity. One of the decisive pieces of evidence is provided by the name of the Amato River, which flows into the sea near Santa Eufemia. "Amato" is in reality an ancient form LAMATO: in the area of the Doric dialect this word preserved the second A intact, as a long vowel, whereas in the Ionic dialect it would have changed into an E. In fact, when in Roman times and later, Hellenistic or Byzantine models made their impact, the original theme replaced the A with an E, and the present-day name, recently added to Santa Eufemia but taken from ancient sources, is LamEzia. The name of the river also appears in a fragment of Hecataeus,[2] already in the Ionic form LámEtos.

Besides this positive datum, we find negative ones. In the first decades of the second century the colonies of Copia (in place of Thurii), Vibo, Medma, Temesa, and *Castra Hannibalis,* later a Gracchian colony with the name Minerva Scolacium, were established. In spite of this, it was not possible to overcome the obstacle of the natural bottleneck in the vicinity of Maratea, where, even up to our own days, a vocalic system of five vowels completely similar to the Sardinian system is preserved (see §90). The Neapolitan system of nine vowels was able to reach central Calabria only later, hurdling the barrier of the Lucano-Calabrese border. From the opposite direction, on the southern tip of Calabria, there are today forms of "Roman" Latin and not "Umbro-Samnite," through the persistence of consonant groups of the type ND, which is not assimilated into NN. This proves that the Roman Latin tradition arrived in Southern Calabria through Sicily and not by means of overland routes through neighboring regions.[3]

79 INFLUENCES OF LATIN

The linguistic unification of Italy was preceded not only by a psychological preparation, but also by the partial acceptance of Roman lexical units and syntactical patterns in juridical texts of the Italic world. The case of the *Tabula Bantina,* one of the principal monuments of the Oscan language from the second century B.C., is typical. Numerous formulas found in this monument are not remains of an Osco-Samnite tradition, but Roman nuclei which were accepted more or less naturally. *Ceus. Bantins* is equivalent to "civis Romanus," but this does not prove that the notion of "citizen" dates back to a presumed Italic community. A series such as *sipus . . . perum dolom mallom* is the "translation" of the Roman formula *sciens . . . sine dolo malo*. *Dicitud* is the Oscan translation of the decisive Roman formula 'liceto'. The names of the magistrates, the censor, the quaestor, as well as that of the senate, go back to Roman labels, which necessarily begin to misrepresent the local traditional material. Even the inscription of the Cippus Abellanus contains the Roman words drawn respectively from *senatus* and *liceto*. But in this cippus we also find a syntactical specimen, an example of the free indirect construction which appears in the Senatus Consultum de Bacchanalibus (CIL I² 581): "that temple and that territory . . . should be in common territory, the income of the temple and the territory should be for common use . . . the treasure . . . they should open it by common agreement."

In this same spirit of sought and desired acceptance, there is the title of the Umbrian magistrate *kvestur,* that is, "quaestor." In this instance we see that the desire to conform to a Roman model results in baptizing with the non-Roman name of "quaestor" a magistrate who, unlike his Roman counterpart, had no duties of a financial nature.

80 INFLUENCES ON LATIN

The general willingness to accept Roman elements even in official texts is found not only among the citizens of Italy. The Latin structures themselves, transported to places far from Rome, were not impervious to the penetration of local elements. From the beginning this penetration was only a matter of small details, thus showing that this local action was an unconscious one, not destined to be projected into the future. Three important pieces of evidence come into this first measure: the inscriptions of Pisaurum and Spoletium, which come from a strongly Latinized environment, and the inscription of Luceria, which is still immersed in a Samnite context.

In the inscription of Spoletium (CIL I² 366) the following forms are noteworthy: *cedito* for 'caedito', which, given the nature of the inscription, cannot be considered (because of its monophthongization) a rustic form which survived in the Latin of Rome. Rather, it reflects an environment which, as we know from other Umbrian evidence, is alien to diphthongization. Similarly, *cedre* for 'caedere' demonstrates a type of syncope which is perfectly well known in the Umbrian world but is quite foreign to the Latin. The following formulas are somewhat less evident but nevertheless valid in proving a certain relaxation away from the Roman models: *res deina, rei dinai* for 'res divina', 'rei divinae', because the loss of the sonant -v- in an intervocalic position is an ancient Roman tendency, which in this particular case had no sequel in the capital.

The inscription of Luceria (CIL I² 401) demonstrates more signifi-cant alterations with respect to Roman patterns; this is understand-able if one thinks about the distance involved and the cultural and linguistic differences that separated the Samnite world from the Roman. The following morphological forms stand out: *loucar,* which corresponds to the Latin 'lucus', expanded by means of a suffix of derivation; the verbal forms *fundatiD, proiecitaD, parentatiD,* of dubious interpretation, which were perhaps influenced by the Oscan models in -TT-.[4] The vocalism of *stircus* as opposed to the normal 'stercus' presents a different case; a dialectal form such as *arvorsum* for 'adversum' is not unknown in Rome (§51). A reaction to the Oscan may appear in the form *macisteratus* with the c and the anaptyctic vowel.

In the inscription of Pisarium (CIL I² 378) the two forms *ma-trona(s)* and *Pisaurese(s)* are conspicuous because they presuppose a nominative plural in -AS which passed from the Oscan world into Latin, as a fragment of Pomponius, *quot laetitias insperatas* (see §141), proves.[5] The perfect *dedrot* for the normal 'dederont' is also clearly of Umbrian inspiration.

In order to find evidence which becomes part of the general de-velopment of Latin, and which therefore has a future, it is necessary to turn our attention to Pompeii at the period of its history when the Latin-Italic fusion has made major strides. The proof of the different strata which come to coexist is given by two inscriptions edited by Diehl (593, 594):[6] (a) *quis amat valeat, pereat qui nescit amare, bis tanti pereat quisquis amare vetat;* here we have a regular text preserved in normal epigraphical conditions; and (b) *quisquis ama valia, peria qui non sci amare, bis tanti peria quisquis amare vota.* The content is identical, but the elimination of the final con-sonants and the transition from EA to IA (§§55, 87) prove at the same time the local adaptation, the elimination of important gram-matical markers, and the beginning of a new tradition destined to blossom into a linguistic system no longer Latin but Italian.

Seventeen

Postclassical Latin

81 AUTHORS WHO ARE STILL CLASSICAL

Even in considering the highest level—the literary—of the languages of Italy, namely, the golden achievements of the Ciceronian age, one never finds an absolute closure with regard to the living forces that exert pressure not only from within the world of literature, but also from society as a whole. If, from a strict point of view, we can say that the Ciceronian model gave weight to the action of rhythm and melody (above all as far as oratory is concerned), at the same time it must also be acknowledged that choice of words, pronunciation, and spelling could have been influenced by other demands. Examples of these needs are found in the linguistic patterns typical of an author like Sallust, whose style Varro defined as *seria et severa oratio*,[1] 'a serious and austere discourse', This definition, which one would give to a harshly selected linguistic system, in fact confirms contributions of various sorts. On the one hand, Sallust accepts words of a rather popular stamp such as the so-called frequentative verbs; that is, secondary derivatives from participial forms of the primitive verb; examples are *agitare* for 'agere', *missitare* for 'mittere' (i.e., 'mandare'), *imperitare* for 'imperare, comandare,' and *negitare* for 'negare'. Forms which are even further removed in this sense are the expressions *fugam facere* for *fugere* 'to flee', and *pugnam facere* for *pugnare* 'to fight'. On the other hand, Sallust tends to appreciate an archaic coloring, which he achieves by the use of a u in place of an i in the middle of a word (e.g., *infUmus* 'lowest'), or, on the morphological plane, by the preference for forms in -*ere* over those in -*erunt*.[2] All this must be understood, not in the sense of a polemic against the detractors of the archaic Roman culture and society, but only as a particular accentuation of the formal archaic tradition, as a kind of ennoblement and accentuation of the dimension of time. For entirely other reasons, the admittance of words of unelevated tradition is promoted in the language of poetry by the needs of prosody.

In Horace frequentative verbs such as *cantare* instead of 'canere' and *captare* instead of 'capere' appear for this indirect reason without helping to delineate an aspect of the popularism of Horace. *Bellus* and *auriculis,* which appear respectively in the *Satires* (I.4.114) and *Epistles* (I.8.16), are diminutives which have become fashionable to the point of later replacing the traditional forms *bonus* and *aures:* the Italian forms *bello* and *orecchia* derive from these diminutives. Accusative plurals of the third declension in -*is* rather than in -*es* are accepted for prosodic reasons, but they can also be understood within the context of the rapprochement of E and I in final syllable (§83).

For Tacitus the prose writer, the problem of archaic models appears in quite a different form, which has to do neither with the motivations of a fad (affected archaism), nor with the internal exigencies of the linguistic system. In Tacitus the archaic model constitutes an availability of different forms to which the author reacts on the basis of personal preferences which are destined to change. The results of the fundamental studies of E. Löfstedt[3] show that in his earliest texts, *Dialogus, Agricola* and *Germania,* the author's preferences generally lean toward classical patterns; in books 1–12 of the *Annals* a clear preference for archaic models is apparent; and finally in books 13 and 14 there is a return to classicism. The following statistical proofs speak for themselves: regarding the use of the two equivalent forms *forem* (archaic) and *essem* (classical), in the earliest texts there are 4 instances of *forem* and 20 of *essem*; in the second category there are 113 instances of *forem* and 48 of *essem*; and finally in the third period we find only one *forem,* but 29 cases of *essem*.[4]

82 GRAMMARIANS

These achievements are accompanied by the speculations of the grammarians. Two important professions of "anomalous" faith appear in Horace and Quintilian. In *Ars poetica* 71 ff., Horace proclaims that usage is the *ius et norma loquendi,* 'the legality and the norm of speech', and in the *Institutio oratoria* (XII.6.4) Quintilian affirms the validity of usage before doctrine. In this period the actions of grammarians appear to move progressively away from the championing of patterns and models to emulate, toward the recording of words and forms in use and the correction of errors. Quintilian is still part of the first phase when he insists on exalting "urbanity"[5] and prohibiting rusticity and exoticism in pronunciation (XI.3.30). He modified, and made more concrete, opinion about the ancient models—they may indeed appear harsher in sound (XII.10.27) but they make the speech richer in dignity, *sanctiorem et magis admirabilem* (VIII.3.24). New forms that appear are presented without explicit condemnation. Suetonius, in speaking of the Emperor Vespasian (VIII.22), relates that he habitually pronounced the diphthong AU (§§53, 87) as a monophthong, o, and defended his pronunciation, addressing as *Flaurus* the grammarian Florus [actually an ex-consul, not a grammarian-translator] who evidently disagreed. As for the atonal internal vowel, Quintilian (I.6.17) prefers the form *audacter* to 'audaciter', which preserves the internal vowel intact, and he relates (I.6.19) that Augustus already preferred *caldus* to 'calidus'.

83 INNOVATIONS IN THE ACCENT

At this point appear the first indications that something is changing in the field of the accent (both from the point of view of its centralizing force and of its nature). As far as the pronunciation of the final vowel is concerned, Quintilian (XI.3.33) observes that orators concentrate on the pronunciation of the preceding vowels *priorum sono indulgent,* and he recommends to them (I.II.8) that final syllables should not be clipped nor *extremae syllabae intercidant.* We note the final orthographic variations of a word like *heri* 'yesterday', which in current usage and even in that of Augustus, appears to confuse the sound I with E (I.4.8; I.7.22). Quintilian makes an important observation on the nature of the accent when he notes the drawbacks of chanting (XI.3.57): "a characteristic which I do not know whether to consider more useless or more ugly." In order for this sensibility to be evident, it is essential that in evaluating accentuation there intervene some new criterion. If this does not exist, it is impossible to find anything to criticize in the succession of musical accents.

It has to do with the first critical, if not constructive, indications which herald change, even if for the moment they do not provoke it. The validity of quantity and of the resulting quantitative rhythm is fully recognized (19.4.61) through the statement that one does not speak except through a succession of long and short syllables, from which come the metrical feet.

Throughout this period, the sense of quantity does not yield; nor does the process of quantitative normalization come to a halt. The action of the tendency toward the abbreviation of iambic series (§68) becomes faint; the indications of a hypothetical conflict between the final syllable and the ictus of the line fades away.[6] The restrictions of prosody call for the replacing in poetry of words that do not fit into the hexameter, with no exceptions: cases in point are *fumeus,* which is more functional than 'fumosus', and *thalamus* or *hymenaeus,* which are used as substitutes for the inadmissible 'nuptiae'.[7]

84 GRECISMS

The action of Hellenism continues from the lowest to the highest levels of the language. It is proved once more by Quintilian (I.5.70) that compound words continue to constitute an obstacle. This accounts for the dictum *magis Graecos decet, nobis minus succedit,* 'it is more suited to the Greeks, for us it is less appropriate'. Yet the phonetic and graphic correspondence of words accepted from Greek is more carefully attended to: *Alcmena* is preferred to Alcumena, *drachma* to dracuma. In fact, a Hellenizing style, to which not even the name of the Tiber is immune, comes into fashion: *Thybris* in the place of the normal 'Tiberis'.

In the field of morphology, the name of the African city Siga can be declined in the Latin form *Siga, -ae,* but also according to the Greek pattern *Sige, -es.* Examples of new declensions more or less "suggested" by Greek models are *Eutyche, -etis, Achillas, -atis,* and *Nicias, -adis,* followed by other more or less contaminated types such as *Psyche, -enis, Lampiris, -inis,* and *Dido, -onis,* in which nominatives of Greek stamp are aligned with oblique cases belonging to Latin forms. Instances of accusatives ending in -N rather than in -M appear in Virgil, for example: *Oronten (Aen.* VI.334), *Tityon (Aen.* VI.595), and *arcton (Georgics* I.138). From the point of view of syntax, the so-called accusative of respect in the Greek style is conspicuous, as for example *oculos . . . in virgine fixus,* 'with his eyes fixed on the girl' *(Aen.* XI.507). A striking Grecism, which is not alien to Italian sensibility, is the use of the infinitive in place of a subordinate clause, as in the *Aeneid: dederat comam diffundere ventis,* 'she had given her hair to scatter in the wind' (I.319), which the grammarian Servius of the fourth/fifth century corrects thus: *ut diffunderetur.* This construction cannot be related to the construction *cupido vivere* in Ennius' *Medea,*[8] in which the action noun still has a link with the verb which justifies the use of the infinitive, while later the nominal construction of the gerund in the genitive case is indispensable. The following passage from the *Aeneid* (VI.411) is cited as an example of a semantic imitation: *per iuga longa sedebant,* 'they were seated on the long "yokes" '. Here we are dealing with a Grecism modeled on the Greek *zygá,* to which the Latin form "transtra" ought to correspond. We have in the French word *aveugle* 'blind', which presupposes as a point of departure the Vulgar Latin expression *ab oculis,* indirect proof of another imitation of the Greek. Although examples of the Vulgar Latin formula have not been found, it must have existed as a copy of the Greek formula *ap' ommátōn,* as E. Löfstedt has well shown.[9] Grecisms are found even in personal names: examples are Virgilius vis-à-vis 'Grēgórios', Constantinus : : Eustáthios, Desiderius : : Himérios, Venantius : : Kynēgésios, and Vincentius : : Nikásios.[10] The bulk of the Hellenism in the early empire, quite apart from the Christian terminology about which we shall speak later (§§91 ff.), does not, however, constitute an Italian episode. Rather, it reflects the great process of Greco-Latin interpenetration by which many Latin words are also Hellenized or translated into Greek. Hellenism as a process of enrichment of the Italian linguistic patrimony and always within the limits mentioned above, is a closed process.

85 POPULAR ELEMENTS IN PETRONIUS

The most striking innovation from the sociolinguistic point of view comes in this period from the work of Petronius[11] and above all the *Cena Trimalchionis,* in which the spoken language, with its quick pace and vivacity, is boldly brought to center stage, on the plane of literary language. The fact that there appears in this work, well-documented, a diffused, paratactical simplicity, which clearly runs counter to the ample prose style of the classical period, is not yet a proof of the approach of new linguistic truths. Rather, we should draw attention to the following points: excessive use of the personal pronoun, even where it would not be strictly necessary; the feature of periphrasis such as *coepi* with the infinitive, almost like a periphrastic form of the inchoative perfect,[12] and the hint of the beginning of a weariness with the traditional perfect; the four examples of *quod* that reappears as a substitute for the accusative with infinitive after a long interruption (§75); indications of the devaluation of the so-called diminutives as we find for example in 63 *hominem . . . valde audaculum,* as if for Petronius there no longer existed *audax,* which alone would have justified the adverb 'valde'; and finally the choices among synonyms, by which *forsitan* ('perhaps') is preferred to 'fortasse', *subito* to 'repente', *invenire* to 'reperire' ('to find'), *occidere* to 'interficere', *homo* to 'vir', and *propter* to 'ob'.

In any case, these innovations, however important, are not found everywhere in the *Satyricon,* but remain confined to the *Cena Trimalchionis* as if in a sort of ghetto. In the development of Italy's linguistic history, this double aspect of Petronius' linguistic testimony remains more relevant to the literary critic than as an effective consecration of new realities and forces.

Eighteen

Innovations during the Imperial Age

86 LINGUISTIC BLENDING

As opposed to the problems of the literary language and to those of grammatical theories, another important problem now comes to the fore, one which is different from those presented by a popularizing author like Petronius: whether the alterations attested by the Latin inscriptions recorded above (§80) are always harbingers of occasional or, alternatively, of definitive innovations, whether, in other words, they are telltale signs of an underground reality, just as buoys floating on the surface of the water are clues to the existence of an unseen net which is suspended from them more or less deep under the water.

Given the variety of political and constitutional structures existing in Italy until the time of the Social War, one might expect an immense variety of reactions. In reality it was not so: in those areas in which direct links with Rome on a political level were most delayed, they were preceded by sociopsychological conditions favorable to their acceptance. The factors in play can be specified in the following terms. Rome by itself had great prestige and was constantly growing in numbers, so that at a certain point its population constituted one-seventh of the Italian population, according to the studies of Beloch and Ciccotti.[1] Instead of resigning itself to uniformity, however, the rest of Italy had to its advantage immense availability of space and a great variety of situations, against which the centralizing prestige of Rome did not work with the same efficacy. In this regard, two large groups can be distinguished: the first is that in which pre-political elements, like the different linguistic structures, functioned to hinder the process of a mutual linguistic rapprochement and blending; the other is that in which political circumstances were already predisposed toward a rapprochement and fusion of the linguistic systems. If this is true in a very general way, it does not mean that the process of rapprochement and fusion varies in proportion to the major and minor differences between the languages with which Latin comes into contact. Etruria, for example, precisely because of the decided difference in linguistic structure between Etruscan and Latin, seems the ideal candidate for the exclusion of any mixing whatsoever. The only doubtful problem is that of the presumed connection between the aspiration of the unvoiced occlusives in Tuscan and Etruscan phonetics (§124).[2]

That said, the regions (besides Etruria) in which linguistic blending has been slight or entirely absent were: Sardinia, where Mediterranean languages were spoken, and here it is not important to specify whether they were of Ligurian or Libyan type; the Salentine Peninsula, where Messapic was spoken; and Euganean Venetia, where Venetic, a language very close to Latin, was spoken (§25). In the rest of Italy, Latin was subjected to very strong linguistic influences by earlier linguistic environments. This is understandable. In central Italy (that is, central and southern Italy with the exception of Tuscany), the affinity between Latin and the languages of Umbro-Samnite extraction and the long tradition of reciprocal exchanges make this fact very easily understood. It appears less easy to understand the intimate rapport which was established in Cisalpine Gaul. But here the tight cultural relations which, in the last centuries of the empire, were established between the schools of Transalpine Gaul and the valley of the Po came into play to define the particular stamp of the "Gallo-Italic" dialects (§97).

One final reservation must be added to this antithesis: theoretically, "unmixed" Latin is in a position to be better preserved. But not even this is a mechanical relationship, because a language can be abandoned to the drift of a rapid development by the unleashing of internal forces that act independently of any blending process whatsoever, as happened with Latin at the beginning of the republic.

87 THE APPENDIX PROBI

Before we go on to speak of the direct signs of changes, accepted within the Latin system as predictions of neo-Latin innovations, it is time to record some observations of certain grammarians who were inclined by nature to register the irregular forms which have already obtained a certain following (§96 ff.). The so-called *Appendix Probi,* which is commonly ascribed to the third century A.D., corrects, and therefore recognizes as existent, the following new forms: in vowels, *columna* and not 'colomna', that is, the existence of an open u (later transformed into an o), which no grammarian, not even a late one, ever recognized; *auris* and not 'oricla', that is, the monophthong-ization of AU to o; *alveus* and not 'albeus', that is, the exchange of v and B; *cavea* and not 'cavia'; *februarius* and not 'febrarius', that is, the consonantization (or suppression) of the vowels I and u before a vowel (§80), as we see in the Italian forms *gabbia* and *febbraio;* the loss of the internal vowel in the series *viridis,* and not 'virdis', *speculum,* and not 'speclum', *calida,* and not 'calda', *frigida,* and not 'frigda', *vetulus,* and not 'veclus'.[3] In the field of morphology grammarians react against the analogical standardization of de-clension: *teter,* and not 'tetrus', *aper,* and not 'aprus', *tristis,* and not 'tristus'; in the field of grammatical gender they recommended *pauper mulier* instead of 'paupera mulier'. As far as Grecisms are concerned, the archaic forms are correct, more so than the forms that are too modern: *tymum,* and not 'tumum', *myrta,* and not 'murta' (§42).

88 CONSONANTAL ASSIMILATIONS

Independent of the testimony of grammarians, there are three inno-vations which, whether they are openly attested or not, define the active new forms within the linguistic system of the Imperial Age. The first of these characteristics consists in the progressive assimila-tion of the group ND, which is resolved into NN: this is a feature be-longing to the Umbro-Samnite world, documented in pre-Roman antiquity from Umbria as far south as the Straits of Messina. The direct testimony is that of the Pompeian inscriptions, nos. 447 and 237 in Diehl.[4] The former, which is completely clear, documents *Verecunnus,* that is the Latin 'Verecundus', distorted according to the valid patterns of the language of Pompeii. The second inscrip-tion, which is less clear, bears the word *Secunnus* instead of 'Secun-dus'. This does not mean that Latin universally accepted the type NN in place of ND. If we bear in mind the fact that, not only in northern Italy and in Tuscany, but also in Sicily there are traces of a Latin tradition without NN but with ND, then we are in a position to make some preliminary conclusions. The introduction of NN is not the automatic result of local pronunciations, but rather the product of Latin currents which absorbed and diffused them in areas where the environment was more receptive. These currents, however, do not correspond to the most ancient Latin. On the contrary they furnish a criterion by which an earlier Latin tradition with ND can be distinguished from a later tradition with NN. This distinction is particularly important for Sicily.[5]

89 FIRST CHANGES IN VELARS

The second of these characteristics is provided by the outcome of the velars. We get our first clue from the word *frigida* 'cold'. While the *Appendix Probi* demonstrates, in the example we have cited, that the velar pronunciation still persists in the third century A.D., the Pompeian inscription Diehl 631 documents the form *fridam*, in other words, with total loss of the consonant. The fate of intervocalic G in the ancient Umbrian language is identical, as we see in the case of *muieto*, which comes from the form MUGETU, or of *iouino* from IGOVINO. The Italian *dito* 'finger', which evidently is a descendant of the Latin form DI(G)ITU- (§121), also demonstrates that in Latin analogous solutions were accepted. But the case of *fridam* is only a point of departure for the consideration of velar changes in general, including voiceless gutturals, before the vowels E and I. This change too is documented in the Umbrian world by an appropriate sign in the alphabet, conventionally indicated by Ç. In Rome, too, there was an indication of this particular pronunciation, marked by the sign C, as opposed to K before A, and Q before U and O. But in Rome this particular pronunciation had no sequel (§42), while in Umbrian the innovation came to be generalized in the third century B.C. This pronunciation was then accepted by Latin during the period of the empire, and subsequently by Rome, by means of successive waves. Here too, as with NN from ND, we must make distinctions on the geographic plane, and therefore also on the historical. The palatal pronunciation of CI and CE never reached the heart of Sardinia; in Dalmatia CI arrived, but KE remained; in the rest of the Romance world both CE and CI became established. Similarly to what we noted regarding NN from ND, we must distinguish between an earlier ancient Latin expansion, still anchored to KE and KI, a second expansion connected with KE and CI, and a final expansion with CE and CI. This last expansion, for example, also reached Sardinia, in the Campidano plain, without penetrating the interior. The first phase is attested even today in the pagan Latin words received into German; examples are *Kaiser* and *keller,* from 'Caesar' and 'cellarium'; the last phase in the Christian words, for example, German *Kreuz* and *Zelle,* from 'crucem' and 'cella', respectively.[6]

90 THE VOCALIC SYSTEM

The most important change, however, is that occurring in the vocalic system, which is founded, as far as Latin is concerned, on the harmonic system of the five vowels A, E, I, O, and U, all alternating as long and short vowels according to their duration. The Umbro-Samnite world is disturbed right from the beginning, still during the life of the regional alphabets, by the fact that these had only four signs for a system of five vowels. In addition, Umbrian sometimes irregularly uses the sign I even when one would expect E, and thus, when the Latin alphabet arrives, uses of U persist in cases where there could be used the sign O, now become available. In the Oscan system there appear instead traces of a new order, through the sign I with an apex (like an acute accent), which serves to indicate a vowel intermediate between E and I, let us call it a closed E. This is the first indication of a distinction which, several centuries later, is destined to have so many consequences within the structure of the Latin system.[7] The need postulated by the comparative grammar of the neo-Latin languages for a "closed E" prototype assumes through the Oscan evidence a historical validity three centuries before Christ and a geographic localization in Campania. As in the examples illustrated above, here also it is necessary to consider the successive stratifications within Latin. The first of these stratifications, limited to the five vowels of the primitive system, survives in Sardinia and in a small area between Bruttium and Lucania, from Maratea on the Tyrrhenian Sea, to Sybaris on the Ionian.[8] There comes to Sicily by sea, and to the Salentine Peninsula along the path of the Via Appia, a vocalic system which, when compared with the "six" vowel system implicitly postulated by the Oscan alphabet, symmetrically postulates a seventh vowel, which we may call the closed O. This vocalic system outlives all subsequent linguistic and ethnic innovations of Sicily and is, therefore, a proof of the Latin continuity that a scholar such as G. Rohlfs maintains was overlaid instead by the Greek tradition and reestablished only in the eleventh century (§151).[9]

In a restricted area of inner Lucania, there are also traces of the arrival of a vocalic system that recognized an eighth vowel, namely, the open I. The importance of this discovery, which we owe to H. Lausberg,[10] resides in the fact that a similar vocalic situation exists in the eastern Latin tradition, as it appears through the Latin of Dacia and present-day Rumania. The Via Appia was the route that spread the seven-vowel system as far as Brundisium, whence it became firmly established in the Salentine Peninsula; it then spread the eight-vowel system, subsequently exported from Brundisium to the Balkan countries. In all the remaining Latin areas of the Western world there spreads instead the last system, founded on the acknowledgment of the distinction between the open and closed u, that is, one of nine vowels (§96).

The differences in the vocalic system have been used by R. Hall[11] for a classification of the Romance language traditions. On the basis of this criterion, he opposes a continental proto-Romance to a southern proto-Romance (Sardinian, Corsican, Lucanian, and Sicilian). The continental proto-Romance is divided into an eastern continental, with outposts in Lucania, and a western. The latter in turn is divided into an "Italo-Romance," which from (and including) Naples reaches the Alps, and a western sector in the strict sense, which comprises all the non-Italian neo-Latin areas.

The classification is valid as a typological classification and as one limited to the vowel system. An analogous classification leads to different results, if it takes as a base other criteria, such as those of the ND group or the guttural consonants. Above all, Hall's classification does not lead to historical and genealogical conclusions, because there remains no trace of organic congealments which permit one to deduce from linguistic situations historical and cultural situations, as for example the objective reality of Roman unity or the reconstructed unity of the Indo-European community.

Nineteen

Christianity

91 CHRISTIAN STRATA

Up to this time, two orders of change have been presented within the structures of the Latin language, as it had been stabilized during the republic. On a more elevated level, within the literary language, the great choice was between the adherence to classical patterns—no matter whether inspired by analogy or by anomaly—in an atemporal vision of the linguistic structures, on the one hand, and a tendency aimed at extracting from archaic models as much as could serve to lend dignity and prestige, on the other hand. This is what has been seen in the passage from the Ciceronian and Caesarean vision to that of Sallust and Tacitus (§81). The establishment of Latin models throughout Italy brought about a new phenomenon; namely, the ascent from the lower to the higher levels of speech, of divergent and unconscious tendencies, some anticipation of which has also come to light.

But a linguistic system, like a society, does not feel the effects only of quantitative changes, expansions and contractions, variability and stability, ascents and descents. It also feels the effects of qualitative innovations, and among these none in ancient times had yet been introduced with the seriousness, the profundity, and the heroism of the Christian message. The moral charge of a vision of life that opposed, if only by its condemnation of slavery, millennia of class-conscious divisions, and the long struggle that engaged the ruling class of the empire for approximately two centuries before it decided to recognize the new cult and the new vision of life, should logically have left a deep impression on the structures of the language of Italy, as it had been shaped in the second century A.D. This, however, does not appear to be the case, at least not at first sight. Nevertheless, before denying that Christianity left any decisive traces on the language, we must first consider the other hypothesis, namely, that it was rather the internal structures of the state that camouflaged a premature identification and immersion of the expressive Christian material in the Latin linguistic structures; in other words, that in essence Latin could have been the normal expressive instrument of the Christians almost two centuries before they were able to achieve political-religious recognition.

The first great Christian author, Tertullian, is born in about 160 A.D. in Africa, and by 180, still in Africa, in a trial against the Christians, there is talk[1] of *libri et epistolae Pauli viri,* in other words, of a Latin version of elements, previously proclaimed as Greek and eastern, arranged around a nucleus of Greek and Hebrew liturgical technicalities. During the papacy of Victor I (ca. 189–98) Latin is established as the liturgical language in Rome; in other words, more than a century before the recognition of Christianity, which occurred in 313.

92 MORPHOLOGICAL CHARACTERISTICS

There suddenly appears in the first Christian linguistic documents a distinction that is only in part chronological. The organic complex of the Vulgate, that is, the translation of the Bible by Saint Jerome (ca. 347–420), is superimposed on the heterogeneous totality of the biblical formulas, as it emerges in isolated form from the earlier texts, collected under the name of "Itala" or, better, "Vetus Latina." Upon careful examination of the differences between the two sources, one realizes that it is impossible to distinguish between an earlier Christian Latin (of the "Vetus Latina") and the later Latin of Saint Jerome. The distinction is of a qualitative order. Saint Jerome translated with a sensibility that was different from that of his predecessors, but this does not mean that Saint Jerome's taste was more modern. Using *iucundari* for 'to rejoice' rather than *laetare* of the Vulgate, *felix* for 'happy' as opposed to the Vulgate *beatus,* *muscipula* for 'trap, deception' rather than the Vulgate *laqueus,* *municipatus* for 'spiritual exchange', as opposed to the Vulgate *conversatio, deridetur* for 'to ridicule' instead of the Vulgate *irridetur,* does not mean that we must distinguish between a series of characteristics proper to early Christianity as opposed to what might be called a classical Christianity. It is rather a matter of recognizing that Christianity had already so deeply penetrated Latin linguistic structures that it was possible to profit from a multitude of choices.

This variety of traditions is transformed into objective reality as soon as one examines the results of the studies of the Dutch scholars begun at Nijmegen under the direction of Schrijnen.[2] The distinction which now appears is founded not on a quantitative documentation but rather on a distribution of functions and meanings; in other words, on a recognition that Latin linguistic structures, applied to the expressive needs of the Christian community, must have responded to two opposed requirements. On the one hand, there was the technical and liturgical need, which was fundamentally stabilizing and conservative. On the other hand, there was the apostolate; that is, the beginning of a dialogue with recent converts and pagans in the midst of whom the Christians wanted to move and with whom they had to participate and communicate, plunging into their ever-changing linguistic world.

93 THE CHRISTIAN LEXICON

The elements that make up the Christian vocabulary are varied, indeed heterogeneous. A first category is represented by Hebrew elements, which were neither adapted nor translated but remained as they were; examples of these are *gehenna, mammon, amen,* and *pascha.* The ultimate fate of these words is varied and can be contrasted with the homogeneity of their origin: the first two words were crystallized in books; the third came to be used, and is still used today, as a symbol of brevity and automaticity; the fourth finally was adapted to a well-known festivity like that of the present-day Italian Easter (Pasqua).

The second category of words, a very large one, consists of Greek technical terms which are just barely adapted to Latin: examples are *eucharistia, catechizare, baptisma, martyr, apostolus, propheta, diaconus*; and similarly *epiphania, evangelium, blasphemare, ecclesia, episcopus, presbyter.* They are all fundamental words, about which it is, however, necessary to make a further distinction. As was the case with the Hebrew words, some of the Greek words remained closed in the technical meaning of the books, while others developed an authoritative spoken tradition which paralleled the written. We thus have in Italian today the learned form *epifania* and the colloquial *befana,* and similarly *evangelico* and *vangelo, blasfemo* and *bestemmia, ecclesiale* and *chiesa, episcopale* and *vescovo, presbiterio* and *prete.*

A third category is represented by "carbon copies," which is to say Latin words modelled after corresponding Greek elements: examples of these are the notions of 'trinity' *trinitas,* 'incarnation' *incarnatio,* and of 'female monogamy' *univiratus.*

A fourth category is made up of Latin words derived with Latin suffixes, which, however, assume an abstract "Christian" value and not a generic abstract value taken from a normal Latin adjective: such is the case of *salvatio* '(Christian) salvation', which is not a formulation associated with the normal value of the adjective 'salvo', nor with the notion of the action noun of the verb *salvare.*

The fifth category consists of Latin words that became specialized, without, however, severing their ancient ties with the pre-Christian lexical system. Therefore, according to Schrijnen's terminology, words such as *humilitas* 'humility', *confessio* 'confession', *confessor* 'confessor', *vigilia* 'vigil', and naturally *deus* 'God', *caro* 'flesh', *scriptura* 'scripture', and *fides* 'faith', belong to this class of "direct Christianisms."

The final category is that of transformed and specialized Latin words: classical examples are *gentiles,* which changes from its original meaning of 'those belonging to the same people' to that of 'non-Christian'; *pagano,* which evolves from 'belonging to the country' to 'pagan'; *plebs,* from 'common people' to 'parish'; *saeculum,* from 'century', in the temporal sense, to 'lay society'. Finally, the complex story of *orare oratio* is of interest to us; these words were on the point of giving way, in lay use, to the more efficacious forms *rogare rogatio,* but instead they took on a religious value and acquired a new and different vitality. In this new sector, however, they again acquire a specialized meaning in the liturgical not the apostolic value, in which sense (apostolic) there becomes prominent instead the word *precari,* whence the Italian 'pregare'.

In its turn this internal diversification of the Christian tradition facilitates overcoming the barriers between itself and the pagan tradition. It acts in such a profound way that the difference between a literary Christian text such as one of Tertullian's and a lay text of Apuleius is less than the difference between Tertullian and the Vulgate. Inversely, there is less difference between the errors corrected by Probus in the pagan sphere and the idiosyncracies of the priest's Sunday sermons than there is between the latter and the elevated formulations of Saint Augustine, even in his *Confessions.*

94 THE PRECOCITY OF TERTULLIAN
Tertullian certainly is in the vanguard as an inventor of new terms that circulated in the environment of Christian vocabulary. But the impetus for their invention did not arise so much from the collective

need of the Christian movement as it did from the strong personality of the author. According to the statistics of H. Hoppe,[3] the words that appear for the first time in Tertullian number 982, of which almost half (438) are exclusively attested as being Tertullianisms. Frequently they are determined by formal needs such as the search for symmetry, alliteration, and even rhyme; in this way the words *reformator* and *consummator* determine the neologism *informator;* the category of action nouns like *statio* facilitates the acceptance of *ieiunatio* along with the form *ieiunum* 'fast'. *Resuscitator,* however, appears much better motivated when compared with the Christian image of 'resurrection' than does the traditional pagan term *restitutor,* which essentially calls to mind the image of the 'restorer'.

In the field of morphology, needs already inherent in the normal Latin tradition become part of Christian innovation. On the one hand, we note the anachronism of markers belonging to so-called deponent verbs, and on the other, the aggressiveness of the new periphrastic constructions. Thus, there appear normal verbs with the value of old deponent verbs, such as *colligere* 'to assemble, gather', *facere* 'to betake oneself', *longinquare* 'to go away'. On the other hand, one discovers the rudiments of periphrastic constructions, as for example in Tertullian *Adversus Valentinianos* 32: *habeo devertere* 'I must turn', which literally could correspond to the Italian construction 'ho da voltare'; and still more in Tertullian's *De Idolatria* 5: *vivere ergo habes* 'you have therefore to live', which anticipates the normal Italian future *vivrai,* derived precisely from *vivere habes.* The Italian future tense differs from this Latin construct not with regard to its constituent elements but only because the postposition of the "auxiliary" verb has not become fixed. This is yet another example of a Christian element's being grafted into a movement that is generically modern.

A similar case of periphrasis is the first type of conditional, which is surely pre-Diocletian, although it is not attested in texts (§98).

Another fertile graft, sometimes exaggerated, is that regarding abstract nouns, which the classical tradition admitted as a possibility of grammatical derivation but which it did not approve on the semantic plane, even though Greek models had already given it a start. The innovation that now appears consists in the use of the abstract noun as an indication of a collective value; examples from Saint Jerome[4] are *fraternitas* for 'brothers', *gentilitas* for 'people', *propinquitas* for 'neighbors', which is analogous to the present-day use of *vicinato* for 'neighbors' or *padronato* for 'masters, owners'. On the other hand, true abstract nouns are the definitions of "sin" that appear in Saint Augustine as "filth" or "corruption" (*Conf.,* II.

1.1.) *recordari volo transacta foeditates meas et carnales corruptiones animae meae,* or "nodosity" for "knot" (*Conf.* II. 10.18) *qui experit istam tortuosissimam et implicatissimam nodositatem?*

Still another use of abstract nouns is that which appears in Palladius, a writer on agriculture of the fourth century, in whose works we encounter *acerbitas* for 'immature grape', *amaritudo* 'a bitter thing', *siccitas* 'a dry place', *novos sapores* 'new oil'.[5]

95 SYNTACTICAL CHARACTERISTICS

The consequences of syntactical grafts are powerful. Participles, whose use is greatly expanded, assume the autonomy that the gerund has, namely, as a prop for an autonomous though dependent clause. In the Tertullian treatise *De Pudicitia* 9, we read *nec notaretur cum Iudaeis communicans victum,* and in *De corona* 8, *passivitas fallit obumbrans corruptelam,* and finally, a little less distant from traditional patterns, in the *Adversus Marcionem* II.24, *nemo enim te sustinebit improvidentiam adscribentem deo.*

This relationship ultimately becomes clarified, but also reinforced in its autonomy, by the association of participles with conjunctions that traditionally should have been accompanied by finite forms of the verb; other Tertullian examples are *ut confirmans . . . Iohannem iam advenisse* (*Adversus Marcionem* IV.18) and *habuerit . . . carnem DUM onmino non natam* (*De carne Christi* 6).

We find more liberal uses of the ablative absolute related to the same line of development; for example, in the *Apologeticum* 18 we find *Instrumentum adiecit literaturae, si qui velit de deo inquirere et inquisito invenire et invento credere et credito deservire,* with homage paid to an apparently classical symmetry, and an opening toward the future which unfortunately was not more fully exploited in the course of time.

On the whole, therefore, it appears that this receptiveness toward innovation constitutes neither a desertion nor a relinquishment of commitment. As far as linguistics is concerned, the Christian factor does not contribute to either the corruption or the weakening of that commitment. Linear structures such as those found in the Gospel according to Luke 1:6 *Erant autem iusti ambo ante Deum incedentes in omnibus mandatis et iustificationibus Domini sine querela,* or in the Gospel according to John 1:1 *In principio erat Verbum et verbum erat apud Deum et Deus erat verbum* represent something strong and vital that permitted the Latin tradition to withstand the rigors of the early Middle Ages much better than the florid Ciceronian models, which were more or less artificially kept alive and which were detached from the normal circulation of both words and ideas.

Twenty

Imbalances Accentuated

96 PRE-DIOCLETIAN GRAMMATICAL PROBLEMS

The alarm sounded by the grammarians, of whom Probus (§87) was a herald, appears in two forms. The first, a critical approach aimed at correcting mistakes, is that of Probus. The second, however, consists of a more cautious confirmation of new phenomena which previously had not yet been verified, or had not been taken into consideration. The fact that Probus corrects 'columna', not 'colomna', presupposes a whole order of phenomena, not all of which had yet been recognized by grammarians, namely, that the Latin u was differentiated into an open u and a closed u, and that subsequently the open u merged with the o (closed). While Probus was already aware of individual instances, the phonetic phenomena pertaining to the vocalic system had been only partially recognized. We know from Terentianus Maurus (end of the third century) that the o was pronounced differently according to whether it was a long or a short o. Servius, in the fourth century, affirmed that there were five vowels, of which two, E and o, had two pronunciations, according to their quantity. Pompeius, in the fifth century, recognized that long E was close to I. Consentius, also in the fifth century, admitted a difference between open and closed I. No one had ever given an account of the difference between open and closed u, which is quite necessary in explaining Probus' correction of 'colomna'. Another decisive argument leads us to believe that this qualitative enrichment of the Latin vocalic system was a relatively early development. The system of nine vowels must have spread from Rome toward Gaul and the Iberian Peninsula even before A.D. 300, that is to say, before the Spezia-Rimini line was transformed from a mere physical watershed into a cultural and linguistic barrier, in other words, in pre-Diocletian times.

As far as consonants are concerned, the vacillation between B and V was already known by Probus; the tendency toward the assimilation of consonants is noted by Servius in a commentary on Virgil's *Georgics* (II.16). Finally, the altered pronunciation of the velars before E and I (§§89, 125), which at a certain point it is necessary to postulate in Vulgar Latin, was gradually recognized by certain authors, Terentianus Maurus, for example, at the end of the third century, and Marius Victorinus, in the middle of the fourth.

97 REFORM OF DIOCLETIAN
Even before the Christian worship was officially recognized through the action of Constantine (A.D. 313) and before the innumerable innovations that can be traced directly or indirectly to the revival of the Christian movement flowed unimpeded, the reform of the Emperor Diocletian modified the constitutional structures of the empire and consequently the currents of traffic, with particularly serious repercussions on what we have called the "languages of Italy." The essential points are these three. First, Rome ceases to be the only capital; therefore, its function as stimulator and regulator in promoting or checking the spread of new trends was destined to weaken progressively, even in the field of linguistics. Second, in place of one single capital, four are substituted, one of which is Milan (the other three are Treviri in Gaul, Sirmium in Illyria, and Nicomedia in Thrace). Third, the distribution of roads is no longer star-shaped, radiating from one single hub (Rome), but rather assumes the pattern of parallel lines from East to West and vice versa. Cisalpine Gaul, which has its largest center in Milan, is traversed by the most southerly of these routes, which has its terminus in Transalpine Gaul, let us say in Lyon. The Spezia-Rimini line takes on a new value as a cultural, economic, and linguistic barrier, while the Alpine barrier, in its function as an obstacle to economic and linguistic communication, grows weaker. The gap not only between the Latin of Tuscany and that of the Po Valley, but also between the latter and Umbro-Samnite Latin is accentuated. Inversely, the Latin of Cisalpine Gaul is opened to the western influences which flow over the Alps along

the important routes of communication, from foci rich in linguistic prestige such as the schools of Gaul, so well illustrated by H. Marrou.[1] The Latin of the Po Valley is distinct from that of central and southern Italy, not only because of its grammatical ties with regions beyond the Alps, but also because of its social prestige.

A century later this imbalance in central and southern Italy became more pronounced, following the sack of Rome by the Visigoths (410). The consequent repopulation worked to take Rome away from its unmixed or hardly mixed environment, to put it in one that was integrally Umbro-Samnite, where it was to remain for over a thousand years, as did Spoletium and Capua.

98 FIRST DIALECTAL DIFFERENTIATIONS

The dialectal classification which at this point can be sketched out, as it pertains to the languages of Italy and disregarding any allusion to genealogy and ramification, is the following: initially, a distinction must be made between those Italian regions in which Latin was intensely mixed with the already existing linguistic heritage, and those areas in which this mingling was minimal or nonexistent. The areas in which the blending occurred to a significant degree were essentially two: Gallo-Italic, that is all of northern Italy with the exception of the estuary zone around Venice, and Umbro-Samnite, central and southern Italy including Sicily, but excluding Tuscany. Besides the Venetic estuary and Tuscany, Sardinia and the Salentine Peninsula can be considered regions in which blending did not take place.

Minor differentiations that develop within these two large "blending" areas, are, as far as northern Italy is concerned, of a rather late date, exceeding the bounds of the Imperial Age, strictly speaking. In central and southern Italy, however, minor distinctions still come to light during the empire. The first group corresponds to Sicily and to that adjacent Calabrian zone that was Latinized by way of Sicily; it is characterized by a primitive system of seven vowels (§90) and by the clearness of the pronunciation of final vowels. The second group is based on a vocalic system of nine vowels, but preserves, as the Sicilian system does, the clear pronunciation of final vowels; this area corresponds to Latium, Umbria, and the Marches. The third group is the Neapolitan and Calabrian area, founded on a system of nine vowels but with an indistinct pronunciation of the final vowels. The fourth group is the Latin of the Abruzzi and of Apulia, which in addition to being characterized by weakened final vowels, undergoes profound changes, dipthongizations, and fractures which perhaps date back to an Adriatic or an Illyrian heritage (§113).

To these yet vague definitions can be added certain further distinctions pertaining to the imperial period. There is a difference between regions in which the final vowels were not only maintained, but also unaffected by metaphony as a qualitative compensation (see §116), and regions which, by means of metaphony, already demonstrate an awareness of the danger of decadence and a consequent need for defense. We shall call the first category a "Roman" Latin tradition belonging to an earlier period, and the second a later "Neapolitan" Latin tradition. The substitution of the group NN in place of ND (§88), which latter survives only in a small triangle in the Messina and adjacent Calabrian areas,[2] is "Neapolitan," as are the forces which brought about the types *cririri* for 'credere', and the conditionals in *-ia,* which are drawn from the imperfect, as we see for example in *avria* from *haber(e hab)ebam* as compared with *averra* from *haber(e habue)ram* (§128).

99 THE ARRIVAL OF THE INTENSIVE ACCENT
While on the lower levels of the linguistic institutions these innovations were developing and spreading, the adaptation of rhythms to the exigencies of the new intensive nature of the accent was also occurring. In this matter the sensibility of the grammarians was quicker than it had been with regard to the phenomena mentioned above (see §96). This is proved by the adaptations applied by the grammarian Caesius Bassus to the system of *clausulae* (rhythmical cadences) as early as the end of the first century A.D. But at the time of Caesius a feeling for quantity still persisted. The real recognition of the intensity of the accent and the introduction of the technical term *sonor, -oris* are due to Terentianus Maurus (end of the third century A.D.):[3] *parte nam attollit sonorem, parte reliqua deprimit; arsin hanc Graeci vocarunt alteram contra thesin* (1. 1345).

Constructive elaboration appears through the *cursus,* which is the accentuative equivalent of what in the realm of musicality had been the *clausulae.* The grammarian Sacerdos (third century) has given a description of the various types, which are grouped into three principal schemes: the final coheredem detraxit, that is, a trisyllabic word accented on the penult preceded by a polysyllabic word also accented on the penult; *modicos coluerunt,* that is, a quadrisyllabic word accented on the penult preceded by a trisyllabic proparoxytone (i.e. accented on the antepenult); *dolores detulerunt,* that is, a quadrisyllabic word accented on the penult, preceded by a polysyllabic also accented on the penult. These basic patterns put down deep roots. When rhetorical studies blossom seven centuries later, they assume the respective names of *cursus planus, cursus velox,* and *cursus dis-*

pondaicus. The only modification will consist in the addition of a fourth model, the *cursus spondaicus.* In the second half of the third century, the Christian poet Commodian produced lines of verse in which the word accents work as ictuses of the line, of a hexameter which has been standardized to meet the new needs: *Dicite/nunc ergo/ quibus/ primum/ sacra fe/ rantur inter u trimque/ vias mors/ imma/ tura va/ gatur (Libri Instructionum* I 16 3 ff).[4] Or else in Saint Augustine the ancient trochaic rhythm appears in the guise of a succession of primary and secondary accents, as in the "Psalmus Abecardius," *ábundántia péccatórum sólet frátres cónturbáre.*[5]

Saint Augustine shows us that all these new aspirations do not spread uncontrollably. In his early writings such as the "De vita beata" and the "Contra academicos," Saint Augustine is still inclined in the matter of syntax toward the classical tradition: as compared with 55 examples of the accusative plus infinitive construction there is only one with *quod.* In the *Confessions,* by contrast, the proportion declines to 11 to 1, while in the *Sermones,* the proportion is no more than 2 to 1. In the *De Civitate Dei* the position of the verb in principal clauses is at the end of the clause in 18% of the cases, while in the *Confessions* it drops to 13%. In dependent clauses the respective proportions are 42% and 22%. This development is not due to polemic or indifference, because Saint Augustine in effect put to himself the theoretical problem, resolving it in favor of usage and against grammar.

100 THE TEXT OF AETHERIA AS RECOGNITION OF NEW FORCES

Aetheria's text[6] is commonly considered to be useful in the evaluation of the spread of colloquialisms. Nevertheless, it must be noted that the zeal of the authoress is at times mistaken; for example, in orthography we note an abuse of initial H, as in *hac* for 'ac', *hostium* for 'ostium', *hivit* for 'ivit', and even *hispatii* for 'spatii'.

In the placement of the verb, the final position (at the end of the clause) normal in classical models is reduced to 25% in principal clauses and to 37% in dependent clauses; this ratio is closer to the classical situation than the one we find in the later works of Saint Augustine. A search for less common constructions appears, for example, in the use of *ut* in a temporal sense: *iam ut exiremus de aecclesia, dederunt nobis presbyteri . . . eulogias* (3.6) 'when we were leaving the church'.

The most conspicuous innovation is the beginning of the Romance declension with the first examples of the genitive marked by *de*: *de terra Aegypti,* which is no longer the classical *terrae Aegypti* and not yet the Romance *de terra de Aegypto.* Striking also is the Grecism *ille locus de Evangelio cata Ioannem* (37.7) 'that passage of the Gospel according to John', which adds itself to the genitival *de*.

Evidences of lexical units and semantic values of the Romance type are numerous: *sabbato sera ingressi sumus montem* (3.1), in which the classical form 'vesper' is abandoned; *gustavimus nobis loco in horto* (4.8) 'there in the garden,' in which *loco* has by now taken on a fixed value as an adverb; *antecessus veniunt* (24.8) they arrive in advance'. *Portare* comes to the fore to the detriment of 'ferre'; *vadere* takes the lead from 'ire'; *plorare* from 'flere'; and *totus,* from 'omnis', as in *toti illi montes* (2.6).

Important Grecisms are *ascitis* from *asketés* and *gyrus* as in *mons . . . per gyro* 'all around'.

Thus, in stepping over the threshold of the fifth century, which is so decisive for political history, the language of Italy goes through an extremely agitated period in which no efforts at efficient coordination were exercised either on a grammatical or on an artistic plane.

The weakening of the final consonants, the pre-eminence of prepositions as morphological markers of declension to the detriment of case endings, the diffusion of periphrastic forms of the verb, the simplification of the sentence, the emergence of new words which can be traced back to socially lower classes: this is the heritage that the language of Italy bequeathed to successive centuries, as the ancient world yielded to the Middle Ages.

Part Three

The Middle Ages:
From 500 to 1200

Twenty-one

The Fragmentation of
the Latin Tradition

101 THE PARISH

When the Emperor Romulus Augustulus died in A.D. 476 and the need to nominate a successor was felt no longer (and here it is not important to specify whether the means used in nominating the successor were legal or illegal), we do not discover behind the curtain of imperial authority an organic edifice of different geographic and structural units out of which the empire was composed. What we find instead are scattered, disordered nuclei that are not capable of constituting a durable even if incomplete structure. Certainly there were the barbarian chiefs; in Italy there was Odoacer. But, the barbaric tribes whose leader he was, were heterogeneous, not tied in a stable way to the soil, and not united by means of steady relationships with the populations of Roman origin. While it is true that these latter were disorganized and dispersed, it must also be observed that they were also almost one hundred times more numerous and above all more civilized. Heruli and the other barbaric tribes, of which Odoacer was the leader, did not provide a framework on which a new structure could be erected. They could not fit neatly into linguistic institutions such as those that had crystallized in the evolution of Latin.

The ecclesiastical organization endured. Important metropolitan seats were Rome, Milan, Genoa, Ravenna, Aquileia, and Cagliari. Dioceses were located in Palermo, Messina, and Syracuse in Sicily; in Naples, Florence, Bologna, Turin, Bergamo, and Verona on the peninsula; and in Vercelli, Como, and Brescia on the continent. Monasteries such as Montecassino (about 530), Vivario in Calabria (from 538), and Bobbio (612), and Farfa (680) certainly exercised a strong attraction, constituting an impediment to the centrifugal forces at work. Schools such as those at Novara, Modena, Lucca, the *Palatium* of Pavia, and the Lateran of Rome[1] ensured an administrative and chancery continuity which answered the scant communication needs that continued to make themselves felt. In short, the schools served to prevent a total breakdown.

But the scattered clergy, linked to the parish and personified by the parish priest, felt the effects of the linguistic currents emanating from the nearest centers of culture less and less; more and more they adjusted themselves to the limited needs of their populations which were anchored to the small territory of the local court, in the shadow of some lord, and hemmed in by the common activities of the peasants, the artisans, and the small merchants or couriers.

The Christian language, for two centuries divided into two opposite aspects—that is to say, ever since the parish priest could carry out his pastoral activity without persecution—throws its own equilibrium off balance, and heightens its own internal contrasts. The conservative aspect of the language of the Christian rite resists the innovative impulses of the language of the apostolate, which does not have to comply with the linguistic models that are valid for the faithful so much as it has to imitate these models in their instinctive, unbridled developments, not controlled or coordinated by permanent contact with other distant citizens. Every linguistic impulse which under normal circumstances would have been neutralized, curbed, and diverted by the needs of a community as vast as it was solid, now had no obstacles in its path in the heart of innumerable small parochial communities. With the end of the western empire, the language of Italy loses the veil of unity which had so slowly and laboriously been woven, and which by now had become so very threadbare; differences appear; the language of Italy is divided into as many units as there are parishes, by means of changes that develop in the shadow of that veil; these changes appear as sharp, unanticipated wounds, but they should not surprise an alert historian.

102 LEXICAL RESISTANCES

The sudden limiting of the horizons results not only in the undermining of the preexisting unit. It also brings about a drastic impoverishment of the lexicon. From among words beginning with *a,* we can utilize a series that we are certain was orally transmitted from classical and late Roman times without any interruption whatsoever. Thus we are in a position to list the following Italian words: *aia, ala, arare, arco, arte, acqua, aceto, aglio, alpe, arena, avena, amara, angoscia, ascoltare, agro, asino, ascia, amo* (bait of the fisherman), *ancora, arma,* and *asse.* These are all words which correspond, if not throughout the entire Italian territory, at least sometimes in one region and sometimes in another, to rudimentary expressive needs of the farmer and the artisan in their work, or to their elementary emotions. Even if all these words tie in perfectly with Latin models— they are in fact "the same Latin words" that have been submitted to the erosion of time—no interruption, however minimal, breaks the continuity present in the evolution of the Italian form *aia* from the Latin *area* for example, of the Italian *angoscia* from the Latin *angustia,* of the Italian *ascoltare* from the Latin *auscultare,* and of the Italian *amo* from the Latin *hamus.*

In certain circumstances the word was so important, not only from the point of view of its meaning as a whole, but also in its constituent elements, that the Latin form was preserved intact. This is the case of the word *anima* which corresponded to a fundamental notion of the Christian doctrine, which implicated thoughts and feelings regarding the 'souls' of Purgatory, which soon had administrative applications in the sense of the number of 'souls' belonging to a certain parish. This form remained intact, notwithstanding all the centrifugal forces of which it could have been a victim. Besides this form, there is the form resulting from the regular alteration of proparoxytones, which as we have seen, tended already during the Imperial Age to eliminate the internal unaccented vowel. This "normal" form is *alma,* which in this initial period of phonetic breakdown and lexical impoverishment probably assumed some metaphorical value, for example in defining the internal part of a pipe, tube, reed, or cannon;[2] in a later period, by means of another metaphor, it was once more applied to the soul as a vital center, not, however, in the religious sense which had never lost its importance, but in the meaning that flourished in Italy in the penumbra of the "dolce stil nuovo" (§162).

103 Lexical Units "Kept in Cold Storage"
     in the Libraries

Although the schools and bishops' palaces of which we have spoken above (§101) could not play the role of linguistic stimulator or coordinator, they did constitute literary, cultural, and, naturally, linguistic forces of conservation, especially in the lexical field.

In contrast to the series of words beginning with *a* that were transmitted from one generation to another without interruption, but that at the same time went through more or less conspicuous changes, we discover an analogous series of words that are substantially "better" preserved. These words owe their superior state of preservation not to their own greater vitality, however, but to the fact that they have been preserved for centuries in books, having become superabundant and superfluous in the small world of the court and the parish. *Augusto* is closer to the Latin form *augustus* than is *agosto,* the name of the month. But in the daily life of the court and the parish one can get along without *augusto,* but not without the name of such an important month. This second list is made up of the following words: *abile, abuso, accusare, acido, aderire, adibire, adulto, adottare, assurdo, atroce, attiguo, atto augurio,* and *azione.* Of these, *abile* and *abuso* with the intervocalic B preserved, and *augurio* with the initial diphthong intact, reveal through their overly faithful preservation that they were kept in cold storage in books, and sheltered from the normal developments that other words "exposed to the light of the sun" could not escape.

The extent of the lexical impoverishment that followed the end of the imperial community of the Latin West is well known to all. The scholar of the Italian language of today, when considering the large percentage of Italian words of Latin origin, must never forget that the majority of these is not made up of words that were regularly transmitted from one generation to another. The majority is constituted by words that returned to the spoken language after an exile that favored their material preservation in the books and libraries of the Middle Ages.

104 TOPONOMASTIC RESISTANCE

One must ask oneself if the testimony of place names confirms or modifies the testimony of common nouns, as regards the narrowing of the horizons to which we have alluded, or indeed with regard to the split that was established between the organization of the imperial society and that of the early Middle Ages. The change in the overall view of the problem appears in this form. While in the nineteenth century great importance was put on the discontinuity between ancient times and the Middle Ages, and the breaks and scars in the connective fabric of the empire were minimized, in recent years we find the reconfirmation of the horizontal breaks and scars (§§101–103) in the results of the studies of G. P. Bognetti[3] on the continuity of the rural communities, and G. D. Serra[4] on onomastic and toponomastic continuity. Thus there are, on the one hand, important cities whose names are popular in form (let us say *Zena* in contrast to *Genova* as an example), and less important cities whose names were established according to the one or the other criterion (for example, *Civita vecchia, Civita Lavinia* as compared to *Città della Pieve,* and *Città San Angelo*); finally there are the remains of the boundaries and the topographic systems of Roman times, such as *Vicano,* the name of a stream, or *Comuneglia,* the name of a territory, derived from the Latin *communis* which evidently indicates a parcel of land which was not privately owned but 'common'. To conclude this series we note the numerous localities which incorporate in their names 'Pieve': *Pieve San Stefano, Pievepelago, Pieve Albignola* and so on, which are vestiges of that parochial unity on which we have put so much emphasis.

105 ECONOMIC REALITIES

The comparison of these conclusions of a linguistic nature must not, however, be restricted only to juridical and constitutional problems. If with regard to both juridical and constitutional problems, the vertical continuity of history seems to be gaining to the detriment of the horizontal geographic continuity, one must not undervalue the importance of economic problems. If the higher forms of unity have diminished, if the life of the individual has fallen into deep isolation, it does not mean that on the economic level Italy tumbled headlong into total autarchy. International trade is not dead; it has only become more aristocratic and closed to those who do not have the means and the power to organize effectively.

Similarly, cultural life was not annihilated, but simply concentrated in those cloisters and schools which, like the ones cited above (§101), were in a position to attract and keep qualified persons. Many cities were depopulated. After the Gothic War Rome's population was reduced to one-tenth of that of the fourth century.[5] Nor were the barbarian tribes that had arrived numerous: the Ostrogoths in Pavia did not number more than twenty thousand.[6] The Belgian historian Henri Pirenne,[7] on the basis of well-founded data having to do with the persistence of commercial exchanges in the early Middle Ages, affirmed that the ancient world ended only with the age of Charlemagne. But if, as far as Italy is concerned, it were legitimate to state that the impoverishment of commerce has not reached the point of an economic breakdown in connection with the disintegration of the western empire, from the point of view of the language of Italy, there was a resolute and decisive turning point. The refined ceremonial garb to which Latin had been reduced, continued to be used in restricted circles. Under ordinary circumstances, however, as many different and threadbare costumes were used as there were parishes. Pirenne was mistaken in not having taken into consideration, in the light of the surviving commercial links, the disintegration of linguistic connections.

This disorder was weakened by three forces: the persistence of Latin as a ceremonial language that was not entirely abandoned (§§106–10); the persistence of pre-Latin heritages and tendencies which now rose to the surface again and contributed to determining differences between great regional customs (§§111–30); and the introduction of factors of linguistic reconstruction through the action of the Longobards (§§131–40).

Twenty-two

Toward Bilingualism

106 Auctores and Artes

The ceremonial garb of language that continues to be used as an exception to the norm, but at the same time is not devoid of traditional aspects is first introduced by two imposing figures,[1] Amicius Manlius Severinus Boethius (about 480 to about 525) and Flavius Magnus Aurelius Cassiodorus (about 480/490 to 573/583), who come to represent the founding of two different traditions. Boethius, on the one hand, has been defined as the last of the Romans and the first of the Scholastics. His prose is of a very high standard, and this standard improves with the years[2] without becoming estranged from the times, insofar as paratactic constructions continue to be preferred by the author.

Cassiodorus, on the other hand, personifies different needs—more technical, less fixed on ancient models, and closer to the tastes and tendencies of Christian authors.[3] The double direction which begins with these two authors has gained a precise title through the contrast which exists in succeeding centuries between the followers of the *auctores,* or those who set before themselves individual models,[4] and the followers of the *artes,* that is, of collective models[5] that leave out of consideration influences and tendencies of the spoken language.

Therefore, the fragile topmost curtain of the language of Italy survives, and indeed continues according to two distinct trends.

107 GREGORY THE GREAT

This superstructure of written language, whether it appeals in a conscious way to preceding models or does not expressly set up canons to follow and imitate, has an unchanging quality, and that is to feel the Latin language as a universal throughout the Latin West and especially in Italy. It does not indulge in local influences, unless precisely to reflect parochialism. Still, continuing our metaphor of Latin as a ceremonial robe, we may say that if the robe embellishes and attenuates details and defects of the human form, this is not to say that the robe itself does not get folded and even stretched out of shape in the process. The tradition of written language, and here it is not important to make a distinction between literary or chancery language, is not hermetically sealed against the possibility of uncertainties, fluctuations, or bold innovations.

Gregory the Great, pope from 590 to 604, and author of dialogs and homilies among other things, employs the following forms: *grandevus* for 'grandaevus', *discendo, clarisco,* and *benivoli* with the I in place of the normal E; and in the field of morphology he uses *abbati de monasterio* for 'monasterii'. His attitude is not rigid and takes into account the social level of the interlocutors when necessary.[6] Moreover, Gregory does not have a false sense of modesty with regard to grammar; he refutes the absoluteness of its discipline, even though the grammarians recommend its strict observation: *unde et ipsam loquendi artem quam magistri disciplinae exterioris insinuant, servare despexi;* in so saying he confirms the position of Saint Augustine,[7] of two centuries before.

These openings, however, do not constitute submission. The tradition of the ceremonial robe of Latin lasts through the seventh and eighth centuries. We can, for example, select a passage such as the following from a medical treatise written at the end of the seventh century by the deacon Crispus[8] *si caput innumeris agitature pulsibus, egrum . . . protinus ex hederae studeas redimere corona.* This shows impeccable external solidity and functionality: the problem of the thickness of the linguistic edifice, as far as the upper Latin stratum is concerned, does not appear here.

108 BARBARIAN INTERVENTION

The dialog between the upper (unitary) stratum of the language of Italy, and the lower (numerous) spoken languages of individual parishes, is enriched at this point in history by a new factor: the participation of the new barbarian ruling class and its acceptance of the Roman world both from the point of view of religious confession and its linguistic structures. This graft occurs first by means of chancery and juridical activity and then through the commentary of grammarians.

The basic example is that of King Rotari's edict of the year 643,[9] from which I quote an eloquent passage: *si quis foris provincia fugire temptaverit, morti incurrat periculum, et res eius infiscentur.* This is certainly not a passage on the level of literature, but neither is it the careless product of the penetration of vulgar or barbaric elements. It is the result of the merging of various needs, on the one hand of modernity and simplicity, and on the other of grammatical propriety, which is of prime importance in a translated text, in which there can never be too much clarity.

Remaining within the framework that has been delineated regarding the Latin tradition, we note that the language of Italy assumes the same double process with regard to barbarian superstructures; on a higher level there is the total acceptance of the Latin tradition by the barbarian world, and at a lower stratum we find not so much the penetration of innovations and mistakes, as that of lexical units and onomastic documents (§§131ff.).

The next century shows us the participation of the barbarians even on the level of grammatical problems, through the work of Paulus Varnefridus, better known as Paul the Deacon or Paulus Diaconus (720 or 724 to 799).[10] Author of a history of the Romans and one of the Longobards, Paul has remained famous in Latin studies for his abridgement of Festus' glossary *De verborum significatione.* Thanks to him, there is a welding with the grammatical tradition of Donatus and Priscian of the fourth and fifth centuries. A proof of the seriousness with which Paulus Diaconus plunged into the Latin linguistic system is given by the fact that there is less difference between a letter written by him and a page of one of his histories than there is between an epistle and a treatise or an oration of Cicero.[11] The structures of literary Latin have lost their elasticity; they are no longer immersed as they once were in the waters of the spoken language on a high level, but still constitute a solid, majestic monolith. Finally, Paul left a document pertaining to rhythm. The line of verse *ut queant laxis resonare fibris*[12] can be considered a Sapphic line from the point of view of classical metrics, but from an Italian point of view, it can already be considered a normal hendecasyllable. Centuries later, the line of verse will be used by Guido d'Arezzo to establish the terminology of musical notation (§145). Even in this, therefore, there is a proof of the tranquil passage from the patterns of Commodianus and

Augustine to those of Italian prosody and the metrics of the "dolce stil nuovo" and of Dante.

109 ALCUIN

Notwithstanding this solidity and continuity, beneath the ceremonial garments of Latin the rest of Italy's linguistic apparel was being worn out and was becoming untidy and diversified even in the fixed written form. The texts, linked to a venerable tradition of literary prestige, or indispensable to the majesty of the cult, sooner or later had to face the problem of revision and improvement. In order for this to be realized on the basis of an organic plan with sufficient consensus and agreement, two situations were needed. On the general plane the reestablishment of a minimum of political will was indispensable, supported by a territorial expanse sufficient to resist municipalism and to lend a sense of authority to the surviving cultural centers. This occurs only when, thanks to Charlemagne, we see once more before our eyes an "empire" that includes all or a large part of Italy. The second necessary condition was the existence of a group of scholars who were aware of the importance of the problem and of the necessity of studying it thoroughly resolving it. The eponym of this movement was a monk of Anglo-Saxon origin, Alcuin (735–804), who proposed a revision of the sacred texts, and the cleaning away from the Bible of encrusted layers that had rendered the texts unrecognizable. The outcome of this operation was indeed the return of the Bible more or less to the original form of the Vulgate of St. Jerome of four centuries before, but it was also proof for the common man that biblical Latin was one thing and the Latin he believed he was speaking quite another. This latter was no longer Latin, even though he still called it Latin.

110 THE LOWER LEVELS

Testimony to the divergent development of this humbler style of dress is not extraordinarily abundant, but it does exist. It is time for some of it to be taken into consideration; after this comes the reconstruction of all those centrifugal forces, but not only the centrifugal forces, that in these four centuries (sixth to ninth) advanced the tendencies already attributed to the spoken Latin of the Imperial Age.

The first testimony, small but genuine, can be traced back to a Spanish monk, Isidor of Seville (570–636),[13] who attributes to the Italians the pronunciation *ozie* for 'hodie', in this way establishing the chronology for the palatalization of the group DJ, which is typical of Italian. Of greater significance are examples drawn from entire texts that are still Latinate, or from words of a stamp that by now is wholly Italian. They are the distant horizons that one can glimpse through the broken seams of a stage curtain that has by now been worn smooth and threadbare.

We also discover nonsacred texts that from a subjective point of view can still be called Latin, but which in reality are deeply eroded in terms of phonetics and morphology. This is the case of the treatise on handcrafts of the eighth century that has been called *Compositiones lucenses* (Compositions of Lucca) and has been the object of an exhaustive study by the Swedish scholar J. Svennung.[14] A characteristic sentence is the following: *Tinctio pellis prasini* [green]. *Tolles pellem depellatam et mitte stercos caninus et colombinus et gallinacium.* Declension is declassed as a result of the inherent uncertainty and above all in the confusion of -US and -UM on the one hand, and of endings in -OS and in -US on the other. Another text, the testament of a Bishop Walprand, of 754, contains *volo ut omnes res meas que ad dictata et non vendita aut non donata remanserint, duas partes abeat.*[15] In addition to these testimonies to morphological disintegration, we find lexical innovations, which to our eyes, appear to be very modern: in documents of Lucca we find *menare* 'to lead' (dating from 770 and 777), *porcello* (777), *terre incolte* (776, 795), and *pascolo* (787). As we can all see, these forms are already "Italian."

Even the attitude of the grammarians develops more in the direction of allowing forms of the written language to coexist with forms of the spoken language, the grammarians limiting themselves to explaining or "translating" these latter. While the *Appendix Probi* "rebuked" with the words *columna non colomna* (§87), the Reichenau glosses (seventh and eighth centuries) were limited to "translating" those words and phrases that contemporary speakers did not use and no longer understood: for example, *transmigrat* 'de loco in loco vadit.'

Twenty-three

The Influence of the
Accent

111 THE EARLIEST CONTOURS OF TUSCANY

A second tempering (§§105ff.) permits a preliminary approach in the attempt to arrange in groups the thousands of mini-Latins that had blossomed in the shadow of the parishes. This tempering is provided by the survival of certain typical pre-Roman linguistic traditions, and of several trends and currents, already reconstructed above, within the Roman community (§§87–90, 96). The many boundaries that were built up between parishes do not lend themselves to comparison with each other. Besides those that constitute only different shades and nuances within a local color, there are others which, for historical reasons, appear already to have been well established, though perhaps only in fluid form, before the disintegration of the Roman world.

Among the many linguistic frontiers that are at times imperceptible, at times just visible, and at other times conspicuous, we must first approach the problem of those boundaries that suggest a definition, even though a negative one, of an entire region, that is to say, of Tuscany. The distant pre-Diocletian premises that were set forth in §96, tell us that two great linguistic innovations had reached Tuscany without difficulty: the palatalization of the guttural consonants, from which only the center of Sardinia had remained immune, and the organization of a system of nine vowels (which subsequently crystal-lized into a group of seven), which remained characteristic of the entire non-Italian Romance world, while in Italy the system had spread only north of the Via Appia. A third great innovation, that of the progressive assimilation of the type ND to NN, of Umbro-Samnite origin, stops at the boundary of Tuscany, which we understand not precisely in an administrative sense, because moving from the east and southeast, the assimilation phenomenon reaches the lower south-ern slopes of Monte Amiata (§138), which is now Tuscan territory.

Post-Diocletian times, and especially the beginning of the Middle Ages, pose two problems that are in large part, but not entirely, innovations, and that implicate the geographic contours of Tuscany. One problem has to do with the effects of the intensive accent, the first indications of which appeared during the period of the empire as indicated above (§99). The other problem concerns manifestations of greater or lesser compression of the word, always achieved through the action of the accent, and producing effects not only on the unac-cented vowels, but also on consonants in final position (§§114, 115). For the characteristics that subsequently develop to define Tuscany further see §149.

112 "INTERNAL" DIPHTHONGIZATION

Quite apart from the changes in timbre which must be accepted as having been evident already during the period of the empire for all accented vowels with the exception of the A, the action of the intensive accent appears through the lengthening of the accented vowel.[1]

In other words, a Latin form such as *dicit*, with its closed pronun-ciation, is not content to be distinguishable from a type with an open I like *picem*, which later developed into the Italian 'pece'. The form *dicit* contains an I that is not only closed, but also "long," so that it is a sort of DIICIT. The linguistic system, however, had just lost its distinctive capacity with regard to the opposition of long and short quantity. The vowels that no longer distinguished between an open and a closed pronunciation adapted to the new situation; with regard to the vowels that showed a distinction between an open and a closed pronunciation, as in the case of the open E and the open O, there developed the temptation further to accentuate the fragile distinction of the open vowels, by prolonging their quantity with an intensity and a stress which could not be protected against dissimilatory tendencies. Thus, when the structure of the open syllable did not pose obstacles of volume and duration (as the closed syllable inter-posed), the result was that PEE-DE was not able to impede that quali-tative imbalance that arose through the dissimilation of E into IE.

Inversely, the closed syllabic structure of PER-DI(T) provided immunity to the vowel in question. The same elaboration occurs in the case of the open o which, in an open syllable, undergoes a lengthening and a diphthongization as for example in the word *cuore,* but which in closed syllable maintains its original features, as in the case of *porta.*

This is the typical case of "internal" diphthongization, which is not determined or expedited by peripheral circumstances such as the pronunciation, the persistence or the decay of the final vowels of words. The following may serve as illustrations: *fiera* Latin FERA, *piede* Latin PEDE(M), *fuochi* Latin FOCI, *duomo* Latin DOMU-; whatever the final vowel, the same innovation occurred in all of them. The precise determination of the internal diphthongization accompanied by the clear pronunciation of the final vowels (even if deprived of the -o/-U opposition) results in Tuscan diphthongization being considered as something closed in itself, as if it were merely sketched out, without being pushed beyond the limits that the whole of the word imposed or allowed, without encountering other tendencies, resolutely differentiated from the diphthongization characteristic of surrounding areas.[2] To this structural definition there must be added a corresponding delimitation that is spatial, temporal, and reflective of the social stratification.

In a spatial sense, Tuscany does not have a monopoly on the phenomenon of "internal" diphthongization. The latter represents, rather, a spontaneous result which was not influenced by external forces and was, therefore, originally much more extended, and on which in some cases subsequent external forces acted, thus shifting preexisting dialectal frontiers. The first of these problems is represented by Venice, which has been recognized above as an area in which Latin was only slightly mixed with other elements (§98); G. I. Ascoli[3] already recognized the existence there of a pure internal diphthongization not unlike the Tuscan one. At a later date, the language in and around Venice was altered by the arrival of external currents, represented by forms of lenition and apocope of Gallo-Italic or Ladin origin. Similarly, as Gerhard Rohlfs has recognized,[4] in northeastern Liguria, and to be more precise near Mount Antola, there survive linguistic remains that were disfigured by a diphthongization of the Tuscan type UO, but this diphthongization was rendered unrecognizable by the arrival of a vocalic system in which mixed vowels are present and which is therefore foreign to the Tuscan system: we are here dealing with the grafting of this Ligurian zone into the larger unit of Gallo-Italic dialects, and therefore we must leave the door open to the possibility of recognizing a "pre-Gallo-Italic" phase in the Ligurian area itself (§140).

This geographic delimitation has two other historical consequences of primary importance that prove the great antiquity of this elementary diphthongization. In order to have reached the Venice area from the balanced world of Tuscan vocalism, it must have been sufficiently ancient first of all to have reached the Po Valley, or at least its most easterly regions, prior to A.D. 300, the period of Diocletian reform; and second, to have preceded the break that occurred in the last two centuries of the empire from the further Gallicization of the intermediary Romagna region, as it appears through the loss of final vowels, even after an occlusive. Consequently, the hypothesis of a Germanic or at least a northern influence, is to be excluded (§131).[5] With regard to absolute chronology, however, the actual evidence is late. In a text from Lucca of the year 761 we find *quocho* and *Quosa* (a place name); from the year 983 we have *aqua buona;* and finally, as a rule we find *cuor* 'heart' and *dieze* 'ten' in Venice.[6]

Finally, with regard to social factors, our attention has been called, thanks again to G. Rohlfs,[7] to the fact that the Tuscan diphthongization is regular but not universal; in other words, it reflects an effort toward precision and attention that was not always accepted by the lower social strata. These latter always said *lepre nove* (not LIEPRE NUOVE), while the Florentine form *bono* could still today be valid and expressive.

113 "VOWEL" BREAKING

Parallel to the "internal" diphthongization of the open vowels, there is the resistance of the closed vowels and of those that do not distinguish between open and closed pronunciation. The conservation of the closed E's and O's is opposed in the large (though not adjoining) Tuscan-Venetian area by that violent phenomenon occurring in all the other Italian regions, and known as "vowel breaking." This is a brusque or "surgical" diphthongization, of which the most elementary type is the passage from E to EI, or from O to OU. In Florence as in Venice, one says *tela* and *vena,* and similarly *croce* in Florence and *croze* in Venice, with the same, unaltered, closed o. In Genoa, though, we find *meise* and *neive* for 'mese' and 'neve'; and in Bologna *vous* and *soul* for 'voce' and 'sole'. In Apulia, we discover *meisë* at Lucera and *soulë* at Barletta for 'mese' and 'sole'. The relationship is obvious: where there is internal diphthongization, the final vowels are pronounced clearly; where there is "vowel breaking," although it is indeed possible for the final vowels to be saved, in the majority of cases they become blurred into an indistinct vowel or disappear altogether. There is connected with the idea of "vowel breaking" an intensity of accent that is much greater than that which appears instead in internal diphthongization.

As we shall see later, the focal nuclei of the fragmentation phenomenon are two: Adriatic "vowel breaking" is at work in a relatively recent period, is valid even after the phenomena of metaphony appear, and also has ancient predictions in prehistory, for example as regards the "mixed" vowel ü. The other type of "vowel breaking"—Gallo-Italic—is connected to innovations that persist in French even to the present day.

114 THE FINAL VOWELS

These changes regarding accent, concentrated as they are in the zone of the accented vowels, are accompanied by processes of compression that influence the compactness of the word as a whole or its greater or lesser individualization in the flow of the sentence. The first of these processes has to do with the problem of the final vowel of the word, which already during the Imperial Age had shown signs, if not of weakness, then at least of less distinctive capacity with regard to the final -I/-E (§83). From the point of view of clarity of pronunciation of the final vowels, conservative areas, in which a more or less complete preservation of final vowel pronunciation is maintained, are opposed to other areas in which we find a weakening effect on the pronunciation of the final vowels, occasionally to the point of total elimination. The large areas that preserve a clear pronunciation of the final vowels are on the one hand the Sicilian, Sardinian, and Salentine group,[8] and on the other hand Tuscany, along with Latium, Umbria (with the neighboring territory of Aquila), and the Marches. Clarity of pronunciation does not mean that the original number of vowels has been preserved. In Sicily, for example, the number of final vowels is three; in Tuscany it is four. In a restricted zone of Umbria and the Marches five final vowels are preserved because the distinction between -U and -O is protected.[9] The texts that demonstrate this are of a much later date, but we must consider the possibility that in this intermediate period morphological distinctions such as that of the neuter gender have consolidated the phonetic vitality of elements which, in terms of the accent, were in similar situations.

Not even the two innovative areas are contiguous. The northern area, which comprises the Po Valley and the northern Marches up to the Esino River, aims at the elimination of the final vowel; but naturally, this tendency is then favored or impeded by the greater or lesser resistance of the consonantal framework. In cases where the latter holds up well the final vowels grow weak, and inversely the final vowels show greater resistance when consonantal lenition is strong. On the whole, we can identify in Liguria and in the environs of Venice the circumstances that are less favorable to the loss of the final vowels. As for the other area, which comprises the Abruzzi (minus the Aquila area), Apulia (minus the Salentine Peninsula), Campania, Lucania, and Calabria, the immediate goal is not so much the destruction of the final vowels as it is their fusion into a single indistinct vowel. Within this overall situation, there are isolated, extremist foci that arrive at the total loss of the final vowel. Yet, these are later phenomena, of which there exist in this historical period only indirect premises.

While during the Imperial Age only the weakening and the loss of internal vowels could be conceived of, in the early Middle Ages a new factor of change and complication is introduced that simultaneously crosses the processes of vocalic and consonantal weakening in such a way that they end up neutralizing each other in part.

115 THE FINAL CONSONANTS

The weakening of the final consonants requires minor intervention on the part of the action of the accent. In ancient times there had been an opposition between urban and rural pronunciation, that is, between a focal nucleus of resistance and autonomy of the word and the tendencies to eliminate the frills at the end of a word, which in the meantime had been discredited from the morphological point of view. The greatest weakening had occurred in the -M, which had been rendered quite invalid as far as prosody was concerned: one isolated resistance to this phenomenon is represented by a word which is not Italian but French, and that is *rien* (Latin REM). In Italian the prepositions *con* and *per* (Latin *cum* and *per*) retain the complete final consonant because they are proclitic; *non* is indeed accented, but it never appears at the end of a sentence. In Rome the -s had certainly grown weaker, as the prosody in the Plautine age demonstrates. The urban reaction had restored it to health; then while the successive weakening appears to have occurred throughout all of the eastern Latin world as far as Dacia, the -s shows vigorous resistance throughout the West, including the Po Valley, which was susceptible to the action of the Gallic culture, and the Friuli region, which was influenced by Transalpine Gaul currents. The traces of an -s that still survived during the Middle Ages in northern Italy confirm this unitary vision.

As far as the -D/-T are concerned, the situation is somewhat different, because the dental consonant was destined to fall without a trace in the isolated word, but found itself in a position of privilege when it was part of a proclitic particle (as the above-mentioned *con* and *per*) and was therefore treated as if it were in the middle of a word. Thus, in that part of Italy which permits assimilation of the consonants and the preservation of doubled consonants that derives from it, the so-called "syntactical doubling" is born which is so characteristic for Italians of other regions, and as regards above all the velar consonants, in clear opposition with the single consonantal forms which are subject to the Tuscan aspiration (§124).[10]

As G. Rohlfs has shown, such a typical process is subject to exaggeration. More important is the fact that the syntactical doubling also appears in other forms, among which the Campania type is to be remembered: singular *o ritë* 'the finger', plural *e ddetë* (§123).[11]

Twenty-four

Metaphony and
Mixed Vowels

116 METAPHONY AS A QUALITATIVE COMPENSATION
The contrast of the two Italys—one with decentralized words, and
the other with words that are more or less strongly centralized—is not
a well-balanced one. It is precisely in this period, one in which we are
still virtually without documents, that we must define, on the basis
of indirect testimony, other processes and innovations destined to
expand the areas in which centralization was felt in a more or less
clear-cut way, as opposed to those zones that remained immune to it.
A reagent allows us to recognize the spread of tendencies directed at
weakening the phonetic consistency of the final syllable, and aimed
at the same time at avoiding the morphological disadvantages that
derive from the less effective "signaling-power" of the final mor-
phemes. This is the so-called metaphony, a fundamental phenomenon
in Italian dialectology, and one which is attested in various forms
throughout Italy with the exclusion of Tuscany and certain parts of
Sicily. By metaphony we understand the alteration of the timbre of
an internal vowel, in such a way that it becomes less distant from or
even identical to the timbre of the final vowel. The latter is tempo-
rarily strong enough to influence the preceding vowel, but at the same
time it feels insecure, as if destined to grow weaker or even to die.
From this it follows that we are not here dealing with a true act of

strength on the part of the final vowel, which prevails over the internal vowel as if it possessed a power similar to that of the accent. On the contrary, at the most metaphony bears witness to a morphological necessity, coupled, however, with a feeling of weakness and therefore even of phonetic invalidity. Metaphony is an instrument which guarantees morphological validity, by substituting one phonetic marker, the fragility of which is evident, with another, the stability of which is certain, as far as clarity and solidity are concerned. Metaphony is defined, moreover, as a "preventive qualitative compensation" actualized before the marker in crisis became unrecognizable or before it disappeared altogether, no longer capable of finding a substitute.

The first variety of metaphony is the precocious type that has the effect of reinforcing the conspicuousness of a morphological opposition, even though the next development of the linguistic system may not come to justify its necessity. In the Sardinian region of Logudoro the masculine singular of the Vulgar Latin type BONU is *bonu* with the closed o, while the corresponding feminine is *bona* with a normal o perceived in opposition to that in *bonu*. The point of departure was this: at a certain point in time the final -U was felt to be destined for weakening; in this situation it acted upon the preceding vowel in such a way that the timbre of the latter approached that of the former, thus determining its "closed" pronunciation. The final -A of the feminine on the other hand, was felt to be stable, and therefore, it did not need to act upon the preceding vowel.[1]

The weakening of the final vowels in Sardinian is not, however, verified, and the precocious metaphony of Sardinian had no other effect but to enrich its vocalic system from five to seven units. In Sicily, especially in the east and southeast,[2] precocious forms of metaphony are found, the result of which is not a raising of the vowel but diphthongization. In contrast to the diphthongized masculine singular *viecchiu,* there is a nondiphthongized feminine *vecchia.* In other words, the relative stability of the final -A resulted in its not needing to reinforce the preceding vowel, while the anticipated weakening of the final -U determined a reinforced pronunciation of the internal vowel. As a result, the reinforced internal vowel had a pronunciation which was first lengthened and then diphthongized. While for Sardinia it can be assumed that the new variant in vocalic timbre is a response to spontaneous local pressure that does not penetrate inland from the coasts, for Sicily we may instead consider that the feeling of fragility of the final vowel and the tendency to resist its consequences by way of metaphony corresponds to that second current of Latin tradition that has been defined above as the "Neapolitan" Latin tradition (§98).

117 PREMATURE METAPHONY

A second type of metaphony can be labelled "premature." Not even this type of metaphony is determined by phenomena of linguistic weakening and foreseeable unrecognizableness; however, unlike Sardinian metaphony, it has such contacts with the areas of classical metaphonetic diffusion that it deserves to be distinguished from the preceding examples of precocious metaphony. In the case of premature metaphony we are dealing with two areas very distant one from the other, but contiguous with respect to the large territory of southern Italy. On the one hand, there is to the north the territory that embraces the present-day regions of Lazio, the Marches, and Umbria including the neighboring territory of Aquila. In Amelia in Umbria, we find the masculine singular form *nero,* to which the plural *niri,* destined to preserve the distinctive morphological value of the -ı as plural ending, corresponds. Not only was there an effective weakening of the final vowels in this area, but it is to be noted that it was precisely in these regions that the distinction between -o and -u was maintained better than in Tuscany itself. At the opposite extreme, in the Salentine Peninsula, the same operation took place. The final vowels -ı and -u maintain their distinctive efficacy, but at the same time there are energetic metaphonic diphthongizations such as *vienti* for 'venti' (twenty), *cueri* instead of 'cuori', and *cueru* in place of 'cuoio'. Here, as in Sicily, the technique of diphthongization reveals a concentration on the internal vowel, after concentration had shifted from the final vowel.

118 CLASSICAL SOUTHERN METAPHONY

Southern metaphony is, for the most part, a phenomenon of the Abruzzi (with the exception of the territory around Aquila), of Molise, Campania, Lucania, and Calabria (with the exception of its southern part). The cause of the process is obvious. Initially all the final vowels are reduced to an -ë, with the exception of the -A. Subsequently, the -A also undergoes this weakening process while the other vowels, in certain more or less restricted zones, cancel out. Thus it happens in Bari, for example, that the masculine singular -u and the masculine plural ending -ı, both destined to weaken prematurely, act preventively and in anticipation on the preceding vowel in order to obscure its timbre, as we see in the case of *chistë,* which, however, in representing the obscured pronunciation of both QUESTU and QUESTI, contemporaneously means 'questo' (this) and 'questi' (these), and therefore no longer makes a distinction between the masculine singular and plural. It was only in the case of the feminine that the final vowel -A, more robust in an earlier period, did not affect the preceding vowel, and even when it did grow weak this nonaction was

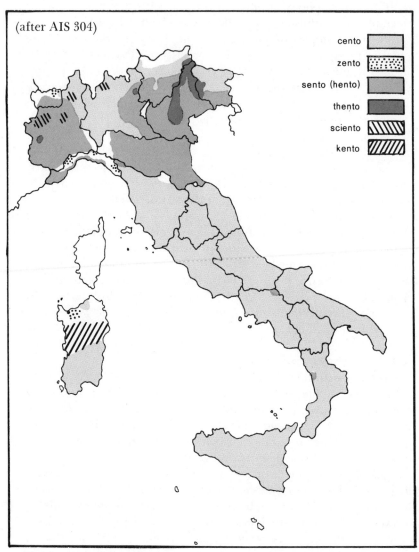

Map 4. Palatalization and Assibilation of C before E and I

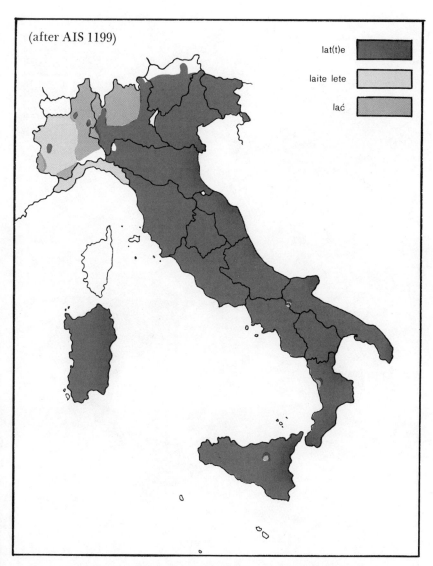

(after AIS 1199)

lat(t)e

laite lete

laĉ

Map 5. Outcome of the Latin Consonant Cluster CT

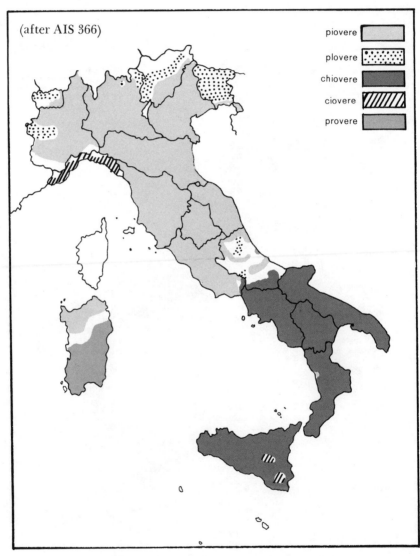

(after AIS 366)

piovere
plovere
chiovere
ciovere
provere

Map 6. Development of the Cluster PL

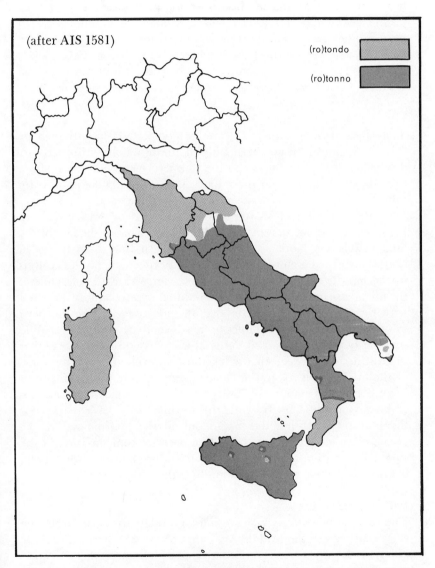

(after AIS 1581)

(ro)tondo

(ro)tonno

Map 7. Assimilation in the Cluster ND, MB in Central and Southern
Italy

important to the distinctiveness of the relationship: *chestë* 'questa' (this, feminine singular) is easily distinguished from *chistë*, the value of which remains ambiguous, however, with respect to both the singular and plural of the masculine form: the metaphonical action has given only partial assistance to the morphological system.

One very important aspect of the problem is chronological in nature. The metaphonical action was precocious in both an absolute and a relative sense. All of the splintering of which we have spoken above (§113) affects the primitive -ɪ's and -ʊ's, as well as the ɪ's and ʊ's that evolved later because of metaphony, in the same way.[3]

119 CLASSICAL NORTHERN METAPHONY

The other great metaphonical area is northern Italy, although by this we do not mean northern Italy in an absolutely uniform sense. The differences with respect to the southern metaphonical area are two. On the one hand, northern metaphonical action does not maintain the same symmetry between the action of the ɪ and that of the ʊ, but rather underlines a greater need to "compensate" for the weakening of the ɪ than for that of the ʊ. On the other hand, the fate of the final vowels was more precarious in northern Italy than it was in southern Italy; therefore, the importance of the metaphonical vowels in the middle of the word becomes even greater with reference to the final marker, which is very often reduced to zero value. Compared with the Bari example cited above, the advantage of the northern solution appears in general lines from this comparison: the masculine singular QUEST(ʊ) is opposed to the plural QUIST(ɪ) in such a way that the distinction between the two is apparent even after the total loss of the final vowels. Note the Genoese examples in which *can* from CANE does not compensate for the loss of the final -E either preemptively or retroactively, while the -ɪ, which is the basic marker for the plural, determines the metaphony of the internal A *into* -E-, giving place to *chen*. Thus there is no need for compensation in the singular *cian* from PLANU, but in the plural we find *cen* from PLANI, because the Genoese system cannot do without this distinctiveness.

120 MIXED VOWELS

The other innovation which we must postulate as dating from the early centuries of the Middle Ages, that of mixed vowels, is entirely different. It has no connection with morphology; rather it represents a different equilibrium within the vowel system. Like metaphony, the phenomenon of mixed vowels also became established in two large areas, although the needs that gave rise to this situation were quite different; one area is the southern Adriatic zone; the

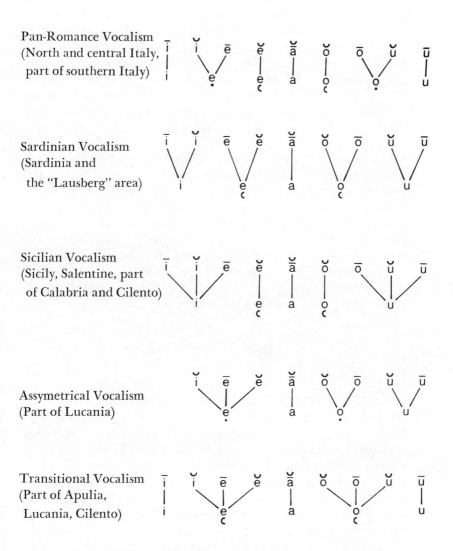

Patterns of Fundamental Types of Vocalism (in Italy) in the Evolution of the Dialects from Latin

other is the northern Adriatic, but restricted to the western Po Valley.

The southern zone, on the one hand, must be viewed within the framework of the vocalic disorder which is characteristic of the ancient Illyrian heritage[4] that left its mark on both sides of the Adriatic; the northern zone, on the other hand, must be considered within the context of its relations with Gaul and the linguistic prestige, which I venture to call orthoepical, that irradiated from it. The two areas—let us say between Taro in Emilia and Tronto in the Marches—are separated by a distance of three hundred fifty kilometers that exclude any possibility whatsoever of genetic or primeval contacts.

A profound difference separates the diffusion mechanism of the one and the other area. In the southern Adriatic zone the development was chaotic, and the mixed vowels are nothing more than a particular instance of the complex phenomena of fragmentation. A different vocalic system can be described for each municipal area. In the northern sector, on the contrary, the pattern for mixed vowels can be introduced in an almost constant and uniform manner: the ü is the result of the ancient closed u; the ö is the result of a diphthong of the type EU, which in turn goes back to the open differentiated o. The pattern could be the following:

$$
\begin{array}{ccc}
 & A & \\
E & Ö & O \\
I & Ü & U \\
\end{array}
$$

Through the diffusion of mixed vowels it is possible to distinguish two areas in northern Italy in which there exists a situation quite different from the traditional zone. The speech forms of Emilia-Romagna east of Taro, Veneto, and Friuli do not in fact have mixed vowels, thus defining a line of demarcation in a north-south direction that more or less corresponds to the flow of the Taro and the Adige rivers and that finds an analogous delimitation in quite another phenomenon, which has to do with the treatment of consonantal groups (§126).

Perhaps the resistance and the prestige of linguistic models radiating from the Byzantine areas of Ravenna and Ancona contributed to this demarcation.[5] It could not have been the exclusive determining factor, however, precisely because the area immune from mixed vowels extends throughout the region east of the Adige and throughout the Giulia region.

Twenty-five

Consonantal Structure

121 LENITION

At this point we come up against a problem. Although contrasting forces such as that of the accented vowel (that is more or less centralizing) and the more or less effective resistance of the unaccented vowels had an effect on the structure of the word, the relationship that came to be established was not determined solely by these forces in play. It was also conditioned by the solidity of consonantal structures. These latter, if solid, permitted the accented vowel greater freedom of action, in comparison with systems in which the consonantal framework was weaker, and therefore exposed to other neutralizing forces. A struggle between syllables is conceivable as long as boundaries between syllables exist; if these boundaries weaken, the primacy of the accented syllable is blocked or deflected.

Taking as our point of departure the Vulgar Latin form FRIGIDU, we have not just one problem of impact on the part of the intensive accent, but three. (1) The first possibility is that the final vowel has greater resistance than the internal vowel, and that the consonantal framework remains solid: from FRIGIDU we get FRIGDU (§87), and we have evidence of this in the Italian form *freddo*. (2) The second possibility is diametrically opposite: that the consonantal framework should give way and result in a type FRI(G)I(D)U, producing the form *frio* in Spanish, and similarly the form *diu* from DI(G)I(T)U in Genoese (§89). (3) The third possibility is that the two atonic vowels should weaken within the same time period and that the consonantal framework should survive, as we see is the case in the Friulian form *fred,* from FRIGD(U).

In addition to the intense action of the accented vowel there is also the greater or lesser possibility that the consonants will be subject to the influence of neighboring vowels. This tendency is called "lenition."

Lenition is a tendency that has existed in the western Mediterranean world since ancient times;[1] it appeared spontaneously in Sardinia in the Latin words that reached its shores, and also in the Gallic world, whence it traveled to the Gallo-Italic world.

To date, the most ancient written texts in Sardinian do not document lenition. In northern Italy is was in the course of developing in a more or less energetic way. Present-day Sardinian examples fall into three categories:[2] (*a*) from voiceless to voiced in Baronia and in the area of Bitti; (*b*) from voiced to fricative (in other words, still partial lenition) in Orani, as we see in the cases of *jughu* 'giogo' (yoke) from JUGU, and codha from CODA; (*c*) and finally from voiced to zero (total lenition) in Dorgali, as we note in *istria* and *coa* for 'strega' and 'coda'. In northern Italy the situation is more simple and clear-cut: on the one hand voiceless consonants show partial lenition in types like *spiga* from SPICA, which exemplifies a passage from voiceless to voiced, or like *cavèi* from CAPILLI, which shows passage from unvoiced to fricative, while in *crèa* from CRETA we have an example of total lenition. Using a voiced consonant as a point of departure, there are only two possibilities: the spirantization of B to V, which is not characteristic of the Gallo-Italic world, but is a feature of Vulgar Latin (§96); or total lenition of the type *istria* (from G) and *coa* (from D). Even from these few examples we have proof of the interdependence between the force of lenition and a relative capacity for resistance of the final vowels. For an account of extreme lenition from -L- to -R- in Liguria see §140.

122 RETROFLECTION

A second phenomenon, that has its roots in Mediterranean (i.e., pre-Indo-European) times and is opposed to an even greater degree than is lenition to the traditional structures of Latin, results from the action of "retroflection," in other words from the presence of articulations generally taking the place of the articulation LL, pronounced with the retroflection of the tongue against the palate. There is evidence of this phenomenon in almost all of Sicily, in Sardinia, and in western

Corsica, which was not exposed to the Tuscan influences in the
second part of the Middle Ages (§146). This articulation also became
established in southern Calabria and in the Salentine Peninsula, in
areas where cases of actual blending with linguistic traditions intermediary between the Mediterranean (i.e., pre-Indo-European) stratum and Latin have not been verified. The pronunciation ḍḍ involved muscular effort and is dictated not by the prestige of the local
traditions but by requirements that are almost physiological in
nature. The classic examples are *cavaḍḍu* 'cavallo' (horse) and
stiḍḍa 'stella' (star), and so on. Yet the fact that this innovation was
not limited by definitive boundaries but rather remained fluid with
the passage of time is demonstrated by the modification of the group
ḍḍ to the simple ᴅᴅ, which occurs in the peripheral Neapolitan of
Ischia and the Monte di Procida, areas which must have first experienced retroflection. In addition to their connection with ʟʟ,
retroflex articulation also appears with the groups sᴛʀ and ᴛᴛʀ, as a
result of which we have the approximate Sicilian pronunciations of
as-ciu for 'astro' and *qua-ciu* for 'quattro'.

Since traces of this development are to be found also in the Apuan
region and even in the area of Pistoia,[3] it is clear that we are faced
with a western Mediterranean phenomenon that survived in peninsular Italy. It will be shown below (§153) that the Gallo-Italic dialects
that were brought into southern and insular Italy in the second half
of the Middle Ages contributed to the reduction of these traces of
retroflection.

123 FROM DENTALS TO LIQUIDS
A third change in consonantal articulation necessarily concerns the
early medieval period, because this phenomenon also has definite
origins in antiquity. In this case we are dealing with phenomena
characteristic of the Samnite world, that we have already seen in
Latin documents (§88). The classical alteration is that of ɴᴅ to ɴɴ;
parallel changes are those of ᴍʙ to ᴍᴍ, as we see for example in
gamma 'gamba' and *chiummë* 'piombo', which are closely followed
by the passage of ɴᴛ to ɴᴅ, ɴᴋ to ɴɢ, and ᴍᴘ to ᴍʙ; examples are
mondë 'monte', *angora* 'ancora', and *rombë* 'rompe'.[4] Naturally this
is not to say that the passage from Oscan to neo-Latin forms was a
direct one. For example, the forms attested in Pompeii, and dating
therefore from the early empire, can derive from foci that spread
these same patterns not as Umbro-Samnite reactions but as Latin
models influenced by Umbro-Samnite. A proof of the necessity for
this distinction is that at Messina the Oscan language was introduced
by the Mamertini, but this language had no effect at all on the forma-

tion of the Latin of the area; in fact the type NN from ND was introduced only in the cities in a later period.

Another very elegant example of this distinction is the one verified in central Calabria. This area received from Neapolitan to the north the type NN from ND, but did not receive the next innovation, namely ND from NT. Therefore, the inhabitants of central Calabria say *chianta* while those of northern Calabria say *chianda* for 'pianta'.[5]

Another element intervenes to confirm the thesis that here we are dealing only in part with the acceptance into Latin of former Umbro-Samnite tendencies. This is the case of the passage in specific circumstances of the voiced dental to the liquid (or to a liquid associated with a sibilant). In ancient times this phenomenon was observed only in the Umbro-Samnite sphere of influence. During the empire and the early Middle Ages the movement swung toward the south and today we find Abruzzi forms of the type *chiure* 'chiude', *vere* 'vedere', and *carè* 'cadere'. The innovation spreads to the south, first affecting the internal and then the initial D. The inhabitants of Gallo, in Campania, still say *o ditë* for 'il dito', but in Naples we hear *o ritë,* or *rurëcë* for 'dodici'. In syntactic phonetics and in literary words there is instead a reinforcement that serves as a protection from this alteration. In Naples, in contrast to the "liquid" singular *o ritë,* there is a reinforced plural *e dditë* for 'i diti' (§115). Thus, in the case of *addèdeca* 'dedica' (he/she/it dedicates) we find an exaggeration, by which there is attributed to the word a sort of article or prefix which protects the initial articulation.

124 ASPIRATION AND PALATIZATION

Aspiration constitutes a case apart. While lenition, retroflection, and progressive assimilation were active linguistic agents in the early Middle Ages, aspiration concerns this period only under one condition, and that is with reference to a movement that had its beginnings in ancient Etruria. The most serious obstacle to this attribution lies in the fact that no author either ancient or medieval, including Dante, ever made mention of this particular feature of Florentine speech or of its neighboring dialects. This phenomenon consists in the aspiration of the voiceless velar consonant in an intervocalic position, considering even proclitic elements such as the article as part of the word. The treatment of the voiceless dental is analogous, though less conspicuous.[6]

A second obstacle consists in the fact that the entire development of the Latin of Tuscany is characterized by its isolation and by the absence of blending; it seems strange that the only blending should have been this one, so isolated and enigmatic. In any case, in order not to justify such a hypothesis at any price, but rather to arrive at a complete picture of the forces in play, we may underline the dissymmetry that exists among the different regions of Etruria. In these different regions the indications of a different degree of adjustment between the superimposed Latin tradition and the preexisting Etruscan tradition can be evaluated by comparing them with regard to the diffusion of the consonantal aspiration. Based on the *Corpus inscriptionum etruscarum* and the *Corpus inscriptionum latinarum*, the ratio of Etruscan to Latin inscriptions in the northern Tuscan zones of Luni, Pisa, Lucca, Pistoia, Fiesole, and Arezzo is 82 Etruscan inscriptions as compared with 505 Latin inscriptions; this means that there are approximately six times as many Latin inscriptions as there are Etruscan ones. In the central Tuscan territories of Volterra, Siena, Cortona, Perugia, and Chiusi, however, Etruscan inscriptions are six times more numerous than Latin ones (4833 to 785).[7] The establishment of the Latin tradition favors the hypothesis of a smooth adjustment and blending; the Etruscan resistance which continued up to a late period supports the theory that on the contrary the two traditions, considered not only linguistically but also from a sociocultural point of view, were for a long time autonomous. The geographic distribution of the Tuscan aspiration corresponds in large part to the northern region. In this sense, it is permissible to state that, in the absence of direct proofs, the geography of the inscriptions eliminates an obstacle and defines a geographical rapport that carries a certain amount of weight.

In terms of palatalization, the early Middle Ages is a period of slow accentuation of the process which was already documented in ancient times; at the same time it is a period in which differences were emphasized, especially as far as the speed of the palatalization process is concerned. The altered pronunciation of the groups CE and CI with respect to groups containing other vowels, a feature which had been part of the Roman tradition from the middle of the Imperial Age (§§89, 90), spreads and becomes established and accentuated. The different degrees of intensity of this development can be represented in the following way. (1) In southern Italy it stops at the palatal occlusive stage, a point of development which is backward with respect to ancient Umbrian, but more advanced in comparison with the Oscan world that had always ignored the alteration. (2) In Tuscany the altered pronunciation becomes established as a fricative articulation, with the result that the rapport between *cena* and *scena* is lively but does not constitute a resolute opposition. (3) In northern Italy there are divergent developments depending on whether a dental articulation is to some degree maintained, or whether the pronunciation approaches a sibilant. Belonging to the first direction are the Veneto types of TH (*thento*) with its interdental sound; to the second the types of the Ligurian mountains *tsentu,* from which follow the totally assibilated forms of the Genoese *sentu* for 'cento'. While in the center of the Gallo-Italic territory there are many gradations of this development, and while in Milan we find that for various reasons even simple palatals become established, the final result is reached in two cities that are not strictly Gallo-Italic, in which there is no longer a distinction between the primitive sibilant and the sibilant derived from the velar. *Santu* and *sentu* in Genoa and *santo* and *sento* in Venice are by now on the same plane as French, which (apart from spelling) makes the identical adjustment for the initial sounds of the words *cent* and *saint.*

125 CONSONANTAL GROUPS

The most characteristic problem in consonantal groups is produced by the encounters among occlusives, and above all among gutturals and labials followed by a dental. The local traditions in Italy, as they appear in ancient times in a conspicuous way are these three. In Latin the rule was assimilation from the point of view of the degree of articulation (voiceless with voiceless, voiced with voiced), the point of articulation remaining intact; *lectus* from LEG + TO shows preservation of the velar in front of a dental, but with the standardization of the former to the voiceless quality of the latter. On the other hand, the original Umbrian tradition consisted in differentiation, in which the preceding occlusive was transformed into a fricative or a spirant (an *h*-type sound) before another occlusive: HAHTU 'capìto' shows the passage from PT to HT; *ahtu* 'agito' shows the passage from the G of AG before a T to AH. Within the Umbro-Samnite group, however, we note signs of weariness in this direction. Assimilation makes headway in the Oscan area in the case of encounters brought about as a result of syncope which took place in a later period (for example, in Oscan *actud* derives from a previous form AG(E)TOD), and also in the Umbrian area, where there is a topographic reference to a form *tettom,* which seems ot be interpretable as TEKTOM and that is, with a total assimilation that is more energetic than the Latin type and at the same time anticipatory of the "Italian" solution. The third tradition is the Celtic one, which is based on a generalized but, unlike Umbrian, a stable differentiation. The Italian tradition which was developed throughout south and central and northeastern Italy (Emilia, Veneto, Friuli) is that of total assimilation: *fatto* from FACTU, *rotto* from RUPTU. In the Piedmontese, Lombard, and Ligurian regions, however, the tendency toward differentiation is inherited and, as far as the consonant cluster CT is concerned, a passage to HT must first be presupposed (§35). At this point, an external condition opens the door to two different solutions. If the final vowel is resistant enough, then the process of palatalization acts upon the final consonant of the group, corroding it as we see in the case in the Spanish *hecho* from FACTU: the type FAHTU becomes a type FAT'(U), from which the Lombard forms *fac'*, *lec'*, *nöc'*, and *tec'*, 'fatto', 'letto', 'notte', 'tetto', derive. If the final vowel does not offer sufficient support, the fricative does not work upon the following consonant, but first becomes a spirant (an *h*-type sound) and then an I: thus there is the pattern FAIT(U), which in Piedmontese (as in French) gives *fait*, and in Genoese produces *fätu* with the final vowel intact and with contraction, and similarly *läte* 'latte', *or* without contraction *teitu* 'tetto'.

Morphological
Phenomena

126 MARKERS FOR THE PLURAL

This period also sees the fulfullment of the destiny of case endings with a final consonant which, because they are weakened, lose all their capacity as morphological markers. The Italian area feels the repercussion in an uneven way, especially as far as the final -s is concerned. Its progressive weakening continued during the period of the empire. At this time an opposition is set up between the greater part of the Italian area which, having lost the final -s, must replace it with another marker for the plural in all the declensions that are different from the second, and the other part of Italy in which the final -s is preserved. There is Sardinia, where the final -s is preserved because of an intrinsic conservative tendency: *tempus, latus, frius,* and *opus* are all normal Sardinian forms. Consequently, the normal Sardinian case endings for the plural are *-os* for the masculine, and *-as* for the feminine.

Friuli is another Italian region in which the final -s is preserved: this occurs not because of a continuing internal vitality but because Friuli was under Celtic influence during the forth and fifth centuries. The validity of -s as a marker for the plural appears by way of oppositions such as the following: *nuf* : *nus'* 'nuovo' : 'nuovi'; *mur* : *murs*; and *timòn* : *timòns* (Tramonti). A still more characteristic case is furnished by an indirect piece of evidence. In Latin, even during the time when the case ending for the feminine nominative plural in -AE, in place of the primitive ending in -AS, had become generally established, there still remained the influence of provincial forms which, on the basis of the Oscan language, maintained the primitive form in -AS.

A few examples of this influence even penetrated the literary language.[1] In a small area of Garfagnana in northeastern Tuscany C. Salvioni discovered a form of the plural like *duo dona* 'due donne' (two women), which evidently presupposes a Latin form DUO DOMNAS.[2] This cannot be a form which can be traced back to the Oscan world; rather we are dealing with a very ancient morphological vestige which was rendered unrecognizable, at least at first sight, by the erosion of the final -s It is a testimony that furnishes a piece of information even on the level of Latin.

127 Periphrastic Past and Future Tenses

Already in the sphere of Latin some use was beginning to be made of the possibilities of periphrastic forms which in the early Middle Ages were progressively morphologized; such were the cases with the present perfect tense, the future, and even the conditional (§128).

The present perfect has remained a periphrastic construction up to our own days, and the only difference between the Italian construction *hostem captum habeo* and the Italian construction 'ho preso il nemico' lies in the area of syntactical structure, so that in Latin *captum* is the predicate complement of the object (*hostem*), while in Italian it acts together with 'ho' as an inseparable predicate ('ho preso'), which is followed by the direct object ('il nemico'). In other words we are dealing with a devaluation of the auxiliary verb which was first taken to indicate a more intense relationship with regard to the simple perfect, then to state a parallel relationship with respect to the past absolute, and finally to undermine the field of influence of the past absolute itself, as occurred in northern Italy.

With reference to the future tense, two forces acted contemporaneously: the one force, a formal one, is the minimal difference between the type *amabo* and the imperfect *amabam;* the other force, a fundamental one, is the need to have alongside the temporal future, an affective future form that underlines the importance or the necessity of placing the action in the future. In comparison with its emotional value, the formal signaling power of the tense declines in importance.

The Latin periphrasis *dare habeo*[3] means precisely 'ho da dare' 'devo dare' (I have to give, I must give). This construction resulted in the Italian 'darò', and the entire paradigm was modelled on the pattern of the first person. Other examples are quoted in §94.

128 THE CONDITIONAL

The problem of the conditional, which did not exist in Latin, is more complex, because it answers to a new need. Here also the affective element is fundamental. The periphrastic formulae, which had already been employed in Latin, are three in number. The first periphrasis decisively accentuates the immediacy of the conditioned action inasmuch as the latter is the result of the infinitive plus the auxiliary verb *habere* in the pluperfect form *habueram*. The pluperfect emphasized an unreality, but at the same time it stressed something that might have been completed already for some time. In Gregory of Tours (ninth century) we read *si fas fuisset angelum de coelo evocaveram.*[4] The clearest Italian example is that of *fora* 'sarei' (I would be), which derives from an original form FUERAM. In Dante we even find the form *sodisfara,* and in Sicily the forms *cantara* 'canterei' (I would sing) and *vulera* 'vorrei' (I should like). The area in which this archaic type became more or less definitively established comprises Sicily, southern Italy, Lazio, Umbria, and even the Marches, but not farther north; it did not receive any substantial literary recognition (§98).

The second periphrasis, arrived at by means of the imperfect, is devoid of any more or less relative determination in a temporal sense and is attested to in the fourth century in the example *sanare te habebat deus si fatereris:*[5] the unreality is entirely in the conditioning formula, and not in the consequence, which has a durative aspect and is therefore strongly intentional, necessary, and deliberate. This construction became fixed in the suffix -IA, and has two foci of origin, Sicily and Provence. From Sicily it became incorporated in Tuscan literary monuments, and from Provence it passed into the literature of northern France. Nevertheless, spontaneous forms in -ea are found here and there, for example, *darea* and *sarea* in Guittone and Ristoro, respectively.[6]

The third solution, which employed the auxiliary *habui,* is the most energetic because it underlines an actual, automatic reality, one that is bound to the verification of the condition. There is a fine example of this type in the Latin of the eighth century[7] *si . . . invenisset . . . Scandalum cum eum committere habuit,* in Italian, 'commetterebbe' (he/she would commit). This solution is not used in southern Italy.

129 THE ARTICLE

The story of the article—that pronominal adjective without semantic weight but still vital even up to our own times—is very important. The raw material consists of two types. The first and more ancient is taken from IPSU and has been retained exclusively by Sardinia: the basis is the singular *(i)ssu, (i)ssa,* and the plural *(i)ssos, (i)ssas.* The Campidanese (in Sardinia) plural is *is* for both the masculine and the feminine. In order to interpret these phenomena correctly, it is of fundamental importance to recognize the analogous documentation of the Abruzzi: *së lupë, së ditë,* 'il lupo', 'il dito' (Pescasseroli), and *sa gallina, sa cauda,* 'la gallina', 'la coda'. In addition to this analogy demonstrating a conservative element in Abruzzi areas, the reader will find below (§137) another example illustrating the conservation of occlusive consonant groups containing L, a characteristic found also in Sardinia.

Of a different nature but nonetheless pertinent to the article is another phenomenon of conservation which preserves the distinction between the grammatical masculine gender and the neuter in a zone that extends from southern Umbria to the Bari-Matera line.[8]

The following oppositions have been preserved up to modern times: in Norcia *lo mèle* 'il miele' (the honey, neuter) as opposed to *ru cane* 'cane' (the dog, masculine); in Nemi (Rome) *o latte* (neuter) but *u lopë* 'lupe' (masculine); in San Felice Circeo (Latina) *ju canë* (masculine) and *lu mèlë* (neuter). Elsewhere there remain traces of the difference between the Latin type (IL)LU(M) CANE(M), which in Naples becomes *o canë* (masculine) without any trace of the final consonant of the article, and *(ill)ud mele(m)* which becomes *o mmelë,* with the assimilation of the final consonant -D, still very much alive.

If we keep in mind that in a restricted "oasis" in central Italy a distinction was maintained between the final -o and -u (which merged throughout the rest of Italy, §114), then it is clear that with regard to the question of the article there coexisted for a long time a network of relationships of both a morphological (as illustrated by the persistence of the neuter gender) and a phonetic order (as for example the resistance of distinguishing vocalic timbres at the end of words or of certain consonants such as the -D, which, with its strong morphological value, was resistant for a relatively long period).

130 REPLACEMENT OF THE DECLENSION

In the field of syntax the transformation of the language of Italy from Latin schema to modern schema is profound and laborious. I shall limit myself here to placing in time the most essential features of three processes. Within the sentence, there is the establishment of a system that takes the place of the declension, through the use of prepositions that almost become prefixes. The system is based on six fundamental prepositions, three local (DA, IN, A) and three modal (CON, DI, PER), of which five continue a Latin tradition and only one, DA, represents an innovation. Here also phonetic conditioning has intervened because it was not possible to escape the necessity of substituting the preposition *a(b)*, which had grown too weak. Naturally, within the group of more morphologized prepositions there is a whole constellation of specific prepositions that have more personality, both semantically and phonetically.[9]

Another effect of the dissolution of the declension is provided by the need to accept a system of indirect syntactical markers, such as word order; in comparison with the free word order in Latin, the pattern subject + predicate + object in Italian is practically binding. A vestige of the traditional final position of the verb appears often only in Sicilian.[10]

Finally, in the syntax of the sentence the most important innovation comes from the development of the gerund as a ready substitute for the dependent causal or temporal clause. The first examples of this construction are of the type *sol calando,* which call to mind the models of the Latin ablative absolute.[11]

Twenty-seven

Germanisms

131 Ancient Germanisms

With regard to the structures of the language of Italy, the contrast between the scarcity of sources and the profundity of the changes that we *must* assign to these "dark" ages could not be greater. It must be noted, however, that while a good deal has been done to bring into the light of understanding the forces that are shrouded in a veil that corresponds to the uninterrupted cultural tradition, other new forces that entered into the network of Italian linguistic traditions and originated not from inherited tendencies but from outside have still not been taken into consideration. We are speaking of the infiltrations and imbalances caused by the barbaric pressures in the long period that stretches from the third to the ninth century, from the isolated arrival of Germanic words to the institutions, organizations, and perturbations that are linked with the establishment of the barbaric states, the most important of which is the Longobard.

These forces have a profound effect: from the negative point of view they destroy the old balances and institutions; from a positive point of view they are the bearers of several hundred new words, which were absorbed both as common and proper nouns by the Roman population; finally, they stimulate the establishment of new institutions, structures, and activities. They are not very important, however, as far as the linguistic structures and their unconscious transformations are concerned, partly because the successive barbarian populations, though they constituted a significant superstratum, never exceeded a few tens of thousands in population and were demographically insignificant. First of all, it must be stated that opinions such as those of W. V. Wartburg,[1] who was in favor of phonetic influences of Germanic inspiration, are unacceptable, not because they are intrinsically impossible, but because there is not sufficient evidence of them in the interplay of the ethnic forces that are in opposition to each other: this is the case above all with regard to the formation of Italian diphthongs, which have been explained above (§112) in quite a different manner.

There are no negative proofs that exclude Germanic words from the Latin vocabulary during the period of the empire. The claim that whenever these words are missing in Sardinian or in Rumanian they cannot have been introduced during the period of the barbarian invasions does not hold up because Sardinian was rather early on cut out of the mainstream of lexical currents—and of linguistic currents in general—emanating from Rome. As for Rumanian, it is evident that from the beginning of the fourth century Roman words no longer reached Dacia within the framework of the internal relations of the empire: Dacia was by now vacated.

If, however, we do not have conclusive arguments that would exclude Germanic words from the Latin lexical system of the empire, neither do we have arguments that would make it possible to accept their entry into the Latin lexicon of the empire whenever they are not directly attested to. Therefore, we must content ourselves with ancient Germanic barbarisms of the following types: *alces* and *urus,* typical animals of the forests of central Europe, and *glesum* and *framea,* as the names for amber and a weapon comparable to the lance. Similarly the Italian names for the marten *martora* and the badger *tasso,* characteristic animals, and the word *vanga* 'spade' definitely date back to the period of Vulgar Latin. The opinion that several names of colors, learned through the terminology of the barbaric cavalries that had been enlisted by the Roman legions, belonged to this group of words, was widespread. But a recent study by Anna Giacalone Ramat has reshaped this assertion and has made a more recent chronology probable;[2] *biondo* is an exception, since, unlike the others, it must be linked with the term *Blondelius* of the Tavola di Veleia (§32) and hence considered as a Lepontic word. The same is true of *bitumen.*[3]

132 GOTHIC WORDS
The first wave of Germanic words after the end of the Roman Empire

is comprised of Gothic words.[4] Within this group of words the geographic distribution permits us to distinguish among Visigothic words (when they are attested to also in France or in Spain) and Ostrogothic words (when there is evidence of them only in Italy). Military terms such as *banda, guardia, elmo, albergo* (which derives from a form of HARI-BERG 'army shelter'), *arredare,* and *corredare* belong to the first group. Domestic utensils are represented in the lexical heritage of western Gothic origin by *(n)aspo, rocca,* and *spola.* Important verbs are *recare,* and *(s)magare;* adjectives are *ranco* 'lamb' —from which we get 'arrancare' (to hobble, limp)—*guercio,* and *schietto.*

The following terms, on the other hand, belong to the Ostrogothic group: *arengo* 'assembly place', *astio* (from HAIFSTS 'dispute'), *lobbia, stia,* and the names of certain utensils such as *stecca, briglia, fiasco, nastro,* and *stanga. Forra* refers to certain land formations. An example of a verb is *smaltire* 'to allow to flow off, to get rid of'; and an example of an adjective is *sghembo.*

The most significant place name is *Goito* (Mantua); others are *Godego* (Treviso), and *Gottolengo* (Brescia).

Hidden behind place names are important personal names of Gothic origin: *Rovigo* comes from a Gothic form *Hrótheigs* 'victorious'; *Vidigulfo* (Pavia) can be traced back to *Widwulfs;* and *Roasenda* (Vercelli) derives from the form *Hrodasindis.*[5]

133 WIDELY DIFFUSED LONGOBARDISMS

The Gothic domination lasted only two decades, in contrast to the Longobard, which endures for two centuries.

Nevertheless, the Longobard population, while it had more opportunity to become established and to allow its lexical terminology to infiltrate or even to take over, also had greater opportunity to allow itself to become absorbed if not into the as yet fluid framework of the spoken language, then at least into the structure of the Latin tradition. Rotari's edict, which dates only seventy-five years after the beginning of Longobard rule, demonstrates this. With respect to the Longobard words that came into Italy, there are at times difficulties in distinguishing them from the Gothic words. The distinction is decisive only when we are dealing with Germanic words showing only the first consonantic mutation and words that also contain the second mutation: the first group is Gothic; the second, Longobard. This is the case with *panca* and *palco,* which are definitely Longobard, as compared with *banca* and *balcone,* which date back to Gothic models that were affected only by the first mutation.

From the point of view of semantic groups, military words such as *strale* and *spalto* must be remembered. The form *sguattero* has mili-

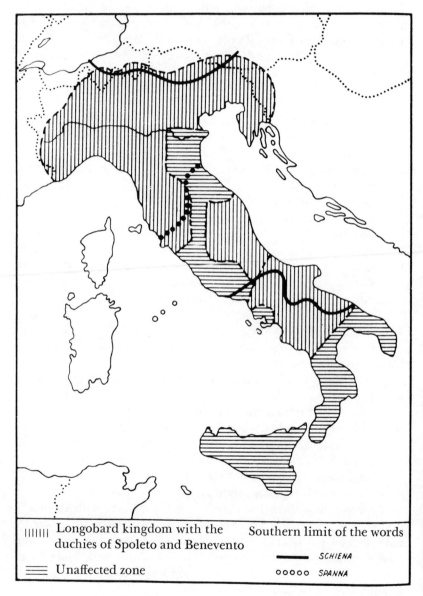

|||||| Longobard kingdom with the duchies of Spoleto and Benevento

≡ Unaffected zone

Southern limit of the words

▬▬▬ *SCHIENA*

ooooo *SPANNA*

Map 8. The Expansion of Longobard

(adapted from Wartburg, *Die Entstehung der romanischen Völker*)

tary origins, because it comes from the Longobard *wahtari* 'guardian'. The forms *staffa* and *predella* can be traced back to the Longobard cavalry, the latter having originally indicated a bridle, which in its Italian form, 'briglia', is a Gothic word, as we have seen. As A. Giacalone Ramat has shown, we derive the forms *bianco* and *bruno* from the colors of horses.[6] Turning to the category of housing, we note the form *stamberga*, which originally indicated 'a shelter made of stones', and therefore something solid. Other words of Longobard origin are *scranna, scaffale*, and *stucco*. Utensils are *gruccia, greppia, spranga, trappola*, and even the word *palla*. Of great importance are the terms that indicate parts of the body; among the most significant that attest to a cohabitation if not exactly a blending we note *guancia, ciuffo, zazzera, grinza, schiena, nocca, spanna, stinco, milza, anca* (and *sciancato*); pertaining to animals are *grinfia* and *zanna*. *Stambecco, tonfano*, and *melma* refer to nature; *gualdo, cafaggio*, and *gaggio* refer to the woods and are used frequently in toponomy. Indicative of social status (and not eulogistic) are *gastaldo, sgherro, scalco (maniscalco)*, and *manigoldo*.

Verbs are *(im)bastire, gualcire, spaccare, strofinare, spruzzare, guernire, (ar)raffare, scherzare, tuffare*, and *russare*. Adjectives are *gramo, ricco*, and *stracco*.

Nouns ending in *-engo*[7] are toponomastic clues to the presence of the Longobards. They constitute three constellations or groups in Monferrato, Bergamasco, and Cremonese: examples belonging to the first group are *Murisengo* and *Marengo* (Alessandria), *Alcenengo* (Vercelli); to the second *Vidalengo, Martinengo* (Bergamo), *Pozzolengo* (Brescia); and to the third *Romanengo* (Cremona). Centrally located with regard to these three groups is Pavia. Other Longobard toponyms are *Fara, Salda*, and *Braida*, with the variant *Brera*.

Personal names of Longobard origin are *Anselmo, Arnaldo, Arnolfo, Baldovino, Bernardo, Bertrando, Ildebrando, Federico, Garibaldo, Giraldo, Umberto, Teobaldo, Gualberto, Guido*, and *Guglielmo*. After the beginning of the Carolingian period, Longobard names do not prove anything about the establishment of Longobard rule or settlement in Italy. In a diploma of 912 we find the following words written about a servant: *nomine Aregisum cum uxore sua Adelinda et filio suo Adelardo*: they indicate that by this time Longobard names had been relegated to the lower classes,[8] and no longer had ethnohistorical value.

134 PARTIAL LONGOBARDISMS
It is impossible to imagine that the vulgar tongue, which was escaping and trickling away in innumerable parochial rivulets, was influenced

by a unitary Longobard accent. We have only two examples in which a blending occurred, not so much between a Longobard model and the many Vulgar Latin models, as between a Longobard model and a "Latin" model. The Latin words in question are *vadum* 'ford' and *vastare* 'to spoil, ruin', the beginnings of which are treated as if they were Longobard words. Indeed, there ought to have existed opposite the forms *vadum* a theme like WAD 'ford', which survives today in the German *waten* 'to ford'; similarly, a theme WOSTI, which survives today in the German form *Wüste* 'desert' ought to have paralleled the form *vastare*. These examples demonstrate an affinity that fostered casual rapprochements, rather than a uniform imposition of a Longobard pronunciation.

The fact that on the linguistic level the Longobard heritage was unilateral, and basically not very important, must not minimize the very great value that the Longobard experience had in the history of Italy. Indeed, even among the Italians of today two types of temperaments are distinguishable: those whose forefathers had lived through the harsh Longobard experience, so full of turmoil, reactions, and stimuli to act and construct; and those who, not having known it, remained in the ultraconservative spiritual and economic sphere of influence of the Roman and Byzantine *latifundium*.

Precisely on account of its variety and mobility, the linguistic tradition of the Longobards was established in a way that differed considerably from the manner in which the Longobard political structure was imposed in Italy. The former gives the impression of an advancing mass in which each of the constituent elements has a different spring that makes it go more or less far.

There are three principal types of partial diffusion. The type *schiena,* on the one hand, spread vigorously as far as southern Lazio and Apulia.[9] The type *spanna,* on the other hand, did not go beyond Tuscany and Romagna. Finally, the third type is exemplified by forms that survived in remote regions but disappeared in original Longobard areas: this is the case of *sarnacchiare* 'to snore', which is found in Tuscany and in the duchy of Spoleto, even if the territorial continuity was interrupted by the Rome-Ravenna corridor (§139).[10] Examples of forms that gravitate even farther toward the south are *uffo* 'flank, side', which extends from Perugia to Taranto, and the Abruzzese form *seneide* 'boundary stone' which is limited to the Abruzzi.[11]

135 INDIRECT CONSEQUENCES
The Longobard linguistic impact was also indirect. In organizing a new state, the Longobards began to overcome the dialectal boun-

daries, not only those between parish and parish within individual duchies, but also between duchy and duchy, thus neutralizing to a certain degree the importance of the boundary which the reform of Diocletian had assigned to the Apennine watershed ridge between LaSpezia and Rimini. Thanks to the unifying action of the Longobards, innovations that were characteristic of northern Italy spread to Tuscany: this happened with lenition which was introduced in a good many Tuscan words. Voiced velars are found in *luoGo, aGo,* and *laGo,* which normally should have produced forms like LUOCO, ACO, and LACO. Voiced, rather than voiceless, dentals appear in *poDere, spaDa,* and *scuDo,* as opposed to the verb *potere,* which was born and developed on the spot, and SPATA and SCUTO, which theoretically should have been the regular forms. The voiceless labial appears as voiced in the case of *Befana* (which represents lenition in the intervocalic position deriving from the form LA(E)PIFAN-) and indeed as a spirant, in accordance with the northern type of development, in *caVezzo* as opposed to "caPestro" and in *VescoVo* in contrast to (E)PISCOPU.

The Genoese term *scöggiu* (Latin SCOPLU) owes its arrival in Tuscany to this capacity of the Longobards to spread and level out; *scöggiu* was adopted in Tuscan in the form *scoglio,* and is opposed to the normal treatment in central Italy of *scoppio,* which survives in place names such as *Scoppio,* a hamlet of Acquasparta (Terni) and in *Scoppito* (province of Aquila).

The current continues to flow even in post-Longobard times along the pilgrimage routes from the Cisa pass to Grafagnana, Lucca, and Siena. In Siena we find a text which contains *fadiga* for 'fatica', just as a Latin text had *madodinos* for 'matutinus'.[12]

Twenty-eight

The Franks and
the Byzantines

136 FRANKISH WORDS

At the end of the eighth century the Longobard era was succeeded by the age of the Franks, which is personified first by the Emperor Charlemagne, and then by the Carolingian dynasty. In this new wave of Germanic terms there are two difficulties present: the first is that Frankish terms are not easily distinguishable from Longobard words on the basis of formal characteristics; the other problem, of an opposite nature, is that Frankish words belong to a Germanic tradition that is by now strongly blended with the Gallo-Roman.[1] From the formal point of view, the only indication of a distinction lies perhaps in the characteristic evolution of the voiced bilabial consonant, which in Longobard words shows a preference for the form GU + vowel, as we see in *guardare, guarnire, guadagnare,* and *guanto,* while we would expect Frankish words to have "French" markers of the type G + vowel, as we see for example in the word *garantire.* Unlike the Longobards, who actually succeeded in blending their linguistic tradition with the Roman, at least in certain zones, the Franks have the characteristic of being a dominant superstratum which exerts an influence from above. Military terms that will serve as illustrations are *battifredo, dardo, gonfalone, schiera, tregua,* and *usbergo.* Colors of Frankish origin are *biavo, falbo, grigio,* and *soro,* which derive respectively from the models BLAWA, FALWA, GRIS, and SAUR.[2] Political and social life is represented by the words *feudo* and *barone;* the word *ligio* also belongs to this group, even if it is a Germanic word imported into France in very ancient times and absorbed in Italy, therefore, as a sort of Gallicism. The term *marca,* which signifies a territory overseen by a "marchese," is similar. As examples of verbs we' find *galoppare, sparagnare* 'to save', *grattare, trescare* 'to dance', *ardire,* and *schivare.*

137 LINGUISTIC EXPANSION IN THE FRANKISH ERA

Precisely because they personified an authority with far-reaching power, the Franks penetrated the Italian culture less deeply than the Longobards had. Nevertheless, they reestablished in large measure communications and distant influences. While the Longobards proceeded mostly in, a southerly direction from the north, during the Carolingian period the major pilgrimage routes were active in both directions, thus spreading linguistic innovations not only in a southerly direction but also from the south to the north. The most characteristic of these southern linguistic features is the palatalization of consonant groups + L. The most simple solution is the Tuscan, which resolves the group in the respective succession of CHJ, GHJ, PJ, BJ, and FJ; examples of these are *clamare, glarea, platea,* BLUNDO-, and *flamma,* which evolved respectively into the Tuscan forms 'chiamare', 'ghiaia', 'piazza', 'biondo', and 'fiamma'. Examples of the type dental + L do not exist because, if they were prehistoric, they had already been transformed into CL, and if they were of secondary derivation (by means of syncope), they had given way to LL, as in *spalla* from SPAT(U)LA.

In northern Italy—in Piedmont, Lombardy, and Emilia—the phenomenon manifested a further evolution in the case of velars, but an arrested development at the Tuscan level in the case of labials. On the one hand, the northern types with labials—*piassa, biond, fiama* —evolve in the same way they do in Tuscany, while on the other hand we find the form *ciama* as opposed to 'chiama' and *gianda* as contrasted to 'ghianda'.

In the south, reinforcement of palatalization is manifested in another way. In the group velar + L, there is a "Tuscan" solution, as we see in types such as *chiave* (Latin *clavis*), or a blocking of palatalization as evidenced in the type *ljuttë* (Latin *gluttus*). In groups of labial + L there is the further palatalization of the voiceless consonant rendering *chianë,* and *chiù* for 'piano', and 'più', thus producing a blending with the results of velar + L. In the case of the voiced labial there is a disarticulation of the occlusive consonant after the palatalization of the L, and therefore we have *janchë* as opposed to the Tuscan 'bianco'. Finally in the case of FL, there is the total palatalization of the group into the single sound of the palatal sibilant, as we see for example in *sciamma* as opposed to the Tuscan 'fiamma'.

We find the most extreme development of these double tendencies in Liguria, where *cian* 'piano', which comes from the group PL, is not distinguishable from *ciama* 'chiama', which comes from CL; nor is it posible to distinguish *giancu* 'bianco', which derived from BL, from *gianda* 'ghianda', which derives from GL. The Ligurian form *sciama*, from FL, corresponds to the advanced southern phase *sciamma*.

The palatalization of groups containing L can intersect or become equated with other tendencies, for example with lenition, when the final vowel is resistant enough to allow lenition to appear and act. Thus there are the divergent results of the Lombard *öč*, without leni- tion and without the final vowel, and the Ligurian *ögiu* 'occhio' (eye) with the final vowel and the internal consonant having been affected by lenition.

The focal nucleus of this process must be sought in the Lazio region,[3] whence it spread along the pilgrimage routes, during the Carolingian period and following. In the process of spreading, how- ever, it came into contact with certain areas in the south and in Liguria that were particularly favorable with regard to the yielding of the labial articulations and where the extreme solutions of which we have spoken above took place. The above constitutes another argument for distinguishing a pre-Gallo-Italic phase from a successive Gallo-Italic phase in Ligurian Italy (§140).

In contrast to the greater or lesser acceptance of the palatalizing tendency of groups containing L, we do find foci of resistance that are more or less organic. They are three in number. The classic nucleus of resistance is "Sardinian" which in fact reinforces the L by changing it into an R: *crae* from CLAVE, *frori* from FLORE,[4] *greva* from GLEBA. As is the case for the article, the compact Sardinian area is matched by a number of isolated conservative areas in Abruzzi, in which the shift from L to R may or may not take place: *flumë* 'fiume' (river), *climë* 'inclinazione' (inclination, slope; from the Greek *klíma*), *plenë* 'pieno' (full), *graccë* 'ghiaccio' (ice); and similarly *planë* (Atri), *fleumë* 'fiume' (Penne), *ploverë* 'piovere' (to rain; Palena), *plazzë* 'piazza' (Teramo), and finally *frumë*, *frammë*, 'fiume', 'fiamma' (in Lanciano).

At the opposite extreme there is the large Friuli area in which we find *plan* 'piano', *flame* 'fiamma'; *claf, clamà,* and *clar* for 'chiave' (key), 'chiamare' (to call), and 'chiaro' (clear); as well as *glazze, glerie,* and *glesie* for 'ghiaccio', 'ghiaia' (gravel), and 'chiesa' (church), respectively.

The Friuli transmission of groups within a word demonstrates not that we are dealing with the passive preservation of an immobile Latin reality, but on the contrary with a process by which the liquid consonant is reinforced, so that the preceding occlusive is weakened, and, under certain conditions, eliminated: thus OCULI is reduced to (*v*)*oli* and GENUCULI to *zenoli* 'ginocchi' (knees). Once again we observe a linguistic parallel between Friuli and France, where the same process of preservation of the initial liquid takes place (as in *clair* and *glace*), as opposed to the simplification of the internal consonant (as in *oeil* from OCLU).

138 THE PAPAL STATE AND THE ROME-RAVENNA CORRIDOR

The spreading of the Longobard hegemony in central Italy did not impede Nature from taking its revenge and reestablishing geographic relationships that mirrored those of prehistory. The return of the marshes along the Tiber Valley resulted in the geographic justification of the linguistic boundaries which, as we have seen above, led to the distinction between a Tuscan Italy and an Umbran and Lazian Italy (§111).

But the eighth century signals yet another change from this point of view. With the beginning of papal temporal power, we witness the resumption of the political and even to a certain degree linguistic influence of Rome. During the Roman Republic, this sphere of influence ended at the frontiers of Etruria, after having established colonies at Nepete and Sutrium (§76); meanwhile it had pushed ahead in a northerly direction along the left bank of the Tiber, more or less along the route of the Via Flaminia. Aided by Byzantine protection, Rome succeeds in maintaining an active line of communication with Ravenna. Its course was analogous to the one that had linked it with the colony of Rimini from 268 B.C. on. The donation of Liutprand in the eighth century and the sense of direction that the papal state derived from it explain the moderate "southern" quality of the dialects of Umbria and the Marches. Roman pressure in the direction of Etruria is limited to two linguistic characteristics: the extension of the shift from ND to NN in Tuscan territory as far as Monte Amiata (§111) but not beyond; and the restriction to Tuscany of the shift from -ARIU to -AIO which, as A. Castellani[5] has shown, at one time extended even into Umbria and northern Lazio.

139 BYZANTINE WORDS

This influence emanating from Rome was greatly assisted by Byzantine efforts, which were aimed at keeping the Rome-Ancona corridor open for commercial and military reasons. From this it follows that the thesis of G. Rohlfs[6] is a legitimate one from a certain point of view; Rohlfs sees in this dividing line a criterion by which to classify Italian dialects. The Byzantine traces which remain in the lexical heritage of the language of Italy are also based on other forces, however, the first being that of our maritime republics. We are dealing here with Byzantinisms that "arrive" and consistently nourish our seacoast cities. In Genoa, for example, the word *basilico,* already well known in Rome at the time of Plautus, appears in reference to a characteristic herb with the Greek accent in the form of *bazgiaikò;* similarly the Greek name of *Philippos,* already familiar at the time of the republic, was accepted in Genoa with the normal Greek accent on the antepenult and gave life to the name Firpo. In the same order of dependence, Venice preserves *Tòdero,* accented like the Greek *Theódōros,* rather than with the Latin accentuation, which rendered the Italian Teodòro. A Neapolitan parallel is the word *Elmo,* which is an adaptation of the Greek *Érasmos,* with the accent on the antepenult, as opposed to the current form Eràsmo.

Quite independent of port towns, we can consider the following Byzantine forms together. First of all, let us list those connected with navigation. *Galea* and *molo* faithfully reflect the late Greek types *galéa* and *mólos; falò,* a hybrid growing from the two Greek forms *pháros* 'lighthouse', and *phanós* 'lantern', reveals its medieval formation by means of the passage from R to L (from *farò to falò*), which is characteristic of the Pisa area; *gondola* appears to be a cross of the medieval Greek form *kondûra,* a type of boat, with the Italian form *(d)ondola(re).* By means of Latin forms, the following words appear: *sartie* (late Greek *eksártion* 'complete ship equipment'), *àrgano* medieval Latin *àrganum,* a Byzantine form taken from the Greek *(t)à (ó)rgana* 'instruments'; *ormeggiare,* which comes from the medieval Latin form *hormizare,* is the Greek verb *hormízein,* taken from *hormós* 'anchorage'. One implement is the *mastello,* a diminutive form of the Greek *mastós* 'breast', a Byzantine noun, born perhaps in Ravenna and indicating a vessel having the characteristic shape. With regard to construction we find *androne,* originally a passageway reserved for men (Greek *andrōn, -ōnos); ancona,* a cross between the Byzantine Greek *(e)ikóna* 'image' and *ánkōn, -ōnos* 'fold, bend, curve', signifying a 'niche for (sacred) images'; *làstrico,* which is the Greek *óstrakon* 'fragment of pottery, shell' crossed with the Italian form *lastra* and themes ending in -ICO *(carico, manico);* and the Venetian form *squero* 'shipyard', which is a cross between the Greek *eskhárion* 'port of call' and the Italian *squadrare.* Going on to fabrics, we discover *bambagia,* which can be traced back to a medieval Greek form *bambákion,* and manifesting the evolution characteristic of the Po Valley (CHJO into GIO by means of SGIO); and *sciàmito,* which dates back to the medieval Latin form *hexàmitum,* which in turn derives from the Greek *heksámiton,* (a six-thread fabric), and contains the normal passage of CSA to SCIA. Vestiges of the Byzantine hierarchy are evident in *catapano* from the name of the Byzantine functionary who acted *kat'epánō* 'from above', whence we derive the name for the province of Foggia called 'Capitanata'; *straticò* comes from the Byzantine Greek form *stratikós,* which is based on the classical form *stratēgós;* finally the name of the province of Basilicata can be traced back to the name of the warrant officer who was called *basilikós* or 'royal (representative)'.

140 PRE-GALLO-ITALIC AREAS

In the light of all these opportunities to communicate and to attenuate and equalize the dialectal differences between more and less important territories, we must keep in mind that in the period of the tenth century, less exposed areas could have maintained a certain personality and autonomy, much the same way Tuscany did. The dialectal physiognomy of the Venetian estuary is striking from this point of view, and in it we include Grado and more or less blurred areas reaching inland. The typical features that have survived up to our own day have been well defined by Giulio Bertoni:[7] the absence of mixed vowels; of nasal, velar, or faucal consonants; of diphthongs in closed syllable; of many syncopes characteristic of the Po Valley. The broad acceptance of lenition and of assibilation were not ever able to impede the preservation and indeed the expansion inland of the Latin tradition of the Venetian estuary which continues up to the present day (§187).

As opposed to the Venetian area, which never became completely Gallo-Italic, there are the Ligurian regions which, according to historical evidence, were strongly influenced by the Gallo-Italic tradition. That a pre-Gallo-Italic Liguria existed is proved by the fact that at one time the Tuscan diphthongization—exclusively characteristic of open syllables—left traces in a small northeastern area, and inversely by the fact that a characteristic development occurred in Liguria which had nothing to do with Gallo-Italic tendencies, either with regard to the extreme palatalization of groups containing PL, or with regard to lenition which totally eliminates first the intervocalic L and then the intervocalic R, producing words such as *dû* 'dolore' (pain), *cû* 'colore' (color), *sû* 'sole', and *sâ* 'sale'.

Twenty-nine

The First Documents
in Italian

141 THE RELATIVE LATENESS OF DOCUMENTS IN THE VERNACULAR
If we consider that the majority of these classifications and reconstructions lack documentary confirmation and that they are based only on comparative historic and geographic considerations, we may ask ourselves why corresponding written documents were so slow in manifesting tendencies toward fixed, standardized forms (i.e., in practice not before the eleventh century).[1]

There are two reasons for this. The first lies in the fact that the distance between the vernacular and Latin became a conscious fact only after the Carolingian renaissance (§109) had propagated Latin texts that were so expurgated and standardized that the difference between them and the vulgar tongue became conspicuous. The second reason is that, notwithstanding the imposition by the Longobards of a new political structure, the cultural capitals of Italy had been maintained in the dioceses and the convents—sufficiently well so that documents and relics were preserved, but not strongly enough so that the newborn dialectal traditions, which were still fragmentary, could be consolidated, coordinated, and standardized. In Italy there is no trace of an ordinance like that of the Council of Tours in France (814), which officially establishes the preaching of the sermon in the vernacular.

142 THE INDOVINELLO VERONESE

The first consequence of this late documentation is connected with the slow and gradual shift from "Latin" structures to "Italian" structures. This makes it difficult to decide when we are faced with a text which is written in the vernacular but which is still rich in genuine Latin elements, and when, on the other hand, we have before us a Latin text permeated by vulgarisms. This is the case of the Indovinello Veronese, the riddle of Verona, discovered by Luigi Schiapparelli in 1924, and here given in the Monteverdi-Migliorini text:[2] *se pareba boves—alba pratalia araba—albo versorio teneba—negro semen seminaba.* This is translated 'they looked like oxen—they were plowing white fields—they were holding a white plough—they were sowing a black seed'; the parts of the riddle indicate hands, paper, a pen, and ink, respectively.

Certainly, the Latin is greatly distorted with the loss of the case endings -NT and -M, and with the vowels E and O in place of I and U(M) in *negro*. Nevertheless, in compensation we do find the final consonants -S and -N, the consonant -T-, which has not been affected by lenition (*praTalia*), and the -B- characteristic of imperfect suffixes. The word 'versorio' is still the Latin *versorium* rather than the vernacular *versor* which, as we can see from the Jaberg-Jud atlas (A.I.S.),[3] is still used today in the area encompassed by Torri del Benaco (Verona), Ponte nelle Alpi (Belluno), San Stino di Livenza (Venezia), Comacchio (Ferrara), and Cerea (Verona again). We are in agreement with B. Migliorini[4] that the Indovinello Veronese is not the first document of the Italian vernacular.

143 THE PLACITI CASSINESI

The texts of Cassino,[5] on the other hand, are decidedly Italian, even though they contain clearly distinguishable Latin elements. The four documents, which are very similar one to the other, are Capua, March 960: *sao ko kelle terre per kelle fini que ki contene, trenta anni le possette parte Sancti Benedicti;* Sessa, March 963 (in two versions): *sao cco kelle terre, per kelle fini, que tebe monstrai, Pergoaldi foro, que ki contene, et trenta anni le possette;* Teano, July 963: *kelle terra, per kelle fini, que bobe mostrai, sancte Marie è, et trenta anni la posset parte Sancte Marie;* Teano, October 963: *sao cco kelle terre, per kelle fini, que tebe mostrai, trenta anni le possette parte sancte Marie.*

These texts are in the vernacular, but not in a vernacular that is drifting aimlessly and splintered in a haphazard way, at Cassino, Sessa, and Teano. Rather, this vernacular has undergone a process of adjustment both from the point of view of space and social stratum.

From the point of view of space, the most famous form, *sao* 'I know', does not correspond to the present-day form *saccë,* which is the Latin sapio, and which the Jaberg-Jud atlas shows to be very diffused in the entire region.[6] M. Bartoli[7] has proposed that the form is a real though precocious literary "Italianism." A rather more prudent hypothesis is that the term was carried along the pilgrimage routes which spread Roman, and also more northern, forms abroad. These forms were valued for use in official documents such as the above-cited Cassino decrees, which were destined to survive and to be understood by all, even though they did not become part of everyday speech.

Similar processes of equalization with regard to fundamental verb forms are well known in the south. More recent and decidedly more relevant is the form *stao* 'sto' (I am, I stay) in Cielo d'Alcamo (§155), while analogous forms such as *abo* 'ho' (I have) and *dabo* 'do' (I give) are found in the diplomatic codex of Cava, which contains documents from the year 790 on.[8]

Another important form is *cco* (*ko*), which means 'that, which', because it balances with the Latin *quod,* which already during the empire was seen to correspond to the classical construction of the accusative plus infinitive (§§75, 85).

The inserted Latin forms *parte Sancti Benedicti,* and *parte Sancte Marie* figure instead as if they were quotations of proper nouns, in which the Latin case endings of the genitive singular are also included. That it is not a device is proved by the fact that similar forms such as Piazza San Giovanni and Via Garibaldi have survived up to the present day without the normal intermediary phrase with the preposition di.

The forms *tebe* and *bobe* are very important as a morphological testimony of the surviving pronominal declension. As for the spelling with b, this is neither a Latinism nor an archaism, but a reflection of the intermediary pronunciation b/v that is typical of the southern regions from ancient times.[9] That these forms were uprooted but surviving is demonstrated by the persistence of the forms *tebe* and *sebe* in the Ritmo Cassinese, a more recent document by two centuries (§48).

An important spelling problem is posed by the question of velars that are not subjected to palatalization. The use of k and of the digraph qu in the forms *ke* and *que* shows that both forms had equal weight in the Cassino texts. Before o, these expedients were not necessary, even though out of a desire for uniformity and an excess of zeal, there are also examples of *ko* alongside *cco* (Latin *quod*).

144 AWARENESS OF THE DIFFERENCE BETWEEN LATIN AND THE
VERNACULAR

Were the persons who wrote the Cassino decrees aware that they were
using the vernacular? As yet no explicit proof confirms this hypothesis. What we do find are indirect references elsewhere which are of
a decisive nature. In the "Gesta Berengarii," a poem dating from
before 923, it is noted that on the occasion of the coronation of King
Berengarius I (915), the senate chanted *patrio ore* (that is, in Latin),
while the masses shouted out *nativa voce* (in the vernacular). In 960
Gonzone, writing to the monks at Reichenau, speaks of the use of
nostrae vulgaris linguae, guae latinitati vicina est, and that is of a
language close to Latin indeed, but autonomous. On the epitaph of
Pope Gregory V, who died in 999, we find written *usus francisca
vulgari et voce latina—instituit populos eloquio triplici,* which
means 'he made use of the French language, the vernacular, and
Latin; he instructed the people in triple language'. Another document dating back to the tenth century but not more closely dated is
the formula of a penitential of Cassino who admonishes *fiat confessio
peccatorum rusticis verbis,* which means 'the confession of sins must
be made in the vernacular'.[10] Finally the Saxon Vitichindo states in
his chronicle that the Emperor Ottone I (died 973) knew the "lingua
romana," which is to say, the vernacular of Italy.

145 A LATIN "COMEBACK" IN THE ELEVENTH CENTURY

In contrast to this ferment and this awareness of Italian in the tenth
century, in the eleventh the evolution of a "new" language of Italy
suffers a setback; the blossoming of rhetorical studies based on Latin
puts a check on the frequency and the spontaneity of the use of the
vernacular.[11]

The attempt to substitute normal bourgeois clothing for togas
and ceremonial garb is slowed down, if not impeded. There appear doctrines and the applications of stylistic schema that are
linked to previous, though not identical, models belonging to the
"cursus" (§99).

The basic models are three in number. The Ciceronian style
abounds in metaphors, overlooks the "cursus," and is, therefore, inspired by classical patterns. The Gregorian style, so named in a
later era after Gregory VII, pope from 1187, fully accepts the "cursus," is inspired by models of the Imperial Age, and becomes the
forefather of the chancery language of the Roman Curia. Finally, the
Isidorian style, which is linked to the doctrines of Isidor of Seville
(sixth and seventh centuries) introduces a new rhythmical character-

istic, the rhyme. It appears in authors such as Guido d'Arezzo (990–1050),[12] Peter Damian (1007–1072), and others.[13]

Thus the resources that the Latin models offer to writers are enormous. The vernacular is something to be reckoned with phonetically and morphologically; but as far as style is concerned it has as yet nothing to say.

Thirty

The Establishment
of Italian

146 TUSCAN EXPANSION IN CORSICA AND SARDINIA
There did not exist a proletarian stasis beneath this high-level Latin mantle. The maritime republics, already making headway, represented elements of interregional cohesion. Because of its linguistic consequences, Pisan expansion at this time in both Corsica and Sardinia captures our attention. In Corsica it has the effect of dividing the island from north to south, so that the eastern forms of speech become substantially Tuscan, while the dialects of the western sector retain their original structure to a greater degree.[1]

From Corsica the Pisan influence spreads to northwestern Sardinia, where it draws the Sassari area under its influence and changes its linguistic characteristics, mostly by imposing upon it the Tuscan vocalic system, founded on the distinction between the two E's and the two O's that was already apparent in Vulgar Latin: thus at Sassari one says *pelu* rather than the normal Sardinian *pilu*, because the Vulgar Latin distinction (and not the Sardinian) between the open and the closed I, as we note for example in *filu*,[2] was introduced (§111).

147 ELEVENTH-CENTURY DOCUMENTS IN THE VERNACULAR
The documents of the eleventh century are six in number, of which

three are Sardinian. Of these the most important is the Privilegio of Lugodoro (1080–85), from which we here quote an excerpt: *E ccando mi petterun su toloneu, ligatarios ci mi mandarun homines ammicos meos de Pisas. . . .* The translation is as follows: 'And when the ambassadors who had been sent to me by friends of mine from Pisa asked me for the exemption. . . .' Basic features are the case endings of the plural in -s, the archaic verb *petterun* for 'to ask', along with an entirely different and isolated word like *toloneu,* which means 'customs'.[3] There are no instances of lenition; however, we do note the syntactical reinforcement that will later be eliminated by orthography.[4] The other two Sardinian texts are documents from Cagliari; one of these can be dated between 1070 and 1080 and is in Latin script, and the other is in Greek letters.

Of the three remaining documents, one is of southern Tuscan origin, another Roman, and a third Umbrian. The first, called the Postilla Amiatina, contains the article *illu,* with the ending still in -u (and not in -o), and a characteristic term such as *rebottu,* which probably means 'the evil one'. The spelling *coctu* for 'cottu' proves that the autonomy of the vernacular as a written language was still feeble and in a certain sense inferior to that of the Placiti Cassinesi that are older by a century.[5]

The inscription of San Clemente in Rome, published by A. Monteverdi in 1934,[6] belongs to the end of the century. It contains examples of final o's, not u's, as for illustration in *fàlite dereto colo palo,* which means 'lift it up with the pole'. We also note the passage of RB to RV in the proper noun Carvoncelle 'Carboncello', and a change of conjugation (from E to I) in the verb *tràere, traìte,* 'you pull'. Finally the confession of Norcia documents two facts that were already presupposed for the Umbrian-Lazio region in previous centuries, the distinction between the final vowels in -o as in *io, accuso, preso,* and *corno* and those ending in -u as in *confessu, battismu, diabolu, Petru,* and *Paulu.* The text also contains examples of metaphony determined by the final -u in *pùseru* 'posero', and by -i in *dibbi* 'debbi' (Latin *debui,* Italian *dovetti*).

148 Documents of the Twelfth Century

The documents of the twelfth century are more numerous, but the gaps to be bridged less important. Let us trace them from the north to the south. A document from Savona, probably dating from 1182, provides us with both phonetic and graphic testimony. Examples of graphic testimony are the use of x for the voiced palatal sibilant (French *j*) as we note in *prixun* 'prigione', and the more vocal digraph GU to indicate the voiced velar, intact before the palatal vowel: *brague,* which is written 'braghe' today. With regard to phonetic evolution we note palatalization linked to lenition (§§121, 123) as for example in *oregèr,* which today has been even further simplified into *uegè* for 'origliere' (cushion) ; and the palatalization of CT into IT, as for instance in *peiten* (Latin PECTEN) (§126), which today has been even more simplified into *peètene* (Italian *pèttine* 'comb').

For Tuscany the first examples of *-aio* (from ARIU) are found in a Volterra document on parchment dating from 1158; these examples are *nappaio* (plural *nappari*[7] and in a text from the mountainous Pistoia area, *dinaio* (of which the corresponding plural ought to be DINARI). In the same text we find the regular diphthongs *tiene* (from E) and *fuori* (from O). In the codicil of a Pistoia will there is the archaic form *arcipreite,* with the diphthong that has not yet been simplified into *-prete.*

The Laurentian Ritmo Giullaresco (1150–71) is clearly Tuscan, but the abundance of verbal derivatives in *-esco,* open the way for comparisons with Umbrian:[8] *Li arcador ne vann'a tesco. Di paura sbagutesco. Rispos'e disse latinesco: –Sten e tietti nutiaresco–.*

There are no traces of metaphony, or of words ending in -U.

Documents of the Marches indicate a broader connection with southern linguistic characteristics. The most important text is the Ritmo di San Alessio,[9] made up of 257 verses that have as a principal feature the distinction between final -U's and -O's; as a result it is possible to make distinctions in the field of morphology (between the masculine gender and the neuter), in pronouns, and in certain demonstrative adjectives. It also contains an archaic feature, namely, the retention of the group FL, as for example in *flore.* It merges with the Umbro-Samnite world by way of the passage from ND to NN. In a document of Fiastra (Macerata) in the Marches, dated 1193, we do find metaphony, both by -I in the case of *Carvone : Carvuni,* and by -U in the case of *questo : quistu.*

The Ritmo Cassinese brings us farther south and is a linguistic example of what has been called "campano illustre." In this text there is no diphthongization of the open E and the open O; the -O is distinct from the -U, and this exercises a metaphonic action; the B prevails over the V. The consonant groups followed by L are intact. *Fora* 'sarei' documents an archaic type of conditional, taken from the periphrastic form with the auxiliary verb in the pluperfect tense (§98).

149 FEATURES OF TUSCAN

From what has been said, it follows that Tuscany corresponded

(§16), as was already indicated in §111, to a region that was isolated in a spatial sense, weak from the point of view of social stratum, and out of the mainstream in a historical sense. The marshes of the Tiber and the Arno and the malaria along the Tyrrhenian coast contributed to the isolation. The absence of blending with preceding linguistic traditions also helps explain this meager quality. On the whole the Latin linguistic tradition was little disturbed.

Although Tuscany was shut off to the outside, within its own boundaries there did exist various degrees of openness. Pisa represented political power on the sea; Lucca had been the capital of a Longobard duchy and was located on an important pilgrimage route that led to Rome. Pistoia was situated close to an easy Apennine mountain pass, Collina. Arezzo was open to transalpine communication by way of Casentino and the upper Tiber Valley and to Umbria and Rome along the lower Tiber Valley and the Val di Chiana. Of all the Tuscan cities, the most isolated and the slowest to develop was Florence. Just as the Tuscan dialects can be defined in terms of the linguistic innovations—both northern and southern—that they did not assimilate, so the Florentine dialect can be called the one least affected by Tuscan innovations. The primary resistance consists of that phenomenon that has wrongly been called "vowel mutation," which is "vowel raising".[11] If in Florence one says 'lingua' and 'unto' (and not LENGUA and ONTO), this does not mean that the open ɪ or the open ʊ of Vulgar Latin, after having become the closed ᴇ and the closed ᴏ, respectively, became the ɪ and the ʊ again. *Lingua* and *unto* correspond to the uninterrupted tradition of Latin pronunciation which has continued up to the present day. Similarly, before a palatal ʟ the forms *conseglio* and *someglio* surround Florence, as do the terms *ponto* and *onghia,* but do not penetrate its boundaries. In the field of morphology, the possessive enclitic is already alive in Tuscany, as it is in other regions; illustrations are *mógliema* and *càsasa* in Florence, and *fratèlma* 'my brother' and *cognàtoma* 'my brother-in-law' at Siena.[13]

The major innovations that came from outside and spread all over Tuscany, such as palatalization of the groups of occlusive consonants plus ʟ (§137), were accompanied by the minor ones, for instance the acceptance of the forms of the voiced sibilant originating from the north. This latter becomes established first in western Tuscany, then spreads toward Florence without becoming firmly established there, although it continues to gain ground even today. A typical Tuscan innovation is that of -ᴀʀɪᴜ, which becomes -ᴀɪᴏ (§148), with the result that there is a dissymmetry between the forms of the singular (e.g., *denaio*) and the plural (e.g., *denari*). These forms are accompanied, therefore, by analogous forms with singulars like *contraro*.

Naturally Florentine innovations also exist, even though they are not very significant: an example is *atro* for 'altro' (other), which soon fell into disuse, and above all the passage of -AR- in internal position to -ER-: *Làzzero* instead of 'Lazzaro' which is then universally generalized in the forms of the future, as in *amerò* instead of AMARÒ.[14] Toward the middle of the twelfth century falling diphthongs are simplified from EI to E: PREITE becomes 'prete'. More than for its permanent characteristics, however, the Florentine dialect of the thirteenth century is interesting because of its grammatical uncertainties, as if dominated by the prestige of external speech forms. through the work of A. Schiaffini and A. Castellani[15] the following forms found in Florentine texts have been put in the proper perspective: *dissoro* 'dissero', *feceno* 'fecero', *metteno* 'mettono', *diceno* 'dicono', and *stra* 'starà', which refer respectively to Prato, Pistoia, Lucca and Pisa, and all give the impression that Florence was still a receptive area, open to broad possibilities of linguistic colonization that were rapidly absorbed only with the social, economic, and political maturation of Florence. Other forms, of a literary nature, are only occasionally documented. Examples of these are the types AU instead of O, snobbish forms modelled on Sicilian patterns: *aulire* for OLIRE (to be *fragrant*), *aunore* for '*onore*' (honor). Similarly, cases of lenition which presuppose the imitation of northern models belong to this category: *imperadore, etade, segondo*. The same criterion applies for imitations such as 'lalda' for *lauda* and 'altore' for *autore*.[16]

An anti-Florentine reaction appears in Siena, however, where, in opposition to the passage from AR to ER, we find the reverse process from ER to AR: this is evident in the type *vìvare,* which is opposed to the original Florentine form *vivere*.

150 THE FIRST ITALIAN PHONEMATIC SYSTEM

It is impossible to speak of an established equilibium and therefore of a linguistic system that is valid for the whole of the Italian territory. But on the eve of the assumption of authority by the Florentine dialect as the symbol of "Italian" in general, it seems opportune to establish the fundamental characteristics of the system that was consolidated in this period, and by this we mean the "first Italian phonematic system" based on Florentine and slowly taking shape from the ninth century on. Its features consist in developments that have been illustrated in preceding paragraphs: (1) Proparoxytones are eliminated in all cases in which the outcome of the ensuing phonetic encounter was in harmony with the speech habits of the speakers:

SOLIDU becomes *soldo* and NITIDU becomes *netto,* as opposed to NUMERU which becomes *novero* and not NOMBRO. (2) The open E and the open o are diphthongized in open syllables, at least in words used by the upper classes: METIT becomes *miete,* and NOVU becomes *nuovo.* (3) Final consonants are eliminated: METIT becomes *miete* and CAPUT becomes *capo.* (4) Consonant groups are assimilated in a regressive sense: CT becomes TT, as does PT: FACTU becomes *fatto,* and RUPTU becomes *rotto.* (5) Consonant groups + L are mildly palatalized as we see in the examples of CLAVE which becomes *chiave,* PLENU which becomes *pieno,* FLAMMA which becomes *fiamma,* GLAREA which becomes *ghiaia,* and BLANCU which becomes *bianco.* Other instances of palatalization belong only in part to an overall pattern: PLATJA becomes *piazza,* and MEDJU becomes *mezzo.* Yet HODJE does not develop beyond the form *oggi,* according to an association that has no parallels within the system and regarding which there is not a clear interpretation not even on a geographic plane. (MODIU becomes 'moggio').

Part Four

The Modern Age:
From 1200 to 1850

Thirty-one

Sicily and the First
Literary Language

151 THE ARABS

In the twelfth century Sicily becomes the most important region in the history of the language of Italy. After the invasion and coloniza-tion by the Arabs, Sicily had for three centuries relived the opposi-tion between an Arab western sector and the eastern coasts that had remained more or less within the Byzantine sphere of influence, just as in ancient times the Carthaginian western part of the island had been set against the Greek eastern part.

The importance of the Arab element in the Italian lexicon is enormous,[1] but it is difficult to establish which Arab forms were transmitted specifically through Sicily. Among this group of words we find *ammiraglio,* which in origin indicated a 'commander' not only in reference to the sea, *sciara* 'deposit of cooled lava (with sub-soil on which only bushes grow)' *zàgara* 'orange blossom', *càmula* 'moths (of various species)', *sciurta* 'sentinel', *bburgiu* 'haystack', *zappa* 'a measure of water', *zammataru* 'manager of a cheese factory', *rabba* 'public granary', *carabba* 'carafe', *cantusciu* 'woman's garment', *tarca* 'mourning veil', *bucecia* 'hen', *macaduru* 'dirty, filthy', *zizzu* 'elegant'. Verbs are practically absent. Family names are Vadalà, Morabito, Molè and others.

The large majority of Arab words in Italian are divided into two large categories: those coming from the Near East by way of the Italian maritime republics and those coming from Spain. In any case, as far as the lexical structure of the language of Italy is concerned, the one category blends with the other when we list words of Arab origin according to subject; words pertaining to technical matters are *azimut, zenit, almanacco, algebra, zero, cifra, alchimia, ricamo, tarsia, racchetta,* and *amalgama.* Those pertaining to foods are *elisir, sciroppo, giulebbe, zibibbo, melanzana, zucchero,* and *arancio;* with reference to commerce we have *arsenale* (in Venice), *darsena* (in Pisa and Genoa), *dogana, fondaco, magazzino, bazar, libeccio,* and *scirocco.* Examples of words referring to social life are *moschea, sultano, califfo, aguzzino, bagarino, assassino, camallu* (in Genoa), *ragazzo, baldacchino, zerbino,* and *giubba,* and two colors are *cremisi* and *scarlatto.*

In the twelfth century the dominant contrast in Sicily ceases to be between east and west and gives way to heterogeneous currents and pressures originating from the north.

152 THE NORMANS

In order to make an assessment of the innovations and trends that were to come in the thirteenth century, it is necessary to take into account the forces that assail and disturb the linguistic equilibrium of Siciliy during the twelfth century, greatly complicating the geographic map of the language of Italy. There are two complicating factors: the first comes from the upper classes, linking distant regions; the other is a force from the lower social stratum, which introduces into the northern part of the peninsula Italian linguistic nuclei that are capable of breaking the inherited continuity of the area, but not strong enough to constitute new bonds.

The first of these factors was the Norman invasion. Their successful establishment in Italy during this period was rapid. In 1030 Rainulf obtained the land of Aversa near Naples. Thanks to the efforts of William "Braccio di Ferro," the Duke of Melfi; Robert Guiscard, the duke of Puglia and Calabria; and finally Roger II, king of Sicily (1130), within the space of a century all of southern Italy came under Norman domination, with the result that the Arab tradition in Sicily was entirely eliminated and the Byzantine influence on the peninsula greatly restricted. The linguistic tradition that the Normans brought with them was French; their social tradition was identified with the feudal system. A considerable number of Norman French terms were added to the Gallicisms that had been imported into Italy during the Carolingian age (§136); however, it must be noted that we are not in a position to distinguish the one group from the other. The Crusades further fostered linguistic contacts with France. At this point it is legitimate to ask if the Normans, in unifying the south of Italy in an administrative sense, were the originators—the distant originators—of a process of linguistic unification. In the main the answer to this question must be negative. When we are dealing with documents of linguistic activity already at the literary stage (§154), as in the following Swabian period, then we can perceive that the preceding unifying force was still in its infancy. The cultural level was high; the linguistic material was often foreign; and Italian linguistic elements found in the Norman society were only occasional. That notwithstanding, a Norman period did exist, and G. Bonfante[2] has illustrated that point quite well.

The elements that allow us to define the Norman phase are as follows. The first is provided by the contrast between the testimonies of the northern Calabrese dialects that preserve lexical units that are more archaic than those of the Sicilian dialects; the latter have *baddaghjari* 'sbadigliare' (to yawn) as opposed to the northern Calabria form *alare,* 'dumani' as contrasted to *craj,* 'lesina' as opposed to *scugghja,* 'testa' in contrast to *capu,* 'avantieri' as opposed to *nustiertsu,* and 'vottsu, gozzo' as opposed to *cagnu.* These elements allow us to justify the arrival in Sicily of linguistic innovations by way of the sea, and more specifically from ports north of Naples and Rome. These elements that can be linked to the Norman movement for "geographic" reasons are accompanied by other elements of a social nature. Although "Norman" linguistic innovations do indeed reach Sicily, they become established only in the upper social circles of the court and the literary milieu, without permeating the lower social strata which continue to use, even today, lexical forms of a previous period. This is the case with the term 'andari', which was accepted into the language of the Sicilian poets but did not filter downward to eliminate the preexisting synonym *iri,* still used today. The same applies for 'sentiri', which did not supplant the form *audiri;* and for 'volta', which was accepted in high society but which did not succeed in eliminating *fiata.*[3]

153 GALLO-ITALIANS IN SICILY

Of an entirely different order is the course of effective colonization that does not impose itself as a superstratum but that becomes established as a demographic stratum beside that already existing. This demographic colonization, already prepared during the twelfth century and further developed in the thirteenth, was certainly broader than the colonization now recognizable through the "Gallo-Italic" dialects of Siciliy. The "Gallo-Italic" dialects recognizable today are differentiated into three areas, the inland region of the Piazza Armerina, the coastal zone on the Tyrrhenian of Sanfratello and Nicosia, and the Tyrrhenian-Ionian region between Patti and Taormina. It is quite natural that these linguistic traditions, totally devoid of cultural prestige, should have been destined to submit to the numerical supremacy of the original Sicilian traditions. Nevertheless, the following forms have succeeded in surviving up to the present day: (a) forms without the final vowel which had already been lost in their northern places of origin (this does not apply to the A); (b) lenition of the voiceless palatal before a palatal vowel producing the voiced palatal sibilant SG, and of the labial -P- producing a -V-; (c) the loss of -L(L)- after a vowel and before an O or E. Examples of these features are as follows: *pet* 'petto' (breast), *dorm* 'dormo' (I sleep), *asg* 'aceto' (vinegar), *savòr* 'sapore' (flavor), *pau* 'palo' (pole), *castue* 'castello' (castle). Moreover, the exaggerated reaction of the initial L- proves that the comparison with Sicilian schema was constant and perhaps even polemic; without any direct influence the initial -L is transformed in an exaggerated way and with regressive action, producing the form *det* for 'letto' (bed).

It has been supposed that the "less southern" quality of the Sicilian dialect can be ascribed to this colonization from the north.[4] But, it must be noted that the "less southern" quality of Sicilian does not reside in the strongly innovative features inherent in the northern patterns, but rather in those conservative original elements that were highlighted as a result of contrast with Norman elements. The northern colonization of Sicily was made up of very many isolated episodes that could not have, for reasons both social and practical, given new life to the linguistic environment that was taking shape in the preceding centuries.

154 GALLO-ITALIANS IN LUCANIA

The linguistic equilibrium reached in Lucania was quite different. It is true that the technique of colonization was not intrinsically different. Still, it must be remembered that the absence of a court and the social inferiority of the region resulted in the sheer numbers of speakers enjoying a greater freedom of action in view of the meager prestige of the preexisting society. In Lucania we speak of a Gallo-Italic "area" west of Potenza, and at Picerno and Tito, rather than of colonies; this Gallo-Italic area constituted an autonomous whole within Lucania that was influenced but not changed by the environment that hosted the "colonies." Its characteristics are three: limited metaphony, that is, metaphony determined only by the final -I (and not even by the -U) which is characteristic of the north; "full-scale" lenition; and the loss (not the reduction) of the final vowels. Thus, at Picerno, we have the nonmetaphonical singular *porchë,* as compared with the metaphonical plural *purc'* 'porci' (swine), and the singular *tsopp* 'zoppo' (lame) and the plural *tsupp* 'zoppi'. We discover similar results at Trecchina even though they are qualitatively dissymmetrical with the overshadowing of the E by I and the diphthongization of the O into UO under the metaphonical action of the -I (but not of the -U): thus we have the normal form *freddu* as contrasted to the metaphonical *friddi,* and the singular *mortu* in opposition to the plural *muorti.* But as we proceed in a southerly direction, we note that the final vowels react according to the tripartite pattern that had been transmitted in Sicily without interruption.

As for lenition, there are partial examples at Tito and at Trecchina such as LOCU, which becomes *luoghu,* STOMACU, which becomes *stomaghu,* or instances of total lenition such as MOLLICA, which becomes *modìa,* or MICA, which becomes *mia.* Parallel changes with dental or labial consonants are all partial: for example, we find NEPOTE, which becomes *nevodhi,* PRE(S)BIT-, which becomes *prèvidhu,* MARITU, which becomes *maridhu;* SAPERE, which becomes *savè,* and finally RAPA, which becomes *rava.*

While the Gallo-Italic colonization in Sicily did not produce repercussions on the classification of the Sicilian dialects, in Lucania the Gallo-Italian colonies constituted a sort of wedge that deepened the division between the northeastern areas, which were clearly very similar to Puglia as far as metaphony, blurred final vowels, and absence of lenition are concerned, and the southern areas, in which the final vowels are still clearly pronounced, as in Sicily.

155 The Court of Frederick II in Palermo

The sphere of influence which the Norman court begins to extend over Sicily reaches its climax in the first half of the thirteenth century with the Swabian court, whose basic quality is its open-door policy toward poets and the most diverse cultural currents—from France, from Provence, and from southern Italy as well as from Sicily itself. In contrast to the variety of dialects available and the Latin revival inherent in the rhetorical studies of the eleventh century, the court of Frederick II offers for the first time a suitable environment, capable of resisting both the prestige of Latin and the fragmentary quality of the local linguistic traditions. It elevates these local forms of speech to a literary level, at the same time rescuing them from traditional geographic limitations. The prestige that the vernacular derives from this process was no longer measurable according to the vertical dimension of tradition and time, but according to the horizontal dimension of space.

For this influx and circulation of ideas and words to be lively and viable, however, it was necessary that this high-level cultural ambient be accompanied by a fairly strong administrative and political structure. This strong political and administrative base was indeed provided by Frederick's court, thanks to the relationships the imperial authority was able to establish, nurture, and defend.

The receptivity to various linguistic models, minor traditions, and individual poetic sensibilities could not have occurred as a result of artificial or impulsive measures; rather they grew out of a nurturing of existing impulses which can be called "Sicilian" though they are heterogeneous, on which the court acted discreetly to coordinate and promote.

The victory over Latin did not occur as a result of the speech forms of the lower classes triumphing over the high-class tradition, but rather by means of a coexisting stratum which was not universal but influential because of the Franco-Norman traditions on the one hand and the lyric poetry that spread from Provence throughout Europe on the other.[5]

The first half of the thirteenth century—and especially the three decades of Frederick's reign—represents the maturity of this process which integrates the Franco-Provençal current with the currents and models of southern Italy, and, through dynastic links, with northern Italy. Pier delle Vigne (1190–1249), who was born in Capua and educated in Bologna and who became Frederick's prime minister, personifies the multiplicity of these traditions.

The coexistence of different traditions assures or imposes the possibility of particular linguistic variants: a Provençal form like 'amori' stands beside a genuine Sicilian form like *amuri*.

In this process of linguistic settling, the Latin tradition acts as a lexical and phonetic reservoir in all cases where, for rhythmical or other reasons, parallel forms are called for; therefore, if not always for reasons immediately evident, we find beside the Sicilian form *chinu* the Latinate form 'plenu', beside the Sicilian *quanno,* the Latinate 'quando', and beside the Sicilian *chiù,* the Latinate 'plu'.

Precisely because political conditions played a decisive part in the establishment of a new but flexible equilibrium, the new tradition cannot be identified with any real locale, not even with the capital city of Palermo. The whole of southern Italy, even beyond Sicily, functioned as the space within which the linguistic encounters took place, with the result that the most varied hypotheses regarding the expansion of the so-called *lingua poetica siciliana* can be justified. Here are some examples of the problems that appear in single authors.[6] The beginning of the tradition coincides with Jacopo da Lentini and his first poem "La amoranza disiusa," whose historical precedents date back to the middle of the twelfth century. In accordance with the author's origins, the poetry of Giacomino Pugliese contains peninsular tràditions. Guido delle Colonne (died 1287) left us two canzoni, "Anchor che l'aigua per lo fuoco lassi" and "Ancor che lungiamente m'ài menato," which Dante cites as examples of native authors capable of writing verse with decorum. The poetry of Stefano Protonotaro, which belongs to the middle of the thirteenth century, contains forms that are typically Sicilian, as in *di chi eu putìa sanari,* and *disìa d'amari e perdi sua spiranza*; Gallicisms such as *ma beni è da blasmare* or *m'eu duttu fortimenti;* and in addition, even an adaptation of the Provençal *mirador* in the line *di chi fa la tigra in illu miraturi.* In the contrasto of Cielo d'Alcamo, we discover a direct confrontation between the spoken and the written forms, for example in the verses *addomannimi a mia màre e a mon peri,* and *arrenneti donna col viso cleri,* in which we find on the one hand the typical southern spoken evolution of ND into NN, and definite Gallicisms such as the erudite forms *cleri* and *peri.*

If it can be said that the circumstances that brought about the success of Sicilian poetry were political, then it must also be pointed out that the circumstances that brought about its downfall were also political. With the end of the Swabian dynasty, the power that had sustained the unstable, heterogeneous, and hardly definitive equilibrium of the language of the Sicilian poets declined. The poetic world of the Sicilians and their linguistic tradition, which had grown only to partial maturity, ended together.

Thirty-two

The Dawn of Literary
Languages Outside Sicily

156 UMBRIAN EXPERIMENTATION

The need for a literary language in the vernacular begins to make itself felt also in other regions. This is the case of the "Cantico di Frate Sole," in which a cultivated man like Saint Francis of Assisi (1182–1226) availed himself of the vernacular not only for expressive reasons. The impassioned religious element which is linked with Umbria swept away the obstacles of linguistic traditions and conventional artistic models and at the same time redeemed the vernacular and elevated it to the dignity of an expressive tool of high quality. Umbria reveals itself to be a favorable climate not only for the passive acceptance of linguistic innovations of this type, but also for their absorption and application. Not being as yet a dynamic society, however, it was not in a position to spread them beyond its own boundaries. A phrase like *Laudato sie mi Signore, con tutte le tue creature, specialmente messor lo frate Sole, (per) lo quale iorna et illumina noi per loi* combines its poetic power with the fascination of something that links the man in an exclusive way to his native land.

If, however, we seek to pinpoint the beginning of a tradition in Umbria, we must look rather to Jacopone da Todi (1230–1306), whose syncopated syntax corresponds to an internal mystical energy. But not even in the poetry of Jacopone do we discover a literary language

capable of rivaling the Latin tradition. Rather, the linguistic innovations of Francesco and Jacopone call the historian's attention to a
statement of principle—to an individualistic form of protest, if you
will—but they do not yet herald the advent of a new class to power.

157 LOMBARD EXPERIMENTATION

Unlike Sicily and Umbria, northern Italy did not have until the
thirteenth century the help of a political power that was sensitive to
cultural prestige, nor did it have the spontaneity inherent in the
Umbrian environment that was so warm and genuine. But northern
Italy was a region open to economic and cultural exchanges with
France, through the Provençal and French literary models that came
to be known and appreciated. As a result, Lombardy and Veneto
were in favorable positions to receive, assimilate, and become adjusted to these patterns. Even if we must reject the hypothesis
cherished by some in the past of the beginnings of a literary language
common[1] to the entire Lombard region, we must recognize an aspiration present in "Franco-Veneti" texts to escape from the provincial
and gaze upon broader horizons.

The following examples will illustrate the successive steps taken
in realizing this aspiration. At the end of the twelfth century the
Sermoni Subalpini show characteristics (§§114 ff.) heralded as typical
of the western sector of the Po Valley, as being already well established. Take for example the seventh sermon in which we read *per que
est apelà povre? Car Dominidè non est mia endeignos . . . de recevre
. . . zo que hom po far*. We already find evidence of the loss of the
final vowel (*hom, far*), lenition of intervocalic consonants, both partial (*povre*) and total (*mia*), and the assibilation of palatal consonants
(*zo* for *ciò*).

A greater effort appears in didactic poetry, for example, in the
work of Bonvesin de la Riva (1240–1313) and that of Giacomino
Veronese (second half of the thirteenth century). Even if we cannot
say that these poets succeed in creating a literary language that goes
beyond the limits of their dialects, still certain concessions with regard
to the Latin or even the central Italian traditions do appear by way
of the rare presence of final consonants other than -N, -R, -L, and -Z.
But a line such as this one of Bonvesin (v. 56)[2] *Quand tu mang' con
cugià* clearly has a local northern stamp, characterized by the energetic elimination of the final atonal vowels, and the palatalization
combined with lenition of the group CL producing G'. Indeed, the
verse "Giama Sancta Maria quella vergen beadha" shows palatali-
zation-lenition in initial position. Lenition of the intervocalic T is
effectively indicated by means of the voiced consonant followed by

H, which is an indication of impending spirantization. But these alterations and changes are still fluid. For example, in addition to the passage of L to R *in tug' li soi perìgori,* we find *miracui* 'miracoli' with total elimination. Inversely, Latinisms that are more or less justified appear. The same motive that applied in the Placiti Cassinesi (*parte sancti Benedicti*) may account for the form *sancta*; and in the phrase *plena plu* with the L intact, an archaizing fad may have been at work. Contradictory solutions appear in *flao* 'fiato', in which, in contrast to the FJ which belongs to the Italian literary language, we find instead the excessively conservative FL, along with the total lenition of the T. We find an extreme example of total lenition in *aiao* for 'aiutato' (helped). This language, which was sought after rather than realized, exhibits patches of conservatism and even Latinized forms destined to be submerged, as well as innovations that are not, however, definitive. Later a sort of normalization modeled after Tuscan forms resulted in the abandonment of forms with total lenition and certain metaphonical features. Thus we have the modern forms *creder* and *vedova,* which appear in place of the earlier forms affected by lenition *crèer* and *vèova,* found in the texts of these authors (§179). Similarly we find examples of plurals in '-osi', which supplant the metaphonical plurals in *-usi.* The heritage of Lombard didactic poetry, more relevant to the genuine speech patterns of the area, comes to an end, overwhelmed by an outside tradition with more prestige and vitality.

158 BOLOGNESE TESTIMONIES

The interest in Latin grammatical and rhetorical studies that matured in the eleventh century did not consist simply in a reactionary quality of detachment from the living linguistic reality. Indeed, it found in one Italian center, Bologna, a way of indirectly becoming part of this reality. This process of liaison had three stages. The first is represented by the *Glossa* of Irnerius (1055–1125), which furnishes the material and living substance, so to speak, by which Latin is linked to real life through legal material; the second stage is represented by Francesco d'Accursio (1182–1258/60) and his *Glossa ordinaria,* which brings to a close this process of rapprochement between juridical material and grammatical exigencies. The third phase, a decisive one, consists in the transfer to the vernacular of patterns that had up to that time been reserved for Latin, as if to indicate that now the vernacular system was comparable with Latin with regard to both uniformity and prestige. Guido Fava (born before 1190, died after 1243) is the first theorist of the vernacular. We possess two of his works: the *Gemma purpurea,* which is a collection of vernacular formulae dating after 1239,[3] and the "Parlamenti ed epistole," a broader work, dating between 1239 and 1243. In the light of this doctrinal prestige, it is not surprising that rhymes of the type 'come'/ lome', which would have been impossible in Tuscany, should appear as perfectly acceptable in Bologna, or that forms of lenition such as *savere* 'sapere' (to know) or *òvere* 'opere' (works), equally foreign in Tuscany, should have taken root in the city to the north.

159 ATTEMPTS IN TUSCANY

The linguistic experiments of Sicily and those of Lombardy (albeit to a more restricted degree) came to be in a position of complementarity with regard to the Bolognese focal nucleus. The former are characterized by a genuineness and spontaneity and constitute creative "anomalies" answering to the inspiration of individual poets; by contrast, the latter, devoid of contacts with a poetic reality and therefore an aggregate of empty units, strive for uniformity and "similarity." It was natural, therefore, that at a certain point a confrontation should take place between the living but disorganized forces of the vernacular systems and the overly organized but abstract patterns of Latin. This encounter was not an easy one. In making a first attempt, it was not enough to recognize the existence of a vernacular as opposed to Latin; it was necessary to realize how cohesive and consistent this structure was that was to be matched against Latin. Slowly the need for what would later be defined with so much severity as the "illustrious vernacular" came to be realized.

The first attempt at an illustrious vernacular form is that of Guittone d'Arezzo (1230–94).[4] He was inspired by Guido Fava in the matter of grammatical fervor. Guittone, however, did not cut himself off from the Latin models and other styles, feeling most comfortable with the "Isidorian" (§145). Moreover, he looked even further back to the "classical" models of Boethius and Augustine. He created a literary language characterized by three elements. First, there are sentences closed in themselves but linked by simple coordinate conjunctions such as *e, ma, però,* and *dunque.*[5] Second, we note a wealth of subordinate constructions within the sentence, with gerund markers which, together with other nominal forms of the verb, were frequently used in Latin texts of the twelfth century.[6] Third, his style is characterized by a broad vocabulary in which we discover widely accepted Umbrian forms such as *ono, alcono,* and *ciascono*; northern forms exhibiting lenition such as *savore* and *savèr*; and finally, Provençal forms such as *aucello, bealtà, miraglio* and *dibonaire.* The results he achieved were not definitive, and Dante, notwithstanding Guittone's receptiveness to nonlocal forms, thought him "provincial." Nevertheless, when we consider that, in an effort to set up a vernacular tradition of literary language, Guittone brought prose close to the language of poetry,[7] then we must recognize his full significance in the history of the language of Italy.

160 Contacts between Sicily and Florence

The fusion of Sicilian poetic efforts and Bolognese grammatical endeavors and the maturation and completion of Guido of Arezzo's attempts cannot be accounted for only by the fact that the court of Frederick and subsequently that of Manfred moved about from one location to another, spreading fashions and stabilizing contacts.[8] The decisive forces must have been something other than the courts, the schools, and the literary activities of isolated writers. They must have been personified by the "readers," who were anxious to familiarize themselves with worthy literary creations whose renown had spread beyond the frontiers of individual regions. This involvement in turn proceeded from a social transformation which, extending beyond the boundaries of restricted circles and becoming sensitive to these fashions and tastes, created a market. This phenomenon is verified in Tuscany where a large class of businessmen and artisans, aroused and interested, produced amanuenses, even before they did poets, gramarians, or scholars. Texts circulated and, in Tuscany, found an audience that read or listened, corrected, bought, and circulated them again in ever larger circles.

Thirty-three

Florence: Its Rise to Prestige

161 FLORENTINE "CONSTRUCTIVENESS"

This circulation of texts immediately posed some problems that were resolved only because the Tuscan reader was not an exclusionist. If the "learned" models of Bolognese stamp such as *podere* and *savere* were accepted for their intrinsic prestige, it must be remembered that forms like *nui* for 'noi', *saccio* for 'so', and *avria* for 'avrei' were also easily accepted, not for practical reasons but only to provide color—exotic, if not strictly Sicilian—to which the Tuscans reacted not with intolerance but indeed with indulgence. In contrast to the Sicilian texts the Tuscan model did impose certain phonetic re-touches, as in the case of the Sicilian rhyme *amuri/muri*, which did not stand up to the Tuscan opposition *amori/muri*. But in general the Sicilian model was not altered, because the two models had the clear pronunciation of final vowels in common and because the Sicilian was not considered foreign with regard either to phonetic structure or to harmony. Farther north the difficulties that result above all from the loss of the final vowels and the lenition of inter-vocalic consonants were greater but not insurmountable. In Tuscany favorable elements existed; therefore, non-Tuscan poetic texts could meet a supportive audience and more concentrated attention than was possible within the strict limits of regional boundaries. Tuscan amanuenses, linked to a culture that was interested in the literary activities of southern Italy, set up the bases for dialectal adaptation and modification which made it possible to accept as an integral part of the Florentine scene the poetry written in exotic regions so far from the heart of Italy. In the battle that subsequently ensued for the language of Italy a tradition of literary vernacular, the anonymous Tuscan artisan who determined the fortune of these amanuenses was the "unknown soldier"—forgotten but victorious.

All this was made possible by the Florentine "miracle," which, viewed from the twentieth century was a reproduction of both the Roman "miracle" of the fourth century B.C. and the contemporary Venetian "miracle" (§178). In Venice the work of reconstruction began on a waning linguistic tradition close to suffocation, with the result that the language was reestablished in Venice, expanded and exported—and here it is not important to specify whether on an international, national, or interregional level.

In addition to individual interests and enthusiasm, a process of political rebirth had in fact taken place, with the result that a remote, isolated city that was behind the times could, within the space of a few decades, come to be praised by Brunetto Latini (1220–94) for its *grande honore e la ricca potenza* (great honor and power), and was assured, with the victory of Campaldino (1289), even political supremacy in Tuscany. The political support that had been a determining factor for the cultural prestige of Palermo was also present, although to a less conspicuous degree, as a determining factor in Tuscany, especially with regard to its geopolitical center which had been established in Florence. Geographic centrality with regard to the rest of Italy constitutes a favorable element in the establishment and consolidation of this preeminence. An additional advantage consists in the relative closeness of Florentine linguistic structures to Latin; it facilitates the introduction of a mass of new words made necessary by the cultural blossoming and taken almost entirely from Latin texts.

162 THE TRADITION OF THE "DOLCE STIL NUOVO"

This cultural prestige consisted not only in poetic excellence but also in doctrinal importance. Guido Guinizelli (1230/40–1276), a Bolognese, after having abided by the ideals of Guittone d'Arezzo, became a follower of the Tuscan models. With the canzone "Al cor gentil ripara sempre Amore," there begins a tradition of poetic language which is associated with a new vision of new life in contrast to the achievements of the Sicilian school; it comes to be known as the "dolce stil nuovo." The poets of the sweet new style, bound as they are from the point of view of content to Provençal models, to scholastic philosophy, and to Umbrian mysticism, create a linguistic tradition that is characterized by strict terminology, bound by a fundamental sense of restraint, and not inclined toward that sort of linguistic receptiveness that in Guittone had given the impression of a certain cosmopolitanism. The word in itself dominates, as does the tendency to play with words and their etymologies, in accordance with a trend that appears in the *Convivio* by Dante.

The Stilnovist group is entirely Tuscan. The poetry of Guido Cavalcanti is distinguished by its particular and limited use of adjectives, a strong propensity for metaphor, an ability to place different styles side by side, and the literary consecration of the popular use of direct discourse.

163 DIALECTAL TEXTS OF THE THIRTEENTH CENTURY

Regardless of how much success the theory and practice of the school of the sweet new style enjoyed, it was necessary for the tradition of Italy's literary language to undergo other experiences in order to become established. The reader must keep in mind two realities. The first, an external one, is that the vernacular dialectal traditions were by now already well established, though not necessarily capable of extending their influence beyond their borders. The second point to be kept in mind is that, in order for the tradition of literary language to spread beyond the limits not only of the city but also of the diocese and even of the region, the prestige of one poetic personality was needed, in addition to the perfection of the doctrinal apparatus. This personality is Dante. The two prerequisites for the establishment of a national literary language are rooted in two problems. First, what was the actual consistency and the reciprocal divergence of the Italian dialects? And second, what position did Dante take with regard to the different dialects? The reconstructed picture, though incomplete, in which Dante had to take a stand, is the following, as it has been taken from a recapitulatory list by G. Vidossi,[1] in addition to the texts that have been taken into consideration above. For the Ligurian dialect there is the bilingual contrasto of Rambaldo di Vaqueiras; for Lombard there are Girardo Pateg, Ugo da Persico di Cremona, Ugguccione da Lodi, and Pietro da Barsegapé. For Emilia we have the regola and the lauda of the servants of the Madonna and the serventese of the Lambertazzi and the Geremei. In Tuscany the Sienese text of the *Libro di Mattasala di Spinello* is fundamental, and for Umbria the vernacular formulae of the notary Rainerio di Perugia; for the Marches we have the document of Fabriano and that of Picenum, as well as the canzone of Castra. For the Roman dialect the *Liber ystoriarum Romanorum* and the *Miracole de Roma* are important, while for Campania the *Inventory of Fondi,* the *Lament of the Virgin,* the *Statutes of the Disciplinati di Maddaloni,* and the *Book of Cato* are basic. The document of Rossano is the text for Calabria, all of the Sicilian poets for Sicily, and for Sardinia the rich harvest of legal documents called *Condaghi.*

164 DANTE'S CLASSIFICATIONS
By common consent the title of father of the Italian language belongs to Dante. In our attempt to describe the beginnings of that linguistic tradition that comes down to us from him, it is not so important to understand the final elaboration of one of his theories about the "volgare illustre," as it is necessary to know something about his psychology in approaching the problem of defining the vernacular. In order to understand this, we must go back to one of his first statements in the *De vulgari eloquentia,* in which he asserts conclusively that the major advantage of the vernacular is that it reflects "nature," while Latin is artificial. Similarly, in the *Convivio*[2] he justifies the use of the vernacular for the internal cohesion it gives when used in the commentaries to canzoni written in the vernacular, for its *pronta libertade* with regard to a larger audience, and finally—and this is very important—for the "natural love of one's own language." This love can be translated into the search for an ideal language that has neither the vulgarity nor the meaningless divergent quality of existing vernaculars, but which seeks instead to embody a certain kind of refinement and distinction, as well as a sense of unity that goes beyond municipal boundaries.

Dante sees the variety of Italian dialects as would one who, placing himself in the center of the Alps, imagines he is gazing down upon the entire Italian peninsula banked by the Tyrrhenian and Adriatic seas, and divided by the Apennines.[3] Dante specifies fourteen dialect varieties, of which seven are located on the western side of the Apennines, and seven on the eastern side. The criteria he uses to evaluate them, however, are neither objective nor functional, but rather dominated by his esthetic reactions, and sometimes by personal resentments. The most typical examples are his harsh judgment of the Roman dialect, which is "the ugliest of the vernaculars," and of Sardinian, which is so close to Latin that Dante thinks the Sardinians "incapable of creating a dialect of their own, and hence compelled by this incapacity to imitate Latin as if they were not men but monkeys." Genoese likewise is condemned; it is so rich in voiced sibilants (z) that if this sound were eliminated the Genoese would be forced to fall silent or look for another language. Despite these personal prejudices, Dante offers us direct testimony of important dialectal characteristics; for example, he documents for the Milan-Bergamo area the form *occhiover,* which exhibits the loss of final vowels typical of the Gallo-Italic dialects, and the palatalizations of the group CTO into CIO. Another example is the Apulian *volzera che chiangesse* 'vorrei che piangesse' (I would like him to cry), which documents both the passage of PLA to CHIA, and the conditional tense taken from a form of the pluperfect, VOLSERAM, which replaced the classical form *volueram.*

165 BOLOGNESE: BEYOND THE CONFINES OF A CITY DIALECT

After having rejected all the Italian dialects, including Florentine and the other Tuscan forms of speech, Dante adopts a rather indulgent attitude toward Bolognese, albeit by a cautious and tortuous line of reasoning and by the process of elimination. He maintains that Bolognese takes from the dialect of Imola a certain lightness and softness (*lenitatem atque mollitiem*), while from the dialects of Ferrara and Modena it takes a certain guttural (velar) quality (*garrulitatem*). In other words, Dante does not prefer Bolognese for its own objectively inherent qualities, but because, having absorbed different elements from different dialects, it automatically avoids the principal defect of an illustrious vernacular, that of being tied to a single "provincial" tradition. This is a necessary step after Dante has given expression to all his spontaneous reactions because it allows him to arrive at a well-motivated theory; according to Dante, in order to achieve linguistic stability it is essential to go beyond the confines of regional speech forms.[4]

Thirty-four

Dante and Petrarch

166 DANTE THE THEORIST
In Dante's eyes, the "illustrious" vernacular is associated only with
some—and not with all—literary genres, and to be precise, only with
the canzone and tragedy. Subordinate to the "illustrious" vernacular
is the "mid-level" (*mezzano*) vernacular, which is to be used for the
ballad and for comedy. Finally, below the "mid-level" vernacular we
find the "humble" vernacular, which is meant to be used for elegies.
The ideal of selection and of unity becomes evident in the details of
"construction" and "vocabulary." His inspiration is not far from
Cicero's: Dante aims at eliminating local dross (for Cicero this would
have meant archaisms and rustic terms), at adding a minimum of
nonlocal elements after careful consideration (for Cicero a moderate
Grecism); and at composing the whole according to a minimum of
artifice (for Cicero the rhythm of the sentence). The attributes
Dante assigns to this vernacular (in addition to "illustrious," which
means "resplendent") are three in number: *cardinale* ("cardinal")
because it is the "hinge" (*cardine*) around which all the other linguistic vehicles of usage—dialects and not—pivot; *curiale* ("curial")
in my opinion inasmuch as it is "worthy of a court" and therefore
not closed to the participation of court officials; and finally *aulico*

("worthy of the royal palace") and that is corresponding to the desires, tastes, and inspirations coming from above.[1]

This system elaborated by Dante is not a reality but only an ideal. What is more, it is not even an ideal that Dante, as a poet, sought to realize. Theoretically, the *Divine Comedy* ought to have been written according to the "mid-level" style since it is a "comedy." In reality, it is written in all styles imaginable. From the *Inferno* to the *Paradise*, and even within individual canticles, the expressive situations are so varied—and I venture to say powerful—that no stylistic casuistry succeeds in adjusting to them automatically.

167 DANTE THE ENRICHER

Despite the fact that it is unsystematic in its structure, the *Divine Comedy* produced immense consequences and results. From the point of view of vocabulary, it represents a very significant enrichment. After the experience of Dante, the vernacular tradition loses in one stroke all of the inferior qualities it had dragged along through seven centuries of poverty, underdevelopment, and parochial restrictedness. This enrichment has nothing to do with the technical process that creates or introduces words as labels or epithets. The vocabulary transmitted by the *Divine Comedy* is applicable to any subject matter whatever—poetic or prosaic, lyrical or philosophical—because the *Comedy* acts as a melting pot not with regard to the well-defined world of specialized works, but in connection with a universality of interests and emotions.

Naturally, we are not in a position to determine which among these lexical innovations were introduced first by Dante and which received from him the consecration and the halo of literariness.[2]

This enrichment process consists not only in the satisfaction of semantic nuances that are increasingly differentiated and subtle, but also in the possibility of evoking new images and new emotions or moods. Examples of these new images and emotions are found for instance in the sixth canto of the *Paradise* in the speech of the Emperor Justinian, in formulae such as *dal cirro negletto fu nomato . . . la morte prese subitana ed atra . . . nel commensurar di vostri gaggi;* or, on Beatrice's lips in the powerful Latinism *cive* for 'cittadino' (citizen). Inversely, we find words that in reality are quotations from venerable texts, such as *agricola*, which goes back to the Gospel parable of the vineyard, or *conservo*, which can be traced to the Apocalypse.

A special case in the process of lexical enrichment is constituted by the variants which create a counterbalance between more and less ancient forms and between high-class and popular forms; naturally these variants are dictated not exclusively by expressive needs but sometimes by rhythmical necessity. Examples of phonetic variants are *padre* as compared with *patre*, *madre* as opposed to *matre*, and the normal *speglio* in comparison with the Latinized *speculo*. Instances of variants of derivation are *rege* as compared with *re*, *imagine* as opposed to *imago*, and *spene*, *speme* in contrast to *speranza*. Morphological variants dictated by rhyme are *diceva* with Eva, and *dicea* with Citerea. Variants in the past absolute tense are *fenno*, *feron*, and *fero* as compared with 'fecero', and *tacette* in contrast to *tacque*. A variant in the conditional tense is the Sicilian form *vorrìa* as opposed to the normal form *vorrei*. Finally, there are variants of derivation which utilize Latin models without constituting Latinisms: *adimare*, *appulcrare*, *ingigliare*, *inurbarsi*, and *sgannare*.

168 DANTE THE FLORENTINE

If now we seek to evaluate quantitatively the lexical additions—the doors that Dante opened, so to speak, in order to escape the bounds of Florentine municipalism—here are the results we come to, as they were concretely analyzed by N. Zingarelli with regard to the lexical heritage of the *Divine Comedy*.[3] Latinisms, in the strict sense of the word, number approximately five hundred; examples are *appropinquare*, *cernere*, *digesto*, and *igne*. There are a few dozen Gallicisms, but most of them were not permanently adopted into the Italian vocabulary; in contrast to *masnada*, which is a definite acquisition, we note *miraglio* 'miracolo', *vengiare* 'vendicare' (to avenge), *giuggiare* 'giudicare' (to judge), which were not. There are a few northern forms such as *brolo* 'orto' (orchard), and *burlare* 'cadere' (to fall). An example of a southern form is *sorpriso* 'sorpreso' (surprised).

Therefore, the vocabulary of the *Divine Comedy* taken as a whole is rich and open and not noticeably corroded by foreign lexical elements. Dante has used a substantially homogeneous lexicon; he did not strain himself to produce a lexical synthesis like the one his theory called for. Dante ennobled the Florentine dialect without building a superstructure. But, if from the external point of view of receptiveness toward lexical forms from other dialects Dante was not locked within the limits of his doctrine and he moved with a certain liberty without contradicting himself, from an internal point of view the contradiction was sharp. Not only does he not attempt to establish a consistent canon at the level of the "illustrious" or even the "mid-level" vernacular, but he even puts into the *Comedy* forms which in the *De vulgari eloquentia* he had specifically pointed out as objects of scornful reproach by Florentines and Pisans alike. This is the case with *manichiamo* 'mangiamo' (we eat), disapproved of in the *De vulgari eloquentia*,[4] but appearing in the thirty-second canto of the *Inferno* (v. 60). This is also the case with the past absolute form *terminonno* 'terminarono' (they finished), which appears in no less elevated a passage than the twenty-eighth canto of the *Paradise* (v. 105), while in the *De vulgari eloquentia* the same ending is disdained in the "Pisan" example *andonno*. As a grammarian, Dante elaborated a theory; as a poet, he did not feel constrained to translate that theory into reality or to repress his creative impulses.

The unitary tradition of an Italian literary language did not have as its basis a sort of Esperanto that the *De vulgari eloquentia* postulated. This tradition is introduced to us for the first time not as the fruit of difficult computations, but as a lofty, magnificent mountain that Nature has fashioned, that a man seized by an ecstatic abandon has attained, and that posterity, admiring, has accepted.

169 PETRARCH AND SELECTION

If we can say that Dante assumes the authority for universality and richness of vocabulary which he passed on to the young tradition of Italy's literary language, this is not to say that he was entirely deaf to the other fundamental need of any elevated linguistic vehicle, that of selection. As B. Milgiorini notes,[5] Dante did not insist so much on the "rules," as on discernment and judgment (in Latin *discretio*). In ancient times Cicero himself stressed this fundamental notion, while in the cinquecento the criterion of "taste" (*gusto*) became more important. In Dante, however, the idea of selection is kept within modest bounds and is limited to suggestions. For example, Dante avoids the use in high lyric poetry of "childish" (*puerili*) words such as *mamma* and *babbo,* "rough" (*selvatiche*) words such as *cetra* and *greggio,* and "indecent" (*lubriche*) words such as *femmina* and *corpo.* Systematic attention to the selection of words (and constructions) is personified by Francesco Petrarch (1303–74). This attention integrates the work of Dante and assures for it the prestige necessary so that his models, rich but inconsistent, are transformed into the elements of an authoritative and conscious tradition. This does not prevent Petrarch from being, in other ways, less modern than Dante; with regard to Latin, for example, this is the case. Unlike Dante, Petrarch recognizes the "greater dignity" of Latin, and he makes use of it, out of preference, in personal marginal notes like the *hic placet* in canzone 268, v. 56. Unlike Dante, who identified with the Florentine vernacular in an instinctive way, Petrarch—with regard to formal characteristics, rhythmical patterns, and choice of vocabulary—always works very deliberately, continuing the tradition of the

Stilnovists, surpassing it, and sometimes going to Sicilian models. The study of variants in Petrarch allows us to see more clearly the lines of development in his personal language, which affect all the structures of the young, growing tradition. We note, for example, the tendency to replace paratactic constructions with the more elaborate and complex "hypotactic," as in canzone 196, which in an early version reads *va mormorando E per la fronte viemme,* and then *mormorando a ferir nel volto viemme* in a later version. In the field of vocabulary, we note *mirare* which, in taking the place of 'vedere', is an example of his practice of selectivity, aimed at attaining a higher linguistic level. To the same end, Petrarch tries to avoid repetitions, even at the cost of substituting the banal *dir cose* for 'parlare', or *aura celeste* for 'aura amorosa'.[6] In order to intensify the metaphor, he substitutes *di sua ombra uscìan* for 'fra i rami uscìa'. The significance of Petrarch's role in the evolution of the tradition of literary language consists in his having been a precursor. Ugo Foscolo[7] has distinguished three phases in Petrarch's development: first, a free, unfettered communication within a restricted sphere of reference; second, an early Latin elaboration; and third, a final perfection of the Italian form "with greater skill" (*con più arte*). Above all, as compared with Dante, who "often creates a new language," Petrarch knows how to "choose . . . the most elegant words and prases," according to Foscolo. According to F. DeSanctis, Petrarch was "capable as no one else was of refining the language and poetry."

170 TOWARD A VERNACULAR PROSE TRADITION

It would seem that prose, because of its greater naturalness and more frequent use, would have been in a position to develop in its vernacular forms more quickly than poetry. This, however, was not the case. Certainly, prose had many more occasions and necessities to be used in very broad circles. Vernacular prose, however, was faced with the obstacle of a solid, massive Latin tradition.

Two currents contributed to the creation of a vernacular prose tradition. The first current is represented by translations into the vernacular. Among these is the famous *Fioretti* of Saint Francis.[8] But more significant from a technical point of view are those translations that begin from classical models and attempt to remain faithful to them, above all as far as the complex structure of the sentence is concerned. A good example is the *Fiore di rettorica* of the Bolognese Fra Guidotto, which is dedicated to Manfred, who was king from 1245 to 1266. This text begins with a concatenation of relative clauses which have been grouped in a higher structure of correlations: *nel tempo che segnoreggiava . . . Giulio Cesare il quale*

*fu il primo imperatore di Roma, de cui Lucano e Salusto . . . dissero
. . . ; in quel tempo fue un . . . uomo, il quale era fatto abitante della
nobile citta di Roma et avea nome . . . Cicerone; il quale·fu maestro e
trovatore de la grande scienza di Retorica.*

The other current completely excludes classical models and takes
as its starting point both the spoken vernacular and the simplicity
of the syntactical patterns of the Gospel. The *Novellino*[9] contains a
passage such as the following: *Marco Lombardo . . . fue molto savio.
Fue a u'Natale a una citta dove si donavano molte robe. Non ebbe
neuna. Trovò un altro di corte il quale era nesciente persona appo
Marco. E avea avuto robe.* Similarly, in a text of a higher linguistic
level such as the *Retorica* of Brunetto Latini we find: *Mercatanti
fiorentini passavano in nave per andare oltremare. Sorvenne loro
crudel fortuna . . . Alla fine arrivaro ad uno porto nel quale era
adorato Malcometto ed era tenuto deo. Questi mercatanti lo adoraro
come idio.*

The relationship between the two currents must not be seen as one
between complex intellectual accomplishments and elementary, instinctive ones. With regard to another form of art like painting,
Latini's recommendation in the *Tesor* (VIII.9) is "to avoid too much
painting, for at times the shunning of color *is* color." While the two
currents are destined to come together with greater or lesser rapidity,
the respective positions of Dante and Petrarch end up belonging to
the past and are reduced to mere points of reference, or, if you like, to
relics. Dante was not inclined to compare Latin and vernacular authors; he placed his trust in the vernacular, in the "pliancy of its
syllables, the propriety of its relations, and the pleasant speeches
which are composed in it".[10] Petrarch, on the other hand, fully valued
the difference that divided the two linguistic worlds. Notwithstanding these differences, the language of Italy took a decisive step forward, thanks to these two great men.

Thirty-five

From Florentine
to Tuscan

171 BOCCACCIO

The experiments and innovations of which we have spoken would have brought into being a unified tradition much less secure and infinitely slower in developing, had they not been assimilated, cultivated, and submitted to the creative abilities of Giovanni Boccaccio (1313–75),[1] who brought them to life. Thanks to his artistic abilities, these simple beginnings, destined to mature very slowly, were transformed into exemplary models. Parallel constructions such as *che* with the finite verb or the corresponding Latin construction of the accusative plus infinitive are deliberately used and appear as the result of a logical choice; similarly we note the preference given at times to adjectives in anteposition according to Latin models, as against those in postposition according to the vernacular. In the *Filocolo* there is still a preponderance of classical elements in addition to those just cited above: verbs in final position, present participles in plenty, and inversion in the position of the auxiliary verb. In the period that embraces the writing of the *Vita di Dante* and the *Decameron,* the two contrasting models are no longer used with rigid preference; both are at the writer's disposition and are harmonized when used together; in the words of A. Schiaffini,[2] the formal moment is liberated and transformed in "harmony, proportion, and music."

With regard to the importance, the completeness and the grandeur of his achievements, Boccaccio is the equal of Dante and Petrarch, giving to Italian prose an archetype not inferior to the *Divine Comedy*. But the intrinsic importance of his model is not adequately matched by a corresponding historical importance which calls for a successive and uninterrupted continuity. This continuity will be evident only much later, after Italy's linguistic vehicles of usage have overcome the test of the humanistic reaction.

172 MORPHOLOGICAL ADJUSTMENT

The linguistic balance at this point in history exhibits its inner distress through numerous morphological phenomena. Florentine forms that are imposed on the rest of Tuscany are *ogni* which replaces *ogne*, and *mila* which wins out over *milia*. With regard to verb forms, the first person plural is generalized in the form *-iamo* in all three conjugations, giving *amiamo, temiamo,* and *sentiamo,* instead of the endings *-amo, -emo,* and *-imo,* which persist in Pisa, Lucca, and Arezzo. The forms *sarò* and *sarai* take the place of the regular forms SERO and SERAI, evidently because the substitution of *-ar-* for *-er-* was a characteristic of the internal syllable. With regard to the article, there is oscillation between the forms *il* and *el,* while the form *lo* is standard after a consonant, and has been preserved up to our own day in the phrase *per LO più.* The superlative *-issimo* is a recent embellishment, but in Boccaccio's day the form was used in a much broader sense as a relative superlative; an example is *soavissima di tutte l'altre scienze,* 'the gentlest of all the other sciences'. With regard to the verb, the use of the pluperfect is freer; it is not only a relative tense as it is today; an example of this freer use is *ebber veduto . . . Andruccio* = videro.[3] The impersonal verb takes the subject *egli* or *el,* as we note in the example *el mi restava molte cose a dire,* as compared with our modern personalized form "mi restavano molte cose da dire." Past participles without suffixes are extracted from those marked in the standard way, as if to emphasize their nonverbal aspect: *cerco* from 'cercato', *tocco* from 'toccato', *guasto* from 'guastato'. Participles and gerunds are widely used and constitute a special facet of the general tendency to favor hypotactic constructions over paratactic forms. Finally, the uses of prepositions are important; for example the partitive use of DI, as we note in *vi ha DI valenti medici,* which has the same meaning as 'vi sono valenti medici' (there are talented physicians); the appositive use of DI, as in the phrase *il cattivello di Calandrino* 'Caladrino, cattivello' (Cala-drino, that mischievous fellow), still used today in the formula 'la citta di Firenze'; the use of A as a marker of relationship of agent *si lasciò vincere A sua femina* = DA sua femina; and the use of A as a marker of relationship of object, which is a southern feature, as we see in *Mandirà AD Eneas a lu infernu*.[4]

173 LEXICAL ENRICHMENT

In contrast to the stamp left by the men who were the founders of the tradition, there were the anonymous victories, so to speak, of the masses. These conquests consist mostly of lexical enrichments which bring with them various problems of a phonetic and morphological order. Scores of Latinisms were absorbed in this period.[5] For an every-day word like 'sorella' we find in the trecento experimental variants such as *suora, suore, suoro,* and *sorore* (which are definite Latinisms), as well as *serocchia, sirocchia,* and *sorocchia;* the everyday form *lepre* was accompanied by parallel forms like *levre, lievre,* and *lièvore;* and the everyday word *sorcio* had parallel forms like *sorice, sorico, sorco,* and *sorgo.* There was experimentation even in derivate adjectives: in this period the standard form *poetico* was accompanied by paral-lel forms such as *poetévole, poetesco,* and *poetale.* Naturally, cases in which variants were due to metrical exigencies were less signifi-cant; examples are 'lepore marina' and 'madre *vetula',* which were imposed by a need for trisyllabic words. Another important element of lexical enrichment is constituted by the technical terms which had to fill the gaps left by the abandoned Latin terminology. For example, with regard to painting, the terms *acquerella* (and then *acquerello*), *a fresco* (and then *affresco*) and *sfumare* were born. The prestige of the Latin tradition, however was so great that in the field of Italian vocabulary many forms were substituted that adhered more strictly to Latin, in addition to others that were Latin in themselves, but altered greatly in the course of their uninterrupted evolution; examples are 'escercito', which replaces *oste,* 'orazione', which sup-plants *diceria,* and 'repubblica', which takes the place of *comune.* Within more strictly formal limits 'pittore' takes the place of *dipintore,* 'cigno' that of *cecero,* 'decimo' of *diecimo,* 'ferire' of *fedire,* 'onorevole' of *orrevole,* 'sinistro' of *sinestro,* and 'Sicilia' of *Cicilia.* We also find instances of exaggerations, like the one Boccaccio employs when he write *preera alla provincia,* which closely follows the Latin formula *praeerat provinciae.* The results were experimental and uncertain from a morphological point of view as well when the model, instead of being the traditional one of the Latin accusative, was the nominative; thus from 'Venus' we obtained *Veno,* in addi-

tion to *Venus* and *Venusso;* similarly we acquired *aspe* in place of
'aspide', *ospe* instead of 'ospite' and *satelle* in lieu of 'satellite'.

174 THE SECOND ITALIAN PHONEMATIC SYSTEM

The consequences of these breakthroughs reverberate against the
Florentine-based phonematic system; the systems that had been built
up between the ninth and the twelfth centuries (§150) are no longer
sufficient. Of this structure there remain only two well-established
features, both negative: the exclusion of consonants in final position,
and the exclusion of the unaccented -u in final position. In contrast
to the old system five important innovations come to the fore: the
indiscriminate acceptance of proparoxytones, which is to say forms
of the type *solido* as opposed to *soldo,* the only admissible form in
the old system; the acceptance of groups of consonant + L, which
before had inexorably been palatalized into consonant + J, an
example being *plebe,* which is accepted along with the type *pieve,*
the only admissible form in the old system; the fusion of the Tuscan
pronunciation of the affricative (*aceto* and *dieci*) derived from the
original Latin κ, with the spirant (*bacio* and *brucia*) derived from
an earlier sJ; the persistence of the intervocalic в, which, in words
having an uninterrupted tradition, were subject to lenition producing v, as in the above-cited case of *pleBe* as opposed to *pieVe;* and
finally the arbitrariness of the open pronunciation of the vowels ε
and o in words introduced from Latin or from other languages. The
open pronunciation of *bello* and *collo* is due to historical considerations that were deep-rooted in Latin, integrated into the first Italian
phonematic system, and as such accepted in the second. But the
open pronunciation of the ε in *problèma* is simply a casual choice,
introduced with the word itself, and devoid of historical justification
(see §239). It prevails as a model of standard Italian pronunciation
not for historical reasons but because of the force of the Florentine
model, which was not contested by the models of other regions. In
the same way the Latin words *iustitia* and *vitium* were accepted as
'giustizia' and 'vizio', because at this point in history no one could
remember that in Vulgar Latin those ι's were open, and therefore
destined to yield the Italian suffix *-ezza,* which we see in the Italian
word *vezzo.*

The independence of the second Italian phonematic system with
respect to the first was determined by the torrent of Latin words
having an interrupted tradition which, in being accepted into the
system, forced enormous changes in the Italian linguistic structures
as they had developed between the ninth and twelfth centuries.

In the field of morphology, the situation is less heterogeneous and therefore, by this time more "Italian" than "Florentine." The only delicate point concerns the forms of the conditional tense, which became established in their more recent structure, resulting from the periphrasis of the infinitive + perfect: AMARE (HABU)I gives us *amerei*. Contributions of a cultural nature enrich and at the same time disturb the system, as we can see for example in the acceptance in literary texts of various forms of the conditionals and in the uncertainty of the plurals of themes ending in velar consonants (whether there ought to be a palatalization before the -I ending or, in accordance with the singular, there ought not to be). For example *manico* and *stomaco* correspond to the phonetic plurals 'manici' and 'stomaci' and the analogous plurals 'manichi' and 'stomachi'.[6] Similarly, in dialects we note the dissimilar plurals *cavagli* and *cavai* for 'cavallo', and the plural *rai* for 'raggio'.[7] A second difference separates the first phonematic system from the second: it concerns sphere of influence. The first system is firmly anchored in the Florentine area. The second phonematic system, unlike the first, becomes important at a time when the separatism of the Tuscan communes was waning. If the second system does not suppress the particular features of individual dialects, at least it creates a public opinion that favors a broader interpretation.

175 THE BEGINNING OF A TRADITION

The writings of Saint Catherine of Siena (1347–80) do indeed exhibit Sienese dialectal characteristics, but these have been strongly tempered. From the phonetic point of view we note the following forms which are Sienese: *oncenso, merollo* 'midollo' (marrow), *giógnare* 'giungere' (to arrive), *pògnare* 'pungere' (to prick), and *pégnare* '(di)pingere' (to paint); however, *lingua* and *famiglia* are already Florentine in form.

From the lexical point of view we still find the Sienese forms *aciare* 'alitare' (to breathe), *ascaro* 'dolore' (pain, grief), *mammolo* 'bimbo' (little child), *papero* 'lucignolo' (wick), and *salavo* 'sudicio' (dirt, filth).

In his comment to Dante[8] Benvenuto da Imola states that there is not a vernacular *pulcrius aut proprius* 'more beautiful and suitable' than Florentine, but he adds that those who have gone beyond the local boundaries speak in a way that is *pulcrius et ornatius* 'more beautiful and elegant' than the others. Francesco da Barberino writes *E parlerai sol nel volgar toscano*. Antonio da Tempo, a Paduan, notes *lingua tusca magis apta est ad literam vel literaturam*.[9]

These definitions establish another aspect of the Italian literary language that is social and not just geographic. Linking it strictly to the manifestations of a literary nature, they ratify a fundamental difference that gives an indelible stamp to the literary tradition of the language of Italy. The language of Italy receives precocious stability, precisely because it is addressed to a closed circle of men of letters. Unlike French and English, which become established because they are solidly anchored in the language used in the royal chanceries, and unlike German, which, on the basis of the translation of the Bible by Martin Luther, penetrated into the consciousness of churchgoers, the Italian tradition is born as, and for centuries will remain, the language of an oligarchic minority (§246).

Thirty-six

The Exhaustion of the
Dialectal Literary
Tradition

176 THE PERSISTENCE OF DIALECTAL TEXTS IN THE NORTH
The following linguistic evidence demonstrates how far regions outside of Tuscany were from realizing similar achievements. In Sardinia
the Statutes of the Sassari Republic (1316) still exhibit salient Sardinian features, like the periphrastic future *aet mitter* 'metterà' or the
articulated preposition *dessa* 'della': *si alcunu iniuriosamente aet
mitter manu contra alcuna dessa famiça dessa potestate* . . .[1] Turning
to northern Italy, we discover that before 1309 the Mantuan Vivaldo
Belcalzèr translated Bartolomeo Angelico's book *De proprietatibus
rerum*. Let us look at the following passage: *Talpa è la topina fata
a similituden de soreg et è çega e senza ocl e ha un musèl a mod de
porçèl* . . .[2] The loss of final vowels other than A, the assibilation of
palatal consonants (*çega, porçèl*), the lenition of intervocalic consonants (*çega*), and the Veneto-Emilian evolution of CT into T (*fata*)
are all northern features. They demonstrate the persistence of structures the overwhelming majority of which are dialectal; only the
inclusion of an extraregional lexical unit such as *similituden* opens a
skylight, through which we can peek at future developments.

177 THE PERSISTENCE OF DIALECTAL TEXTS IN THE SOUTH
In Rome, the very southern dialect that had appeared in the preceding century as a vernacular translation of a Latin text in the *Storie di*

Troja et de Roma (1252–58) persists in the fourteenth century with the *Vita de Cola de Rienzo* (1313/14–54) with its three basic southern characteristics: noncontiguous metaphony as in *dienti* (plural) as opposed to the singular *dente;* the prevalence of V over B in forms like *vagno* and *varva,* 'bagno' and 'barba'; and the palatalization of the group PJ in *via Acia* for 'Appia'.

In Naples, notwithstanding the bonds that Boccaccio could have established there with the Tuscan tradition, we still find in the fourteenth century the poem "I bagni di Pozzuoli" in which diphthongization in a closed syllable appears with all of its familiar characteristics, for example, in the passage *che una cosa facza multi effiecte—nuy lo vedemmo per li soi proffiecte* while from a point of view of necessary lexical enrichment the scope of Latinisms is much greater than the range of Tuscanisms. In Sicily the local tradition is not only still stable in the fourteenth century, but, according to S. Debenedetti,[3] exhibits the "the fixedness, the stability and all but the unity of literary languages"; an example is the *Libru de lu dialogu de Santu Gregoriu* of the first half of the fourteenth century. To give an example of poetic language we cite from the "Profetìa" or the "Lamentu di parte siciliana": *O fortuna fallenti, pirkì non sì tutt'una?* in which we note the conspicuous ı in place of the normal Tuscan ε.

178 MIRACLE IN VENICE

Between the two extremes of Tuscan constructivism (approaching a definitive crystallization) and the persisting dialects of both the north and the south, one can place the Venetian area, and more precisely the Venetian estuary, on the strength of its intermediary nature. On the one hand we note indications of the subjection of Venetian speech forms to more or less intense neighboring currents even during the fourteenth century; on the other hand we see signs of a recovery of Venetian that is destined to have consequences that are not only structural but also sociogeographic (§187).

In reference to the first category of phenomena, we note the Gallo-Italic pressure on the whole of the Euganean area, which was able miraculously to save itself (noted in §§121, 125, and 126), although it paid dearly for it by absorbing, even in the heart of Venice, the strong lenition of intervocalic consonants and numerous losses of final vowels, and, along with Friuli, saving itself only from the introduction of the mixed vowels ö and ü and from the palatalization of ст.

Besides this action which comes from the south, another form of subjection coming from the north also leaves its mark on the Venice of the fourteenth century. It probably is related to influences dating back to the action of the patriarch of Aquileia, which was still linked to the Friulian world in which it had been founded, even though it passed to Grado in A.D. 568. An early example of this pressure is the palatalization of the velar even before A, which is identified in Friuli by means of the acceptance of Friulian words in Slovenian from the tenth century on and which appears in the form *chian* 'cane'.[4] Another example appears in the declaration of Ser Michele Zancani (1307), in which the author uses *glesia* for 'chiesa';[5] and in the pact with Ramadàn, lord of Crimea, in which the form *sclavo*[6] appears intact, without counting the Ladin form *autro* in the *Atti di Lido Maggiore*.[7]

The recovery of Venetian occurs not so much with regard to the Gallo-Italic tradition that was systematically accepted and not correctable, as it does in the purging of Ladinisms, so that for 'cane' we now find *can* and not 'cian' (chian). External circumstances which occurred immediately afterward completely modified the area, with the result that linguistic models spread from Venice. In the middle of the fourteenth century Venice becomes the capital of a larger inland area, and Venetian linguistic models, as if endowed with a certain prestige, are introduced in all the administrative centers of the region. This prestige is not destined to subjugate or to destroy local forms; rather it constitutes a sort of coverlet which spreads over the area and facilitates partial uniformity and reciprocal understanding. Even today, a century and a half after the end of the Venetian Republic, the metropolitan action of Venice still continues, undermining dialectal areas including Udine and Trieste. Even without projecting into the very distant future, we can see that the Venetian linguistic tradition is gaining not only in geographic extension but also in social level and stability; in the sixteenth century it reaches the level of chancery language (§187).

179 DECLINE OF THE DIALECTS

The first foci of extraregional reconstruction outside of Tuscany were the courts and centers of culture that were forming around Ferrara, Mantua, and Milan, in addition to Urbino and Rome. We must begin to understand the situation through the sermons of Saint Bernardino of Siena (1380–1444). Saint Bernardino preached in the vernacular in Tuscany, while in the north of Italy he remained faithful, at least in intention, to Latin.[8]

Of the territories cited above, the first to emerge from the greyness was Ferrara. In the second half of the fifteenth century we read in the preface to the biography of Filippo Maria Visconti, written by P. C. Decembrio (1392–1477): *non saperìa io adriciare la lingua se non al ferrarese idioma;* in this text we note on the one hand a conditional tense influenced by Sicilian (hence distant) models, and at the same time an excess of zeal in substituting for the standard form *addrizzare,* an overly conscientious correction containing a palatal consonant, *adriciare.* This does not preclude the possibility of strongly palatalized or assibilated dialectal forms as in *non si meterìa li piedi in giesa* (for 'chiesa') and in *l'arco che in cielo zase* (for 'giace') appearing in other parts of the text.

Even more than through the texts that were associated with more cultivated settings and authors, the action of the courts and cultural centers is seen through the tendency to correct the obstacles of lenition and assibilation that were features of the northern dialects and especially of Lombardy. Whereas, at the height of the Middle Ages one said *crèer* and *vèova* with the total lenition of the intervocalic D (§157), today we find the forms *creDer* and *vèDova* reestablished through a process of adjustment toward more conservative models emanating from the courts. Similarly, it is probable that the tendency toward assibilation as exhibited in the evolution of *ce* into *çe* was already advanced in the Middle Ages, while today in Milan we hear *cent* and *cinc* for 'cento' and 'cinque'.

180 THE FIRST INSTANCES OF ADOPTION OF A LITERARY LANGUAGE
There were three decisive events in this march toward normalization. The first took place in the south in 1476 with the publication of the *Novellino* of Masuccio Salernitano. Certainly we cannot speak of a language that is perfectly balanced in the coexistence of Latinate and analogous forms, between the variants of *debito* and *dovuto, dubitare* and *dottare, credette* and *credé.* But from the dialectal point of view, the step has been taken, and if any anomaly remains, this is due not to concessions made to local speech forms but to a persistent propensity for archaic Latinate models. In 1483 a parallel event takes place with the publication of the *Porrettane,* a series of short stories by the Bolognese Sabbadino degli Arienti; the *Porrettane* represents the grafting of the tradition of "illustrious Bolognese" to the mainstream of Italy's literary language which by now goes beyond the confines of regionalism.[9]

In the meantime, however, an event of fundamental sociolinguistic significance took place in Tuscany; this was not the publication of a text in a standardized language (Tuscany had already reached this point on its own), but rather an acknowledgment such as the introduction of the obligatory use of the vernacular in the commercial courts (1414).[10] Even more characteristic of this trend was the "Certame coronario"; this debate was so named by Leon Battista Alberti, who, at the height of the humanistic period, sanctioned the equal literary dignity of the vernacular and Latin, which had in that period enjoyed a recovery because of the humanists.

Thirty-seven

Humanistic Reactions

181 THE FIRST HUMANISTS

The recognition owed to the "Certame coronario" was all the more surprising in view of the fact that the period that spans the end of the thirteenth century and the beginning of the fourteenth coincided with efforts for the consolidation and unification of a literary language in the vernacular and at the same time with a radical change in taste, dominated by a renewed sympathy for models of classical antiquity in all areas and not just that of language. It is not that the taste and sensibility for classical forms had ever waned. But in the second half of the fourteenth century—that is to say after Petrarch and Boccaccio—Medieval Latin came to be thought of as something crude and incapable of refinement; as a result a purified image of an amended, redeemed classical Latin was delineated opposite the vernacular, and so the gap between the two was filled. The "new" Latin image was not just the object of detached contemplation; it was also the object of meditation and comparison. A figure of no less stature than Boccaccio dared to say that Dante's contribution, far from representing the glorious beginning of the vernacular literary tradition, would have been "more artful" (*più artificioso*) and "sublime" (sublime), and therefore more prestigious, if it had been written in Latin.[1]

Even before the legal recognition of the vernacular in 1414 of which we have just spoken above, a chain of events begins that are identified with the well-known period of humanism, and these, as far as linguistic equilibrium is concerned, lead to that famous event, the linguistic reaction of the humanists. The first event took place in 1396 with the beginning of the teaching of Greek in Florence by Michele Crisolora. Notwithstanding his ties to the medieval doctrines of the *dictamina,* Coluccio Salutati (1331–1406) fights against the first obstacle to the return of classical models, namely, rhymed prose; in this struggle he acts as a pioneer for the rebirth of chancery Latin prose style. Leonardo Bruni (1370–1444) adopts an epistolary Latin style that is less artificial than Salutati's and accepts the principle of admitting new words, insisting, however, that they must harmonize with the system as if they were "not found, but freed from the shadows of antiquity."

182 CICERONIANISM

Gasparino Barzizza (1370?–1431) sought to define in a rigorous and restrictive way the Latin model that was once again proposed to these authors. According to him, this model had to be not just generically classical, but precisely "Ciceronian." It was with this thesis that the desperate debate began; during its course the Ciceronian theory was formulated and reformulated in an increasingly rigid way, and its applications were always more difficult if not completely unrealizable. This position was an abstract one, however, because it did not take into account the achievements of the vernacular, beginning with the practical goals already realized with the *Decameron.* The insistence on Ciceronianism in spite of these achievements justifies the attribute of "reactionary," which has been given to the movement.[2] In any case, Ciceronianism continued with Poggio Bracciolini (1386–1459), who in concentrating on stylistic patterns was at times ungrammatical with regard to details. In this debate Lorenzo Valla (1407?–57) attaches importance to the disquisitions concerning the use of individual Latin particles. The trend continued in this direction in a coherent and extreme manner up to Paolo Cortesi (1465–1510).

In comparison with this central current Francesco Filelfo (1398–1481) represents an extreme wing; at the age of eighty he declared that we write in the vernacular only that which we do not want to come down to our descendants (*quod nolumus transferre ad posteros*). This does not detract from the fact that other writers were steeped in such a balanced and organic way in the linguistic structures of Latin that they were able to write with equal ease in Latin and in the vernacular; Agnolo Poliziano (1454–94) and Giovanni Pontano

(1426–1503) are examples of such writers. But these were extraordinary men. Their linguistic virtuosity had to come to terms with collective forces and needs, against which these exceptional spirits could not play a decisive role.

183 COMPARISONS BETWEEN LATIN AND THE VERNACULAR
Precisely because the interest in the ancient world continued to be alive and profound, its pole of attraction ought to have gravitated toward the literary and architectural art forms rather than toward the arid linquistic structures that were not very functional in themselves, not very responsive to the needs of the times, and anachronistic. Doctrinal investigations and comparisons based on criteria and norms replaced real achievements in Latin prose. The principles around which these discussions centered were basically four. First, the superiority of Latin or the vernacular was discussed, on the basis of milieu, that is, of the territory in which their use could be valid. On this argument Gerolamo Muzio (1496–1576)[3] stated that Italian was known in France, Spain, and even in Turkey, while Latin was limited to maintaining its hold in Germany and England. The second criterion, eminently subjective, was that of intrinsic worth. With regard to this, Leon Battista Alberti (1404–82) maintained that the perfection of a language resided not in its substance but in its use. The argument was specious, and still in 1524 Vittoria Colonna (1490–1547) dared to assert that Latin was comparable to an object made of gold, while a text in the vernacular could correspond only to copper. The third criterion had to do with autonomy, that is, the prejudice that Italian was a "corruption" of Latin and therefore not an independent language. The right response to this argument was given by Benidetto Varchi,[4] who in 1570 wrote that the vernacular is a new language, "not corruption but . . . generation". The last criterion is that of overall uniformity, in which Latin obviously prevailed because it was "stable" or in Dante's terminology imputable to an "art," while the vernacular is changeable or in Dante's words a "usage." But in this last criterion of comparison the value of stability is not matched against the defects of mutability; it is rather the opposition of that which is living against that which no longer is.

Very slowly the polemic becomes less intense. The last well-structured defense of Latin was that of Uberto Foglietta (ca. 1518–81), who in 1574 published a book entitled *De linguae latinae usu et preastantia*. In the meantime, on a political level, an important innovation had been introduced in 1561; Emanuele Filiberto, duke of Savoy, adopted Italian instead of French as the language for official documents.[5]

184 THE CORRECTIONS OF SANNAZARO AND ARIOSTO

In addition to these academic discussions, the fifteenth century brought to the development of Italy's literary language a contribution of an entirely different sort, the invention of the printing press by Johann Gutenberg (1453). This invention meant the possibility of greatly increasing the numbers of copies of books and at the same time called for consistency and coherence in spelling. From this point of view it is instructive to look at a sample of the corrections that were introduced in successive editions of works of the period; these corrections were motivated by the single basic impulse of a unity that was both extraregional and graphic. The following examples are taken from *Arcadia* by Jacopo Sannazaro (1456–1530) and *Orlando Furioso* by Lodovico Ariosto (1474–1533). These works are examples of Tuscan models that spread beyond Tuscany, the former toward the south and the latter in the direction of Reggio and Ferrara.

The Vatican manuscript version of Sannazaro's *Arcadia*[6] is followed twenty years later in 1504 by a printed edition known as the *Summonte*. The most significant revisions are the following: from the southern metaphonic forms *nuovo* (masculine) and *nova* (feminine) to the standard forms 'novo : nova'; from diphthongated forms such as *priego* to nondipthongated forms like 'prego'; from the Latinized J at the beginning of a word as in *Julio,* for example, to the standard palatal of 'Giulio'; and finally from the non-Florentine types *onto* and *longo* to the Florentine forms 'unto' and 'lungo'.

There are three editions of *Orlando Furioso*: 1516, 1521, and 1532.[7] The corrections that appear in the second and third editions, though not of great significance, all attest to an aspiration for consistency. We note an evolution from *in l'altra* and *in la terra* to 'ne l'altra' and 'ne la terra'; instead of the articles *el* and *li,* the forms 'il' and 'i' are introduced; the modern inverse versions 'ti lodo' and 'te la dono' replace the atonal pronouns in *te lodo* and *ti la dono.* Corrections regarding questions of pronunciation are less coherent; in 1516 the correct forms with the Tuscan palatal s already appear (*scevra* and *sdruscito*), but the Emilian forms with the normal s still persist in *settro* and *trassinare.* Dialectal forms *gianda* and *giotto* for 'ghianda' and 'ghiotto' are still to be found in the 1532 edition. Examples of hypercorrections in the 1521 edition are *ciucca* for 'zucca' and *roverscio* for 'rovescio'.

185 LEONARDO AND CELLINI

The works of two other authors of this period who are very different one from the other, Leonardo da Vinci (1452–1519) and Benvenuto Cellini (1500–1571), pose other uncertainties which are at the same time proofs of vitality. Leonardo reaches the height of reason and aims at creating in his *Trattato della pittura* not so much an exemplary model of the scientific treatise as a didactic model that contains dialogue and is pleasant and lively; for this reason the literary language is subjected to a special kind of tension. The text contains dialogue with aphorisms in the third person and with suggestions in the second: *el pittore è padrone di tutte le cose . . . periciocché s'egli ha desiderio . . . egli è signore,* with a style that calls to mind the exhortatory letters of Saint Catherine of Siena. An example of inclusion of dialogue in the second person is *a colui che piange s'aggiunge ancora l'atto di stracciarsi . . . non farai il viso dichi piange . . .* Another example of the second person, this time in the imperative, is *Farai uomini morti, alcuni ricoperti mezzi dalla polvere ed altri tutti. La polvere . . . convertirsi in rosso sangue. . . .* Leonardo's *Trattato della pittura* is an abridgment of a budding linguistic tradition that is spontaneous and does not need older models for inspiration, either in the sense of the parataxis of the *Novellino* (§170) or of the hypotaxis of the *Decameron.*[8]

Even more foreign to grammatical and stylistic doctrines, Cellini from the beginning assumed authority as a champion of a free and easy style that was not unworthy of the writers of the trecento. In reality this innocence, which can more accurately be labeled impulsiveness, is divided into two different attitudes; according to the one attitude Cellini stays within the limits of the stylistic choices admitted by the tradition and according to the other he goes beyond the rigidity of standard syntactical structures to engage openly in the field of grammatical errors found in spoken speech forms. On the one hand, an excerpt like *e quivi è gran gentili uomini: ancora ne è in Pisa, e ne ho travato in molti luoghi . . .* exhibits simplicity—indeed poverty—of style which is well within the stylistic limits of the period. On the other hand, the use of the gerund as an inflected form of the verb, as in *il signore non gli rispondendo a proposito, ma faceva,* is an illustration of how Cellini goes beyond the limits of accepted structures; in so doing he emphasizes the expressive power of his vehicle, but he does not cooperate in the reinforcement of the tradition, the consistency and stability of which it is in the interest to everyone to insure.[9]

Thirty-eight

The Debate on Language

186 MACHIAVELLI

The person who victoriously brings to a conclusion the troubled process of forming an Italian prose tradition is Niccolò Machiavelli (1469–1527).[1] The progress made in a century and a half beginning with Boccaccio is effectively outlined by the following opinion of Leonardo Salviati (1540–89), who in commenting on the prose of the *Decameron* wrote *tutto candidezza, tutto fiore, tutto osservanza, tutto splendore,* while with regard to Machiavelli's prose he praised *la chiarezza, l'efficacia e la brevità. . . Nella prima a Cesare, nell'ultima a Tacito da paragonare.*

The intrinsic Florentine quality of Machiavelli's prose is apparent in his intentions even before we find it in fact. Although he was averse to theorizing according to schema that were cherished even by Dante, he succeeded in associating the idea of Florentine with that of linguistic honorableness; those who aimed at Italian models were considered by Machiavelli to be "most dishonest," while those who aspired to Tuscan models he tolerated as "less dishonest." His vocabulary was unitary, even though a certain number of Latinisms were present: we find "graphic" Latinisms like *descendere, miraculo, populo,* and *iusto;* "lexical" Latinisms like *accidente, allegare,* and *cogitazione;* and "semantic" Latinisms like *chiamare* for 'acclamare', *impeto* for 'assalto', and *appetito* for 'tendenza'. Fortuitous and officially adopted Gallicisms also appear; examples are *fauta* for 'errore', *ostello, lingi* for 'tovaglia' (tablecloth), *seggio* for 'assedio' (siege), and *villa* for 'città'.[2] Naturally, the homogeneity of the vocabulary was possible only because technical words could be formed out of ordinary ones; note for example the fate of *ruinare* 'to ruin, spoil', which according to Machiavelli technically defines the final outcome of an erroneous policy.

Sentence structure is still quite complex and corresponds to a phase of objective transition in which, according to Luigi Russo,[3] there is an evolution from the *ragionamenti a piramide* (pyramid-style reasoning) typical of medieval academics to the *ragionamenti a catena* (chainlike reasoning) characteristic of the new times; the result, which has been well illustrated by F. Chiapelli, was the coexistence of complexity and freedom in sentence structure.[4]

Morphology is neither traditional nor improvisational; rather it goes back to the old Florentine popular source as it appears in the *Regole della lingua fiorentina,* which has been attributed to Lorenzo the Magnificent;[5] examples are the use of *lui* as the masculine singular subject, and *le* as the plural feminine subject.

Machiavelli's greatest victory with regard to the consolidation of the prosaic linguistic tradition lies in the fundamental unity of his image, so that the author of a prose style of high level is not out of harmony with the image of the man[6] who for fourteen years was the secretary of the Signoria of Florence and the master of a mature and excellent chancery style. Machiavelli might be considered the founder of Italy's prose literature as much as Boccaccio, if the ban of which his writings were an object had not closed him off for many decades in a sterile limbo.

187 VENICE

The process of Florentine and Tuscan linguistic maturation is matched, although at a distance, by an analogous process in the area of Venice, where political circumstances made it possible for the Venetian linguistic system to spread progressively as a superstratum as far as the Alpine frontier, and in more adjacent regions to blend with preexisting speech forms. The most interesting linguistic development of the period is the one that took place in Padua, in the evolution from "pavano" to "padovano," and by the latter we mean "the Paduan dialect with Venetian elements." As late as the sixteenth century, Angelo Beolco, known as Ruzzante (ca. 1502–42), is a symbol of ancient "pavano." Beginning with the genuine "pavano" base, Ruzzante works in his capacity as a playwright to coordinate more than one linguistic tradition into a superior synthesis. Thus in his early comedy *La pastorale* the original Paduan dialect appears with its final *-ò*'s instead of -ATO, as in *acolegò* 'coricato' (in bed), *amalò* 'ammalato' (taken ill); with strong diphthongization not only in open syllable as for example in *bruolo* 'orto' (garden), but also in closed syllable as in *govierni* 'governi' (governments); and with strong palatalization of the L before I, as in *cavigi* 'capelli' (hair), and *friegi* 'fratelli'. But the "pavane" forms are fitted into a broader sociolinguistic body, in which other levels, both inferior and superior, are contrasted. The lower social level is personified by the rough peasant who speaks in the dialect of Bergamo; high-class Venetian appears in forms like *agiuto* for 'aiuto' or *si scorze* for 'si scorge'. Both lexical (*tuti* 'sicuri') and graphic (*victo, stricto*) Latinisms are present.[7]

Once it has grown in a geographic sense, the newborn tradition of Venetian literary language rapidly increases in importance through its use as a chancery language; ambassadorial letters written in Venetian demonstrate both the maturity of a political class and the adaptability of Venetian linguistic vehicles to new needs.[8] The Neapolitan Benedetto di Falco, a contemporary of Ruzzante, hopes that the Signoria of Venice will "reform Italian speech by making one language for everyone . . . as there was once one Latin for the whole world."[9] If the political events connected with the League of Cambrai had concluded favorably for Venice, di Falco's hope could have become a reality according to the same process by which a national language based on chancery, and not on literary, style developed in both France and England.

188 ROME

Roman development is much more moderate, and rather more passive than active. In the period of the two Medici popes, Leo X (1513–21) and Clement VII (1523–34), the new element on the Roman scene consists in the prestige accruing to Florentine models of all sorts, including linguistic models, and in the solidarity and vigor of the retinue that accompanied them from Florence. Thus it happens that in the sixteenth century the Roman dialect loses its most conspicuous anti-Florentine features such as diphthongization in closed syllable (§176), but it continues to remain distinct from Florentine, as a variant that is not so antithetical as before. On the psychological level, through the modified Tuscan accent that made an impression in Rome, the saying *Lingua toscana in bocca romana* ('Tuscan as spoken by a Roman') was born, which has been a model of a pleasant, tempered Italian accent almost up to the present time, although it has now been superseded (§236). From this rapprochement there grew a theoretical parallel in the same period. At the beginning of the century Angiolo Colocci (1474–1549) had elaborated a theory about the vernacular which could be traced by way of imperial Rome to four sources: Picenum, Oscan, Tuscan, and Sabine; this was a synthetic interpretation destined to be taken up again in modern times, although in a duly altered form.

These changes in the Roman dialect of the cinquecento, however rich in consequences, were not immediate. In a comedy dating from the end of the century, the *Stravaganze d'amore* by Christoforo Castelletti, presented in 1585, the Roman dialect survives in the words of one humble character, a certain Perna.[10]

189 BEMBO'S THEORIES

Thus the time came when it was necessary to respond consciously not to the question of whether or not the vernacular was to be preferred, and not even to which vernacular was preferable, but to the question of how *the* vernacular was to be defined. The first answer to this question is found in the *Regole della volgar lingua* of Gian Francesco Fortunio, which is dated 1516. In spite of its substantial validity, it was soon obscured by the *Prose della volgar lingua* (1525) of Pietro Bembo, which, in its dialogue form, had an immediate and profound effect. According to Bembo, now that the vernacular was established, that vernacular must be Tuscan. Moreover, this Tuscan must also be "archaic," that is, inspired by the models of Petrarch, Boccaccio, and other writers of the trecento. Dante must not be held up as a model; this is understandable if we remember that Dante, precisely because it was he who enriched the Italian lexical heritage, was not at the same time selective from the point of view of vocabulary (§168).[11] Then Bembo states that every word must be in harmony with the mood the material calls for: serious words for grave matters and light words for popular material. Adjectives that describe words recommended by Bembo are *pura, chiara, monda, bella, grata,* which we translate roughly as 'pure', 'clear', 'limpid', 'beautiful', and 'pleasant'; adjectives that qualify words of which Bembo disapproved are *languida, densa, rinserrata, pingue, arida, morbida,* which we translate as 'weak', 'dense', 'closed-in', 'heavy', 'dry', and 'soft'. With regard to clauses and sentences, the aim was always for an effect of gravity or of pleasantness, according to a rigorous standard not unlike that to which poetry was subjected.

190 CASTIGLIONE'S THEORIES

In contrast to Bembo's theory stands the thesis of Baldassarre Castiglione (1478–1529), stated with valid reasons but with less coherence. In Castiglione's view as it is presented in his *Cortegiano* (editions in 1508, 1519, and 1528), language is but a special instance of a civic, social, and world vision that excludes any form of provincialism whatever, whether geographic or chronological, even at the cost of being forced to become discriminatory with regard to social class. The differences in the positions of Castiglione and Bembo are not so much matters of quality as they are ones of quantity. In contrast to Petrarch's "heraldic" selection, Castiglione is less removed from Dante's pragmatic unitary policy. It is not possible, therefore, to illustrate Bembo's line of reasoning, but only to comment on a few examples of his open policy which are not always commendable. For example, it is not accurate to state that non-Tuscan Latinate forms such as *populo* and *onorevole* are more decorative than the corresponding Tuscan forms 'popolo' and 'orrevole'. Contrariwise, in our view Latinisms such as *abusione, argumento, captivo, divorzio di acque, documento* for 'insegnamento', and *esito* for 'uscita' do not lend themselves to criticism. Archaic Tuscanisms that Castiglione accepts are *avvilito* for 'ribassato di prezzo', *diffidato* for 'disperato', and *manco* for 'manchevole'. Acceptable northern dialect forms are *biastemar* for 'bestemmiare' (to curse), *capigliara* for 'capigliatura' (hairstyle), and *sentare* for 'sedere' (to sit). Examples of forced exoticisms are *brida* for 'briglia' (bridle), *debatto* for 'dibattito' (debate), and *visaggi* for 'facce' (faces).[12] Lesser contributors to the debate on language are Giangiorgio Trissino (1478–1550), who does not restrict himself geographically to Tuscany but aims at the (theoretical) contribution of all Italy, and Claudio Tolomei (1492–1556), who adopts an intermediate position, concentrating his attention on an ideal that is "Tuscan" rather than rigidly Florentine.

Bembo's thesis received an important impetus through the work of Leonardo Salviati (1540–89), who in 1564 wrote the "Orazione in lode della fiorentina lingua" and later "Degli avvertimenti della lingua sopra 'l Decamerone."[13]

Salviati's efforts, however, were most important in transferring the Florentine doctrine into the circle of the academics of the Crusca in such a way that the first edition of the *Vocabolario degli Accademici della Crusca* (Venice, 1612; see §196) appears as the application and final outcome of the doctrine that was coherently formulated for the first time by Pietro Bembo eighty-seven years before.

Apogee and Satiety

191 PHONETIC AND GRAPHIC EVOLUTION
The opposition between static and dynamic phases, as they can appear through the difference between the first two phonematic systems of Italian, is less evident in the cinquecento. Nevertheless, we do not arrive in this century at the state of stability that is predicated and expected. Remnants of ancient disturbances appear, sometimes connected with the problems of adapting late Latinisms. The most elementary cases[1] consist in the standardization of the atonal U's, which still survive in forms such as *vulgo/volgo, sustanza/sostanza,* and *capitulo/capitolo;* or in the delayed palatalization of the J as in *iocondo/giocondo* and in *Iulio/Giulio.* The processes of palatalization, however, pose two problems of a more complex nature. On the one hand we have the lateral L (GL), which replaces the types GHJ and GHI; *ragliare, mugliare,* and *Figline* take the place of the forms *ragghiare, mugghiare,* and *Figghine.* On the other hand, we have the cases of deviation of the palatals which, as the tongue moves forward toward the teeth, finally produce a new group of real dentals that are characterized by an element of plebeian extremism; examples are *stiavo* as compared with 'schiavo', *diaccio* in contrast to 'ghiaccio', and similarly *mastio* and *diacere* as compared with 'maschio' and 'giacere'.[2]

The passage from a phonematic system which imposes the passage from PL to PJ to one which accepts the continued existence of PL is not entirely free of difficulties. There is an intermediate solution in the form PR, which is present in the forms *compressione, frutto,* and *pepro* for 'complessione', 'flutto', and 'peplo'. Less significant attempts also appear, as for instance ALTRU, which could have evolved into *aitro,* and AU before the accent, which became A- in words of uninterrupted tradition (§106); one of the last traces is *arora* for 'aurora'.

From the point of view of adjustment to the characteristic features of other regions, we must remember the exaggerated diphthongization of the type *spiero* 'spero' (I hope) in Venice, *crudiele* 'crudele' (cruel) in the Emilian region of Boiardo, and *tieco* 'teco' in Bologna. The weakening of metaphony outside Tuscany is an additional factor; for example, in Sabbadino degli Arienti we note *genoìsi* but also "bolognesi," and *amorusi* but also 'religiosi'. We must also take note of the confusion that results from the blending of forms that have been affected by lenition and those that have not, as well as related excesses of zeal; in the north we find the type *deliberaDo* as well as the form 'deliberaTo', and even *daTo* for 'dado' (die).

192 MORPHOLOGICAL CHANGES

Apart from phonetics there still remain a few "rough spots" to eliminate. One of the first transitions of some structural value is the decline of the so-called Law of Tobler and Mussafia,[3] which confirmed in the Italian world the weak nature of the second syllable, this weakness having a remote Indo-European origin. As a result of this rule, the atonal pronominal particles had to be placed in second position; in other words, they were "enclitic" with respect to the preceding fully accented word. Up to this time the standard construction had been *pregovi* and not 'vi prego'. Now this relationship loses its rigidity; forms like 'vi prego' begin to spread and today are still valid and the only ones in use, apart from the style adopted in telegraph messages in which the economy of the word makes the former type preferable. The forms *mi* and *ti* are still used, and they are accented as in *misera mi,* instead of the form 'misera ME', which we use today. Notwithstanding its long history, the article maintains the validity of the pronoun in some cases: *la vita di Gesù . . . e LA di Maria,* for which we today would be obliged to substitute ' "quella" di Maria'. As for the verb, it is only in this period that the regular paradigm 'dissero' took the lead over the other variants, the strongest of which was the form *dissoro* (§149). The nominal forms of the verb had a more "verbal" framework than do the present-day forms which are fitted into nominal relationships; today we ought to say "restata la femmina contentA," while in that period it was permissible to say *restatO la femmina contenta;* another example is *gli operai vistOsi in vergogna,* which today would be defined in a nominal form 'vistisi', as if it were the predicate object. Finally, the polite form of the pronoun was taking shape in this period through a process consisting of three phases: in the first phase, which dates from the quattrocento, the pronouns *quella, essa,* and *lei* always refer to an understood *vostra signoria* or *vostra magnificenza;* in the second phase, the Spanish usage of 'Signore' becomes widespread, and the forms *Ella/ Lei,* with 'Signoria' understood, still survive. In the third stage, *Lei* takes on a shape and an autonomous value and is parallel to 'Voi' and 'Vostra signoria'. With regard to "structures," it is in this state of affairs that the sixteenth century ends.

193 THE MELODY OF THE SENTENCE

The progressive clarification of theories and the rapprochement of the large provincial areas seemed to forecast a period of tranquility in the second half of the cinquecento similar to that of the Latin language under the spell of the Ciceronian model. Just as Latin in the first century B.C. began to absorb the seeds of future changes, so the literary language of Italy had then to face two grave problems: its "extension" to nonliterary fields in which the use of Latin still persisted and the exaggerated use of those tools and vehicles of a peripheral nature, such as rhythm and melody.[4]

Beginning with the second point, we note that the taste of the times was influenced by the young Petrarch, who was enthusiastic in his reading of classical authors and who prized the *dulcedo* 'sweetness' and the *sonoritas* 'sonority' of their words. Certainly, Ariosto was not deaf to this sweetness and sonority, but straddling the fifteenth and sixteenth centuries as he did, it seemed to him that his first priority was to try to attain a sense of unity in the literary language which at the time was, as we have seen, still furrowed with more or less troublesome regional forms. It was only with Torquato Tasso (1544–95), a man of the second half of the cinquecento, that the rhythm of the ottava rima could exercise an uninhibited charm without phonetic or grammatical interferences and that melodic potentiality could have free rein. Tasso, however, did not blindly abandon himself to melody; in fact, he was often more moderate than his own father, Bernardo Tasso (1493–1569). Torquato theorized on schema that were similar to Dante's; he distinguished the "magnificent" style from the "mediocre" and the "humble," extolling above all the lexical aspects of the first. He openly adopted the position of favoring foreign words, so long as they were taken from congeneric languages, such as French and Spanish as well as from Latin. He even admitted the principle of artificial or "simulated" (*finte*) words, among which he sought extrinsic qualities such as "roaring" (*rimbombo*) or "murmuring" (*sussurro*), even more than clear derivation or metaphorical meaning. He did not resist the temptations of onomatopoeia and as a result saw his poetry criticized as "base" or "cacophonous." In revising his epic poem, which was called the *Gerusalemme conquistata* (1593), Tasso did not achieve results equal to his intentions[5] and consequently was bombarded by harsh attacks from Salviati (§196).[6] Nevertheless, precisely because of his formal preoccupations that were not necessarily linked to theories and because of his internal scrupulousness with regard to formal questions, Tasso not only contributed to a tradition but also worked toward the exaltation of a tradition of literary language that continued well into the seicento.

194 THE LANGUAGE OF SCIENCE AND GALILEO

The extension of Italian to nonliterary fields consists in its application of the literary vernacular to philosophical and scientific texts. Let it suffice here to point out three stages of this process. The first stage is typified by a mathematician of scant humanistic learning, Nicolò Tartaglia (1499–1557), whose *Nova Scientia* of 1537 was translated into French. Despite the fact that the idea of writing in the vernacular was considered premature and not very honorable, the bare fact that Tartaglia did so is enough to assure him a place in the history of Italy's linguistic evolution.

The second stage is built around Giordano Bruno (1548–1600), who wrote his *Dialoghi* in the vernacular in 1586. From a historical-linguistic point of view, the *Dialoghi* constitute a document of revealing significance, precisely because of the effort they represent, the terminological imprecision, and the contrasts in tone, which is at times literary, at times humble, and sometimes frankly vulgar.

In contrast to the difficulties and torments of these pioneers, there stands with a magnificence, a maturity, and a perfection worthy of Boccaccio the tradition of scientific language personified by Galileo Galilei (1564–1642): calm, solid, mature, and definitive. The synthesis that Galileo produces is of a very high order. The spoken language of his dialogues is disciplined and adapted to the formulation of scientific precepts. Direct discourse alternates with indirect, not as a means of producing external variety, but with the symmetry of crystals. The transfiguration that Galileo wrought is such that we cannot speak with regard to his writings of a tradition of special language for science, but only of a literary language that is so flexible to be able to bend to the needs of science without becoming deformed in the process. His expertise resides then in the area of vocabulary and above all in his ability to make technical use of ordinary words, in much the same way that it is possible to do with great naturalness today in the English language. Examples of Galileo's technical application of everyday words are the use of *candore* as 'lunar light', *momento* as applied to physics, *macchie solari* 'sunspots', and the substantival use of *pendolo* 'pendulum'. This did not impede his creating, when needful, new words such as *apogeo* and *parallasse*. His influence appears all the greater and more decisive inasmuch as he epitomizes the person who perfected Italian scientific language, although ironically he did not employ Italian in his writings until he was fifty years old, his first work in his native language being the discourse "Intorno alle cose che stanno in su l'acqua" (1612). Nor was Galileo deaf to the theoretical positions taken regarding language. His "poetics" consisted in conciseness and was very distant, for example, from the sensibility and the achievements of Torquato Tasso.

195 SEVENTEENTH-CENTURY STYLISTIC MANNERISMS
The impulses and tendencies that Tasso had exhibited continued through the sixteenth century and on into the seventeenth, in still more extreme forms. The ottava rime of G. B. Marino (1569–1625) combine the search for melody with all that can excite the fantasy: etymological extremes (for example, the Dora River is associated with gold), rhetorical questions, series of metaphors and exclamations; in short, all that can lend to the language of poetry a sense of constant wonderment. The trend toward ornamentation and melody blends with a preference for Spanish words, which was widespread in this period. This in turn provokes an influx of Spanish words, subsequently solidly grafted onto the language, such as *creanza, sussiego, premura* and *lindo,* which form part of the cult of forms that characterized Spain at that time. The history of Italian sacred oratory, of which the work of Father Paolo Segneri (1624–94) is the most important representative, is no different. The obsessive exclamations that occur in succession—*oh cecità! oh stupidezza! oh delirio! oh perversita!*—are accompanied by frightening descriptions, apocalyptic visions, and terrifying invectives that rain down from the pulpit, intoned not so much at the masses, who were not refined enough to appreciate them, as at the grandeur and opulence of the baroque churches.[7] These more extremist expressions do not lead to a real break with the traditions of the preceding centuries. In addition to these exaggerated expressions more moderate ones continue that do

not pose any form of contrast with the patterns of the preceding century. Examples of more moderate forms are the travel stories written subsequent to those geographic discoveries which greatly increase our knowledge of India, China, and Japan. The testimony of accounts of India by Filippo Sassetti (1540–88) is not refuted, contradicted, or corrected by the splendid letters of Daniello Bartoli (1608–85) from the Far East.

Apart from these, the *Arte della guerra*, by Raimondo Montecuccoli (1609–80), deserves mention, because of its Tacitean sentences reminiscent of aphorisms and epigrams; an example is *Le battaglie danno e tolgono i regni, pronunziano le sentenze decisive e inappellabili tra i potentati, terminano le guerre e immortalano il capitano. Esse si cercano, si fuggono o si danno.*

Forty

Toward a New
Bilingualism

196 THE ACADEMY OF THE CRUSCA
The linguistic theories of individual scholars and the preferences of individual authors do not exhaust our description of the forces that affect Italy's linguistic usage. These forces bring about another stage—one that is normative, collective, and no longer individual. The symbol and instrument of this activity is the Academy of the Crusca. Its history dates back to 1541, when Cosimo I recognized the Florentine Academy by assigning to it the task of translating all learning into the Tuscan vernacular. In 1583 the Accademia della Crusca ('chaff, bran') was born; in the beginning its name was interpreted in a humorous sense. It was only through the action of Leonardo Salviati (see §193), who saw in its members, the Crusconi, not just convivial companions who think only of having a good time, but men who are capable of sifting the flour and separating it from the "bran," that the new academy took up its first task, the publication of the *Vocabolario degli Accademici della Crusca*, the first edition of which saw the light in Venice in 1612; it was inspired in choice and acknowledgment of words by the archaic Florentine model that Bembo had advocated (see §189).[1] The second edition came out in 1623, and the third, in three volumes, in 1691 in Florence. This last edition contained the vocabulary of several other authors;

particularly conspicuous was the acceptance of material originating from Torquato Tasso. The impact of the *Vocabolario* was profound even outside Italy. It became the archetype of all modern language dictionaries, especially the dictionary of the Académie francaise (1692), which, however, excludes the acceptance of material before the seventeenth century, for reasons peculiar to the French language. The first period of activity of the Accademia della Crusca ends with the fourth edition of the dictionary, published in six volumes in Florence between 1729 and 1738.[2]

197 ARCADIA AND METASTASIO

The ornamental and emphatic tension that had made itself manifest during the seventeenth century carried with it the seeds of a reaction which occurred in two stages. The first deals above all with the question of images and tastes and does not cut directly into the structure of the Italian literary language. This change is identified with the founding of the Accademia dell'Arcadia (1690). The promoter of the academy was G. V. Gravina (1664–1718), and its aim was to oppose the taste for the marvelous and the monumental with rustic images and moderate and refined emotions. Born only as a formula, Arcadia came to define an opposite mannerism, but one that was not substantially different from that imposed by the baroque of the seicento. In any case, a special quality that characterized the beginning of the settecento was faithfulness to rhythm in the field of poetic language. Pietro Metastasio (1698–1782), with his preference for Tasso's schema over those of Ariosto and his fondness for Marino's poetry rather than the lyrics of the cinquecento, was the one to continue the seicento. But he is the champion of a tradition renewed by the specialized poetic language of the melodrama and gravitating toward an elementary vocabulary and a dependency on rhythm even in the use of interjections: *Ah, che né mal verace—né vero ben si da— prendano qualità—da' nostri affetti.*

198 G. B. VICO AND L. A. MURATORI

The real rebellion against the seicento, inasmuch as it is a century of linguistic confidence and expansion, is manifest in quite another, more resolute, form, through the documentation of a linguistic torment that is still more apparent than that of Giordano Bruno (§194), namely, in the writings of G. B. Vico (1668–1744).

The *Scienza nuova prima* (1725) and its later version the *Scienza nuova* (1730), so rich in speculative intelligence and lyric power, are not inspired by any seventeenth-century model; they are not content with the affectedness of Arcadia and remain distant even from the now classical models of Galileo. For Vico it is the Latin models that are exemplary. After having returned to writing Latin in an earlier period, Vico was inspired by these models, characterized by complex sentence structure, fluctuation between indirect and direct discourse, a tendency toward infinitive construction, a preference for adjectives in anteposition in pairs or in threes, a search for compound verbs, and the insistence on the affective value of prefixes, even when writing in Italian.

Apart from Latin, Vico was aware of the prestige of Tuscan models and among these he preferred the archaic types, as we can see from his choice of words such as *maestrato* for 'magistrato', *propio* for 'proprio', and *notomia* for 'anatomia'. He also accepted Neapolitan models, though without ever giving his sentence structure any local coloring. On the other hand, precisely because of its inner turmoil, Vico's style, for all its complexity, could not match the harmonious and controlled style of Boccaccio.

A further expansion in the field of Italy's literary language occurred in this century with regard to antiquarian erudition, thanks to Ludovico Antonio Muratori (1674–1750). Muratori was not, however, to erudite language what Galileo had been to scientific language. While his attitude was antibaroque, Muratori was certainly not considered the champion of a new vision. Indeed, he has the dubious distinction of being remembered for giving little thought to the rational use of linguistic structures. In short, he left us examples of pedestrian prose. Within the more strictly linguistic problem, apart from its esthetic aspects, Muratori had real concerns. He recognized and seized the opportunity of enriching the terminology of the field of erudition. In his *Trattatello della perfetta poesia italiana* (Modena, 1706), he emphasized the good qualities of sixteenth-century models, not as Florentine, but as Italian. In his *Antichità del Medio evo,* he dedicated his thirty-second discourse to the origins of the Italian language. He was aware of the problem of the relationship between dialects and standard language and recommended experimentation in translating the former into the latter. With regard to isolated words, he preferred those that were not banal: *garofani* for 'garofoli' (carnations), *scudella* for 'scodella' (soup plate), and *cadino* for 'catino' (basin).

199 GALLICISMS IN THE VOCABULARY
The legacy of the seicento was not, therefore, brought into a new balance either by Arcadia or by the uneven accomplishments of Vico and Muratori. The linguistic continuity that had flowed uninter-

rupted since the time of Dante now entered into crisis. Not having had a constructive outlet, it left a wake not only of relaxation but also of deliberate slackness (§203) that was destined to end in what Giuseppe Toffanin[3] called *lo sciopero della lingua* 'language on strike'.

In the area of scientific language on the one hand, a prominent author such as Francesco Redi (1626–98) neglected the tradition of Galileo but did not know how to begin a new one. On the other hand, a man of letters such as Lorenzo Magalotti (1637–1712) played an important role in opening the language of Italy to a new and almost fatal resource, the Gallicism. His part later acquired for him the attribute of "one of the first corruptors of the language."[4] But Magalotti's action was not a caprice. The dialogue with Latin having recently come to an end, the biases of dialectal centers having been curbed, the melodic and ornamental possibilities having been exhausted with the seicento, and Arcadia's protest having slipped into mannerism, a new sap, enriching and rejuvenating, was present in the Gallicism, in a way not unlike that which Latin had represented in Dante's time. The principal foci from which the Gallicisms spread were Piedmont and Parma.[5] As early as 1625 the first French grammar appeared, edited by Pietro Duranti; in the settecento these grammars multiplied. Fifteen editions of Racine's *Iphigénie* appear between 1708 and 1799.

French words became rooted in Italy's linguistic tradition beginning with the field of apparel and fashion; extreme examples are *disabigliè, bonè, dominò, falbalà, fisciù, ghette, mantò, surtù* 'overcoat', *flanella,* and *frisatura.* Examples of Gallicisms having to do with cuisine are *bignè, fricandò, ragù, sciampagna, cotolette,* and *fricassea;* concerning interior decoration we have *burò, bidè, cabarè, ridò,* and *trumò.* Turning to industry we find *calotta, cerniera, ghisa,* and *zinco;* and in the field of navigation *manovra, scialuppa,* and *andare alla deriva.* With regard to social life we have *abbordare, cochetta, madamosella, condiscendenza, allarmare, finezza, imparzialità, irritabilità,* and *vanitoso;* and with regard to the military *ingaggio, mitraglia, baionetta, tappa, rango, picchetto, massacro,* and *montura.* But many Gallicisms were not permanently accepted into Italian; examples of these are *partaggio* for 'divisione', *visaggio* for 'viso', *portreto* 'ritratto', *bordosa* 'ricamatrice', *paressoso* for 'pigro', *regrettare* for 'rimpiangere', *polito* for 'cortese', *volare* for 'rubare', *lutta* for 'lotta', *mantenire* for 'mantenere', and even *pesàno* for 'contadino'. Just how deep-rooted this interweaving was, even in the work of individual authors, is demonstrated by the case of Francesco

Algarotti (1712–69),[6] who criticized the then-current use of *dettaglio, regretto,* and *debosciato* and himself employed *capo d'opera* and *cochette.*

One particular sector of Italian life, that of economy, now takes on greater importance, gravitating in large part toward French models. After Antonio Genovesi (1712–69) had initiated a course on "civil economics" at the University of Naples in 1754, the abbot Ferdinando Galiani (1728–87) employed a technical language that was already more mature and contained Gallicisms that were destined to find a permanent place in Italian, without much difficulty of a technical nature; examples of the Gallicisms he used are *materie prime, mano d'opera, analisi, dettaglio, fermentazione, and raffinazione.* Finally, although there were in this field Gallicisms that were provisional and short-lived, such as *egualità, monetaggio,* and *aumentazione,* there were also words of fundamental importance belonging to this period, such as the following: *esportare* as an economic term, which is specialized in comparison with the generic 'estrarre'; *importare,* which is specialized in comparison with the generic 'immettere'; and last *milionario,* as a symbol of personal wealth, which in that period began to have consistency.

French fashion did not introduce Gallicisms alone into Italy. It was also the intermediary for Anglicisms[7] such as *constituzione, comitato, commissione, maggioranza, opposizione,* and *petizione.* As we can all see, however, these are really cases of Anglo-Latinisms that were easily assimilated first by the French (the intermediary) and then by the Italians (consignee).

200 GALLICISMS IN CONSTRUCTIONS

It is important to be aware of violent Gallicisms in constructions like *vengo a dire* for 'sto per dire', *vengo di leggere* for 'ho appena letto', *in leggendo,* which is modelled after the French *en lisant,* and *il poema* IL *più galante, le pene* LE *più acconce, passare a esaminare, discendere a ordinare.* But formulae such as *fare il diavolo a quattro* or *mettere una cosa sul tappeto* or *occorre più* DI *energia* were excessively criticized by Algarotti.

Constructions that were perfectly integrated were *i polli* ALLO *spiedo* and the reinforced phrase *È lui che l'ha detto*[8] instead of 'l'ha detto lui.' But in the sentence as a whole, the beneficial influence of the Gallicism appears in the introduction of a pattern that was much more linear, in comparison with the traditional Italian sentence structure, which was complex, hierarchical, and "architectonic."

The French tradition had, therefore, a profound and innovative effect on Italian and resulted in the settecento's being called the century of "new bilingualism" (no longer Latin).[9] This tradition continued and finally united with the French current inspired by Napoleon, which was so different in its ideals. Naturally, and notwithstanding its profound penetration and great authority, it also provided occasions for satire; we find an example of such satire in the writings of Giuseppe Parini (§204), who in his ode "Il giorno" (lines 200–201) writes *misere labbra che tempra non sanno—con le galliche grazie il sermon nostro.*[10]

Part Five

Italy United:
From 1850 to the Present

Forty-one

Hypercriticism

201 SELECTIONS

Although the theoretical debates waned and were discredited, the vast world of linguistic experimentation did not grow calm, not even to the extent of sinking into indifference. Other criteria of comparison, discrimination, and devaluation took the lead. The language is analyzed and judged no longer according to the unidimensional criterion of conformity to the spatial concept of Tuscan territory, nor with respect to the temporal standard of the archaic Florentine tradition, but rather according to the criterion of social strata. Words are analyzed and selected, dissected and reclassified from time to time in either an upward or a downward social direction.

Here is how Scipione Maffei (1675–1755) classified words, and here it is not important to determine whether it was in a way that reflects or offends our present-day sensibilities; for example, he excludes from the vocabulary of poetry words such as *appetito, confutare, congratularsi, dimenticanza, magnificenza, misericordia, operare,* and *tribolato.* Similarly, according to Eustachio Manfredi (1674–1731), on the poetic level, *diligenza* must be substituted with 'cura', *divertimento* with 'piacere', *salario* with 'mercede', *disgrazia* with 'sventura', *collera* with 'disdegno', and *sodisfatto* with 'pago'.

202 RESISTANCES

Not even the negative positions enjoyed undisputed success as, in another sense, the exaggerated tendency toward melody and ornamentation had in the seicento.

An unmotivated and perhaps unconscious stand appears in the prose style of a lively essayist, Gaspare Gozzi (1713–86), with the "portraits" of the *Osservatore Veneto;* in these portraits we find a true sample of an easy, concise style which was somewhat in harmony with the French style of composition and which was basically useful in neutralizing in a nonreactionary sense the consequences of pessimism and linguistic disintegration just illustrated.[1] On a constructive level, a direction of some interest was defended by another essayist, Giuseppe Baretti (1719–89), who was inspired by a strong polemic spirit. The middle road which he proposed, halfway between the nihilism of the "Caffè" group (§203) and the literalism of the Crusca traditions, consists in his recognition of the validity of a model consecrated by history; as opposed to the banality of a contemporary writer like the economist Antonio Genovesi (§199), Baretti invites his generation to look to the past. This past is not, however, the past of the trecento; still limiting himself to Tuscany and Florence, Baretti looks to the style of Cellini—*semplice, chiaro, veloce*—as worthy of imitation. At the same time he strictly defined this frame of reference, excluding on the one hand the authority of a model like the overly courtly style of Boccaccio, who is defined in the *Frusta letteraria* of 1763 as the "ruin of the language of Italy." On the other hand, he eliminated from contemporary Florentine, defined as a "lousy . . . language," every normative or imitative tendency. Moreover, Baretti did not spare the *Vocabolario degli Accademici della Crusca,* which he describes as full of *stomachevoli vocaboli e modi di dire, parte tratti da molti dei loro ribaldi prosatori e poeti, e parte raccolti nei chiassi e nei lupanari di Firenze.*[2]

203 NEGATIONS

At the same time, with reference to its sphere of application, the Italian language records its last conquest, in the only field in which Latin had resisted. We are speaking of studies of classical antiquity, in which the abbot Luigi Lanzi (1732–1810), with his fundamental work, *Saggio di lingua estrusca e di altre antiche d'Italia* (1789), demonstrates that Italian is by now perfectly suited to any branch of learning. The geographic expansion of its use was shown in 1764 when Italian was adopted as the official language of Sardinia[3] in place of Spanish.

Though overbearing, disorderly, and paradoxical, the influx of Gallicisms still continues to have a limited importance in light of the new outlook on linguistic problems. These problems are now introduced in a challenging form that is contrary to all that had been the travail of Italian authors from their first attempts to create a vernacular literary language.

This attitude was negative in comparison with the validity of the linguistic debates and had as its nucleus in Milan the readership of the review *Il Caffè* (1764–66). The famous positions that Pietro Verri (1728–97) took in the periodical are two in number. The first is: "Every word that is understood by all the inhabitants of Italy is, according to us, an Italian word; the authority and consenting opinion of all Italians, in the matter of their language, is greater than the authority of all grammarians." The second position is: "Whenever a writer says reasonable and interesting things and states them in a language that is understood by all Italians and writes with such artistry that his language can be read without trouble, that writer must be called a good Italian author." A document written by Pietro's brother, Alessandro Verri (1741–1816), can be related to these propositions; appearing in the July 1764 issue of *Il Caffè*, it solemnly renounces "the pretended purity of the Tuscan tongue," although in a private letter dated four years later Alessandro had some second thoughts on the matter.[4] Similarly, Francesco Algarotti (§199) had written a couple of decades earlier, "He who says . . . things that are good and useful to society can do without beautiful words."[5]

The transition from theory to practice was not, however, a simple one. Cesare Beccaria (1738–1794), the famous champion for the abolition of the death sentence, tried to elaborate a linguistic theory in his "Ricerche intorno alla natura dello stile" (1770), by seeking to reconcile a style of writing that was "guided by certain principles and by inalterable norms" with the recognition of the evocative powers of language. Unfortunately, he did not succeed in being consistent even in his own spelling, as is demonstrated by his use of the forms *diffenderlo*, *gueReggiare*, *diFusamente*, *sfoGio*, and *diriGGano*.

204 RHYTHMS

In the language of poetry, the race towards ornamentation and exaggerated expressive intensity reached its climax above all in the melody and rhythms of Pietro Metastasio (§197). As often happens, extreme goals provoked reactions. The abbot Giuseppe Parini (1729–1799), younger by a generation than Metastasio, symbolized a total reversal of interests with respect to the fatuous, external world of the century. Because of Parini's different vision of life, Italy's language experienced profound repercussions, particularly with regard to the language of poetry. The first victim of these repercussions was the traditional insistence on rhythms that were ever more stimulating and accentuated. From the point of view of metrics, Parini preferred the ode to the canzonetta and the free hendecasyllable to rhyme. He did not adhere to the centrifugal or free *(lassistici)* models, but, like Horace, always held to the principle of moderation; he felt the Dantesque models, which at times appeared capricious or grotesque to him, to be remote. If necessary, he indulged in a few syntactical Latinisms, for example, with regard to word order. He did not indulge in reformist tendencies with regard to lexical or grammatical material, as he had in the matter of rhyme. Nevertheless, Parini had enough authority to become the founder of the modern tradition of the free hendecasyllable, which was nobly continued by Alfieri, Foscolo, and Monti; the first of these writers was rebellious and unaccommodating; the second, austere and mature; and the third, resonant and sometimes melodramatic.

205 THE SUPPRESSION OF THE ACCADEMIA DELLA CRUSCA
The problems of linguistic structures and their coordination are put in a state of crisis. Nevertheless, specific uncertainties continue to diminish. They are reduced to variants in spelling, in the sense of alternatives between single and double consonants in words having an interrupted tradition, such as *a(b)bate, uf(f)izio,* and *rob(b)a,* as well as in the sense of the introduction of the double consonant as a result of a different analysis of a word, as in *immagine* and *innalzare.* With regard to the use of the article, IL still appears before a z.[6] For the pronoun employed as an adjective the form *mia* appears instead of 'mie' and 'miei'.[7] Turning to verb forms, we note that the conditional tense modeled after the Sicilian form in *-ia* is still frequent in poetry. As verbal auxiliaries there are forms like *si hanno preso la briga,* for which today we would substitute 'si sono presa la briga'. The nominal form of the verb *in dipignere* 'in painting', in part echoes the French type *en peignant* (§200). *Che* with the meaning 'quanto' is of Spanish origin.[8] Formal uncertainties are reduced to mere trifles. Because traditional preferences have been devalued and discredited, the moral authority of the Accademia della Crusca grows weaker. Girolamo Gigli, in his *Vocabolario cateriniano* (from 1717 on), reproaches the academy for not having taken into account, in various editions of its dictionary, material originating from Saint Catherine of Siena, and in this way opens the door to disputes and retorts. But the final consequence of this unpopularity was that in 1783 the Grand Duke of Tuscany suppressed the academy by uniting it with the Florentine Academy.

The language of Italy now opens to a thousand horizons; it now experiences new crises.

Forty-two

Language and Nationhood

206 THE DIALECTS "MAKE A COMEBACK"

The notion of "linguistic stratification" and the discrimination of higher and lower levels that is connected with it are made manifest according to entirely different criteria. In explicit opposition to preceding attitudes, the century of illuminism and rationalism does not block the literary use of the dialects, notwithstanding the fact that their literary hopes had ended with the cinquecetto. The principle that made them appear on the horizon was a negative one, namely, the elimination of exclusivism, of barriers that had no visible constructive scope.

For reasons that are entirely literary, the Venetian dialectal area, being the most imposing and practical, now takes the lead. The author who symbolizes this great turning point is Carlo Goldoni (1707–93).[1] He is the author of comedies that are written not only in the Venetian dialect, but also in literary Italian, and even in French; for this reason, his use of dialect does not represent a provincial mentality and even less a return to parochialism. Nevertheless, in the matter of practical application, Goldoni does not employ Italian and Venetian in the same way in his plays. On the one hand, the passages in dialect all appear in their full spontaneity and are in total harmony with the psychology and the expressivity of the personages and situations. On the other hand, the standard Italian of Goldoni's comedies often appears to be an extraneous, conventional, and artificial creation that does not satisfy the requirements which in the dialectal form find such free and spontaneous representation. An Italian formula like *converrà che lo soffra* 'it is necessary for me to endure it', meant to be spoken by the personage Giacinta in the comedy *Le smanie per la villeggiatura* as she turns to her maid, does not produce the same effect that another literary formula such as *bisognerà che mi adatti,* for example, would have produced. Goldoni's formulation, though meaning the same as *bisognerà che mi adatti*, reads as though it were a stage direction instead of a sentence in a dialogue; in other words it is an element apart, like the caption of a painting or a label at the side of a statue, existing on a different plane. For this reason, we cannot speak of a general linguistic resurgence of Venetian, but only of a supportive situation, in which Goldoni uses the dialect occasionally in situations which call for a feeling of closeness or of intimacy. In contrast to this, the literary language, although handled in a clumsy way, does not function effectively but rather serves as an abstract and pedestrian link whenever external commentary and illustration are needed.

We find a parallel use of dialectal structures at the opposite end of the peninsula, in Sicily. Here Giovanni Meli (1740–1815) took up the use of the dialect for the same reason that Goldoni did, namely, for a closer contact with his expressive world.[2] Indeed, unlike Goldoni, who with regard to dialect was able to make use of structures suited to his world, Meli did not depart from the dialect in an equally exclusive way. What he has left us is not a sample of a new dialectal achievement on a literary level, but rather paradoxically, an example of a tradition of Italian literary language that is specialized, or better yet diluted, by means of Sicilian elements and lexical units.

207 NATIONAL SYMBOL

From every process of disintegration a new order is born. A strong, new, inspirational principle replaces every negation. The social stratification factor functions not only with regard to making distinctions between social classes. A linguistic system can be related to the rapport between nations in an even more striking way than it can to the interrelationships between social classes. Between the eighteenth and the nineteenth centuries people escape from their old definition of being the *greggi dei re,* to become autonomous units that are not hierarchical except within the limits of necessity. Each political state or unit desires or demands to be supported by a parallel linguistic unit. Every linguistic system, as a condition of reciprocal understanding and fellowship, is a motivating force toward a political design of independence and unity.

This interpretation of linguistic systems as nuclei of national significance is not born suddenly and unexpectedly, but is rather the result of a process that has its origins precisely in the pressure of French on Italian, which seemingly ought to have produced effects quite other than that of encouraging an Italian national linguistic consciousness.

The first stage of this movement consists in the comparison of the structures and the functional capabilities of the linguistic vehicles of the two countries. In the second half of the eighteenth century a "balance of trade" seemed justified, however, at the expense of French, because of its orthographic instability and the tyranny of the Académie française, which, unlike its counterpart in Italy, could not compare and temper its contemporary sensibilities through the study of ancient texts. Because of the very rapid natural evolution of the language between the Middle Ages and the Renaissance, ancient French texts did not furnish material for useful comparison. There followed, again to the disadvantage of French, criticisms that were directed toward its rigid word order in the sentence, the sterility of its derivations that were devoid of superlatives and diminutives, its monolithic compactness that impeded a distinction between the language of poetry and that of prose, and finally the monotony of its rhythms. The mechanism of this debate can be reduced to the following three stages. In the first stage it is ascertained that a comparison of the two languages is impossible because of their different historical developments. In the second phase practical criteria of judgment are introduced. In the third, linguistic unity is linked to values that are no longer quantitative but qualitative; that is, by the idea of a linguistic system for the national community. In the light of these developments, the subtleties and the proclamations of faith in Florentine must have appeared not just old-fashioned but also futile, at least for a certain period of time.

The Italian author who was most conscious of this problem was Vittorio Alfieri (1749–1803). In the sonnet "L'Idioma gentile," written on the occasion of the suppression of the Accademia della Crusca (1783), and in his rigid declaration that all language can be found in Dante and Petrarch, Alfieri was not a precursor of that discreditable exclusivism known as purism (§211); rather, he expressed a point of view that was proudly nationalistic. Because of this he was able to declare that, within the framework of this sentiment, it required greater loftiness of soul to observe grammatical trifles than to disparage them.[3] But from the point of view of language scholars, the stands taken by nonmilitant men of letters are more significant; an example of such a man of letters is the Piedmontese Gianfrancesco Galeani-Napione (1748–1830), who in writing about the "Uso e dei pregi della lingua italiana" (1791), sought to initiate some action by suggesting that, in those semantic sectors in which it was most appropriate, such as the toilette, cuisine, and ornaments, Gallicisms be accepted into Italian. For Galeani-Napione, these categories constitute, because of their indispensable and exceptional nature, special cases akin to those in which "the Church permits even robbing."[4]

208 THE PHILOSOPHY OF LANGUAGES
The national interpretation of linguistic institutions ties in naturally with the problem of the interpretation of linguistic phenomena as a whole. It is precisely the existence of general stands taken within this frame of reference that gives weight and reality to specific interpretations. Even before the work of Napione, the publication that opens the door to these debates is the *Saggio sulla lingua italiana,* published in 1785 by Melchiorre Cesarotti (1730–1808) and republished in 1800 under the new title *Saggio sulla filosofia delle lingue.*[5] Some of his statements are, within human limits, definitive: "Initially no language is either elegant or barbarous"; "No language is pure"; "No language was ever formed on the basis of a preexisting model"; "No language is perfect"; "No language is unalterable"; and "No language is uniformly spoken in its region."

Similarly, Cesarotti states that the written language "must have usage as its base, example as its adviser, and reason as its directive." And regarding written language he states, "Jurisdiction over written language belongs undivided to three reunited authorities: philosophy, erudition, and good taste."

This is not all. The distinction acknowledged to exist between "memorative" and "representative" words aligns itself precisely with the difference recognized today between "evocative" action and "representative" action of linguistic vehicles of usage.[6] The essential inadequacy of linguistic systems is defined with the judgment, "even if we imagined that all possible objects were already discovered and named, human language would still be very poor." This, however, does not hinder language from sometimes appearing superabundant in linguistic forms. The relationships between morphology and syntax are recognized, through the distinction between the "content" and the "form" of syntax, understood in a general sense. The distinction between "semantic" and "syntactical" verb tenses is also suggested.[7] Moving against the nineteenth-century trend toward ramification, Cesarotti dares to state that languages are destined to come closer together.

With regard to details, Cesarotti defined neologisms such as *incompassione, disragione, infugare, rimbaldire, rischievole,* and *sceleranza.*[8] But he criticized medical vocabulary for being "perpetually corrupted by Hellenisms," citing the uses of *sintonia* for 'accidente', *narcotico* for the standard Italian form 'sonnifero', and *diatesi* instead of 'disposizione'. He defended "on the basis of analogy" the form *elettrizzare,* because the form 'elettricità' existed, and *magnetico* on the basis of the existence of 'magnetismo'.

At the height of the period in which all the normative forces of language had been deprived of authority, however, Cesarotti proposed the foundation of a responsible "national council on language," in other words, an equivalent of the disqualified Accademia della Crusca.

209 THE NAPOLEONIC AGE

Quite apart from theory, the Napoleonic age did indeed represent a trauma, even on the linguistic level. Among other events, the adoption of the Napoleonic Code afforded a more organic opportunity than there had ever been before for the absorption of words, just as French legal structures were being absorbed into the Italian system. It is impossible to make proportionate lists;[9] with regard to the miiltary we have *affusto, ambulanza, appello, avamposto, buffetteria, casermaggio,* and *marmitta;* words pertaining to administration are *borderò, controllo, parafare, regìa, timbro, cassazione,* and *giurì;* pertaining to cuisine we find *griglia, casseruola, tartina,* and *trattoria;* from the world of fashion *bretelle, calosce, paletò,* and *percalle;* and from theater there is the word *debutto.*

In addition to these words, there are the suffixes; the old form *-aggio* becomes more active again and is still very vital, and the suffix *-ista* spreads. These trends do not end with the Napoleonic period, but continue and are strongly influenced by Italy's industrial development and by Italy's contact with English society. Other technical terms, which do not always adapt well in Italy, arrive, always by way of France and then Austria. Examples of these are Anglicisms such as *leader* and *meeting,* which are used in their original forms, and *conservatore, radicale,* and *assenteismo,* which are adapted forms. We also find the psychological terms *humour* and *spleen,* and the railway terms *tender* and *tunnel* intact, while *vagone, locomotiva, viadotto, ferrovia* are adapted or imitated forms.

210 THE RECONSTRUCTION OF THE ACCADEMIA DELLA CRUSCA

Reason and symmetry had to "win out" over capriciousness and impulsiveness. The suppression of the Crusca, which the legitimistic Grand Duke had intended to be a manifestation of opportunity and modernity, was met by the disapproval not only of a single scholar like Cesarotti (§208). Indeed, its suppression was nullified by the sovereign "subversive," Napoleon. The Accademia della Crusca, which had been dissolved before the French Revolution, was reconstructed by Napoleon in 1808 within the framework of existing academies in Florence and was recognized as autonomous in 1811 at the height of the Napoleonic period. Moreover, Napoleon did not hesitate to assign it the task of supervising the literary language, particularly with regard to its "purity."

Naturally it was easier to bring an organization back to life than it was to make it resume responsibility for an operation that was already undergoing new trials, one in opposition to the other. In taking the problem in hand again, the initiative of Vincenzo Monti (1754–1828), author and poet, was useful, even though he was by nature very removed from debates concerning linguistic doctrine. Immediately after the Austrian restoration, he defined the goals of an Italian dictionary as being those of "purging the language, enriching it in a legitimate way, and molding it in a permanent way." In order to help the Crusca, which was basically perplexed about having to resume its responsibilities, Monti published his "Proposte di alcune aggiunte e correzioni al Vocabolario della Crusca" (1817–24). His attitude is defined by the basic premise that he was raising questions about words and not about authors, who in his opinion ought to be either universally accepted or universally rejected. In essence he was courting an "illustrious" Italian; he admitted a distinction between written and spoken language; above all he improved the old category of analogy, stating, on the one hand, that if *giullare* was acceptable, so was *giulleria,* and that for the same reason the forms *bibliotecario* and *biblioteca* had to be accepted together. On the other hand, it was necessary to limit analogy; for example, agreement in the formula *eccettI i figli* cannot be accepted, because "eccetto," in ceasing to function as a participle, became a preposition, and the indeclinable nature of the preposition must be assumed.

Forty-three

From Purism to
Manzonianism

211 PURISTS AND NONPURISTS

Monti's attitude was determined by the fact that he was a writer who did not think much about the principles involved in writing and even less felt the necessity of applying them rigidly. The case of the scholar who is steeped in the problems of language but who does not participate in their creative aspects—which are by definition open to the possibility of irregularity—is quite different. The doctrine which objectively accepts such an approach is called "purism." Purism aspires to the "purity" of language, regardless of how the criteria (historical, geographic, or social) used to define it are established. During this period in Italy it is represented by two authors who are a little younger than Monti. The first is the Veronese Antonio Cesari (1760–1828). Rigid in his dogmatic expression, he became emotional in his approach when he wrote about it; the following sentence is an effective example of both his theoretical approach and his passionate expression of it: "In that blessed period of the fourteenth century, everyone spoke and wrote well; . . . everyone was precise and correct, and there shone from within a certain natural honesty and the graciousness of simple and sweet manners, which no longer exist."[1] He promoted an unofficial edition of the *Vocabolario degli Accademia della Crusca,* which was published in 1806, and he was honored by the Accademia di Livorno for his "dissertazione sullo stato presente della lingua italiana (1808)," which was a sort of gospel of new purism.

The second of these men was Basilio Puoti, a Neapolitan (1782–1847); he was somewhat less rigid in setting up chronological boundaries limited to an ancient epoch. He was more arbitrary, however, in selecting authors and texts, and he was not very scrupulous as an editor because he changed and selected words according to how they sounded.[2] In 1833 he published the "Regole elementari della lingua italiana," which had certain praiseworthy aspects. But, since neither he nor Cesari had the ability to enforce purism universally, and since the Accademia della Crusca was during those years blindly groping without visibly progressing in its work, the first half of the nineteenth century appears to the eye of the historian, at a distance of a century and a half, like a great hiatus in the broad defensive front of the traditional Italian language.

This strict purism must be compared with certain unsystematic stands that were taken by authors in the beginning of the ottocento. Independent of their status as critics, writers, or poets, the essential points of view are the following. From Pietro Giordani (1774–1848), who is primarily a critic, we have certain polemic statements which still retain some interest value today. Giordani took a hostile attitude toward French sentence structure, which he found to be too analytical and epigrammatical in comparison with the complexity and harmony of Latin sentence structure, which he called true "logic in action."

Turning his attention to Florentines, he declared himself with equal impulsiveness to be against Florentine (and Tuscan) models. In a letter dated 16 March 1817, he writes: "There is no place in all Italy where one writes worse than in Tuscany and in Florence, because there is no place where language is studied less." Notwithstanding this impulsiveness, Giordani has the merit of having formulated for the first time the need for a history of the language, as a "first draft of a history of the civic spirit in Italy . . . as seen through the vicissitudes of language," in other words, a scientific thesis of primary importance, a pioneering effort.

The following thoughts of Ugo Foscolo (1778–1827), more reflective of his poetic temperament, are worth citing: "Language is the mistress of mediocre minds, but the servant of great men." "Every nation has a language. Each man of letters must speak to his nation in the language of his fatherland. Thought is not represented if not through words. Therefore, in order to represent thought it is necessary to know the value of the word. . . ."

Giacomo Leopardi (1798–1837) saw the problem of linguistic stability correctly; namely, that a language does not attain that stability until it dies. He observed the golden mean, believing in naturalness which is opposed to the two extremes of artificiality and colloquial expression. He aimed at elegance, seeking to avoid the ordinary and the banal. He made a distinction between "words" that were capable of evoking emotion in and poetry and "terms" that were confined to the limits of literal "representation" (§208). For this reason, he was able to accept the principle of "linguistic propriety" and at the same time deny that languages could evolve into one single language that was "almost pure mathematics, corresponding to a universal grammar." From this point of view he emphasized the difference that exists between Italian and French, the former being more evocative and the latter more literal; and for this reason, he found Galileo's stylistic patterns to be cold. Galileo, defined as being so "precise" and "mathematical," unconsciously reminded Leopardi of something Cartesian, and therefore French and foreign.

212 MILAN AND PORTA

In light of these positions, interesting and fortuitous, but not tied to any particular city, Milan takes on a special significance in the first quarter of the century. Among the many causes for this importance, the most conspicuous is dialectal poetry, as exemplified by the work of Carlo Porta (1776–1821). Porta's poetic language surpasses that of Goldoni, because of the genuineness of his testimony which is closed in the world of dialect and which does not attempt to confront foreign literary accomplishments in either Italian or French. He also surpasses dialectal creations in Sicilian because he demonstrates that dialect is much more impervious to the processes of dilution. A small government clerk devoid of inhibitions, Porta was not tempted to look beyond his world toward the affectedness of the aristocrats or the prestige of those who imitated the French style. Life, people, and language form an inseparable whole through which the geographic determination of the dialect and the social delimitation of the people constitute a historical-cultural unit closed off in itself.

213 THE POETIC LANGUAGE OF MANZONI

But this genuineness and integrity of documentation, instead of remaining within a quasi-folkloristic framework of exclusively dialectal documentations, is absorbed and by contrast becomes conspicuous not through a collective Milanese effort, but through one man who lived a linguistic experience so profound and rich that he came to formulate, if not a doctrine, a "directive" that was organic and complete and that answered to the needs of the times.

This illustrious Milanese was Alessandro Manzoni (1785–1873). Although he belonged to the upper class of his society, his first linguistic experiences were outside his class, taken in a strict sense, namely, in the Milanese dialect and in French. This early experience as an outsider nurtured a fundamental experience which applied not only to Italian problems. Like a hothouse plant, a feeling for poetic language developed in Manzoni, which was realized on a very high level in his *Inni sacri*, in "Cinque maggio," and in his tragedies. In all this Manzoni was a traditionalist in his choice of words and in his strongly accentuated rhythms which were proportioned to the epic themes he treated.

Nevertheless, the traditionalist period ends for Manzoni before 1825. The problem of prose concerned Manzoni the man and the user of language even before it concerned him as a novelist and an artist. If as a man he could have contented himself with being the last representative of eighteenth-century bilingualism, as a writer Manzoni had to follow ideals that were both new and conscious, because of his calling, his ambition, and the seriousness of his convictions. Not being able to elaborate the tools he already had at his disposal Milanese and French, Manzoni had to take into consideration and submit to scrutiny the problem of how much artificiality and indeed foreign matter there was in the current literary language. He reflected; and the new doctrine was not born in his mind as an organic whole but very slowly and in phases. The first stage was that of a generic language that went beyond the confines of the dialect and resembled the Dantesque vision; the second stage was a language that was generically Tuscan; and the third and final stage was a rigorously Florentine vision, not as the purists, emblamed in the contemplation of an archaic Florentine, had conceived it, but rather integral, pulsating, and steeped in the living models of his time.

214 Manzoni's Ideas on Prose

At the age of forty, Manzoni's position already appears constructive, even though it is still far from its final crystallization. In a letter to Luigi Rossari dated 1825, Manzoni speaks of that "Tuscan-Milanese" language, which, in his opinion, both men had been courting for some time. In the concrete reality of "Fermo and Lucia," which was written between 1821 and 1823[3] but never published by Manzoni, the author demonstrates that he had already reached his goal with regard to sentence structure. But the situation was comparable to a concentration camp as far as choice of vocabulary was concerned; phrases such as *tenere il libro socchiuso nella destra mano* and *arrivare a una rivolta della strada* are conspicuous clues that prepare the reader for wave upon wave of vulgarisms, dialectalisms, and lexical banalities, one more unfortunate than the other; all of them are destined to be swept away by the detailed, unrelenting work of subsequent revisions. The first authorized edition of the *Promessi Sposi* (1827) does not show much progress in this regard. But two years later, in two letters dated February and April 1829,[4] the decisive crisis is foretold, which Manzoni overcomes in his famous sojourn in Florence. That Manzoni's vocabulary underwent a radical rebirth is apparent as soon as one opens a page of the definitive edition of 1840. Moreover, this "Florentine" reconstruction is not a lexical or phonetic translation into Florentine linguistic units; it is a revision made according to Florentine taste and sensibility and with concreteness, acuity, and a sense of humor. It is precisely for this reason that at a distance of 130 years, Manzoni's literary language does not show any traces whatever of local color, which would make it seem not so much a part of the past as provincial, outmoded, and alien.

From the age of sixty to the age of eighty, Manzoni continued his battle as a "language user," that is, from the period of his letter to G. Carena requesting a methodical dictionary of the Italian language (1845) to the successful conclusion of a commission to propose better means for the diffusion of proper language and correct pronunciation (1868). No author, whether writer or grammarian—not even Dante—fully grasped the problem of the language of Italy as did Alessandro Manzoni.

215 MANZONIAN APPLICATIONS

Italian linguistic vehicles of usage reached goals that have never been surpassed, thanks to the masterful restraint[5] that Manzoni knew how to exercise on all the linguistic structures and their constitutive elements, however minimal, and the judgment with which he distributed the different levels of narrative in dialogue, and idealized the landscapes, transforming them from ugly, anecdotal topographic reality into universal vision. Personages of all social classes in the *Promessi Sposi* speak the same Italian language of Florentine extraction. But this is evidently only a filter; in reality, for example, the two protagonists Renzo and Lucia, who do not know how to read or write, would have spoken in a horrible brand of Lombard dialect, structurally entirely different from Tuscan. Don Abbondio would have spoken in a modified dialect, while Cardinal Borromeo would have used the integral literary language, though somewhat altered by the Lombard accent and by a desired simplicity of construction. And yet the four protagonists, even though they have been filtered through the rigid structure of the literary language, are not deformed; they appear to be real persons. To the rigid discipline of restraint, Manzoni added a kind of ideal twist or flavoring by which these same structures, apart from the geometric relationships that are intrinsic to them, emanate a special aura of confidentiality or emotion which in fact liberates the expressive power from all formal limitations. In addition to being a champion of restraint, Manzoni is therefore also a champion of linguistic "evocation"; we need make no effort whatever to enter into the individual linguistic systems that belong to the different characters.

Inversely, with regard to landscape, Manzoni has no interest in describing the mountains, rivers, and villages with photographic exactitude. The restrained description is developed with supreme care, but the individual mountains, streams, lakes, and dwellings are introduced in a whole framework by relative, not absolute, values, thus freeing the reader of the necessity of having to consult a topographic map or of having to transfer himself to the narrative level of the inhabitant: their value is relative (and at the same time universal), not absolute (and at the same time personal).

Forty-four

The Manzonian Vision
and Political Unity

216 MANZONIAN DIRIGISMO AND ASCOLIAN LAISSEZ-FAIRE

If Italy's language as it existed after Manzoni's achievements is something crystalline and definitive that does not give occasion for uncertainty, the outcome of the corresponding theoretical positions taken is quite different. With the passage of time and with the revolutionary innovations that were interposed in Italy's political institutions, these theoretical positions quickly passed from principles formulated in the light of artistic applications (reserved for a minority of authors if not exactly for one author) to the primary needs of the users of Italian, in which they were interested not just as minority cultivators of a literary language, but as citizens desirous of supporting the unity of their political institutions and the newly realized historical unity with a unity of language.

Almost without realizing it, Manzoni had given to the theory of the literary language an interpretation that was no longer artistic but juridical and political. The result of this stand was not limited to offering an occasion for a theoretical debate but to decisions in the field of action, to the confrontation, that, is, of a problem of "linguistic politics."

While up to that time the debate had attacked questions of taste in which there had been possibilities for an infinite number of nuances, preferences, and definitions to manifest themselves, under this new light the problem became rational and at the same time historical. It was not possible to dispute the matter or take a position on the basis of preference but only on the basis of "experience." It was a challenge, and the person who accepted it was the most important Italian linguist of the time, Graziadio Isaia Ascoli (1829–1907).[1] The publication of his review, the *Archivio glottologico italiano,* destined to become famous, afforded him this opportunity. In the introduction to the first volume he acknowledges the problem and indeed the disadvantage of "the lack of unity of language among Italians." Still he states that this is not due to fate or caprice, but that it had historical justification that could not be corrected from one day to the next with artificial means; in fact, the causes lay in "the concentration of knowledge in the few and in the fussy demands of the delicate, unstable, and restless sense of form."[2] The remedy could not be an immediate one. Moreover, the solution lay in "renewing and enlarging the mental activity of the nation" and not in creating a new "preoccupation with form."

217 THE HISTORICAL-POLITICAL PROBLEM

Ascoli's line of reasoning was correct. By studying the histories of the French or English literary languages and comparing them with Italian, it is easy to see that, since the former had spread as administrative languages through the royal chanceries, they had enjoyed a diffusion and an acceptance that was precocious and so to speak democratic. The situation in Italy was quite the opposite. The establishment of the literary language, very precocious on the literary level, did not seep down to the lower social classes, because there was neither an opportunity nor a need for this. Up to the middle of the nineteenth century[3] the Italian literary language had not been the language of a nation, but rather that of a caste of "letterati" or an oligarchy. If Ascoli's position was unobjectionable on a theoretical plane, on the historical-political level of the citizen it ought to have taken into account the fact that the problem was one which man must face even at the cost of correcting Nature. If man can correct Nature by drilling into mountains and by bridging the sea in order to create new roads of communication, he must also seek to build bridges made of ideals so that men of the same national community can communicate among themselves using linguistic vehicles that are adequate, valid for all the citizens, and that do not lend themselves to hateful confrontations, derision, and discrimination.

While the practical difficulties involved in putting into action a policy of linguistic intervention and *dirigismo* (for example, through the idea of exporting from Tuscany throughout all of Italy elementary teachers who would propagate the new unitary linguistic legitimacy) remained unresolved, Ascoli's renunciatory position was a little too reminiscent of the person who, finding it difficult and tiresome to resolve the problems involved in building an immense freeway network of communication, gives up and waits endlessly until innumerable pedestrians transform the footpaths into trails and the trails into roads. The need to promote linguistic unity already existed, and the technical reservations of the linguists could not eliminate them.

The drawbacks of an unsuccessful linguistic policy following political unification were reduced also for another reason, namely, that the national revolution was accompanied by social ultraconservatism. While it cannot be denied that communication within the ruling class, among members of parliament, among teachers and state civil servants who carried out their duties throughout all of Italy, was facilitated, the problem centered around that small minority that succeeded in completing their secondary school education. The overwhelming majority of Italians were content to limit themselves to their dialectal world, which instead of being a fount and a reserve of genuineness and expressivity, constituted—until the end of the century and for the first decade of the following one—a ghetto.[4]

218 DIALECTOLOGICAL PREFERENCES

Besides the historical reasons that imposed a restraint on Ascoli's good judgment, there also existed in his mind a mood determined by the times. The linguistic science of the period, born in an atmosphere of curiosity and romantic sensibility, looked at problems with greater interest in proportion to how these problems reflected the pure, unadulterated nature of man, unrelated to the deformations of so-called civilization. From this point of view, it was not the literary language but the dialects that seemed to lead the scholar to relive the spontaneous developments of the people within the sphere of influence of the home town and under the shadow of the local church spire; and for the same reasons the scholar was led further back into prehistory to all those traces of unknown civilizations (and languages) that had not been deformed by Greek and Roman classicism. The *Archivio glottologico italiano,* which theoretically ought to have been consecrated to linguistic documents of any type, was for decades in reality a storehouse for investigations into Italian dialects. Ascoli was the principal cultivator of these investigations, which up to the First World War constituted what might be called the only area of work and creative research in the field of Italian linguistics. A testimony to these interests was Ascoli's celebrated article "Dialects of Italy," published in the *Encyclopedia Britannica*.[5]

The tradition of dialectological studies continued for four decades through the contributions of Francesco d'Ovidio (1849–1925) on the dialect of Campobasso, of Carlo Salvioni (1858–1920) on the Milanese dialect, of E. G. Parodi (1862–1923) on the Ligurian dialects, of Matteo Bartoli (1873–1946) on Dalmatian, of Clemente Merlo (1879–1966) on the dialects of the south and those of Ticino, of Carlo Battisti (born 1882) on Ladin dialects, and of B. Terracini (1886–1968) on those of Piedmont.

Sacrificed by these interests which were directed toward dialectology on the one hand and toward the literary language on the other, dialectal poetry became increasingly more closed in its folkloristic frame of reference. Even the high quality dialectal poetry of G. G. Belli (1791–1863) was a victim; Belli's sonnets, though effective and genuine, are by the author's own admission, capable of reflecting only an "abject and comical" language and not one into which the Gospels, for example, could be translated.[6]

219 GRAMMATICAL CHANGES

The grammatical uncertainties that exist in the middle of the nineteenth century are minor ones. The form *ne* for 'ci' as atonal pronoun of the first person plural[7] falls into disuse; and the form *li* as plural definite article yields. The forms *Il zio* and *I stenti* become standardized with the substitution of *lo* and *gli* as articles.[8] The forms *qualche speranzA* and *qualche decinA,* instead of 'speranzE' and 'decinE', come to be used generally. The nominal value of the present participle grows; *presidente* DEL *tribunale* takes the place of 'president IL tribunale'. Two Tuscanisms appear: *eri* for 'eravate'[9] and especially *noi si dice* for 'diciamo'.[10]

220 LEXICOGRAPHICAL ACTIVITIES

The disadvantages of not having been able to impose the Manzonian thesis with force, and the impossibility of entrusting the problems of linguistic unification to the future were mitigated by two very different situations. The one situation was represented by lexicographical undertakings, two in particular. The first of these, of genuine Manzonian inspiration, is the *Novo vocabolario della lingua italiana* of G. B. Giorgini and E. Broglio (4 vol., Florence, 1870–97), which, even in its spelling of the title (*Novo,* a Florentine form, is preferred to the standard 'nuovo') illustrates in a polemic way the informing principle that governs its choice of vocabulary. The other lexicographical enterprise did not come from the Accademia della Crusca, as one might have anticipated, even though that organization did publish the first fascicle of its fifth edition in 1863.[11] Rather, the second current was represented by an eccentric personality, Niccolò Tommaseo (1802–74), who, not bound by any theory and combining an energy for work with a lexical sensitivity of very high quality, completed two classical works. The first was the *Dizionario dei sinonimi,* which was first published in 1830–32; the second, the great and not yet entirely superseded *Dizionario della lingua italiana,* was made in collaboration with B. Bellini. The validity of Tommaseo's judgment and choices is not diminished by the whimsicality or the vivacity of his judgments. Born in Šibenik in Dalmatia, Tommaseo acquired a perfect command of the Florentine accent[12] and was in a position to judge the language of his time in an autonomous though acrimonious way, as we can see from the following passage: Italian is "a jargon composed of exotic words and manners, oddly reshaped, affected in their lack of elegance, and ridiculous to one who knows the original."[13]

Forty-five

The Consequences of
Political Unity

221 CLASSICAL INSPIRATION
The death of Alessandro Manzoni (1873) came soon after the liberation of Rome and the actual unification of Italy (1870). The polemic that had developed between Manzonian *dirigismo-populismo* and Ascolian *liberismo* waned. Ascoli concentrates on the study of dialects; and while the position of the latter remains static owing to the immobility of social structures, the debate is centered on the upper linguistic strata. In the forty-year period that follows (1870–1910), the doctrinal alternative between *populismo* and *liberismo* is replaced by the alternative between the epic and the musical in the field of literary achievement. Of the two it is the epic moment, closely linked to the emotions that had accompanied the unification of Italy, that first makes itself manifest. After the Rome of the popes and the emperors, *la Terza Roma* did not come to belie but rather to synthesize the ancient traditions and in particular the imperial, classical ones. The dialectal tendency toward fragmentation that was characteristic of the Middle Ages was parallel to the erosions that Christianity had wrought in the vision of life, in the competitive spirit, and the life of comfort and ease in the homes and spas. Neither the cult of linguistic unity, understood only from a material point of view, nor a poetic language which posed only external problems of prosody

was enough to counter this explosion of emotion. The interpreter, indeed the transformer, of these emotions was Giosue Carducci (1835–1907).

Carducci's anti-Manzonian sentiments soon became evident—and for a psychological reason; Carducci the Tuscan, full of political fervor, reacted against the Florentine monopoly that was championed by a Lombard who was a political moderate. Manzoni's was a vision that was destined to appear to Carducci as an artificial one even in the light of the most favorable interpretations. If on the one hand Carducci mitigated the external austerity of Manzonian forms and accomplishments, in this way exhibiting a considerable sense of moderation, on the other hand, he greatly accentuated the pathos of prose by introducing in a powerful way the images and myths and harmonies of classical antiquity: its metaphors and personifications, its sumptuous solemn sentences, its invectives, and its eloquent polemics. His oration in memory of Garibaldi—at once a literary comment and a historical-political debate—was transformed by his pen into an epic narrative, in a supreme testimony of the possibilities inherent in Italian linguistic structures.

222 Carducci's Schema

Although he professed to be against rhetoric, Carducci did have a rhetoric of his own. While he did not elaborate a grammatical doctrine of his own, he did reflect and describe the linguistic ideals he believed in, which were for a cinquecento language that was freed from the "barbaries" of the Middle Ages, for a modern language which "would take off the makeup of the academies, would discard foreign fashions as well as provincial habits," and would recover qualities that were "at least strong and pure, national and popular." This attitude did not prevent him, however, from resorting in special cases to contradictory and extreme solutions: on the one hand extreme Latinate forms such as *cerula* or *Addu-a* instead of the standard Italian 'Adda', and on the other equally extreme Italianizations such as *Voltero* from the French 'Voltaire', or *Cromuello* from the English 'Cromwell'.

The models of poetic language Carducci took as a starting point were not the strongly rhythmic ones of Manzoni (§213) but rather the free hendecasyllables of Parini (§204), which had been developed by Leopardi in the severe form of his canzoni, not entirely adverse to rhyme but full of antimelodic reservations. It is from these models that Carducci proceeded, searching in classical rhythms for something that could bear new fruit in contemporary poetic language. He does not limit himself, therefore, to restraining traditional melodic excesses; rather he builds new rhythms with the *Odi barbare,* beginning with the ode dedicated to the Adda (1873) and culminating in the "Fonti del Clitunno." Carducci's inspiration consisted in following classical metrical schema, identifying the main beats of the classical line with the intensive accents of Italian words, and at the same time renouncing the distinctions of vocalic quantities; he reconstructed hexameters, Sapphic and Alchaic odes, and other poetic forms. Naturally, expertise was required to produce a synthesis that was not merely a juxtaposition or a contamination. If on the one hand it cannot be said that as a result a lasting continuity was established, on the other the Carduccian models certainly do represent an addition in the history of the Italian poetic language and a change that is superior to the step which Dante took, though not more permanent.[1]

223 MUSICALITY

The golden age of the Carduccian tradition as the authoritative and prestigious stylistic model encompasses only the fifteen-year period from 1875 to 1890. At a certain point the epic influence came to be opposed by the melodic and lyrical trend that was personified, even before the beginning of the twentieth century, by Gabriele D'Annunzio (1863–1938). From a formal point of view, the principal difference between the two lies in the fact that, while in the writings of Carducci the language of prose is something intrinsically different from the language of poetry, in the writings of D'Annunzio, musical inspiration dominates both traditions equally, in such a way that the two currents are brought closer together. A justification of a negative order lies in the fact that Italian society, after having been dominated by the great novelty of unification and by the temptations of an epic interpretation of it, slowly turns toward other interests. In the grayness of contemporary life, Italians made themselves comfortable with a vision of life that was positivistic with regard to science and philosophy and hedonistic with regard to the arts and life in general. Through the musicality of prose, D'Annunzio was the supreme interpreter of this hedonism; in this sense the novel *Il trionfo della morte* (1894) was his masterpiece. This novel is truly the best example of that type of linguistic achievement in which a certain aura is evoked through the melody of the sentence, a melody that, indeed, has never been surpassed. From the lexical point of view from time to time precious words are fashioned in the excess of a rare talent, or exhumed with historical fidelity, being taken verbatim from other sources.[2] Unlike Manzoni, D'Annunzio's dialogues are always stylized, as if they were part of an ideal and permanent performance, and never referable to reality, either with regard to particular forms or to human content.

Given these circumstances, the novelty of D'Annunzio's poetic language is somewhat less prominent than that of his prose. It begins precociously with the *Canto novo* (1882), which is less original and coherent than Carducci's language; it is defined with supreme care, characterized by rhythms that are less daring and by a precious vocabulary. The musicality of the play *La figlia di Jorio,* drawn from the sources, is just as extreme. It reaches the height of artificiality in the *Canzoni di oltremare,* which, set against the background of the African war of 1911–12, represent a unitary context between linguistic accomplishment and the affairs of a society interpreted and influenced by an aesthetic vision. Unlike Carducci and Manzoni to a greater degree, however, the stylistic schema that D'Annunzio employed soon faded. By the end of the First World War, D'Annunzio at the age of fifty had limited himself in his "Notturno" to elementary and idyllic schema that ran counter to his actual sensibilities. His new tack assured him the praise of the critics, who were still in tune with a sensibility that was far from that of traditional ornamentality, but his historical-linguistic contribution had already been made, twenty years before the end of his mortal cycle.[3]

224 ORDINARY DISCOURSE

The bourgeois prose that paralleled these literary trends does not need exhaustive analysis. On the whole, the trends we must investigate are two, the older and more grandiloquent of which is linked to the dignity of the Carduccian tradition. The philosopher Francesco Acri (1836–1913), a contemporary of Carducci, and Manara Valgimigli (1876–1965), one of Carducci's last and closest disciples, may be considered the extreme representatives of this trend. Acri directed his sensibility for linguistic dignity toward an immaculate syntax and an ecstatic contemplation of the great trecento models, almost as if in an attempt to equal the dignity of the personages of Plato's *Dialogues,* which he translated. At the other extreme, Manara Valgimigli, in both his essays and his translations, maintained an exalted and harmonious classicism, purified and softened by a temperament that was less pugnacious than that of his master, more receptive to convivial popular forms, and modern in the best sense of the word.

The other current—nontraditional, averse to any form of rhetoric, and characterized by simple sentence structure and an intrinsic respect for linguistic traditions not bound to any archetypal model or disposed toward purism—is realized by three authors who are most important in delineating an intermediary prose style that is averse to strange forms and innovations and still genuine in the adherence of its words to both objects and emotions. The first phase is represented by Edmondo De Amicis (1846–1908), who became famous for his children's book entitled *Cuore*—unjustly disparaged in more recent times—a work that is fundamental for the elementary paratactical structure of its sentences. In the theoretical field, De Amicis polemicized about purism and dedicated a well-known little book, the *Idioma gentile* (1905), to this romantic cult. The second stage is represented by Alfredo Panzini (1863–1939), who until the First World War was the champion of a natural and subdued sentence style and showed an interest in lexicon, being the first to collect Italian neologisms and submit them to the more or less spirited criticism of the *Dizionario moderno,* and finally becoming the standard-bearer—even though he was less authoritative than De Amicis—of purism. The third writer was Ugo Ojetti (1871–1946), who came from journalism and not from literature and who precisely for this reason was more detached from mannerism and at the same time more painstaking in the discussion of linguistic phenomena that went beyond superficial professions of puristic faith and the terroristic attacks and the anathemas that usually accompanied them.

225 BUREAUCRATIC PROSE

In addition to the most modest kind of literary prose, the political unity of Italy also brought up the problem of administrative prose, which realized its most important accomplishments in legal texts.

Debate over the defects of Italian juridical language had gone on even before political unification, and, like the arguments regarding literary language, those concerning juridical language consisted in the criticism of inaccuracies, neologisms, and foreign words. T. De Mauro[4] has given us a very interesting summary of this polemic.

More important than the material facts of the matter are the symbols, as they are exemplified for instance by the work of Gaetano Valeriani.[5] The causes of these specific difficulties regarding administrative language are more evident in juridical language, because from the point of view of the judge, juridical language must above all take into account precision and shall we say, technicality and specificity, while from the point of view of the lawyer it must emphasize the art of persuasion that culminates in the plea, characterized by emotion, universality, and popular appeal, which the lawyer makes to the jury.

We find efficacious examples of the pathos that accompanied these debates in the book by Valeriani; for example, on page 10 we read: "How will it ever be possible for us to carry out the laws you impose upon us, if . . . you do not write them in Italian? At least write them in Arabic, in Sanskrit, or in any existing language whatever. . . ." On page 24, under *contabile* we find: "How can we observe and obey your laws if they are not understood? because *contabile,* according to the author means 'that which can be counted'. This zeal does not prevent the author from writing that one cannot "neglect" (*negligentare*) spelling (p. 27) or that with regard to using a word that is definitely "vulgar," one does something unworthy of the law "even in pronouncing it" (*in pronunziandola ancora,* p. 36).

Forty-six

First Evasions

226 Sentimental Evasions

The linguistic system in which the language of Italy took shape at the end of the nineteenth century and the beginning of the twentieth is characterized by two features: a certain degree of elasticity, which permitted the actualization of restrictive measures, and sufficient solidity to support mechanisms of "superelevation" (i.e., the steady raising) of the linguistic edifice, and indeed of evasion. Man's expressive need is in fact a living thing, and it is normal, therefore, that he could find himself in conflict with the system. For a long time this need was not recognized; instead poetic canons were accepted with greater or lesser discipline, in the area of literary languages as well as with regard to the visual arts and music. All this began to be reconsidered a century ago.[1]

With regard to language, all of these impulses together are grouped under the common title of "phenomena of evasion." One mechanism of evasion consists in going beyond the normal geographic limits of the literary language, in supplanting the symbolic elements that have defined it, and in establishing a more direct link with the images. This occurs through the use of onomatopoeia in cases of acoustic images that are capable of being translated into words. Evasion is dominant in these cases not only because the author has gone beyond the bounds of normal literary language, but also because he has basically exceeded the limits of *any* literary language by following an emotional impulse in order to affirm an ideal of total liberation from linguistic structures consecrated by history.

The writer who most coherently and most audaciously gave free rein to this tendency was Giovanni Pascoli (1855–1912). In his *Canti di Castelvecchio* we read, for example in the poem "L'uccellino del freddo," the recurrent verse *trr trr trr terit tirit*[2] (pp. 13–14); and in "Pania" we find *E me seque un tac tac di capinere, e me segue un tin tin di pettirossi, un zisteretetet di cincia, un reverere di cardellini . . .* (p. 21). This adherence to nature on the part of Pascoli was directly linked to one environment, that of Garfagnana, in the Apennines near the city of Lucca, a mountainous country region from which significant numbers of the population had emigrated. This situation furnished Pascoli with another opportunity for evasion, through the use of words of the Italian-American jargon, which had been absorbed into the language of the area and which Pascoli put in his poetry; examples are *Re Erode* and *la stima*, which are adaptations of the English words "railroad" and "steamer," respectively.

Pascoli's approach gave rise to controversy and severe criticism, not on theoretical grounds but because Pascoli's somewhat embarrassed and childish retreat into the realm of the ineffable gave many critics, Benedetto Croce[3] among them, the chance to refuse to recognize Pascoli's poetic validity that is obviously based on universal values. In any case the boundaries of a linguistic system are not rigid, and it is permissible for each user to utilize its components, by sometimes giving preference to the more general and open—if not to say universal—elements, and at other times choosing to employ those elements that are more particular and restricted. This is a matter of fashion rather than one of principle. According to the spirited metaphor of Renato Serra,[4] at a certain point, when the fashion changed, "the people removed from their windowsills the many bird cages that they had displayed in Pascoli's honor."

227 REALISTIC EVASIONS

In the meantime another evasion mechanism, colder and more calculated, had been put into effect by Antonio Fogazzaro (1842–1911) by means of scrupulous linguistic fidelity with regard to certain of his personages who, in the reconstructed reality of his novels, actually spoke in dialect. In Fogazzaro's case it is not so much a matter of "evasion" from an organized system, as it is one of nonentry, that is, an anticipatory, legitimate evasion. The contrast with Manzoni's technique, particularly with regard to landscapes and dialogues, is clear. Whereas Manzoni "constrains" the common language system in order to describe landscapes that are severed from local topographical reality, and thus transfers them to the level of universal images, Fogazzaro individualizes them by means of their specific names which almost become their onomatopoeia; in Fogazzaro's writing every mountaintop, every hamlet, every stream resists and rejects generalization that goes beyond its own individuality. Here we are dealing not so much with evasion as with the renunciation of constraint. In handling dialogue between characters of different social background, Manzoni transforms them, by aligning them on the single plane of the national literary language, while Fogazzaro refuses to indulge in any transfiguration whatever and limits himself to recording in genuine dialectal form, either integral or attenuated, the presumed words of the interlocutors; he lets objects prevail over words, following a trend of realism that is, however, renunciatory.

The dialectal elements which here permit an evasion, albeit a rational one, from the system of the literary language, inversely suffer an "invasion" of literary forms in the genre of dialectal poetry, which increasingly shuns ambitious attempts to express values other than strictly local ones. A statistical comparison of the numbers of Italianisms in Roman poets such as Belli or Salustri (Trilussa) indicates that the percentages of words phonetically identical to the corresponding Italian ones are 60 percent in Belli but 71 percent in Trilussa, while purely vernacular words constitute 4 percent in Belli and 1 percent in Trilussa, and words that are slightly discordant on a phonetic level are 36 percent in Belli and 28 percent in Trilussa.[5]

228 EXUBERANT EVASIONS

The different levels of narrative,[6] as they exist according to the traditional structures of the Italian language, are (*a*) a series of personal experiences and memories, marked by the first person of the personal pronoun (I, we), and therefore of a predominantly lyric content; (*b*) a dialogue between two or more interlocutors, marked by the second person of the personal pronoun (you), and therefore of dramatic content; (*c*) a series of events acted out or experienced by other persons and marked by the subject of the verb in the third person, and therefore of substantially narrative or epic content.

Fogazzaro's *Piccolo mondo moderno* (1900–), in confronting delicate themes of religious awareness, relates situations in which the traditional rapport between the narrator and the things narrated no longer suffices. The figure of the narrator is bound up with those of the personages, and as a result the text exhibits uncertainties, a dispersive quality, and a humble, uncultured literary language. This disharmony, these stammerings are comparable to the uncertainties of the ancient Placiti Cassinesi—on the threshold of a new language in which idiosyncratic expressions, Latinisms, and nonregional forms are mixed in an inorganic way, in anticipation of the introduction of new structures.

With reference to the third category, however, there had been established, already in the Roman era, a subordinate variant (§79), through the so-called "free indirect construction." The reduction of markers indicating indirect discourse (that is, the realm of the third person) constituted a rapprochement toward the system of the second person and represented something intermediary between the realm of the epic and the realm of drama.[7]

In his novel *I Malavoglia,* Giovanni Verga (1840–1922) introduces other distinctions in this area. The first sentence of the book is: "The Malavoglia had once been as numerous as the stones on the old Trezza road." Although the formal structure is conventional, namely, like that of the epic narrative, the nature of the simile employed puts us on our alert. Normally a simile is used to open a broader world to the reader. This statement on the contrary serves to close off the restricted world in which the narrative takes place. That is, the simile is in reality spoken by the personages who live in that area; it is direct discourse, or a chorus, placed on a narrative level which is no longer that of the epic. The same technique of presenting on the level of a narrative and in the third person words that in reality are spoken by single personages or by groups and are therefore on the level of *tu* or *voi* is found throughout and, in effect, creates a new category within the framework of expressive possibilities of the language of Italy at the end of the nineteenth century.

229 POOR EVASIONS

Evasion can also be unintentional, that is, determined by a preexisting inadequate adaptation on the part of the author to the linguistic vehicles of usage of his time, a testimony to a shortcoming. This is the case of Italo Svevo (1861–1927), a writer from Trieste who was dominated, not unlike the young Manzoni, by the dual concept of local dialect/closest foreign language, which in his case was German. Svevo's documentary value resides, therefore, not so much in congenial or favorite formulae as in the blemishes of his experience, his weaknesses, and lack of sensitivity. Unlike Manzoni, Svevo had neither the will nor the opportunity of debating the problem and even less of resolving it with normative criteria. He was a pioneer inasmuch as he transferred certain essential difficulties of the common language to the level of the literary language, but he did not propose or impose any solutions, much less establish a new tradition. For reasons of content, Svevo instead attacked problems regarding levels of narrative, but with this difference: instead of adopting the alternation of narrative and dialogue that characterized the writing of Verga, he substituted an alternation between narrative and memory; in other words between the third person and the first person, in an epic-lyric blending that in Italy had no other models. He was aware of the difficulties involved, but he was able to produce only consequences of a negative order, as is demonstrated by the fact that when he consented to republish a revised edition of his novel *Senilità,* his corrections reflected neither a verification of a growing sensibility of his own nor the organic vision of another author.

230 FUTURIST EVASIONS

Thus we come to the one real organic evasion: that represented by the Futurists and by their recognized leader, Filippo Tomaso Marinetti (1872–1944). This form of evasion is identified with a struggle against all structures that are deemed superfluous and oppressive, and was fought on both the technical and the emotional plane. The movement is not limited to Italy nor to linguistics, because it implicates international circles, especially in France. The manifesto of the Futurists was published in the Paris newspaper *Le Figaro,* on 20 February 1909. Nor was Futurism limited to linguistic conventions, because it also attacked conventions in the fields of music and the visual arts. The Florentine periodical *Lacerba* was for a brief time its spokesman. At their rallies the Futurists resembled present-day models of protest but with the difference that, unlike the shabby and bearded spectacles of today, there was always something roguish and humorous about the Futurists. Moreover, since the traditional classicism of Italian society was a reflection of a social traditionalism, the proposed linguistic revolution constituted only one particular fact within the framework of an overly ambitious political-social revolution aimed not only against the bourgeoisie but also against the organizations of the proletariat. The struggle for liberation championed the destruction of traditional harmonies in music in favor of noises, of any representation or imitation of nature in painting in favor of the juxtaposition of geometric forms and colors devoid of any formal character whatever, and of all superfluous grammatical markers (for example, punctuation, accessory words, and word endings that are too specialized) in favor of the general use of a telegraphic style. To use the images of the times, "violent outbursts of emotion-steampower will blow off the exhaust pipe of periods, the valves of punctuation, and the bolts of adjectives,"[8] and also "we must destroy syntax, arranging nouns by chance as they are born."[9] With regard to rhythm it is necessary to take an additional step beyond free verse, in the direction of *parole in libertà.*

While the Futurists' criticism of pictorial and musical conventions left impressions that were fertile, in the field of language the explosion was noisy but hardly conclusive. Not only did the Futurist movement not establish a revitalized tradition, but it must be noted that sports and war, the two pivotal points of the Futurists' vision of life, were sources of clamorous rhetorical degradation, as the soccer chronicles of the years 1910–15[10] and the correspondence of both the African war (1911–12) and the First World War, attest.

Forty-seven

From Evasion to
Classicism

231 THE HERMETICS

A second point of departure for evasion—an entirely different one—
made itself manifest as soon as the context of the dialogue shifted
from the ultraconservative society of the late nineteenth century to
the totalitarian society of the two-decade period between 1925 and
1945. In contrast to D'Annunzianism, in which the emphasis was on
a search for melody, Hermeticism, as it appeared above all in the
milieu of the Florentine review *Letteratura* (1937–), searched for and
cultivated amelodic ideals. Unlike the Futurists, who preferred noise,
the Hermetics favored pauses, silences (for instance those of Giuseppe
Ungaretti, 1888–1970), tenuous words, and austere sentences. Metaphors were frequently taken from technical vocabulary, not in an
attempt to mechanize both poetic statement and reader, but rather
in order to reinforce imperturbability with regard to emotions; an
example of such metaphors is *la costante* to indicate 'characteristic',
taken from the terminology of physics and applied to literary criticism to define an author. The metaphor *istanza,* however, comes from
legal language and takes the place of 'exigency' or 'revendication'. Let
us not speak of the obstreperous political terminology of the period,
which within the Hermetic context could never have found a place,
not even an emasculated or attenuated one. Beyond its actual mean-

ing in the context, words in themselves becomes the object of exclusive attention, almost of a cult. Satellite words, which are grouped around a central or "essential" word like the stars of a constellation, receive from the latter a certain coloration. Three lines of verse from Eugenio Montale such as *viaggiano la cupola del cielo/non sai se foglie o uccelli / e non son più* have the same evocative power in this trend as does the rapprochement of Luzi's forms such as *stelle che esorbitano* and *capriolo che esulta* and *cipressi equinoziali.* Its most extreme development consists in the following phenomenon, to use the words of M. L. Altieri:[1] "the word, now removed from the flux of melody, rhythm, and syntax, . . . is left alone to 'tremble' in the line, which expires in that very word, isolated by the white space and by the silence." At the opposite extreme, the Hermetics subscribe to a kind of humble ineffability, rather than to a proud isolation, thus reaching the absolute limit of protest.[2] Born out of a polemic exigency, Hermeticism could not survive the fall of the totalitarian society. If on the one hand Hermeticism ceased to exist as an organic tradition, on the other, certain particular tastes and traditions continued to subsist. I shall make reference to two of them: the agility with which words from any technical language are transferred into a literary language, a procedure to which Gianfranco Contini (born 1912) has brought great distinction, and extreme parataxis—indeed, according to Altieri "obsessive" parataxis—in which the judgments of Giuseppe de Robertis, a thoughtful and subtle critic in the study of the formation and development of the texts of his authors, are realized.[3]

Other processes of linguistic enrichment gravitate around Hermeticism, two of which are worthy of mention. The first process is related to the course of action taken by Carlo Emilio Gadda (1893–1973) who, both in pre-Fascist times and today, combined the technique of linguistic accomplishment with the exuberance of his own expressive needs; to this end he first of all brought together, in a bold combination with literary language, the resources of the jargon of First World War soldiers and those of his native dialect, Milanese; then he enriched the whole with technical terms that come from his profession of engineer; he integrated it with a somewhat artificial Roman jargon, which he acquired during his residence in that city for the last thirty years. The result, with its luxuriant vocabulary, calls to mind a tropical forest.[4] That this is the product not of an uncontrolled instinct but rather of a precise, reasoned act of will is proved by the following quotation: *I doppioni li voglio tutti, per mania di possesso e per cupidigia di ricchezze: e volgio anche i triploni e i quadriploni.*[5] Not only does the author control the linguistic structures, but he also assumes authority in the pre-Hermetic, Hermetic, and post-Hermetic community, just as in the pre-Fascist, the Fascist, and post-Fascist era, his personality, in its formative principles, remained substantially coherent and unchanged.

232 NEOREALISTS

The opposite trend is born not out of an individual but rather a collective need. It is immersed in and conditioned by Italian society as it was emerging from the Second World War. Under the pressure of the obvious consequences of the war was born the trend, at times masochistic, of analyzing reality in a pitiless way, not only with regard to literature. It was the moment of so-called neorealism, which enjoyed immediate success in the world of cinema. Films such as *Riso amaro* or *Due soldi di speranza,* which went beyond *Roma città aperta* or *Ladri di biciclette,* suggested models for linguistic vehicles of usage. On the literary plane this was evident in the shift of interest from the pompous environments of the well-to-do to the world of the poor. It was also evident in the position taken with regard to the linguistic equivalent of the lower social levels, namely, the dialects. Unlike their use in the ottocento, when the dialects appeared as a testimony to a reality that was more real, more natural, and more genuine, now they were considered as a social testimony. The psychological immediacy and objective accuracy in everyday activities suddenly became obvious to writers in search of new realities. Indeed, in addition to the dialectal structures which characterized a geographic unit, there also appeared linguistic structures that corresponded to sociotechnical units; that is, beside the dialects appeared the work jargons of occupations. Broad horizons of rejuvenescence and reawakening of the linguistic tradition appeared. The person who more than any other assumed the role of interpreter of this need and who dedicated himself to developing it in a constructive and coherent way was Pier Paolo Pasolini. Of course, his novels *Raggazzi di vita* and *Una vita violenta* do not lead to a linguistic reawakening because for artistic reasons they must remain confined to a peripheral, shantytown, dialectal environment. A linguistic system is not, however, made up only of permanent structures that are valid for the whole of the national territory and for all normal daily circumstances, as we have already seen in the case of Pascoli (§226). The structures are also made up of optional units, which can be used occasionally and which do not make any claim for national citizenship and the rights of majority in a definitive way. Pasolini's skill lies then also in the fact that the dialectal and jargon elements he introduces into his writing do not consist only in violent and crude expressions but also in euphemisms and minimization. The possibility or the legitimacy that an evasion of this sort could "rejuvenate" the traditions and the structures of the Italian linguistic system does not exist.

233 THE AVANT-GARDE

The problem is posed with greater clarity with regard to avant-garde movements, of which the most meaningful testimony is the so-called anthology of the Novissimi.[6] There are two reasons for this. The first lies in the prejudicial, protesting nature of the avant-garde movements which consists in the "communication of the negation of existing communication." It is clear that, at the conclusion of a process of this nature, one ends finally by accepting "silence," as one of the exponents of the movement, Angelo Guglielmi, recognized.

But, the true weakness and insignificance of the avant-garde movement lies in the fact that it was set into motion by an internal contradiction, deluded as the followers were into believing that by provoking the linguistic structures of a community into a state of crisis, they are coming to terms with one particular instance of that global confrontation of the entire society, which confrontation is one of the tenets of their faith. The actual situation is quite different. As Altieri has demonstrated very well,[7] the experimentations of the avant-garde are aristocratic phenomena which presume a closed circle accessible only to a few initiates and totally outside the tastes and possibilities of the masses. Under these circumstances not only have the avant-garde movements not effected any change, even a negative one, in the field of linguistics; indeed, they have revealed themselves to be in total opposition to the tendencies and tastes of today. As an example of these experiments I shall limit myself to citing one of the more moderate examples, of Alfredo Giuliani:[8] *Ma io-qui-ora, dolorosa sospensione,so=che non basta, non ammetto la conclusione=, non indulgo, è lo stesso, la noncuranza=si corruga. Con gli anni tutto diviene=simbolico, capire è un sentito dire, poesia=nient' altro che paralogia dei soliti discorsi.* This sentence, which is among the least scattered of the collection, must be compared with the theoretical position taken by the same author.[9] *La visione schizomorfa con cui la poesia contemporanea prende possesso di sè . . . tipici caratteri la discontinuità del processo imaginativo, l'asintattismo, la violenza operata sui segni. . . .*

This is no longer chance or deliberate evasion, but rather total evasion, which ranges from the disassociation between lexical units and their semantic values to the confused entanglement of intersecting levels of narrative.

234 INSTANCES OF LEXICAL ABSORPTION

These evasions that aim at "limiting" the exercise of the linguistic faculty into very restricted circles can give rise to strange innovations, though not necessarily capricious ones. A fine example of coherent displacement is provided by the metaphors applied to images of the human body by the beat group and inspired by the instrumental and mechanistic view. The 'elbows' are called *angoli* (corners), the 'teeth' become *avorio,* the 'navel' the *centro,* the 'skin' the *fodera* (lining), the 'hands' the *tentacoli,* the 'brain' the *motore,* the 'eyes' the *fari* (beacons), the 'breath' is *gas,* and even a person's 'name' becomes a *stanga* (lever).[10]

Apart from these extreme cases, the sort of evasion that consists in utilizing lexical units that surface from dialects or from certain jargons can lead to an advantageous enrichment of the lexicon, without a shock effect.

Such is the case with the emergence of expressions that have a certain affective impulse toward an intentional confidentiality; they are divided into two large groups. The first consists of terms that are taken from dialects inasmuch as they are creations of history crystallized in more or less limited areas. These terms would never have been used outside the dialectal area if for social reasons there had not been occasions for encounters and comparisons, with the result that one dialectal form had a particularly effective and expressive, which is to say favored, outcome; I am referring, for example, to the Genoese term *mugugno* 'grumbling', meaning a kind of protest that is not intended to be successful and is limited to function as a venting of feelings, without any real consequences. If there had been no contacts with the Genoese dialectal vocabulary through the broader context of men immersed in the First World War, there would never have been an occasion for this word to be compared with others in such a way that brought it recognition and fame. This is also the case with the form of greeting that is first Venetian and then Milanese, and then generalized throughout all of Italy, and then carried beyond Italy's borders, that is *ciao;* today it means nothing other than 'good-bye'.

The other contribution that penetrated the literary language of the last twenty-five years since the Second World War consists of southern forms such as *paisà* for 'compaesano' (fellow villager), *scippo* (theft with adroitness) for 'strappo' (wrench, jerk), and *fasullo* 'worthless (because not authentic)'. An interesting Anglo-American stamp is left by the expression *sciuscià* (from the English "shoeshine"), which spread from Naples and refers to the boys who polished the shoes of American soldiers. Even the term *segnorina,* which has the restricted meaning of 'streetwalker', is indeed the Italian *signorina* but the pronunciation E of the protonic vowel has remained as a trace of the standard accent of the Anglo-American soldiers in Naples, that is, of the social current that assured the word success.

These systematic evasions that come into collision with the "system," are counterbalanced by innumerable lesser evasions that constitute, as it were, migrations within the system and consist in the transference of single elements of linguistic structures from one professional semantic sector to another.

This is the same technique which for other reasons was applied by the Hermetics when they transferred words from the world of science to the literary language. There are an infinite number of examples of this technique, but here their quantity and abundance is not important.

Of greater interest are the special cases in which the selection of vocabulary from various sources assumes a less "quantitative" or technical character. This appears in sectors in which the linguistic tradition is not yet solidly established, in connection with theoretical or at least intellectual innovations. Art criticism (both of the visual and musical arts) does not have a linguistic tradition comparable to that of literary criticism. Its vocabulary is being formed not only wth new words but also through metaphors taken from other arts; the expressions *una sinfonia di colori* and *i colori squillanti* 'blaring colors' show the application of a musical notion to the visual arts. But the expression *un impasto di note e di toni* 'a medley of notes and tones' is an illustration of the reverse, namely, a musical notion defined with pictorial terms. Naturally a tradition is not born without pain. We know of some instances of even keen criticism in which the faltering language style of certain art critics has been the object of criticism on the part of the artists. The latter have felt themselves to be repudiated by the unfortunate or immature terminology of the critics, because that terminology was created by "people who spoke of paintings and statues with the phraseology of pastry-cooks".[11]

235 THE FINAL CLASSICAL FORM
The reaction to the imbalances determined by the need for evasion did not consist only in a return to an exclusive classicity. It also made itself manifest in three other forms. The first of these consisted in the rejection of ornamental traditionalism through the elimination of all that was superfluous, without resorting to the subversion of the Futurists. This aspiration, linked to the *prise de conscience* of contemporary foreign ideals such as American pragmatism, aimed at bringing the linguistic traditions back to their functional purpose

of acting as tools of communication. This was first evident in the last years of the first decade of this century and the first years of the second decade. Isolated in the succession of tastes and fads in Italy, the Florentine circle of the *Voce* embodied an antirhetorical attitude between the years 1908 and 1916 and functioned as a model and guide, although it did so through incursions into the exaggerated and impulsive sector of the polemic. The second current was less spectacular. After the cult of the "big," which was followed by the cult of the "disordered," some gentler poets and men of letters were attracted by the cult of the "little." In the poetry of the Piedmontese Guido Gozzano (1883–1916) and that of Marino Moretti (born 1885) of Romagna, diminutives—both semantic and morphological—were emphasized; examples are *alberini* instead of 'alberi', *solicello* instead of 'sole' (sun), *capanna* (hut) for 'casa', *orto* for 'podere' (farm), *aioletta* (flower bed) for 'giardino,' and *bugigattolo* (cubbyhole) for 'stanza' (room).[12] In the area of syntax, the equivalent of this minimalization was represented by a new wave of parataxis pushed to the extreme. Let us cite these verses of Sergio Corazzini[13] as an example: "Why do you call me a poet? / I am not a poet / I am only a little boy who cries / I have but tears to offer to the silence."

These poets were called the Crepuscolari; they were only potential evaders, ready to return to the fold, humble but purified.

The third current—the real reaction to both the sentimentalism of Pascoli and the sonority of D'Annunzio—consists in the movement that was called by the name of the review that was its representative, *La Ronda*.[14] Principally through the work of its founder, Vincenzo Cardarelli (1887–1969), *la Ronda* advocated a sort of "poetics of restraint," which cut not so deeply into linguistic structures as it did into their functionalism. In this regard the following propositions of Cardarelli are worthy of citation: "Light without color, existence without attribute, hymns without interjections, impassibility and distance, orders and not figures."

Precisely because it is dominated by a sense of moderation, however, the linguistic tradition left us for example by Cardarelli with reference to the nominal sentence offers to the scholar of structures fertile[15] and partially new material gradually adopted by the Italian language.

A prose that is defined by more classical limits and that does not yield to the temptations or dangers of distraction and transience is in a position to set for itself ideals of prestige, and after many uncertainties a pole of attraction and a tradition capable of imposing itself can be established. Even without taking into consideration schema and proportions, Manzoni had succeeded in leaving behind a tradition of Italian literary language that was at once youthful and durable. The problem of modernization and rejuvenation was more applicable to nonnarrative prose (the prose of criticism, erudition, and history) in short, to that prose style that had to fill the void between literary and scientific prose which had existed since the time of Galileo.

This was the framework within which the Crocean experience must be viewed. Benedetto Croce (1866–1952), unlike Manzoni, reached linguistic maturity quickly, as is evident from the first editions of the review *Critica* (1903–). He was opposed to Manzoni in evading any doctrinaire or normative aspiration with regard to language. The tradition he established was excellent with regard to the consolidation of paragraphs (both in their coordination and their opposition) in a harmony in which common and less common words were easily combined. The reader who compares the paragraph structure of three very different Crocean works, such as *Storia d'Europa, Logica,* and the criticism of Pascoli, will recognize a basic unity that exists in all of them despite the diversity of subject matter: the fluid, harmonious nature of a narrative told with consummate art and a constant balance between participation and distance on the part of the author.

As with Manzoni, the validity of this classical prose was not immediately recognized, much less continued. A hostile attitude toward Manzoni's Florentine theories and toward Croce's idealistic historicism has kept the public distant from these writers' linguistic models. Yet this situation does not diminish the obligation of the student of the history of the language of Italy to align these two authors— writing at a distance of many decades—as the creators of valid, insuperable models.[16] Just as the Manzonian model, despite everything, has survived unscathed the two intervals of Carduccianism and D'Annunzianism, both of which now seem so distant from us, so the Crocean model has survived unharmed the period of linguistic "evasions" constituted by Hermeticism and Futurism and transmits to successive generations a classical model worthy of Alessandro Manzoni.

Forty-eight

Phonematic Structures

236 THE TEMPERED FLORENTINE MODEL

Out of these contrasting forces from within the system, which are added to external forces linked to rapid change of social structures, emerges this approximative tableau of the languages of Italy, as they appear six thousand years after the first traces, and twenty-five hundred years after the first monuments.

To avoid the danger of unjustified oversimplification, it is necessary first to consider the different aspects that constitute the linguistic system valid today. There prevails the biased notion that Italian is a Tuscan dialect, to be precise the Florentine dialect, to which the duty, the honor, and the burden of becoming a literary superstratum (subsequently extended and recognized throughout all Italy) have fallen. As a consequence of this extension and recognition, the characteristic features of Florentine have been modified; hence it is not correct to speak of the Italian system as being only an "illustrious" Florentine. It would be more correct to say that it is a system of "tempered" Florentine, in view of the numerous flaws that have been introduced into the rigidity of the original structures, the lexical variety which one encounters (§246), and the musicality of the sentence which now reveals a dozen varieties of regional Italian languages—from Piedmont, Liguria, Lombardy, Veneto, Emilia, Tuscany, Umbria and the Marches, Abruzzi and Puglia, Lazio, Campania and Lucania, Calabria, Sicily, and Sardinia.

First of all, Tuscany is a region (*a*) that preserves the orthodox Italian system of seven vowels (north of the Via Appia) reduced from the system of nine of Vulgar Latin; (*b*) that is opposed to both the north and the central southern regions inasmuch as metaphony is absent;[1] (*c*) that can be contrasted to northwestern Italy and to the central and southern Adriatic coast, in that it does not contain mixed vowels or the processes of disintegration; (*d*) that is in accordance with northern Italy in rejecting progressive assimilation of ND to NN; (*e*) that is in accordance with the rest of southern and central Italy in rejecting lenition and maintaining and developing the process of regressive assimilation in groups of occlusives, specially of CT and PT into TT; (*f*) that introduces its own solutions in the moderate palatalization of the velars; (*g*) that is distinguished from other regions with regard to the diphthongization of the accented E's and o's in open syllable, in agreement with Euganean Veneto; (*h*) that is distinguished from all the other regions for the moderation of its accent, which does not devalue final vowels, much less nullify them; (*i*) that demonstrates an excess of conservation (Florentine) through the so-called vowel mutation (*anafonesi*); and finally (*k*) that exhibits an excess of innovation in the aspiration of the occlusive consonants in intervocalic position.

Notwithstanding the clear delimitation of its structures and its deeply rooted identity of cultural superstratum, however, the traditional Tuscan model is not identified with the third Italian phonematic system, which had to make numerous concessions to the pressures—not only non-Tuscan but also non-Italian—of the majority of its users, who have adapted themselves to it without conscious resistance.

Tempered by these currents, pressures, and peripheral influences, which are heterogeneous but representative of a numerical majority of 90 percent and of the even greater political and economic weight of Rome and Milan, the Tuscan system nevertheless remains the most recommendable from the point of view of balance, harmony, and flexibility and because it is naturally unrelated to any form of didactic imposition or fad.

A parallel postulation of an Italian system based on the Roman dialect, even if tempered, is neither legitimate nor feasible (§188).

237 THE THIRD PHONEMATIC SYSTEM: THE VOWELS
Thus we come to the problem of delineating the third and current morphophonemic Italian system (see §§149, 174). At this point it no

longer suffices to point out essential distinctive characteristics as we have done for the preceding systems. Rather, it is necessary to give a more detailed description on the basis of absolute values, the principal elements of which have been gathered by Ž. Muljačić. According to Muljačić, there are thirty presentday Italian phonemes,[2] twenty-two of which do not require any discussion, and only eight of which are subject to any doubt.

The present-day Italian vocalic system consists of seven vowels. The objection of those who maintain that only five of these ought to be recognized is premature, even if we can presume that within a century this pentavocalic system will be established. Even now the heptavocalic system is limited to the accented vowels; in atonal position the difference between the open and the closed E and o does *not* exist.[3] Moreover, it must be remembered that it is only in a minority of cases that the bipartition of the E and the o into open and closed vowels is historically justified. In the majority of cases, it is a matter of arbitrary attribution, in which words which were taken from books and which therefore did not have the possibility of a spontaneous allotment were given either an open or a closed pronunciation. An empirical formula states, *Vocale incerta vocale aperta*,[4] and it is this rule that is applied for example in words of the type 'problèma', which we of the north of Italy pronounce 'probléma', without feeling that we are in error; it is another example of those uncertainties and difficulties that only the fusion of the two E's can resolve, even if there is no particular reason to hasten this fusion.

A difference of quantity in Italian vowels does not exist on the pan-Italic phonematic level, but only in certain dialects such as Genoese which clearly distinguishes between *baagiu* 'yawn' and *bagiu* 'toad'. In any case, in the regional pronunciation of Italian, there are differences between the long pronunciation which is conditioned by the position of the open syllable and the short pronunciation in a closed syllable. The difference between *faato* 'fato' and *fatto* (with the short pronunciation) is valid in the regional Piedmontese, Lombard, Ligurian pronunciation, while the short quantity is pronounced indistinctly in Tuscany and in Veneto. Similarly, the single or double pronunciation of words such as *bagno, fascio,* and *aglio* (*ññ, šš, l'l'*)[5] can be traced back to regional patterns, with the possibility of corresponding alternations, in certain regions, of the preceding vowels, respectively long and short.

238 THE SEMIVOWELS

On the one hand, T. Franceschi has maintained that the phoneme *i,* as found for example in the plural noun *bivî* 'junction, road-fork',[6] is autonomous, on the grounds that in these cases we are not dealing with a long vowel but only with the beginning of a diphthongization toward JI. On the other hand it would be absurd to consider the final vowel of *dormii* 'I slept' as long, because this is clearly a case of two independent vowels.[7] Similarly, in *ossequiai* we have not a "tetraphthong" but "two" syllables, -*quia-i*.[8] There is also a distinction of syllables in *pi-ano* 'di Pio', and the 'piano' which comes from the Vulgar Latin PLANU, though how lasting I do not know; similarly *sci-a-re* 'to ski' is trisyllabic, while in the word *la-scia-re* 'to leave', -*scia*- constitutes only one syllable.

It is indispensable in Italian to distinguish a double category of semivowels. On the one hand, we have the vocalized elements that are part of a diphthong and are therefore considered and dealt with as if they were vowels, in view of a possible elision of the article. On the other hand, there are the elements that do *not* constitute diphthongs and which therefore are not capable of elision; indeed, these elements demand the use of the article LO, almost as if they were the equivalent of a group of complex consonants like SP and at the same time fragile. Thus we note the opposition between the types *l'uomo* and *l'ieri* of the first group, and *lo iato, lo Jonio,* and *lo uadi* of the second. A correct spelling system would make a distinction between the entities through the signs I/J and U/W.

Another example of a semivowel is the vocalized R in *brr* (how cold it is).[9]

Into these oppositions come the treatment of the article before foreign words beginning with H (which is really articulated); examples are *lo Hegel* (German), *lo Haldane* (English), *lo Jäger* (German), and *lo Watt* (English).

239 THE CONSONANTS

With regard to consonants, the major problem consists in the difference between single and double (or better "intense") consonants. The difference does not justify the acknowledgment of a different phonematic nature.[10] The overall tableau which on a descriptive level involves the distinction of degree and of articulation, as well as of lenition on the evolutive plane, constitutes a compact unit; it seems difficult to postulate a quadripartite series PP, BB, P, and B, rather than one that would be PP/P BB/B. The doubling of the consonant in the Italian *attimo* from the Latin ATOMU is an opposite phenomenon, but one which is comparable to the phenomenon of the passage from NUBULU to *nuvolo*.

The doubling of consonants is one of the fundamental features of the Italian system. The people of Veneto are branded by their inability to pronounce, distinguish, and articulate double consonants. In Italian there are fifteen phonemes that are susceptible to gemination.[11] Once again in agreement with T. Franceschi,[12] we note that the types *faccia* and *maggio* must not be considered as autonomous phonemes but only as intense variants of the presumed forms FACIA and MAGIO. In any case this alignment is acceptable only if we take a tempered Tuscan stratum as a base. It is only in the milieu of Tuscany that the pronunciations *cena, gente, dice* and *regina* can definitely presuppose a different phoneme—one that is not only palatalized but also affricative. It is always a matter of a single articulation as in the case of *zio, mézzo* 'saturated', *zinco,* and *mèzzo* 'half', in which the transcription TS/DS cannot be recommended.

With regard to the relationship between voiced and voiceless consonants, apart from the hardly valid axiom *consonante incerta consonante sonora,* the most evident anomaly is the tendency to lenite the intervocalic voiceless consonants in the present-day standard pronunciation of southern Italians, a tendency that corresponds to that of doubling the voiced consonants, almost as if to save them from being confused with the voiceless lenited consonants: examples are the modern Roman pronunciations of *àbbile* and *cuggino* for 'abile' and 'cugino'.

The situation regarding the voiced S is a confused one; it is standard in intervocalic position in the pronunciation of northern Italians, absent in the pronunciation of southern Italians from Arezzo down, chaotic in Tuscany and even in Florence, although it is slowly tending toward the voiced patterns of the north. For example, the pronunciation is shifting from *così* to *cozì,* with the S having become voiced.

In addition to the vacillation in the relationships of voiced and voiceless consonants in intervocalic position, three other typical cases must be remembered: the resistance of diphthongated forms of the type *buono* as opposed to the nondiphthongated form of the Florentine type 'bono'; the resistance of the southern pronunciation of the type *sci-enza* as compared with the central and northern pronunciation which is tending toward 'scenza' (written *scienza*); the non-Tuscan symmetry of the pronunciation *pace, faccia,* and *vince,* which in Tuscany is disturbed by the fact that the first example, an (apparently) pure palatal, is attracted by the series of affricated palatals, as found in *pesce,* for example. Even here it is predictable that *pace* and *vince* will in the future be drawn into the unitary system of 'faccia'.

Uncertainties of a social order are less important; the uvular R is frequently used in the snobbish milieu of diplomacy and plutocracy,[13] but is also diffused throughout all social levels in certain areas, for example, Parma.

With regard to the word as a whole, the persistent preference for words ending in vowels assures them a solidity and a significance which are of an entirely different constitution from that of French words, which have been felicitously defined by C. Segre[14] as having been now reduced to an ideogram.

240 CONSONANT GROUPS

In any case the principal characteristic of the third Italian phonematic system is its regulation of the consonantal endings of foreign words: consonantal endings are accepted in the case of isolated consonants, as in *baR*, *gaS*, or *gaP*, or in the case of groups of consonants in which the first is a continuant and the second an obstruant, or more continuous than the preceding. "Sport" and "film" are grafted onto the language intact, whereas adaptations of the French words *act(e)* or *t(h)eatr(e)* would be unthinkable.[15]

With regard to groups of consonants, we are still far from any definitive solution. We cannot restrict ourselves to speaking only of groups that have been accepted and groups that have been excluded; we must also recognize groups that are partial, intermediary, and optional; and those that have been accepted into certain technical sectors, but not everywhere, and not in a definitive way.

Consonant groups made up of a nasal plus a liquid (for example, aNLa), of VL and DL (aVLa, aDLa), of a voiceless consonant plus a voiced consonant (aPBa) or of a voiced plus a voiceless (aBPa) are persistently incompatible. In technical vocabulary, however, we find nonassimilated series of a voiceless plus a voiceless as in *PTerodattilo* or in *CTonio;* or a voiced plus a voiced as in *BDellio*. A group such as PN has no possibilities of expansion, and yet it appears in as fundamental a word as *PNeumatico*. There are extreme cases of occurrences such as *suBSTRato, feLDSPato,* and *tuNGSTeno,* which are again technical words, but it would be grotesque to state that the Italian system tolerates the consonantal groups BSTR, LDSP, and NGST.

To be sure, there is a growing trend toward greater flexibility, and the abandonment of the optional prothetic vowel in words such as *(I)spagna* and *(i)scuola* is proof of it. But one must recognize here another aspect of the process (which we shall see again with regard to procedures of derivation) by which there is a tendency to evolve from a "closed" linguistic system to an "open" one, both in the phonematic field, as well as in the morphological field of the derivation of words (§242).

Forty-nine

Morphological Structures

241 DERIVATION: PREFIXOIDS AND SUFFIXOIDS

The greater phonetic elasticity and adaptability also produce indirect effects on the individuality of the word in the sentence. The temptation to elide or to cut off the end of a word, as well as the temptation to introduce prothetic vowels (already noted in §240), diminishes. There is even less inclination to combine the preposition with the articles in the form of "articulated" prepositions; from the language of ordinary conversation there seeps into the literary language the preference for the type "con il" to the detriment of the type "col."[1]

With reference to the derivation of words, Italian had a certain abundance of traditional characteristic suffixes, especially when one considers the scarce resources of French; for adjectives, for example, there is the formation of the superlative with endings in *-issimo;* and for nouns a variety of augmentatives and diminutives, including those implying a sense of endearment (*vezzeggiative*), exist, as exemplified by the type *casona, casina,* and *casetta,* all formed from 'casa'. Turning to the composition of nouns, we note that there had already been a certain possibility of development in the preceding system, when, under the influence of Latinisms, one became aware of the usefulness of certain prefixes such as RI- to indicate a repetition. These prefixes, however, had never constituted a functional resource, as the so-called separable prefixes of German do, for example; the prefix is easily recognizable in Italian words such as *risentire* and *premettere,* and yet it does not succeed in assuming the automatism of a paradigm, as, on the contrary, occurs for instance, in the humorous quip *ri-buon giorno.* Spontaneous composition in Italian is that in which the first element is verbal, as for example, in *mangia-fuoco* 'fire-eater'. The German construction *Morgen-gabe,* which literally means 'morning-gift' is inadmissible in Italian and must be "translated" into the decidedly more complex syntagma *dono del mattino.* But against this significant resistance of the system press the semantic exigencies of our time, namely, the Anglo-Saxon influence and the European frame of reference which is growing (§250). These semantic needs are beginning to be satisfied by the technique of "prefixoids,"[2] which are units intermediary between nominal themes and prepositions or pre-fixes. We cannot imagine an Italian lexical-derivative equilibrium without considering the part now played by types formed with *auto-* 'by itself' or with *tele-* 'at a distance'; examples are *auto(combustione)* and *tele(communicazioni).* Yet even this technique shows traces of difficulties and ambiguities, because the prefixoids are by now split. The primary prefixoid, as it appears in these examples, is one matter; quite another is the secondary prefixoid which results from the abbre-viation of a word of which the prefixoid had become a normal com-ponent; *autorimessa* does not mean 'automatic repair' but simply 'garage for auto(mobiles)'; similarly *telespettatore* does not mean a 'distant spectator' but rather 'one who watches tele(vision)'.

Primary prefixoids are employed to create "motivated" non-arbitrary) words with a technique of composition that does not go beyond the "attributive" compound word. Secondary prefixoids are introduced to "abbreviate," and they go beyond the traditional pat-terns of composition; in this case we are dealing with compounds in which the stable ruling element is *not* verbal, and is therefore on the level of the German *Morgengabe,* which has just been defined as foreign to the Italian tradition.[3]

In any case, changes are taking place also in the second part of future compound words, through elements that are definable not as "suffixoids" but rather as "predicatoids." Latin formulae of this type, which were created in part on the model of Greek compounds have been illustrated in §63; we note *agri-cola, igni-fer,* and *arti-fex* as examples. In place of the form *mangiatutto* we find the Latinate types such as *onnivoro* and *erbivoro;* modelled along the same lines are *avicolo* 'chicken farmer', *pestifero* 'pestiferous', and *vermifugo* 'vermi-fuge', which constitute a providential resource for needs that are increasingly more deeply felt and diffused.

242 THE MORPHOLOGIZATION OF SYNTAGMS

Within the framework of the trend toward motivation, whether or not associated with the search for brevity, we note three different tendencies today. The first of these aims at substituting arbitrary words or cumbersome phrases with words that are motivated (non-arbitrary) or shorter. The second trend aims at substituting morphological derivations for syntagmatic relationships. The third procedure is based on the telegraph model, in which words are juxtaposed without formal markers that specify whether or not we are here dealing with a real alignment or with the elimination of one or more understood markers.

Examples of the first category are particularly numerous in the language of bureaucracy which by its nature prescinds from the expression of emotion and aims not so much at real functionality as it does at an economic ideal of minimal effort. An example that has taken root even outside the world of bureaucracy is *evidenziare* instead of 'mettere in evidenza', which apart from its obvious justification also has the functional advantage of greater brevity. More indicative of this loosening of ties are the words *relazionare* in lieu of 'referire', and *revisionare* in place of 'rivedere'. This type aims at "motivating" its form through a link with the noun which in the Latin tradition was contained in the "suppletive" and arbitrary relationship of the infinitive *referre* to the supine *relatum*. Other members of this series are *sensibilizzare* for 'render sensible', *ipotizzare* for 'fare l'ipotesi', and *strumentalizzare* for 'usare come strumento' (actually *strumentare* would be better).

Belonging to the second category are constructs that are gaining ground every day, such as (*stato*) *confusionale*, and (*potere*) *decisionale* for '(state of) confusion', and '(power of) decision'. This trend is the object of criticism, but in reality it represents neither an anomaly nor a source of disorder for the present-day living system. It is a trend that one may or may not like, but a negative aesthetic judgment is not valid solely on the grounds that the expression in question deviates from our habits.

The third category is the most abnormal, because it does not belong to the traditional inflected type, but rather clashes openly and enthusiastically with both morphological and syntactical relationships and thus comes closer to an uninflected linguistic type. It arises both from ordinary relationships devoid of special importance, as for example *la gente bene,* in which the adverb takes the place of the adjective, as well as from technical terms which constitute real telegraphic forms; examples of these are *borsa valori* and *cassa pensioni,* in which 'dei' and 'delle' are understood, respectively; similarly we note 'movimento testa-coda' and 'missile terra-aria', which with a renunciatory attitude "make do" without markers signalling relationships of reciprocal dependency. They entrust to the reader or listener the task of integrating on a "word" level but not on a "language" level the relationships that have been deprived of markers. On the phonematic level, this mobilization of morphological procedures produces a result parallel to what we have noted, on the phonematic level, with reference to *feldspato* and other words containing similar abnormal juxtapositions of consonants (§240); indeed, such a process leads to the possibility of coining occasional, open, short-lived words that can be justified in an appropriate context but that do not aspire to national recognition and registration in the lexical treasury of the language. The principle that from every abstract noun and adjective ending in *-ale* can be drawn, or that from every adjective an abstract noun ending in *-ismo* and indicating a doctrine or custom can be drawn, should in theory deserve the same acknowledgment as the possibility of forming a past participle from every verbal form. Thus, through a richer paradigmatic system, one can aim at a more "open" linguistic system (§240). Similarly, through the alignment of certain notes the musician makes "chords" which are nothing other than "words" created one at a time in accordance with patterns that have been more or less generally accepted.[4]

Nevertheless, this idea of the integral possibility of creating new paradigms (*paradigmaticità integrale*) is still foreign and distant to Italian. The most extreme testimonies of this search for brevity, indeed of this impatience, are nothing other than the internalized implication of the external factor of the "speed" with which European formulae typical of our civilization are spreading.[5] On the one hand we find mutilation within the word, as exemplified by *cine(ma)* for 'cinematografo', or of the syntagma as in *federale* for '(segretario) federale', or *direttivo* for '(consiglio) direttivo'. On the other hand, there exists in Italian as in all other languages the unlimited access to the monogram.[6] The great popularity of the monogram has resulted in the fact that those who coin them do not always respect the criteria and limits which alone can make them useful. The three basic types are: (*a*) the practical semantic monogram, which we illustrate with FIAT, in which a correspondence is created between the monogram "F(abbrica) I(taliana) A(utomobili) T(orino)" and an auspicious Latin word; (*b*) the monogram whose function and value is solely practical, as exemplified by CED for C(omunità) E(uropea di) D(ifesa); (*c*) the monogram which is neither semantic nor practical, like CLN for C(omitato di) L(iberazione) N(azionale), which calls for an integration with vocalic elements in order to be pronounced and has given life to the integrated derivative *ciellenistico*. Monograms simplify, but they are closed off to the uninitiated. They produce a vicious circle in the following way: first of all they concentrate on the essential elements necessary for rapid recognition —to the advantage of the initiated—and then time and effort are required to decode them for the uninitiated.

243 SYNTACTICAL CHOICES

In the field of morphology a salient characteristic of Italian as compared with French, for example, is its superior conservation of markers, which permit stylistic choices that are not possible in French. In Italian, verb endings are sufficient to indicate the "person" without the intervention of the respective personal pronouns. The use of these latter, in itself superfluous, offers an important variant in concentrating attention on the subject whenever this seems opportune; in Italian one can choose between *dico* and *io dico*, while in French one can only use *je dis* unless one resorts to complex circumlocutions. These appear also in Italian in the case of atonal pronouns which allow a triple stratification: *ti obbedisco, obbedisco a te*, and *è a te che obbedisco*. With regard to word order it is possible to alternate *mio amico* with *amico mio*, according to both the insistence one wants to associate with the attribute, and also from the point of view of regional preferences; in French on the contrary, *ami mon* does not exist alongside *mon ami*. With regard to declension of nouns, we are now witnessing the beginnings of indeclinableness of the relative pronoun, at least in the spoken language; we find *una donna che suo marito è scomparso*, as well as the standard form *una donna il cui marito è scomparso*.

The superior conservation of morphological markers also leads to unfavorable syntactical consequences. The overcomplexity of agreement in Italian is conspicuous in comparison to French simplification. In the Italian sentence *i bravi soldati avanzano,* there are fully four markers of the plural. In the French equivalent, *les vaillants soldats avancent,* the four markers are evident on a graphic level, but only one of them is pronounced.[7] Turning to verb forms, we note that the subjunctive is in decline, but not to the degree it is in French. But in surviving, the subjunctive does permit the adequate signalling of relationships of clausal dependence, and so also for this reason the Italian sentence continues to be more complex and flexible than its French counterpart. Even the past absolute tense is in decline, and has entirely disappeared from northern usage. Precisely for this reason, we are dealing with a regional, and not a national, decline. There is no indication that this process is spreading to southern Italy.

Somewhat analogous situations can also be noted in the syntax of the sentence, above all under the influence of the emotion-charged language of advertising. This consists mostly in forms of affective, abbreviated sentences which insist on either a command or on a prohibition. In the series *basta tintarella, niente Africa, tanto nero, via le catene, vota socialista,* and *mangiate snello,* we note an omission of markers, which more or less cuts into the actual structure of the sentence. In these cases, there are three degrees. The first is the basically nominal sentence, in which only the prepositional markers have been omitted: 'basta CON la tintarella'. The second phase requires the integration of a verbal predicate: 'NON VOGLIAMO . . . l'Africa', 'ADOPERA tanto nero', 'METTETE via le catene'. The third stage is no longer a sentence with reduced markers, but rather a telegraphically visual sentence: 'vota PER LA LISTA socialista', 'mangiate IN MODO DA RIMANERE snello'. Here we are faced with a form of syntactical abbreviation which is increasingly more accentuated, but always determined by emotional needs.

The other side of the question goes much deeper and consists in the general trivializing of the spoken sentence. From this point of view we are dealing with schema—for the most part bureaucratic—which are distributed in convoluted sentences that abound with nominal forms of the verb and in abstract nouns that nominalize the performed action, or in denominative verbs which submit the action to an abstract motivation. It is a form of egocentricity, by which, even against one's own self-interest, one forgets that one is speaking in order to be understood. The traditional principle that requires us to write with the naturalness with which we speak is counterbalanced by the habit of speaking as if we were writing, without seeing the interlocutor before us. We are faced with a search for statistical justification that is as exaggerated as it is shortsighted and inefficient.

244 SUBSIDIARY ACCENTS

Over the isolated word, as over the sentence, there hovers a coordinating force which is the accent. With regard to its nature, the accent in Italian has been intensive from the first centuries of the Roman Empire. Historically, this intensity has been greater in the north, but little by little, it has moved in a southerly direction, and today we of the north hear the accent of southern Italians as being more intense than our own. With regard to its position, once again Italian is at the extreme opposite of French. In French the accent is linked to the last pronounced vowel, but in Italian its position is free, which is to say it is determined by history, with the exception of alterations due to analogy; an example of these possibilities is provided by the following series: *desiderò, desideriamo, desìdero, desìderano.* Moreover, if we consider enclitic particles, we come up with a striking series like *telèfona, telèfonami, telèfonamela.* In most Italian words the accent falls on the penult. According to statistics, 60% of Italian words are accented on the penult, 32% are enclitic or proclitic particles, 4% are accented on the antepenult, 3% are accented on the last, and 1% on the syllable preceding the antepenult.[8]

The Italian word is not made up only of the opposition of accented and unaccented syllables, however. In every series of two or more syllables, we must recognize syllables that are clearly accented and syllables that have a secondary accent; in fact, by developing a suggestion of R. Hall[9] we ought to distinguish between a full accent, a syllable which has no accent, an intermediary accent, and even one that is emphatic. In the case of words that are accented on the fourth or the fifth to the last syllable, another criterion must be taken into account, which in Italian normally does not play a part, namely, quantity; in the example *telèfonamela,* there is, in addition to the opposition of the accented and the unaccented syllables and in addition to an opposition of force, an opposition of quantity; in *telèfonamela* the accented syllable is long, the four unaccented vowels are very short except for the last one which stands out as a possible intermediary accent. The intensity of the accent is then relative and not absolute; two fully accented syllables cannot be contiguous; before an accented syllable at the beginning of a word, it is difficult to introduce a word accented on the last syllable, or one that is subject to apocope; in a series like *andare lì,* it is certainly possible to cut off the final (atonal) unaccented E. But in doing so one pays a price: instead of the normal succession of accents found in *andàre lì,* one is left with the retrogression of the accent in the pronunciation of *àndar lì.*

In addition to the quantitative problems of accentuation in a strict sense, there exist the qualitative problems of the so-called melody of the sentence. Through the observations of A. Camilli and of R. Hall,[10] three melodic intonations have been distinguished: the ascending, the descending, and the ascending-descending. The first two are important inasmuch as they have the value of syntactical markers, the first for the normal interrogative sentence and the second for the interrogative introduced by pronouns or by interrogative adverbs; in fact, the intonation of *vieni?* is exactly opposite to that of *chi viene?* The third type is that of the normal assertive sentence.[11] Within this category, we must distinguish between the purely indicative statement (for example, *non c'è niente da fare: è pazzo*) and the statement that is more or less strongly emotional (for example, *quel corridore è un pazzo*). We must also add the special melody of the segmented statement, as exemplified by *lo conosco bene, l'amico,* which is entirely different from the melodic sequence of the sentence *conosco bene l'amico.*[12] A further comparison with French makes us aware of yet another opposition: the interrogative sentence *lo conosce?* which we mark only by means of an ascending melodic form, needs a syntactical marker in the corresponding French form; note the interrogative formulation *le connaît-il?* as compared with the affirmative *il le connaît.*

Melodic varieties distinguish the great regions of Italy rather clearly, even when one does not consider the use of the dialect (§236, 246). It is a field in which there still remains a great deal to investigate. In any case, on the basis of certain analogies that were believed to have been discovered between "melodies" along the Adriatic coast and the Po Valley region, the legitimacy of a (still surviving) "Gallo-Italic" melody was proposed.[13]

245 "GENIUS" OF LANGUAGE?
On the basis of these considerations, we can say that a linguistic system is neither geometric nor immobile. Rather it results from the balancing of a great many contrasting forces; it is like a ship, which can remain relatively stable, but is not immobile, because its buoyancy is the result of many individual balances. To use the words of a distinguished contemporary scholar,[14] languages are not "natural codes"; those scholars who use the "synchronic method" cannot allow themselves the luxury of leaving the history of the language out of consideration.[15] To repeat an old formula of mine, synchrony is nothing other than disguised or microscopic historicity.[16]

In contrast to these leveling tendencies, however, the notion of a "genius" of language has been elaborated (though from opposing points of departure), as if linguistic institutions as a whole justified an analogy to a living being: we need only remind ourselves of Karl Vossler's vision.[17] The expression *genio della lingua* is inappropriate; a living being, on the one hand, can be more or less efficient, but he always represents a type of organized life which is the fruit of selection and which has rendered him fit for the tasks in the world of nature. A language, on the other hand, is a product of convention, in which the viscosity of tradition has rendered the forces of selectivity almost invalid.[18] Linguistic institutions, inasmuch as they are conventional, are always inadequate or overpowering, with respect to the expressive needs of their users,[19] that is, they are half tool and half prison. With regard to the Italian language, in defining this "genius" there has been an insistence from time to time on the traditionalistic hallmark linked with the similarity of Italian to Latin, on the traditional recognition of its variety and harmoniousness (wrongly devalued by a recent author[20]), and on the sophistication connected with the agility and richness of its poetic vocabulary and the clumsiness and poverty of its technical vocabulary—all characteristics which are closely connected with the structure and affairs of Italian society, which is quite heterogeneous. If these features merited the comprehensive attribute of "genius," then it would apply to the society and not to the Italian language.[21]

Fifty

Future Prospects

246 THE SOCIETY

These linguistic structures, on the one hand consolidated and on the other submitted to so much unrest and turmoil, now pose problems pertaining to their relationships with the society. From this point of view, the great turning point did not occur in connection with political unification. The latter was simply superimposed on a society that was substantially static and unchanged. The fundamental statistical fact, elaborated by T. De Mauro,[1] proves that at the moment of political unification, the Italian literary language was a matter of concern to only 3% of the population, while 97% lived exclusively in the world of the dialects, which constituted real linguistic ghettoes. Other statistical data is less significant: for example, that the population of Italy was 17 million in 1770, 28.5 million in 1881, and 55 million today; that cities with a population exceeding 100,000 numbered five in 1770, 10 in 1881, and more than 40 today; that 17% of the population lived in the cities of more than 50,000 inhabitants in 1861, and by 1961 this percentage was 34%.[2] These are all figures that are not directly related to linguistics because the large urban centers certainly favor the formation of a unitary linguistic community in a geographic sense, but not always in a social sense. Because of the fluidity of the present-day situation, it is impossible to determine the relationship that exists today between the users of the standard language and the users of dialect, as compared with that of 3% and 97% a century ago.

Three forces have contributed to the following accomplishment: that within half a century the literary Italian language (at least potentially) concerns all 55 million inhabitants of Italy today without distinction, as compared with the 750,000 of one century ago. These factors are the First World War, which brought millions of Italians into contact with each other; the organization of trade unions, which brought all workers into a single coalition; and television, which daily presents millions of Italians with a largely uniform standard language. This process has not merely had the effect of unifying the language; in addition, the opposition between the standard language and dialect has become more articulated because this opposition is not being modified only to the advantage of the standard language and to the disadvantage of the dialect. On the one hand, there is the traditional dialect which accentuates its (even social) ghetto nature, but its use is becoming ever more restricted in extension and profundity. On the other hand, there exists the dialect which is applicable to the needs of cultured society; it was used in large cities, from Turin and Genoa, to Milan, Rome, and Naples; in most cases it was used in a somewhat diluted form, but in certain centers, such as Venice, it is still very much alive. In a parallel fashion, there exists the literary language which on the one hand is locked in its oligarchical tradition, but on the other accepts certain regional aspects, especially from the point of view of certain accents or a median melodic structure (§§236, 244). Pairs of synonyms which link the user to one particular Italian region rather than another are maintained without influencing the sociolinguistic dignity of the users. I list here a certain number of pairs of synonyms[3] regarding which I should like to recommend to foreign users (as well as to Italians) the most absolute indifference: *intendere/sentire* 'to hear', *uscire/sortire* 'to go out', *comò/cassettone* 'chest of drawers', *cassetto/tiretto* 'drawer', *armadio/guardaroba* 'wardrobe', *lavandino/acquaio* 'sink', *gruccia/ometto* 'clothes-hanger', *rubinetto/chiavetta* 'faucet', *stringa/fettuccia* 'ribbon', salvietta/asciugamano 'towel', *mezzanino/ammezzato* 'mezzanine', *balcone/finestra* 'window', *tavola/asse* 'plank, board', *trapunta/imbottita* 'quilt', *adesso/ora* 'now', *giocattolo/balocco* 'toy', *granata/scopa* 'broom', *gota/guancia* 'cheek', *riga/scriminatura* 'part(ing) of hair', *bollito/lesso* 'boiled meat', *sottana/gonna* 'skirt', *pelare/mondare* 'to peel', *cacio/formaggio* 'cheese', *midolla/mollica* 'crumb, soft inside of bread', *infreddatura/raffreddore* 'cold' (n.), *saetta/fulmine* 'lightning', *sasso/pietra* 'stone'. The coexistence of tempered forms both of a literary language which rejects the role of tyrant and of nondogmatic dialects will give the language of Italy the possibility of reaching a new flexible, and valid equilibrium in the fascinating but profound crisis which it is now experiencing.

247 THE SCHOOLS

After society, the most important protagonist in this crisis is the school. The first rudimentary need was to eliminate illiteracy; this struggle began immediately after unification, and in ninety years has succeeded in reducing the percentage of illteracy from 75% to 14%.[4]

It is up to the schools—first of all only on the elementary level and later in what has been called the *scuola dell'obbligo* 'compulsory secondary-school education'—to compare the linguistic structures with the needs of the users, growing in number at a dizzying rate. Linguistic teaching continues to have an indirect effect even later, at least on those students who in their roles as teachers or in their offices or factories will be in a position to require the increasingly more frequent use of the literary language.

At one time the linguistic norm continued to be presented in the Italian schools as something authoritarian and determined, if not by an official authority, then at least by what survived of the ever decreasing traditional authority of the Accademia della Crusca, and later by what we might call the median use of writers and journalists. In 1923 the Italian educational system began its great reform. As far as language was concerned, this reform moved away from the authoritarian vision in a dramatic way and promoted on the elementary school level the use of the local dialect and of textbooks suited to build a bridge between the genuine speech of the area and the written form. In any case, this reform did not have favorable results, above all because it was not continued long enough. The evolutionary step taken by the Fascist regime, which diverted the organization of the state in a resolutely centralizing sense, resulted in the dialects' being considered as dispersive elements and therefore their being banned. But this turn of events, which arose so suddenly, did not lead to a new authoritarian regime as far as language was concerned. Given that creativity, proclaimed as the fundamental requirement of the personality of the pupil, had to allow the latter the greatest liberty of expression, it followed that as soon as the terms of comparison with the dialect were taken away, there was nothing to maintain and sustain through constant comparison that linguistic stability without which a society remains crippled. Thus by the middle of the century Italy was suffering from the effects of a dissymetry—indeed of a divergence—between social necessities and psychopedagogical precepts which constituted the inspiration of Italy's scholastic reform. Exactly when the clientele of the literary language had expanded to, let us say, fiftyfold (see §246), the structures that governed it or at least were present in Italy's collective consciousness were demobilized. It was as if the number of girders and beams of a building destined to house fifty times more people than it had previously housed, were reduced because they had been deemed nonessential. With regard to the whole of the Italian linguistic system, all considerations of a descriptive order must take into account this intrinsic crisis and therefore the necessity of gradually establishing a new order within the limits of possibility.

Even though the spirit of the old reform of a half a century ago is no longer present in the Italian school system, still the linguistic damage has been done, and even persons who do not insist on the myth of creativity and of language-poetry find it difficult to submit themselves to a linguistic discipline, even one that is not oppressive. To this end it is vital that the teaching of the literary language, both in its rigid structures and in its many possibilities of evocation and choice, be intensified without skepticism and without dogma on all scholastic levels.

In light of this literary language founded on tempered and open models, the dialect is not destined to be either a trademark of inferiority or a romantic symbol of bygone noble times[5] or a misplaced symbol of autonomistic or separatistic degeneration. The dialect still preserves its validity as a legitimate, permanent, and antidogmatic term of comparison with the literary language. It is a liberating alternative to the growing depersonalization and the trivialization of the literary language, which has now come into general use.

248 Linguistic Dirigisme: Language Use Controlled by Authority

There are two equal and contrary forces that are working against the unifying tendencies promoted, at least on the regional level, by society and against the striving toward national uniformity that ought to be aimed at by the educational system; they are civic insensitiveness and the pressure of foreign systems. Thus, for higher reasons, the problem of language use controlled by authority (*dirigismo linguistico*) is posed. This control must be defined in its informing principles as well as in the ways and means that are capable of translating the innovations and proposals of individuals into linguistic facts and relationships acceptable to the whole community. This *dirigisme* is identified with that activity which Bruno Migliorini had called *glottotecnica,* a calk which has been modeled in an unobjectionable way on *glotto-logia* 'language engineering' as opposed to 'the science of language'. In theory the action of language engineering is not limited. Theoretically, it could even set itself the task of creating an artificial language, inspired by given principles which have been established from the beginning. Language engineering must, however, take into account the circumstances that can facilitate or hinder its suggestions and proposals. Above all, in consideration of those difficulties which for social reasons the Italian linguistic system is now experiencing, the "language technician" (*glottotecnico*) of Italian must limit his intervention to those cases in which he feels he would be able to count on the conscious or unconscious consensus of the users of the language. For this reason, he rejects traditional, archaic, and class-conscious "purism" and accepts the tempered, functional purism that has been called "neopurism."[6] Italian linguistic institutions feel the effects of their historical formation in both a favorable and an unfavorable sense. The desirable conservation of many markers has resulted from the fact that as theoretical tools they represent something valid today. But the heaviness of syntactical agreement in Italian makes the system overly complicated; a scant predisposition toward the use of abstract words in a society which needs them for technical reasons is an onerous impediment. The origins of the language and its oligarchical history block the possibility of creating metaphors that are taken from everyday discourse, which practice is indeed the power of the English language. The strong points of the Italian language are only its clear pronunciation and its decent spelling; regarding this latter the reader will find proposed below only a few modifications aimed at eliminating uncertainties.

The appropriate marking of accents on proparoxytones (when the final syllable begins with a consonant) and on paroxytones (when the final syllable begins with a vowel) is of the utmost importance; therefore, *màcchi-na* and *malì-a* ought to be marked with accents, while *risa-ta* and *bali-a* ought not. Next, it would seem advisable that the use of the x be reduced to a minimum and that we write and say *tassì* and *silografia* rather than 'taxi' and 'xilografia'; that the diphthong UO be eliminated after an I, whether phonetic or graphic, so that the pronunciation and the writing of *aiola, piolo,* and *gioco* (in lieu of *aiuola,* etc.) be standardized; that the spelling of the plural form of nouns ending in -CIA and -GIA be -CE and-GE after a consonant and -CIE and -GIE after a vowel, as in *provinCE, facCE* and *franGE,* as opposed to *audaCIE* and *valiGIE;* that the article before groups beginning with PN or PS be LO, as in *lo pneumatico* and *lo psicologo;* that the plurals of nouns ending in -CO and in -GO, be left to develop as they will, and that time not be wasted in disputing whether *stomachi* ought to be prefered to 'stomaci', or *filologi* to 'filologhi'.

With regard to the formation of words, we must take into account not only the preferability of suffixes that are already "functioning" and therefore more functional, but also the need for simplification and brevity; *automazione* has already won over 'automatizzazione', but 'lemmazione' (reception of a word as an entry in a dictionary) has yet to impose itself on 'lemmatizzazione'. Similarly, *anglismo* is to be preferred to 'anglicismo' although this latter is more corect from the point of view of traditional morphology.

In his handling of foreign words, the "language engineer" proceeds according to three directives: (*a*) he "reproduces" those words whose structure is compatible with that of Italian words: such as *gap, bang, test, ring,* and *boom* (§240); (*b*) he "adapts" the words when their incompatibility is limited: in this category we find such words as *gol* from 'goal', *lider* from 'leader', *tosti* from 'toasts', *mochetta* from 'moquette', *taièr* from 'tailleur'; (*c*) he "translates" words in the case of total incompatibility: examples are *flash* which ought to be rendered by 'lampo' or another equivalent word.

249 National Linguistic Authority

In the matter of language, legislative activity is not enough; executive action is also necessary, which for three centuries and with a diversity of energy and prestige was identified with the Accademia della Crusca. Here also a question of number has upset the traditional equilibrium; faced with an oligarchy of men of letters, the Crusca was able to impose rules or at least to discuss problems or engage in controversy. In the present-day situation of Italian society, none of this is possible. The lack of success of the Accademia d'Italia, in a period in which it could even have availed itself of the support of a totalitarian power, is an example of this.

Significant success cannot be realized if not through the collaboration of three forces, even if these forces do not operate within the same space and with the same intensity. They are the RAI-Televisione,[7] for the attenuation of certain excessive differences of pronunciation that are too regional; the teachers' unions, which would require of instructors that they insist on standard spelling and grammar at all scholastic levels; and finally, the major newspapers together with the unions of the printing industry, which could visually translate the suggestions and proposals of the "language engineers" and at the same time collaborate in keeping Italian syntax agile and efficient. Finally the legislative office of the prime minister could be furnished with a linguistic section authorized to regulate the terminological bedlam typical of the different ministries and bureaucratic offices, naturally limiting this authority to "technical" words.

Cultural organizations such as the Accademia della Crusca can today set for themselves only goals that require contact with a limited number of researchers; an example of such an undertaking is the great collection of entries for the historical dictionary of the Italian language, which requires approximately fifty years of work and which, with regard to the first two centuries of Italy's literary history, will constitute a virtual "thesaurus", that is, the complete collection of all lexical units attested to (including dialectal variants). Less monumental, though not less worthy, undertakings are those which have to do with the editing of ancient texts, a valuable process for our understanding of the languages of Italy, because without reliable editions it would not be possible even to make reliable dictionaries. Finally, the grammatical institutions of today's Italian must be described by a grammar that suits the times.[8]

250 LINGUISTIC COORDINATION ON THE "NEO-LATIN" AND THE "EUROPEAN COMMUNITY" LEVELS

The future problems of the Italian language, as well as of all other national languages, are not limited to internal ones. L. Spitzer[9] and G. Nencioni[10] have already demonstrated that a European semantic community is now in the process of being formed, and E. Peruzzi has made further investigations into the matter.[11] Peruzzi has demonstrated well how this expansion has been progressive, promoted first under the Anglo-French label and then under the Anglo-American. Even here we can see how we have passed from the old oligarchical situation to a convergence of masses. The popularity of the expression "Iron Curtain" (in Italian *cortina di ferro*)[12] is one of the best examples of this comprehensive European outlook. On the formal level of meanings, we are here dealing not only with the adaptation of foreign terms, but with the adoption of parallel positions with regard to the application for example of the suffixes of denominative verbs (e.g., Italian *-izzare*, French *-iser*, German *-ieren*[13]) to new formations.

On the international plane, the problems of language *dirigisme* consist above all in the possibility or impossibility of adapting the words pouring in from the Anglo-Saxon world to the languages that are closest to Italian in morphological structure, like French, which in this matter is more open than Italian, and Spanish, which is more closed. The fate of the American word-image *skyscraper*, which has come into Italian through the French form *gratte-ciel*, will serve as an example of the problems involved. The Italian solution, *grattacielo*, imitates the French both from the point of view of phonetics as well as of semantics; the Spanish solution *rascacielos* adheres to the French only on the semantic level, while the German *Wolkenkratzer* corrects the original image even on the semantic plane by substituting the image of "cloud" for the original "sky." Agreements with the Conseil international de la langue française, and possibly with the Spanish Academy are in the process of being formulated so that in the future the problem of a reciprocal coordination of words through FITRO (Fond international pour la terminologie des langues romanes) can be confronted.

Another aspect of the situation concerns the problems of rapport between languages that are intrinsically different, but which together form part of a common political-economic system, such as the European Common Market. In this case it is not so much a matter of regulating possible neologisms which spread within the community. Rather the problem is one of easy translatability, and above all concerns the treatment of compound German and Dutch words with regard to the possibility of their correspondence with other compound words in Italian (or French) or to the use of simple derivatives.

It is with these far-reaching prospects that we bring to a close this panorama of historical events and structures through which the language of Italy has slowly been realized, and is now predisposed to evolve in the near future. It has been a contemplation which, notwithstanding lacunae and obscure points, constitutes an incomparable picture of serenity and efficiency. In contrast to the constant fluctuation of individual and social forces in conflict, the scholar keeps himself free from philosophical or nationalistic tutelage, from the tyranny of specialization, and from the utilitarianism of specialists. With unflagging attention and understanding he sees passing before him the weight of anonymous medieval masses, the refined choices of the founding fathers of a tradition, as well as the uniform and depersonalized patterns which, because of our computer civilization, loom up today and threaten the future.

Notes

CHAPTER ONE

1. *Piccola guida alla preistoria italiana* (Florence, 1962).
2. *Historia mundi* 1 (1952):118.
3. Rust, *Historia mundi* 1:294.
4. Eickstedt, *Historia mundi* 1:129.
5. *Preistoria italiana*, table 7.
6. See Kälin's table in *Historia mundi* 1:60.
7. *Preistoria italiana*, tables 13–19.
8. Mercando, *Le iscrizioni rupestri di Monte Bego* (Turin, 1957).
9. Ribezzo, *Rivista indo-greco-italica* 4 (1920):83 ff.; Terracini, *Pagine e appunti di linguistica storica* (Florence, 1957), pp. 41–52.
10. *Bulletin de dialectologie romane* 3 (1912):1–18, 63–86.
11. See Giacomo Devoto, *Scritti minori* 2 (Florence, 1967):20 ff., and Giacomo Devoto, *Studi etruschi* 37 (1969):93 ff.
12. Krahe, *Sprachverwandtschraft im Alteuropa* (Heidelberg, 1951).
13. Hubschmid, *Thesaurus praeromanicus* 1 (Bern, 1936):9 ff.

CHAPTER TWO

1. Devoto, *Scritti minori* 2:21.
2. *Ibid.*, 22.
3. Niedermann, *Essais d'étymologie et de critique verbale latine* (Neuchâtel, 1918), pp. 17 ff.
4. *Historia mundi* 1:225 ff.

Notes

5. Devoto, *Scritti minori* 2:44–49; Jud and Jaberg, *Atlante italo-svizzero,* table 424.

6. Devoto, *Scritti minori* 2:44 ff.

7. Alessio, *Studi etruschi* 9 (1935):133 ff., 10 (1936): 165 ff.

8. Devoto, *Scritti minori* 2:17, 59.

9. Ribezzo, *Rivista indo-greco-italica* 15 (1931): 155 ff.

10. Hubschmid, *Mediterrane Substrate* (Bern, 1909), p. 35.

11. *Ibid.,* p. 27.

12. *Ibid.,* pp. 37 ff.; Devoto, *Scritti minori* 2:16.

13. Terracini, *Archivio glottologico italiano: Sezione Goidanich* 20 (1926):131.

14. Devoto, *Scritti minori* 2:29–30.

15. Pizano, *Scritti in onore di Alfredo Trombetti* (Milan, 1938), pp. 199–213.

16. Durante, *Annali dell'Istituto orientale di Napoli: Sezione linguistica* 3 (1961):59–77.

17. Terracini, *Gli studi linguistici sulla Sardegna preromana* (Rome, 1936), p. 12.

18. *Die Indogermanisierung Griechenlands und Italiens* (Heidelberg, 1949), p. 32.

19. Herter, *Minos* 9 (1960):219 ff.

20. Giacomo Devoto, *Origini indeuropee* (Florence, 1962), p. 94.

21. *Ibid.,* p. 125.

22. Devoto, *Scritti minori* 1:70 ff.

23. *Preistoria italiana,* table 22.

24. *Ibid.,* table 23. Cf. Laviosa Zambotti, *Le più antiche culture agricole europee* (Milan, 1943), p. 500.

25. *Preistoria italiana,* table 23.

26. *Ibid.,* table 24.

27. *Ibid.,* table 32.

28. Zambotti, *Antiche culture agricole,* pp. 351–83.

CHAPTER THREE

1. Devoto, *Origini indeuropee,* pp. 15 ff.

2. Meillet, *Linguistique historique et linguistique gènérale,* 2d ed. (Paris, 1936), pp. 165 ff.

3. Devoto, *Origini indeuropee,* p. 18.

4. Schwyzer, *Griechische Grammatik* (Munich, 1934–53), 1:645, 2:303.

5. Devoto, *Origini indeuropee,* pp. 191 ff.

6. *Ibid.,* pp. 263 ff.

7. *Ibid.,* pp. 292 ff.

8. L. R. Palmer, *The Latin Language* (London, 1954), p. 32.

9. Giacomo Devoto, *Atti delle giornate sociolinguistiche* (Rome, 1970).

10. Devoto, *Origini indeuropee,* pp. 382 ff.

11. *Ibid.,* pp. 193 ff.

12. *Preistoria italiana,* table 18.

13. Devoto, *Origini indeuropee,* p. 109.

14. *Preistoria italiana,* table 31.

15. Devoto, *Origini indeuropee,* p. 109.

16. Rellini, *Bullettino di Paletnologia* 48 (1925):32 ff.

17. *Preistoria italiana,* table 32.

18. *Ibid.,* table 35.

19. Devoto, *Origini indeuropee,* p. 148.

20. *Ibid.,* p. 384.

21. *Ibid.,* p. 151. Cf. Dumitrescu, *L'età del ferro nel Piceno* (Bucharest, 1929).

22. Zambotti, *Antiche culture agricole,* pp. 402 ff.

CHAPTER FOUR

1. Devoto, *Scritti minori* 2:200 ff.

2. *Rivista indo-greco-italica* 17 (1933):197–211.

3. Pisani, *Le lingue dell'Italia antica oltre il latino,* 2d ed. (Turin, 1964).

4. Pauly-Wissowa, *Realenzyklopädie,* suppl. 9, col. 1779; Pisani, *Lingue dell'Italia antica,* pp. 225 ff.

5. Camporeale-Giacomelli, *I Piceni e la civiltà etrusco-italica* (Florence, 1959), pp. 93–104.

6. Pisani, *Lingue dell'Italia antica,* pp. 317 ff.

7. *Ibid.,* pp. 318 ff., 323.

8. Battisti, *Studi etruschi* 8 (1934):193 ff.

9. Livy 5:33; Pliny, *Naturalis historia* 3:133.

10. *Corpus Inscriptionum Etruschorum* (1970), vol. 2, section 1, fasc. 4:5607–6324.

11. See Pallottini, *Etruscologia,* 6th ed. (Milan, 1968), pp. 385 ff.

12. *Revue des études grecques* 80 (1967):41.

13. *Antichità romane* 1:30.

14. *Saggio di lingua etrusca e altre antiche d'Italia* (Rome, 1789).

15. C. O. Mueller, *Die Etrusker* (Breslau, 1828), ed. W. Deecke (1877).

16. *Beiträge zur Lehre vom indogermanischen Charakter* 1 (Heidelberg, 1929); *Neue Beiträge zur Lehre vom indogermanischen Charakter* (Vienna, 1931).

17. *Etruskische Wortdeutungen* (Vienna, 1937).

18. *Glotta* 14 (1925):300 ff.

19. Devoto, *Scritti minori* 1:63–69.

20. *Ibid.,* 2:185 ff.

21. *Ibid.,* 2:79–87.

22. *Saggio di lingua etrusca* (Florence, 1947); *Nuovo saggio di lingua etrusca* (Florence, 1966).

23. Georgiev, *Hethitisch und Etruskisch* (Sofia, 1962).

24. Pallottino, *Etruscologia,* p. 385; Olzscha, *Interpretation der Agramer Mumienbinden* (Leipzig, 1939); Pfiffig, *Studien zu den Agramer Mumienbinden* (Vienna, 1963).

25. *Beiträge* 1:12, 13, 24 ff.

Notes

26. Giacomo Devoto, *Tabulae Iguvinae,* 3d ed. (Rome, 1962); Devoto, *Scritti minori* 2:254 ff., 289 ff.

27. Devoto, *Scritti minori* 2:99 ff.

28. Pallottino, *Etruscologia,* pp. 354 ff.

29. The form *prumths* 'grand-nephew' pedantically repeated by various authors, does not exist. See *Studi Etruschi* 38 (1970):142 ff.

30. Ferri, *Rendiconti accademia Lincei* 13 (1958):323.

31. Pallottino, *Etruscologia,* pp. 403, 414 ff.

32. Devoto, *Scritti minori* 2:97–119.

33. Giacomo Devoto, *Storia della lingua di Roma,* 2d ed. (Bologna, 1944), pp. 67 ff.

CHAPTER FIVE

1. Devoto, *Scritti minori* 1:63–69, 2:80 ff.

2. Devoto, *Studi etruschi* 35 (1967):180; *Gli antichi Italici,* 3d ed. (Florence, 1967), pp. 33, 118; cf. Palmer, *The Latin Language,* pp. 43 ff.

3. Tusa, *Kokalos* 6 (1960): 34 ff., 12 (1966):207 ff., 13 (1967):233 ff.

4. Durante, *Kokalos* 7 (1961):88.

5. Alessio, *Kokalos* 7 (1961):33; Parlangeli, *Kokalos* 7 (1961):20.

6. Ambrosini, *Studi e saggi linguistici* 8 (1968):160–72; Schmoll, *Die vorgriechischen Sprachen Siziliens* (Wiesbaden, 1958).

7. Lejeune, "La langue élyme d'après les graffites de Ségeste," in *Comptes rendus de l'Académie des inscriptions et belles lettres,* 1969, pp. 237–42.

8. See L. Agostiniani, Appendix A, in Devoto, *Il linguaggio d'Italia,* p. 375.

9. Pisani, *Le lingue dell'Italia antica,* p. 126 n., p. 294.

10. Thurneysen, *Kuhn's Zeitschrift für vergleichende Sprachforschung* 35 (1897):212 ff.

11. Devoto, *Lingua di Roma,* p. 56; see also Campanile, "Note sulle glosse sicule," in *Studia classica et orientalia A. Pagliaro oblata* (Rome, 1968), pp. 293–322; see also Appendix A, *Il linguaggio d'Italia,* p. 375.

12. *Lingua falisca* (Florence, 1962).

13. Devoto, *Scritti minori* 2:362 ff.

14. G. B. Pellegrini and A. Prosdocimi, *La lingua venetica,* 2 vols. (Padua and Florence, 1967). The Venetic inscriptions are cited according to the numeration of this edition; cf. Beeler, *The Venetic Language* (Berkeley: University of California Press, 1949); Palmer, *The Latin Language,* pp. 41 ff.

15. F. Altheim, *Vom Ursprung der Runen* (Frankfurt, 1939).

16. Pauly-Wissowa, *Realenzyklopädie,* suppl. 9, col. 1764 (Radke).

17. F. Altheim, *Vom Ursprung der Runen,* pp. 47 ff.

CHAPTER SIX

1. Devoto, *Scritti minori* 2:217 ff.

2. Blumenthal, *Indogermanische Forschungen* 47 (1929): 48–72.

3. Pauly-Wissowa, *Realenzyklopädie,* suppl. 9, col. 1779 ff. (Radke); Pisani, *Le lingue dell'Italia antica,* p. 226.

4. Pauly-Wissowa, *Realenzyklopädie,* suppl. 9, col. 1780 (Radke).
5. Devoto, *Tabulae Iguvinae,* 3d ed.
6. Bottiglioni, *Manuale dei dialetti italici* (Bologna, 1954), pp. 121 ff.
7. M. G. Bruno, *I Sabini e la loro lingua* (Bologna, 1969).
8. Devoto, *Lingua di Roma,* pp. 77–78.
9. Bottiglioni, *Dialetti italici.*
10. Devoto, *Studi etruschi* 35 (1967):179 ff.; Pisani, *Le lingue dell'Italia antica,* pp. 46 ff.
11. Parlangeli, "Le iscrizioni osche di Messina," in *Bollettino del Centro di studi filologici e linguistici siciliani* 4 (1956):28 ff.; De Franciscis and Parlangeli, *Gli Italici del Bruzio* (Naples, 1960), in the epigraphic documents.
12. Giacomo Devoto, *Profilo di storia linguistica italiana,* 4th ed. (Florence, 1964), pp. 12 ff.

CHAPTER SEVEN
1. *Athenaeum* 42 (1964):118 ff.; *Rendiconti dell'Istituto lombardo* 100 (1964):3 ff.
2. Pisani, *Le lingue dell'Italia antica,* pp. 281 ff.
3. Pauly-Wissowa, *Realenzyklopädie,* suppl. 12, col. 2067 ff.
4. Terracini, *Archivio glottologico italiano: Sezione Goidanich,* 20 (1926): 126 ff. In this regard I cannot renounce the term as Lejeune does in *Studi etruschi* 40 (1972): pp. 259 ff. In any case see A. L. Prosdocimi, Appendix B, in *Il linguaggio d'Italia,* p. 377.
5. Devoto, *Scritti minori* 2:332 ff.
6. Devoto, *Origini indeuropee,* pp. 395–402.
7. *Studi etruschi* 11 (1937):263–69.
8. *Gli antichi Italici,* p. 110.
9. Parlangeli, *Studi messapici* (Milan, 1960). The numbers in the text refer to the pages of the aforementioned work. See also Haas, *Messapische Studien* (Heidelberg, 1962); De Simone in Krahe, *Die Sprache der Illyrier,* vol. 2: *Die messapischen Inschriften* (Wiesbaden, 1964).
10. Ribezzo, "La originaria area etno-linguistica dell'albanese," in *Rivista d'Albania* 2 (1941):129 ff.
11. Parangeli, *Studi messapici,* pp. 23 ff.
12. *Ibid.,* p. 25.
13. Haas, *Messapische Studien.*
14. *Ibid.*
15. Pisani, *Le lingue dell'Italia antica,* pp. 331 ff., and n. 141.
16. Devoto and Giacomelli, *I dialetti delle regioni d'Italia* (Florence, 1972), pp. 1 ff., 20 ff., 54 ff.

CHAPTER EIGHT
1. Pugliese and Carratelli, *I micenei in Italia* (Fasano, 1967).
2. Pugliese and Carratelli, *Micenei,* p. 24.
3. *Historia mundi* 3:337.

4. Devoto, *Scritti minori* 1:65, 67, 69; Devoto, *Origini indeuropee,* pp. 376 ff.

5. Pallottini, *Relazioni del X Congresso internazionale di studi storici* (Rome, 1955), pp. 34–38.

6. Eusebius in St. Jerome, p. 69; Helm, cf. *Velleio,* 1:14.

7. Pauly-Wissowa, *Realenzyklopädie,* suppl. 9A (1961), pp. 538 ff. (Wüst).

8. Hesiod, *Theogony,* lines 1011 ff.; cf. Pauly-Wissowa, *Realenzyklopädie,* 1, col. 1013.

9. Pauly-Wissowa, *Realenzyklopädie,* 1, col. 1014 ff.

10. *Ibid.,* col. 1009 ff.

11. Wikén, *Die Kunde der Hellenen von dem Land und den Völken der Apenninenhalbinsel bis 300 v. Ch.* (Lund, 1937).

12. For this conservative evaluation of the tradition see Pallottino, *Relazioni del X Congresso internazionale di studi storici,* pp. 29, 40.

13. Strabo, VI, pp. 278 ff.; Pauly-Wissowa, *Realenzyklopädie,* 11, col. 2476.

14. Slotty, *Silbenpunktierung und Silbenbildung im Altetruskischen* (Heidelberg, 1952); cf. Pallottino, *Studi etruschi* 22 (1953):478–81.

15. Vetter, *Glotta* 24 (1936):114–33, 27 (1939): 157–62.

16. Pfiffig, "War di erste Schrift der Etrusker eine Silbenschrift?" in *Kadmos* 2 (1963):142–49.

17. Lejeune, *Revues des études grecques* 82 (1967):40–59.

18. *Gli antichi Italici,* p. 84.

19. For Timmari see *Preistoria italiana,* table 35.

20. For Milazzo see *Preistoria italiana,* table 35.

21. For Chiavari see Lamboglia, "La necropoli ligure di Chiavari," in *Rivista di studi liguri* 26 (1960):91 ff.

22. For this image I am indebted to F. Rittatore-Vonwiller, who proposed it during a meeting of the Primo Simposio di Protostoria, organized by the Centro Faina in September, 1967, in Orvieto.

23. Whatmough, *The Foundations of Roman Italy* (London, 1937).

24. Devoto, *Scritti minori* 2:349 ff.

25. Duhn, *Italische Gräberkunde,* vol. 1 (Heidelberg, 1924).

26. R. Mac Iver, *Italy before the Romans* (Oxford, 1928).

27. Varro, *De lingua latina* 5:45; cf. Pauly-Wissowa, *Realenzyklopädie,* 1A, col. 1021 ff. (Graffunder).

28. Peruzzi treats this matter principally in the following articles: "Il latino di Numa Pompilio," in *Parola del passato* (1966), pp. 15–40, and "Onomastica e società nella Roma delle origini," in *Maia* 21 (1969):126–58.

29. Peruzzi, *Maia* 21 (1969):142; cf. *Le origini di Roma* (Florence, 1971).

30. *Dalla monarchia allo Stato repubblicano* (Catania, 1945).

31. Devoto, *Scritti minori* 2:352 ff.

32. Devoto, *Lingua di Roma,* p. 62.

CHAPTER NINE

1. *Gli antichi Italici,* pp. 138 ff.; Bottiglioni, *Dialetti italici,* pp. 106–13, 159. ff.

2. Sommer, *Handbuch der lateinischen Laut- und Formenlehre* (Heidelberg, 1914), pp. 615 ff.

3. Pisani, *Grammatica latina*, 3d ed. (Turin, 1962), p. 11, with bibliography.

4. Peruzzi, *Maia* 21 (1969):126–58, 244–72.

5. Hammarstroem, "Beiträge zur Geschichte des etruskischen lateinischen und griechischen Alphabets," in *Acta Societatis scientiarum Fennicae* 49 (Helsinki, 1920); Buonamici, *Epigrafia etrusca* (Florence, 1932), pp. 133 ff.

6. *Corpus Inscriptionum Latinorum*, I, 1222.

7. G. Pasquali, *Preistoria della poesia romana* (Florence, 1936), pp. 59 ff.

8. Castagnoli, *Studi e materiali per la storia delle religioni* 30 (1959): 109 ff.

9. See §48.

10. Devoto, *Scritti minori* 2:117 ff.

11. O. Castellani-Pollidori, "I più antichi grecismi nautici in latino," in *Atti della Accademia Toscana: La Colombaria* 21 (1957):181 ff.

12. Pisani, *Le lingue dell'Italia antica*, p. 115, n. 47.

13. Devoto, *Scritti minori* 2:123 ff.

14. *Ibid.*, 2:35, 115, 130, 234.

15. Pasquali, *Poesia romana*, p. 1 ff.

16. Meillet, *Les origines indo-européenes des mètres greques* (Paris, 1923).

17. Pasquali, *Poesia romana*, p. 76.

18. Meillet, *Esquisse d'une histoire de la langue latine* (Paris, 1928), pp. 87 ff.

19. See §47.

20. Polybius, III, 22.

21. Dionysus of Halicarnassus, IV, 26, IV, 28; Pliny, *Naturalis historia*, XXXIV, 14.

22. Cicero, *Pro Balbo*, 23, 53.

23. Livy, IV, 7.

24. *Corpus glossariorum latinorum* (Leipzig, 1888–1923), 8:28.

25. Giacomo Devoto, *Geschichte der Sprache Roms* (Heidelberg, 1968), pp. 71 ff.

26. See Palmer, *The Latin Language*, pp. 346 ff., in which the reader will find a splendid collection of essential archaic documents.

CHAPTER TEN

1. Arnaldo Momigliano, *Rivista storica italiana* 81 (1969): 5–43.

2. *Gli antichi Italici*, pp. 109, 118 ff.

3. Pauly-Wissowa, *Realenzyklopädie*, 3 col. 1555 ff. (Huelsen); *Gli antichi Italici*, p. 113 ff.

4. *Gli antichi Italici*, p. 113 ff.

5. Sommer, *Handbuch*, pp. 215–40.

6. See the following works: Giacomo Devoto, *Adattamento e distinzione nella fonetica latina* (Florence, 1924), pp. 24 ff.; Devoto, *Geschichte der*

Notes

Sprache Roms, p. 95; and Lepschy, "Il problema dell'accento latino," in
Annali della scuola normale superiore di Pisa 31 (1962): 199–246.

7. Palmer, *The Latin Language,* pp. 214 ff.
8. *Ibid.,* p. 233 ff.
9. *Ibid.,* p. 261 ff.
10. Alessandro Ronconi, *Il verbo latino* (Bologna, 1946).
11. Palmer, *The Latin Language,* p. 278.

CHAPTER ELEVEN

1. Devoto, *Scritti minori* 2:359 ff.; cf. §39.
2. *Ibid.,* 2:355 ff.; for the value of *plebs,* see *ibid.,* p. 367.
3. This according to the jurist Pomponius (second century A.D.); see
Sommer, *Handbuch,* p. 190; Palmer, *The Latin Language,* p. 230.
4. Pisani, *Lingue dell'Italia antica,* p. 117, n. 50.
5. Pisani, *Lingue dell'Italia antica,* n. 55.
6. Sommer, *Handbuch,* p. 79; Palmer, *The Latin Language,* p. 218.
7. For a different interpretation see my *Scritti minori* 2:141 ff.
8. Cf. Peruzzi, *Parola del passato* (1966), p. 25.
9. Quintilian, *Istitutio oratoria,* I, 4, 8; cf. Sommer, *Handbuch,* pp.
104 ff.; Palmer, *The Latin Language,* p. 219.
10. Sommer, *Handbuch,* p. 194.
11. *Ibid.,* p. 30.
12. *Ibid.,* p. 156. Also see §67.
13. For this section Palmer's collection of texts is useful. See Palmer,
The Latin Language, pp. 346–57.

CHAPTER TWELVE

1. See Peruzzi, *Parola del passato,* chap. 11.
2. J. Marouzeau, *Quelques aspects de la formulation du latin littéraire*
(Paris, 1949), pp. 37 ff.
3. Ronconi, *Il verbo latino,* p. 153.
4. *Ibid.,* p. 16.
5. Marouzeau, *Formulation du latin,* p. 111.

CHAPTER THIRTEEN

1. J. Marouzeau, *Traité de stylistique* (Paris, 1935, 1946), p. 128.
2. *Ibid.,* p. 131.
3. Sommer, *Handbuch,* pp. 199 ff.
4. Palmer, *The Latin Language,* pp. 81 ff.

CHAPTER FOURTEEN

1. Stolz-Leumann, *Lateinische Grammatik* (Munich, 1928), pp. 181 ff.
2. *Iktus und Akzent im lateinischen Sprechvers* (Berlin, 1928).
3. *Rivista di Filologia classica* 58 (1930):157–88.
4. Devoto, *Geschichte der Sprache Roms,* p. 104.
5. Sommer, *Handbuch,* p. 93; Palmer, *The Latin Language,* p. 213.

6. Cf. De Groot, *Handbook of Antique Prose Rhythm* (Groningen, 1919).

7. See my *Geschichte*, p. 143, and compare Palmer's clear explanation, *The Latin Language*, pp. 130 ff.

8. Palmer, *The Latin Language*, p. 211.

9. Servius, *De accentibus*, IV, p. 525, 18.

10. *Notti attiche*, XIII, 26, 1.

11. *Rivista di filologia classica* 58 (1930):185.

12. Cicero, *Orator*, 8.27.

13. Pisani, *Grammatica latina*, 3d ed., p. 11, with bibliography.

14. Palmer, *The Latin Language*, pp. 211 ff.

15. Marouzeau, *Traité de stylistique*, p. 64.

CHAPTER FIFTEEN

1. Lucretius, *De rerum natura*, I 139, 832, III 260.

2. Cicero, *Brutus*, 72, 258.

3. Varro, *De lingua latina*, bks. 8–10.

4. Cf. my *Geschichte*, p. 135.

5. Marouzeau, *Traité de stylistique*, p. 12.

6. Eduard Norden, *Antike Kunstprosa*, 3d ed. (Leipzig, 1915–18), p. 190.

7. Marx, "Beziehungen des Altlateins zum Spätlatein," in *Neue Jahrbücher* 23 (1909):434 ff.; Ronconi, "Arcaismi o vulgarismi?" *Maia* 9 (1957): 7–35.

8. Blatt, *Die lateinischen Bearbeitungen der Acta Andrea et Matthiae apud anthropophagos* (Giessen and Copenhagen, 1930), pp. 190 ff.

9. Ed. Pascucci (Florence, 1965), pp. 207, 356.

CHAPTER SIXTEEN

1. See the excellent exposition in Ernst Pulgram's *The Tongues of Italy* (Cambridge, Mass., 1958), pp. 268–76.

2. Pauly-Wissowa, *Realenzyklopädie*, 12, col. 544.

3. Devoto and Giacomelli, *Dialetti delle regioni*, p. 135.

4. Stolz-Leumann, *Lateinische Grammatik*, p. 323.

5. Löfstedt, *Syntactica* (Lund, 1933), 2:329.

6. *Pompeianische Wandinschriften*, 2d ed. (Berlin, 1930).

CHAPTER SEVENTEEN

1. See my *Geschichte*, p. 156.

2. See my *Storia della lingua*, p. 243.

3. Löfstedt, *Syntactica* 2:206.

4. *Ibid.*, 2:283 ff.

5. See my *Geschichte*, p. 199.

6. *Ibid.*, pp. 187 ff.

7. *Ibid.*, p. 188.

8. Eduard Norden, *Kommentar zum VI Buch der Aeneis*, 4th ed. (Stuttgart, 1957), p. 163.

9. *Syntactica* 2:376.
10. See my *Geschichte,* p. 217.
11. *Ibid.,* pp. 217 ff.
12. *Ibid.,* p. 219.

CHAPTER EIGHTEEN

1. *Biblioteca di storia economica* 4 (1909):394.
2. Giacomo Devoto, *Atti del V convegno di studi umbri* (Gubbio, 1970), pp. 118 ff.
3. Terracini, *Archivio glottologico italiano* 27 (1935):145.
4. *Pompeianische Wandinschriften,* 2d ed. (Berlin, 1930).
5. Devoto, *Atti del V convegno,* p. 121; cf. §98.
6. *Ibid.,* p. 113. For the testimonies of the grammarians see §96.
7. See the interesting considerations of T. Franceschi on the principle of "exaggeration" here applied: *Archivio glottologico italiano* 54 (1969): 59 ff.
8. Devoto, *Atti del V convegno,* pp. 98 ff.
9. *Scavi linguistici nella Magna Grecia* (Rome, 1933).
10. "Die Mundarten Südlukaniens," in *Beihefte zur Zeitschrift für romanische Philologie* 90 (1939):84 ff.; De Felice, *Atti Accademia Colombaria* 26 (1961–62):233 ff.
11. *Language* 26 (1950):6–27.

CHAPTER NINETEEN

1. See my *Geschichte,* p. 262.
2. J. Schrijnen, *Charakteristik des altchristlichen Lateins* (Nimega, 1932).
3. *Beiträge zur Sprache und Kritik Tertullians* (Lund, 1932), p. 148.
4. Marouzeau, *Quelques aspects de la formation du latin littéraire,* p. 123.
5. Svennung, *Untersuchungen zu Palladius . . .* (Uppsala, 1935), p. 518.

CHAPTER TWENTY

1. H. Marrou, *Histoire de l'éducation dans l'antiquité,* 6th ed. (Paris, 1965), pp. 425 ff.
2. Devoto and Giacomelli, *I dialetti delle regioni d'Italia* (Florence, 1972), pp. 136, 147.
3. See my *Storia della lingua di Roma,* 2d ed., p. 273.
4. *Ibid.,* p. 325.
5. *Ibid.,* p. 331.
6. *Ibid.,* p. 334.

CHAPTER TWENTY-ONE

1. Viscardi, *Origini,* 4th ed. (Milan, 1966), pp. 227 ff.
2. Giacomo Devoto, *La Bibbia nel Medio Evo* (Spoleto, 1963), pp. 58 ff.
3. G. P. Bognetti, *Sulle origini dei comuni rurali del Medio Evo* (Pavia, 1927).

4. G. D. Serra, *Contributo toponomastico alla teoria della continuità nel Medio evo delle Comunità romane e preromane dall'Italia superiore* (Cluj, 1931).

5. Lot, *La fin du monde antique* (Paris, 1927), p. 313.

6. *Ibid.,* p. 280.

7. *Mahomet et Charlemagne* (Paris, 1937).

CHAPTER TWENTY-TWO

1. B. Nardi, *Origini* (Milan and Naples, 1956), pp. 1–25.

2. Eduard Norden, *Antike Kunstprosa* (Leipzig, 1918), p. 586.

3. Viscardi, *Origini,* 4th ed., pp. 334 ff.

4. Norden, *Antike Kunstprosa,* p. 690.

5. *Ibid.,* p. 680.

6. Norberg, *In registrum Gregorii Magni studia critica* (Uppsala, 1937).

7. Devoto, *Geschichte,* p. 278.

8. Viscardi, *Origini,* p. 47, n. 1, pp. 48 ff.

9. G. L. Barni in *Origini,* p. 66, n. 1, pp. 67 ff.

10. *Ibid.,* p. 92, n. 1, pp. 93 ff.

11. See my *Profilo della storia linguistica italiana,* 4th ed. (Florence, 1964), p. 29.

12. Monteverdi, *Studi romanzi* 28 (1939):152.

13. *Etymologiae,* ed. Lindsay (Oxford, 1911), XX, IX.4.

14. *Compositiones lucenses* (Uppsala, 1941).

15. Devoto, *Storia linguistica italiana,* p. 24.

CHAPTER TWENTY-THREE

1. See Richter, *Beihefte der Zeitschrift für romanische Philologie* 27 (1911):120 ff.; Meyer-Lubke, *Einführung in das Studium der romanischen Sprachwissenschaft* (Heidelberg, 1920), pp. 141 ff.; Vidos, *Handbook tot de Romanse taalkunde* (Florence, 1959), pp. 244 ff. For the fundamental part, the following work is important: L. Romeo, *The Economy of Diphthongization in Early Romance* (The Hague, 1968).

2. Castellani, *Atti del V convegno di Studi umbri* (Gubbio, 1970), pp. 57–62 with bibliography; compare the stubborn resistance of Schürr in *Revue de linguistique romane* 9 (1933):203 ff.

3. G. I. Ascoli, *Archivio glottologico italiano* 8 (1882–85):110.

4. Gerhard Rohlfs, *Historische Grammatik der italienischen Sprache* (Bern, 1949), 1:192.

5. Wartburg, *Die Entstehung der romanischen Völker* (Halle, 1939), pp. 149 ff.

6. Ascoli, *Archivio glottologico,* pp. 110 ff.

7. Rohlfs, *Historische Grammatik* 1:152 ff., 185 ff.

8. *Ibid.,* pp. 239 ff., 243 ff.

9. *Ibid.,* pp. 240 ff.

10. *Ibid.,* pp. 290 ff.

11. *Ibid.,* p. 258.

CHAPTER TWENTY-FOUR

1. Wagner, *La lingua sarda,* p. 310; *Zeitschrift für romanische Philologie* 93 (Halle, 1941):15.

2. Rohlfs, *Historische Grammatik* 1:178.

3. *Atti del V convegno di Studi umbri,* p. 112.

4. Devoto, *Scritti minori* 2:214 ff.

5. Schürr, *Revue de linguistique romane* 9 (1933):203 ff.; Vidossi, *Origini* (Milan and Naples, 1956), p. xxxix.

CHAPTER TWENTY-FIVE

1. Devoto, *Atti del V convegno,* p. 116. For Sardinia, see Wagner, *La lingua sarda,* p. 311.

2. Wagner, *La lingua sarda,* p. 311; *Historische Lautlehre des Sardischen* (Halle, 1941), 106.

3. Rohlfs, *Historische Grammatik* 1:390.

4. *Ibid.,* 1:425 ff.

5. *Ibid.,* 1:418–27.

6. *Ibid.,* 1:327 ff.

7. Devoto, *Atti del V convegno,* pp. 118 ff.

CHAPTER TWENTY-SIX

1. Löfstedt, *Syntactica* 2:325 ff.

2. Salvioni, *Romanischer Jahresbericht* 4, 1, 178; Rohlfs, *Historische Grammatik* 2:44 ff.

3. Rohlfs, *Historische Grammatik* 2:380 ff.

4. *Ibid.,* 3:36.

5. *Ibid.,* 28.

6. *Ibid.,* 2:388.

7. *Ibid.,* 3:30.

8. For the various results of the hypothetical period in the south see Rohlfs, *Scavi linguistici nella Magna Grecia* (Rome, 1933), p. 80.

9. Rohlfs, *Historische Grammatik* 2:133.

10. *Ibid.,* 3:101–24.

11. *Ibid.,* 3:209.

CHAPTER TWENTY-SEVEN

1. Wartburg, *Die Entstehung der romanischen Völker,* pp. 73 ff.

2. *Memorie dell'Accademia Toscana di Scienze e Lettere la Colombaria* 32 (1967):105–211.

3. See my *Scritti minori* 2:333.

4. Bruno Migliorini, *Storia della lingua italiana* (Florence, 1960), pp. 78 ff.; Bonfante, *Latini e Germani in Italia* (Brescia, 1963), pp. 31 ff.

5. Gamillschegg, *Romania Germanica* (Leipzig and Berlin, 1935), 2:14.

6. *Memorie dell'Accademia Toscana,* pp. 126 ff., 150 ff.

7. Gamillschegg, *Romania Germanica* 2:72 ff.; Bonfante, *Latini e Germani,* p. 55.

8. Devoto, *Storia linguistica italiana,* p. 26.

9. Sabatini, *Riflessi linguistici della dominazione longobarda nell'Italia mediana e meridionale* (Florence, 1963).

10. Wartburg, *Die Entstehung,* pp. 145 ff.

11. *Ibid.,* p. 148.

12. See my *Storia linguistica italiana,* pp. 31 ff.

CHAPTER TWENTY-EIGHT

1. Bonfante, *Latini e Germani,* pp. 41 ff.

2. Giacalone and Ramat, *Atti della Accademia Colombaria* 32 (1967): 105–211.

3. Devoto, *Scritti minori* 1:357 ff.

4. Rohlfs, *Historische Grammatik,* p. 295.

5. *Archivio glottologico italiano* 35 (1950):141 ff.

6. Vidossi, *Origini,* p. xxxix.

7. *Italia dialettale* (Milan, 1916), pp. 110 ff.

CHAPTER TWENTY-NINE

1. Migliorini, *Storia della lingua,* p. 88.

2. *Archivio storico italiano* I (1924):113; Vidossi, *Origini,* pp. 164 ff., Migliorini, *Storia della lingua,* p. 64.

3. *Atlante italo-svizzero,* map, 1434.

4. Migliorini, *Storia della lingua,* pp. 61 ff.

5. *Ibid.,* p. 93.

6. See my *Storia linguistica italiana,* p. 33.

7. M. Bartoli, *Lingua nostra* 6 (1944–45):4.

8. *Codex diplomaticus cavensis* (Naples, 1873), vol. 1.

9. Terracini, *Archivio Glottologico italiano* 27 (1935):133 ff., 28 (1936): 134 ff.; also see §87.

10. Migliorini, *Storia della lingua,* p. 110.

11. Schiaffini, *Tradizione e poesia nella prosa d'arte italiana dalla latinità medievale a Giovanni Boccaccio* (Genoa, 1934).

12. Ronga, *Origini* (Milan and Naples, 1956), pp. 322 ff.

13. Viscardi, *Origini,* pp. 162 ff.

CHAPTER THIRTY

1. Bottiglioni, *Italia dialettale* 2 (1926):156 ff., 3 (1927):1 ff.

2. Wagner, *La lingua sarda,* p. 248 ff.

3. See my *Storia linguistica italiana,* pp. 40 ff.

4. Migliorini, *Storia della lingua,* p. 284.

5. *Ibid.,* pp. 97 ff.; Ruggieri, *Lingua nostra* 10 (1949):20 ff.

6. Migliorini, *Storia della lingua,* p. 98.

7. *Ibid.,* pp. 102 ff.

8. See my *Storia linguistica italiana,* p. 41.

9. Migliorini, *Storia della lingua,* p. 109.

10. *Ibid.,* pp. 110 ff.

11. Schiaffini, *Testi fiorentini del Dugento e dei primi del Trecento*

(Florence, 1926); Castellani, *Nuovi testi fiorentini del Dugento* (Florence, 1952), p. 21.

12. Migliorini, *Storia della lingua,* p. 157.
13. *Ibid.,* p. 161.
14. *Ibid.,* p. 106.
15. See my *Storia linguistica italiana,* p. 60.
16. Migliorini, *Storia della lingua,* pp. 157, 224.

CHAPTER THIRTY-ONE

1. G. B. Pellegrini, "L'elemento arabo nelle lingue neolatine con particolare riguardo all'Italia," in *L'occidente e l'Islàm nell'alto Medio evo* (Spoleto, 1965), pp. 698–844, esp. pp. 731 ff.; G. B. Pellegrini, *Parole arabe* (Brescia, 1970).
2. *Bollettino del Centro di studi filologici e linguistici siciliani* 1 (1953): 45ff., 2 (1954):280 ff., 3 (1955):305 ff., 4 (1956):296 ff.
3. Bonfante, *Latini e Germani* 1:47 ff.
4. Rohlfs, *Scavi linguistici nella Magna Grecia* (Rome, 1933).
5. Schiaffini, *Momenti di storia della lingua italiana,* 2d ed. (Rome, 1953), p. 10.
6. Devoto, *Storia linguistica italiana,* pp. 44 ff.

CHAPTER THIRTY-TWO

1. See the objections of Gianfranco Contini in *Italia dialettale* 2 (1935): 54, and also cf. Vidossi in *Origini,* p. lxiii ff.
2. Gianfranco Contini, *Cinque volgari di Bonvesin de la Riva* (Modena, 1937).
3. Monteverdi, *Saggi neolatini* (Rome, 1945), pp. 94–101.
4. Devoto, *Storia linguistica italiana,* pp. 48 ff.
5. Segre, *Memorie Accademia dei Lincei,* S. VIII, 2 (1952):59, 73.
6. *Ibid.,* p. 73.
7. *Ibid.,* p. 65.
8. Devoto, *Storia linguistica italiana,* p. 50.

CHAPTER THIRTY-THREE

1. *Origini,* p. liii–lvii.
2. Migliorini, *Storia della lingua,* p. 184.
3. *De vulgari eloquentia,* ed. Marigo, I, X–XV (Florence, 1957), pp. 80–129.
4. Migliorini, *Storia della lingua,* p. 185.

CHAPTER THIRTY-FOUR

1. *De vulgari eloquentia,* I, XVII.
2. Migliorini, *Storia della lingua,* pp. 190 ff.
3. *Studi di filologia romanza* 1 (1884):1 ff.
4. *De vulgari eloquentia,* I, XIII, 2.

5. Migliorini, *Storia della lingua*, p. 183.
6. Gianfranco Contini, *Saggio di un commento alle correzioni del Petrarca volgare* (Florence, 1943), p. 25.
7. Ugo Foscolo, *Opere edite e postume* (Florence, 1859), p. 41.
8. Devoto, *Storia linguistica italiana*, p. 52.
9. *Ibid.*, p. 63.
10. *Convivio*, I, x, 13.

CHAPTER THIRTY-FIVE

1. Migliorini, *Storia della lingua*, pp. 207 ff.
2. Schiaffini, *Tradizione e poesia nella prosa d'arte italiana*, p. 187.
3. Migliorini, *Storia della lingua*, p. 229.
4. *Ibid.*, p. 231.
5. *Ibid.*, pp. 233–38.
6. *Ibid.*, p. 161.
7. *Ibid.*, p. 225.
8. *Ibid.*, p. 214.
9. Devoto, *Storia linguistica italiana*, p. 51.

CHAPTER THIRTY-SIX

1. Bruno Migliorini and Gianfranco Folena, *Testi non toscani del Trecento* (Modena, 1952), p. 9.
2. *Ibid.*, p. 6.
3. *Studi romanzi* 22 (1932):12.
4. From the treatise *De regimine rectoris* in Ascoli, *Archivio glottologico italiano* 1 (1873):463.
5. Migliorini and Folena, *Testi non toscani*, p. 9.
6. *Ibid.*, p. 45.
7. Ascoli, *Archivio glottologico*, p. 471.
8. Devoto, *Storia linguistica italiana*, p. 73.
9. Migliorini, *Storia della lingua*, p. 276.
10. Devoto, *Storia linguistica italiana*, p. 71.

CHAPTER THIRTY-SEVEN

1. Devoto, *Storia linguistica italiana*, p. 74.
2. *Ibid.*, p. 75.
3. *Ibid.*, p. 77.
4. *Hercolano*, 193.
5. Devoto, *Storia linguistica italiana*, p. 87.
6. Gianfranco Folena, *La crisi linguistica del Quattrocento e la Arcadia di Jacopo Sannazaro* (Florence, 1952).
7. Debenedetti, *I frammenti autografi dell'Orlando Furioso* (Turin, 1937); *Studi romanzi* 20 (1930):217 ff.; Debenedetti and Segre, *Ludovico Ariosto: L'"Orlando Furioso"* (Bologna, 1960), pp. 1649 ff.
8. Devoto, *Storia linguistica italiana*, pp. 91 ff.
9. *Ibid.*, pp. 92 ff.

CHAPTER THIRTY-EIGHT

1. Chiappelli, *Studi sul linguaggio del Machiavelli* (Florence, 1952); and *Nuovi studi sul linguaggio del Machiavelli* (Florence, 1969).

2. Chiappelli, *Nuovi studi,* p. 38.

3. Machiavelli, 3d ed. (Bari, 1949), p. 68.

4. Chiappelli, *Nuovi studi,* p. 52 ff.

5. Devoto, *Storia linguistica italiana,* p. 82.

6. Chiappelli, *Nuovi studi,* p. 168.

7. See my *Storia linguistica italiana,* p. 93.

8. Segarizzi, *Relazioni degli ambasciatori veneti al Senato,* 3 vols. (Bari, 1912–16).

9. *Ibid.,* p. 71; cf. Kristeller, "L'origine e lo sviluppo della prosa volgare italiana," in *Cultura neolatina* 10 (1950):152.

10. Merlo, *Italia dialettale* 7 (1931):115.

11. Devoto, *Storia linguistica italiana,* p. 83.

12. *Ibid.,* pp. 83 ff.

13. Migliorini, *Storia della lingua,* pp. 358 ff.

CHAPTER THIRTY-NINE

1. Migliorini, *Storia della lingua,* p. 386.

2. *Ibid.,* p. 387.

3. Massafia, *Miscellanea Caix-Canello* (Florence, 1884), pp. 255–61.

4. Migliorini, *Storia della lingua,* p. 392.

5. Giacomo Devoto, *Nuovi studi di stilistica* (Florence, 1962), pp. 143 ff.

6. Migliorini, *Storia della lingua,* p. 367.

7. Devoto, *Storia linguistica italiana,* p. 98.

CHAPTER FORTY

1. Migliorini, *Storia della lingua,* p. 450.

2. *Ibid.,* pp. 517 ff.

3. Devoto, *Storia linguistica italiana,* p. 104.

4. Migliorini, *Storia della lingua,* p. 392.

5. *Ibid.,* p. 525.

6. *Ibid.,* p. 528.

7. *Ibid.,* p. 664.

8. *Ibid.,* pp. 543 ff.

9. Devoto, *Storia linguistica italiana,* pp. 101–4.

10. *Ibid.,* p. 109.

CHAPTER FORTY-ONE

1. Cf. Devoto, *Storia linguistica italiana,* pp. 101 ff.

2. Migliorini, *Storia della lingua,* p. 513.

3. Wagner, *La lingua sarda,* p. 187.

4. Migliorini, *Storia della lingua,* p. 512.

5. *Ibid.,* p. 506.

6. *Ibid.,* p. 538.

7. *Ibid.,* p. 470.

8. *Ibid.*, p. 542.

CHAPTER FORTY-TWO

1. Devoto, *Storia linguistica italiana*, p. 109.
2. *Ibid.*, p. 110.
3. *Ibid.*, p. 112.
4. *Ibid.*, p. 113.
5. *Ibid.*, p. 115.
6. Giacomo Devoto, *Linguistics and Literary Criticism* (New York, 1963), pp. 77–102.
7. Giacomo Devoto, *Studi di stilistica* (Florence, 1950), pp. 138 ff., 163 ff.
8. Devoto, *Storia linguistica italiana*, p. 116.
9. Migliorini, *Storia della lingua*, p. 660.

CHAPTER FORTY-THREE

1. Migliorini, *Storia della lingua*, p. 604.
2. *Ibid.*, pp. 605 ff.
3. See the edition by Chiari and Ghisalberti, vol. 2, no. 3 (Milan, 1954).
4. Barbara Reynolds, *The Linguistic Writings of Alessandro Manzoni* (Cambridge, 1950), pp. 44 ff.
5. Devoto, *Nuovi studi di stilistica* (Florence, 1962), pp. 73 ff.

CHAPTER FORTY-FOUR

1. Devoto, *Nuovi studi*, pp. 169 ff.
2. Migliorini, *Storia della lingua*, pp. 673, 687–90.
3. De Mauro, *Storia linguistica dell'Italia unita* (Bari, 1963).
4. *Ibid.*, pp. 21 ff.
5. And in the *Archivio glottologico italiano* 8 (1882–85):98–128.
6. Devoto, *Storia linguistica italiana*, p. 121.
7. Migliorini, *Storia della lingua*, p. 706.
8. *Ibid.*, p. 629.
9. *Ibid.*, p. 630.
10. *Ibid.*, p. 706.
11. Up to the first part of vol. 11 (to the entry *ozono*) in 1923, and remaining unfinished since that time.
12. Migliorini, *Storia della lingua*, p. 594.
13. *Ibid.*, p. 691.

CHAPTER FORTY-FIVE

1. Devoto, *Storia linguistica italiana*, p. 133.
2. A document of the deafness of Italian men of letters is the *Atti della Tavola rotonda;* "D'Annunzio e la lingua letteraria del Novecento," in *Quaderni dannunziani* 40–41 (1972).
3. Devoto, *Storia linguistica italiana*, p. 135.
4. De Mauro, *Storia linguistica*, pp. 424–35.
5. Valeriani, *La lingua dei nostri legislatori ossia Dizionario degli errori di lingua intrusi nel codice penale del Regno d'Italia* (Naples, 1867).

Notes

CHAPTER FORTY-SIX

1. Giacomo Devoto, *Civiltà del dopoguerra* (Florence, 1955), pp. 57 ff.
2. Citations from the Zanichelli edition, 12th ed. (Bologna, 1926).
3. *Giovanni Pascoli* (Bari, 1920).
4. See Giacomo Devoto and M. L. Altieri, *La lingua italiana* (Turin, 1968), p. 196.
5. De Mauro, *Storia linguistica*, p. 137.
6. See Devoto, *Linguistics and Literary Criticism*, pp. 63 ff.
7. See Herczeg, *Lo stile indiretto libero in italiano* (Florence, 1963); cf. Zeppetella, *Archivio glottologico italiano* 54 (1969): pp. 260–66.
8. Migliorini, *Storia della lingua*, p. 680.
9. Devoto and Altieri, *La lingua italiana*, pp. 145 ff.
10. *Lingua nostra* 1 (1939):17 ff.

CHAPTER FORTY-SEVEN

1. Devoto and Altieri, *La lingua italiana*, p. 164; and see Schiaffini in Devoto, Migliorini, and Schiaffini, *Cento anni di lingua italiana* (Milan, 1962), pp. 36–68.
2. According to M. L. Altieri, in *La lingua italiana*, p. 173.
3. *Ibid.*, p. 201.
4. *Ibid.*, p. 259.
5. *Ibid.*, p. 258.
6. Edited by Alfredo Giuliani (Milan, 1961).
7. Devoto and Altieri, *La lingua italiana*, p. 268.
8. Taken from *Novissimi*, p. 190.
9. Devoto and Altieri, *La lingua italiana*, p. xviii.
10. *Ibid.*, p. 316.
11. Thus Ardengo Soffici as cited by M. L. Altieri, *La lingua italiana*, p. 205; for the broad view of the problem see De Mauro, *Il linguaggio della critica d'arte* (Florence, 1965), which provides many statistics.
12. Devoto and Altieri, *La lingua italiana*, p. 131.
13. *Ibid.*, p. 135.
14. 1919–23; see Cassieri *Antologia della Ronda* (Turin, 1969).
15. M. L. Altieri, *La lingua italiana*, pp. 227–31; cf. Herczeg, *Lo stile nominale in italiano* (Florence, 1967).
16. Devoto, *Storia linguistica italiana*, p. 142.

CHAPTER FORTY-EIGHT

1. Notwithstanding the stubborn resistance of F. Schürr in the article "Epilogo alla discussione sulla dittongazione romanza," in *Revue de linguistique romane* 36 (1972):311–21.
2. *Fonologia generale e fonologia della lingua italiana* (Bologna, 1969), p. 379 ff.
3. *Ibid.*, pp. 425 ff.; cf. Malmberg, *Orbis* 11 (1962):173; Devoto, *Storia linguistica italiana*, p. 150.
4. Muljačić, *Fonologia generale*, p. 417.
5. *Ibid.*, p. 429.

6. *Bollettino dell'Atlante linguistico italiano* 9–10 (1964):43–4; cf. Muljačić, *Fonologia generale*, p. 436.
7. Muljačić, *Fonologia generale*, p. 437.
8. Against Muljačić; *ibid.*, p. 455.
9. Very difficult to put into the system, because it is obviously interjectory; however, cf. *ibid.*, p. 442.
10. Unlike Muljačić; *ibid.*, p. 433.
11. According to Muljačić; *ibid.*, p. 428.
12. *Ibid.*, pp. 46–47, n. 6.
13. Which Muljačić overrates; see *ibid.*, p. 445.
14. Segre in Bally, *Linguistica generale e linguistique francese* (Milan, 1963), p. 449.
15. Devoto, *Storia linguistica italiana*, p. 149.

CHAPTER FORTY-NINE

1. De Mauro, *Storia linguistica*, pp. 414–15.
2. Bruno Migliorini, *Lingua contemporanea*, 4th ed. (Florence, 1963), pp. 84 ff.
3. For a schema of the syntactical bases of compound Italian verbs, see Ambroso, *Atti del I e del II Convegno di Studi delle Società di linguistica italiana* (Rome, 1969), pp. 97–98.
4. See my *Civiltà di dopoguerra* (Florence, 1955), pp. 59 ff.
5. *Saggi di linguistica europea* (Salamanca, 1958), p. 10.
6. Altieri in Devoto and Altieri, *La lingua italiana*, pp. 274 ff.
7. Segre in Bally, *Linguistica generale e linguistica francese*, p. 444.
8. Muljačić, *Fonologia generale*, p. 491.
9. *Descriptive Italian Grammar* (Ithaca and New York, 1948), pp. 11–12.
10. Camilli, *Prouncia e grafia dell'italiano*, 3d ed., ed. P. Fiorelli (Florence, 1965); Hall, *Italian Grammar*, p. 14.
11. Muljačić, *Fonologia generale*, pp. 495 ff.
12. De Mauro, *Storia linguistica*, pp. 418–22, with a detailed bibliography.
13. Battisti, *Fonetica generale* (Milan, 1938), p. 251.
14. Muljačić, *Fonologia generale*, p. 460.
15. *Ibid.*, pp. 460 ff.
16. Giacomo Devoto, *I fondamenti della storia linguistica* (Florence, 1951).
17. *Lingua e nazione* (Florence, 1936).
18. See my preface to Stalin in *Il marxismo e la linguistica*, trans. B. Meriggi (Milan, 1968), pp. 5 ff.
19. Devoto, *Fondamenti*, passim.
20. De Mauro, *Storia linguistica*, pp. 288 ff., 322.
21. Cf. Parodi, *Lingua e letteratura* (Venice, 1957), p. 313.

CHAPTER FIFTY

1. De Mauro, *Storia linguistica*, pp. 41 ff.
2. *Ibid.*, pp. 65–72.

Notes

3. R. Ruegg, *Zur Wortgeographie der italienischen Umgangssprache* (Cologne, 1956); cf. De Mauro, *Storia linguistica,* pp. 140 ff., 234 ff., 384–402.

4. De Mauro, *Storia linguistica,* pp. 81–96.

5. See the opposing points of view of T. De Mauro (against the social glorification of the dialects) and G. Rossi-Landi (against the literarary language understood as the long grasp of the hegemonic, perverting class).

6. Migliorini, *Lingua contemporanea* (Florence, 1963), pp. 125 ff.

7. Instrumental in the publication of the important *Dizionario di Ortografia e Pronuncia,* ed. P. Fiorelli, B. Migliorini, and C. Tagliavini (Florence, 1970).

8. The Accademia della Crusca has in the meantime founded a Centro di grammatica italiana (1970).

9. *Essay on Historical Semantics* (New York, 1948), p. 7.

10. See *Atti e memorie dell'Arcadia* III, V (Rome, 1950), pp. 33 ff., with regard to Europeanisms.

11. *Saggi di linguistica europea* (Salamanca, 1958).

12. Peruzzi, *Parola del passato,* pp. 97–104.

13. *Ibid.,* p. 27.

Index

Index

Ice Age, and postglacial migrations, 3–4

Idioma gentile, 286

Iguvine tablets, 38–40

Il Caffè, 263

Illyrian heritage, 45, 163

Imola, Benevenuto da, 230

Imperial age, 101; consonantal assimilation during, 118–19; fall of, 137; grammars of, 117–19, 128–29; linguistic blending during, 116–17; velar modifications during, 119, 152–53; vocalic innovations during, 120–21

Indo-European languages: archaeological relics of, 21; articulation of, 17–18; consonants in, 16; contrasted with Mediterranean languages, 17, 20, 22; diffusion of, through markets, 31; heritage of, 5; innovations of, 17–18; lexical strata of, 18–20; morphology of, 7, 17–18; relation of, to Etruscan, 26–27; tribal cultures of, 22; vowel treatment in, 16. *See also* Pre-Indo-European

Indo-Iranian, 19

Indo-Mediterranean, 13

Indovinello Veronese, 191

Inni sacri, 274

Iphigénie, 255

Irnerius, 212

Iron Age, 21–22

Isidor of Seville, 146; style of, 193–94

Italian: Arabic contributions to, 203–4; democratization of, 278–79; dialectal texts of, in trecento, 217–18; first phonematic system of, 199–200; Gallic influence on, in ottocento, 267–68; national linguistic consciousness in, 266–68, 272; national education in, 277–81; oligarchic tradition of, 230–31, 278; Sardinian adoption of, 262; second phonematic system of, 229–30; third phonematic system of, 303–4; vowels and semivowels in, 304–5. *See also* Dialects; Vernacular

Italy: contemporary social statistics of, 317–18; linguistic foci of, 14; linguistic unification of, 104–10; national revolution in, 277, 279; Norman invasion of, 204–5; political unification of, 282. *See also* names of specific Italian cities and regions

Jerome, Saint, 123, 126

Jaberg-Jud atlas, 191–92

Jud, Jakob, 5

Krahe, H., 6

Kretschmer, P., 27

Lacerba, 292

Language, as product of social and historical forces, 315–16

Language engineering, 277–78, 282, 320–23

Lanzi, Luigi, 26, 262

Latin: accentuation and rhythm in, 94–98, 101, 113–14, 131–32, 148–53; alphabet of, 57; ancient Germanisms in, 177–78; articulation of, 64–65; aspiration in, 65, 80, 90, 107; Christian influence on, 122–27, 138–40, 190; coexistence of, with Etruscan, 55–56; colonies of, 106–7; dialects of, 34, 130–31; in eleventh century A.D., 193–94; in fifth century B.C., 63–65; gallic remnants in, 47; gerunds and gerundive forms in, 84; after Gothic war, 138–39, 141–42; Greek influence on, 57–61, 89–93, 108, 114–15; during humanist renaissance, 235–40; hyperarchaism in, 79; during Imperial age, 116–22; influence of, on Oscan, 108–9, 120, 167; internal resistance in, 74–76; lexical derivations in, 84–85; lexical problems of, 88, 92–93, 101–2; lexical roots of, 20; linguistic blending in, 116–